A Social Laboratory for *N*

D0642638

∼

A Social Laboratory for Modern France

THE MUSÉE SOCIAL & THE RISE

OF THE WELFARE STATE

Janet R. Horne

❧

Duke University Press ~ Durham and London 2002

© 2002 Duke University Press   All rights reserved
Printed in the United States of America on acid-free paper.
Typeset in Quadraat by Tseng Information Systems, Inc.
Permissions and Library of Congress Cataloging-in-Publication
Data appear on the last printed page of this book.
Frontispiece: *Progression des sociétés mutualistes en France. 1852:
2,488 Stés; 1906: 24,000 Stés. Représentant 4 millions
d'individus.* Composition par A. L. Copyright: Collection Viollet

FOR ISABELLE

Contents

∽

Je vais le plus rarement possible dans les grandes bibliothèques. J'aime mieux me promener sur les quais, cette délicieuse bibliothèque publique. Néanmoins je visite parfois la Nationale ou la Mazarine et c'est à la Bibliothèque du Musée social, rue Las Cases, qui je fis connaissance d'un lecteur singulier qui était un amateur de bibliothèques.

Je me souviens, me dit-il, de lassitudes profondes dans ces villes où j'errais et afin de me reposer, de me retrouver en famille, j'entrais dans une bibliothèque.

C'est ainsi que vous en connaissez beaucoup.

Elles forment une part importante de mes souvenirs de voyages.

—GUILLAUME APOLLINAIRE, *Le flaneur des deux rives*

I go as rarely as possible to big libraries. I prefer to stroll along the banks [of the Seine], that wonderful public library.

Nevertheless, I sometimes visit the Bibliothèque nationale, or the Mazarine. But it was at the Musée social library, on the rue Las Cases, that I met an extraordinary reader who was an amateur of libraries.

"I recall," he told me, "feeling moments of deep lassitude in the cities where I roamed; so, in order to rest, to find myself in a family, I would enter a library."

"So that is how you know so many of them."

"They form an important part of my travel memories."

Acknowledgments

∾

While embarking on graduate study in New York, I found myself equally if not more engrossed by the restoration of an abandoned nineteenth-century tenement building. With each layer of plaster, paint, and wood that I removed, my curiosity grew about the immigrants who once lived there and who raised the walls brick by brick, burying plastic Madonnas, horse hair, playing cards, and bits of Ukrainian and Italian newspaper as they worked. My curiosity also grew about a few odd architectural features, such as the set of double-hung lead-weighted windows that were installed on the interior walls. As I later learned, these windows—as well as the building's overall design (a double-decker dumbbell)—were part of a late-nineteenth-century public hygiene campaign to reduce tuberculosis by allowing for more light and air circulation throughout the apartments. With each blow of my hammer, I contracted an abiding interest in the development of low-cost housing, first in the United States, and then in France, an interest that gradually expanded to include the evolution of social policy more generally. From a tenement in New York's Lower East Side, my concerns grew to encompass the Musée social and the French reformers who aspired to make the social policies for which they lobbied in such earnest a landmark of the twentieth century.

Many people on both sides of the Atlantic have shared this extraordinary adventure with me. The Musée social became enmeshed in my life not only as a subject of study but also as a nexus from which I have met a congenial group of colleagues, friends, and fellow travelers from many countries. The exchange and collaboration I have enjoyed with them over the years have enriched my life as well as the pages of this book. To all of them I owe a profound debt.

In Paris, Françoise Blum, Colette Chambelland, Anthony Lorry, and Michel Prat of the Musée social made every trip to the rue Las Cases intellectually stimulating. I thank the administration of the CEDIAS-Musée social for allowing me to reproduce photographs from the library's collection. The Siegfrieds graciously opened their family archives to me; and members of the Chambrun, Gruner, Métin, and Seilhac families invited me into their homes and offices to speak about their ancestors. It is a pleasure to thank Christian Topalov for having invited me to present part of my work to his research seminar in Paris, and the seminar participants for their thought-provoking comments. Christophe Prochasson generously pointed me toward important archival sources at a key juncture in my research; and Antoine Savoye shared his research, ideas, and amicable support from my earliest days in Paris.

Among my mentors in France, I would particularly like to acknowledge my gratitude to Louis Bergeron, who directed my D.E.A. thesis on low-cost housing at the École des hautes études en sciences sociales and who served as my honorary thesis advisor for the Ph.D. Since then, he has always found the requisite dose of encouragement, humor, and what I can only call "inspired impatience," while urging me to finish my manuscript. To him I am deeply indebted. My gratitude extends to André Burguière, Jacques Julliard, Michèle Perrot, Madeleine Rebérioux, Pierre Rosanvallon, and Michel Winock, all of whom have been my teachers, have generously shared of their time, and have helped open new vistas on my work.

Of course, without the support of a variety of institutions, it would have been nearly impossible to complete such a study. New York University's Institute of French Studies provided a dynamic interdisciplinary and cross-cultural milieu for my research interests and supported me along the way. The late Nicholas Wahl, director of the Institute, left a lasting imprint upon my thinking and understanding of France and the ways of the French. For his lessons, of an intellectual but also of a more personal nature, I will always be grateful. I also benefited from a predissertation travel grant from the Council for European Studies, a French Government Chateaubriand Fellowship, and a Jacob Javits Fellowship from the U.S. Department of Education. The University of Virginia granted me a research leave and several summer stipends to help with the completion of this book. I thank each of these institutions for playing such an important role in supporting historical scholarship.

At Duke University Press, Valerie Millholland has been a delight to work with. I thank her for her patience, unfailing confidence, and goodwill in helping bring this book into the light of day. I am also grateful to Pam Morrison, to the anonymous readers who called my attention to matters both big and small, and to Nancy Green, who first recommended that I knock at Duke's door.

Along the way I have accumulated numerous debts toward those who have generously read or commented on parts of this manuscript and offered their critical suggestions and encouragement. My heartfelt thanks to Marva Barnett Sr., Michel Beaujour, Lenard Berlanstein, Laurent Dappe for photographic assistance, Jon Guillot, Deborah Hurtt, Richard Kuisel, Vincent Michelot, Alison Murray, Pap N'Diaye, Shanny Peer, Roland Simon, Christopher Thompson, and Olivier Zunz. François Weil, who spared me neither critical nor cajoling commentary, deserves special thanks for having read an earlier draft of this book. I am also indebted to Alice Conklin, who has been a pillar of support and friendship, and to Paula Schwartz, who bore witness to every twist and turn in the plot of my research with such empathy and humor. Without Harriet Jackson's extraordinary editorial and book midwifery skills or her shared curiosity about social reform, this book would have been a very different one.

I am deeply grateful to the friends and colleagues in Charlottesville, New York, and Paris who have done everything possible to encourage me and make my life easier while finishing this project. Particular thanks to Kathryn and Zvi Bareket, Eric Garfunkel, Laurence and Pascale Gouy, and Rémy Taïeb. I also thank my parents, Robert Horne and Marilyn Magenheimer Horne, for having allowed my seemingly inexplicable passion for France to enter their lives as well. During the final preparation of this manuscript, I could not have done without my mother's generous help with child care in Paris, or that of Holly Jones in Charlottesville.

By now my husband, Richard Holway, has learned far more than he probably ever cared to about the French social reform. Without the haven of his complicitous humor and compassion the completion of this book would have been far more arduous and less pleasurable. Finally, our infant daughter Isabelle, perhaps my harshest critic, shredded every page she could get her hands on. Her deft sense of punctuation, clearly marking the beginning of a new chapter, has helped me find my way out of this manuscript. It is to her that I dedicate this book.

Introduction

∽

Welfare states everywhere are the targets of controversy. Crippling financial strains and uneven demographic pressures are forcing all industrialized nations to reevaluate the viability of their social welfare provisions. Deep in the throes of a national debate, Americans have dramatically overhauled the legislative edifice comprising the system we have come to know as "welfare." But nowhere else does "welfare" mean quite the same thing as it does in the United States. Our system targets discrete segments of the national population more than the citizenry at large. Our debate focuses on the legacy of the New Deal and the War on Poverty and is rooted in what has been described as "a collapse of confidence in the public sector."[1] Dependency on government programs is widely seen as undermining family life and generating a social pathology among poor, young, unwed mothers. Discussions about human nature are frequent, and proposals are framed with the intent of transforming individual behavior. In a nation that takes pride in its tradition of pragmatic consensual politics, the American debate on welfare reform has been unusually probing and ideologically charged.

Whether referring to Europe or the United States, systems of public welfare are clearly much more than a set of regulations defining eligibility and payment schedules. Underlying the social policies of welfare are deepseated, often unexamined suppositions about the relationship of the individual to society. Welfare has also acquired cultural meanings that extend far beyond the realm of public policy and into the realm of social imagination, where boundary lines of class, race, and gender are frequently drawn. To reexamine welfare is to reexamine our identities as individuals and as nations.

My purpose here is to explore the cultural underpinnings of another system of welfare—the French welfare state—and to suggest that public policy is the product of multiple historical and cultural factors, many of which are not visible at first glance. Recent scholarship on the rise of welfare demonstrates how helpful an understanding of historical precedent can be in shedding light on today's debates as well as on the limits and possibilities of future policy making.[2] Each welfare state has its own "personality," and each has developed its own characteristic blend of institutional elements and political compromises. Each welfare state reflects a particular national context and history. But social welfare of any ilk is more than a legislative history of bills passed and amended. To examine a nation's welfare state is also to open wide the history of that nation's value systems—to investigate, for instance, not only the political pressures but also the religious, philosophical, and cultural influences exerted on policy makers.

France presents a curious irony. It is a nation with a proud tradition of ideological sparring, where social debate is often raised to a form of high public drama and where political disputes are easily paraded through the streets or across the pages of newspapers, manifestos, and petitions. Partisan debate on the crisis of the French welfare state, however, has been curiously muted. Granted, *consensus* is a word scarcely uttered with reference to contemporary France. Yet there is one major phenomenon of the twentieth century on which Left and Right appear to have agreed for quite some time: the ultimate goals of the welfare state. Even the massive strikes and demonstrations in defense of the public sector that paralyzed France during the fall and winter of 1995 cannot be understood if analyzed merely according to long-standing political and ideological divisions.[3] Specialists and government officials in France may quarrel intensely over how to avert financial disaster, liberals may propose individualized solutions to retirement pensions, but the general public remains overwhelmingly committed to the ideal of a system that guarantees social protection to its citizenry. So thorough is acceptance of the welfare state in France that the system appears as a normal, "obvious," and necessary feature of social life; almost everyone benefits by it; almost everyone accepts it. Mere mention of the absence of a comprehensive welfare system, as in the case of the United States, provokes reflex utterances in France about the American "struggle for life," straight from a Herbert Spencer-like primer on social Darwinism. As an American observer of contemporary France, I have found this observation to be both unsettling and intriguing.

My concern in this book has been to query the historical and cultural underpinnings of consensus on the French welfare state. What forces have contributed to this apparent consensus? This question cannot be answered fully through an analysis of traditional French political formations. Although politics is certainly a crucial element of the story, agreement on the goals of the welfare state in France crosses political, class, and gender lines. The basis for such widespread consensus must therefore also be sought in more general cultural and historical factors.

Terminology used to speak of welfare in France embodies this broader cultural and historical bias in a compelling fashion. Even today the French welfare state is still commonly referred to as "l'État-providence" or "the Providential state," an early-nineteenth-century term suggesting that welfare is rooted in the long intertwined history of church and state in France. The historian Jean-Baptiste Duroselle has linked, for instance, the history of French social Catholicism—an essential ingredient of the social welfare compromise in France—to the traditions of the legitimist monarchy. But why today, in a country that adamantly defends its secular and republican values, is the term "État-providence" still culturally meaningful? This question warrants a brief detour through history.

After the French Revolution of 1789, l'État-providence invoked a new representative order of society. The secular state, revolutionaries believed, should replace both the Catholic Church and the monarchy in their traditional roles as protectors of the poor. But during the nineteenth century, liberal republicans initially fought any proposal that portrayed the state in a providential role. They distrusted the centralizing, potentially authoritarian capacities of central government. It has taken more than two hundred years for the French to collectively transfer their expectations of social protection from the king and the church to the secular state. But French citizens today look to l'État-providence as an essential agent of social cohesion.

This book addresses the problem of French social welfare from the perspective of an early "think tank" that emerged in the aftermath of the 1889 Universal Exhibition, held during the year of the French Revolution's centennial. The Musée social (or "Social Museum"), known to many present-day researchers as a splendid archive in Paris on French social and labor history, has a rich history of its own: it played a crucial role in the unfolding debate on social welfare reform in France during the early years of the Third Republic (1870–1940).

A precursor to modern policy foundations such as the Brookings Institution or the Russell Sage Foundation, the Musée social assembled a professionally and ideologically diverse group of reformers, beginning in 1894, to study contemporary social and economic problems. It attracted experts in the nascent social sciences, financed research groups and study missions both in France and abroad, and intended to have an impact on social legislation. Thus, the Musée social was often referred to by contemporaries as "the antechamber of the Chamber" since it worked outside of government to effect change. Although they are widely accepted today, mediating institutions such as the Musée social, which gather data, analyze arguments, and "help form the knowledge base for public policy," were novel inventions in the nineteenth century.[4] Musée social members saw themselves as embarking on a modern quest since the need for social reform was a consequence of industrial and urban growth. The Musée, therefore, unlike any other institution of its day, offers a penetrating vantage point from which to understand the social, political, religious, and professional networks that undergirded the quest for a renewed social contract in republican France. These networks are at the origin of the rise of the French welfare state.

Traditional histories of the French welfare state often begin in 1945 when the first general ordinance of Social Security became law.[5] But social welfare reform did not, of course, spring full-blown from the forehead of Zeus in 1945. As the political scientist Douglas Ashford has pointed out, although the institutional and political compromises were not worked out until 1945, the basis for a philosophical and ideological consensus on modern social welfare in France had been mapped out as early as 1910, the year Parliament passed a national pension law.[6] This book's primary focus is on this early debate. Although the two World Wars undeniably played catalytic roles in propelling social welfare legislation into existence, their impact does not fall within the scope of this book. Instead, this history of the Musée social assesses the broad implications of the period before the First World War for the social thought and policies that laid the foundation for the rise of the French welfare state. The history of this early period, moreover, serves to illuminate contemporary debates both in the United States and in France.

The Musée social provides a lens for understanding this crucial process of transformation in late-nineteenth- and early-twentieth-century France. But much as a telescope both affords a new angle of vision and is an instrument of measure, the Musée social opens new vistas on the origins of the welfare state but also gauges and defines that vision. By using the Musée social as the primary lens through which to analyze transformations in French social welfare, I shift the analytical focus of this book away from the formal arena of parliamentary politics and argue that the extraparliamentary debate on social politics at the turn of the century, which often preceded the parliamentary debate, was central to the rise of the French welfare state.

During the late nineteenth century a dense network of extraparliamentary reform groups emerged in France, attracting individuals who were often not directly involved in politics and giving them a strong voice in the ensuing debates on social reform. The sociologist Christian Topalov has labeled this close-knit network of organizations a "reformist nebula" and has, moreover, pinpointed its international dimension.[7] In this book I study a "parapolitical sphere" that existed in the interstices of government, philanthropy, and industry, midway between the public interests of the state and the private interests of individuals. Ideas generated within this parapolitical sphere helped achieve the transition in France from nineteenth-century concepts of charity, to twentieth-century concepts of social insurance. The historian Sanford Elwitt previously identified "bourgeois parapolitical associations," including the Musée social, as the "offstage precincts" of a conservative ruling-class bloc.[8] I contend, however, that the importance of these groups goes far beyond providing a vehicle for a class-based ideology of social peace or a mouthpiece for industrial and business lobbies. They delve into the heart of French civil society. The reform groups comprising the parapolitical sphere channeled a vital process by which the French reexamined the basis of the Third Republic's social contract and their collective identity as a nation; it was a debate that involved every level of society.

Within this parapolitical sphere, the Musée social sought to coordinate the efforts of voluntary reform groups focused on "the social question" addressed in chapter 1. The fact that so many reform groups emerged on the fringe of government in fin de siècle France suggests that the process of defining social politics in the early Third Republic was occurring beyond the traditional purview of the parliamentary hemicycle. Parliament became an echo chamber for debates rooted in civil society. Consequently, our notions of what constituted the boundaries of government must be re-examined if we are to understand the conceptual changes that ultimately gave rise to the French welfare state.

One original aspect of the French system of social welfare is its "hybrid" nature, which sought from the outset to integrate private initiative and the public sector. The history of the Musée social helps to shed light on the means by which civil society exerted pressure on the political process to negotiate a solution to the social question in France—a solution that bears the marks of this early period, that is complex and curiously "non-statist" in a country where state centralization has such a long tradition. To focus on the Musée social, a group formed in this parapolitical sphere on the margins of traditional government, is to focus on the tension between the central state and civil society that is such a characteristic feature of French politics, history, and culture. This tension is palpable, too, in the formation of the French welfare state. Central government's role in providing social services in France has been mitigated, both historically and presently, by mutual aid societies, cooperative associations, private contractual arrangements, and elected social security boards. A main theme of this book is therefore to analyze how the members of the Musée social understood the role of central government in social policy. The rise of the particular model of French social welfare was shaped by this tension between a strong Jacobin state and the liberal republican desire to achieve national unity and identity, but not at the expense of regional, local, or private interests. Because of its status on the periphery of government, the Musée social offers a unique vista on this process of state building.

Recently, general historiographic debates have centered around the causal role of culture, language, and identity in the processes of historical change.[9] In light of these debates, it is also necessary to reframe the problem of the emergence of the French welfare state within the larger context of discursive practices and the struggle for representational hegemony in fin de siècle political life. Such questions are important to this study of the Musée social. Reformers who engaged in debate on the social question during the final decades of the nineteenth century did so with a heightened awareness of the power of public discourse. Throughout the period under study, they carefully used rhetorical conventions, cultural symbols, and political traditions to promote their agendas for reform. They operated within the highly charged political arena of a still-vulnerable republic and manipulated discerningly both new and old media forms to further their ends: journals, newspapers, public meetings, posters, slide shows — and later, even the cinema — were used to promote causes such as public hygiene. Musée social reformers considered the public reception of reform ideas to be crucial to their implementation. Therefore, the deliberate shaping of public opinion was never absent from their strategies and rhetorics of reform. These republican reformers were consciously engaged in the formation of a new public discourse on the role of the individual in modern industrial society.

The contours of this new public discourse were also a gendered construction. Because of the exclusion of French women from the body politic of the Third Republic, women who wished to engage in reform politics were forced to so do from within a highly circumscribed sphere of action. The limits of this public sphere of activity were determined as much by the traditions of a male-dominated republican political culture as they were by the rules of citizenship and parliamentary democracy in the Third Republic. As a result, although gender constituted a primary structuring vector of reform discourse, women were denied membership in the Musée social until 1916.[10] The absence of women from the Musée only highlights how male reformers shaped social policy from within the guarded preserve of their gender-exclusive political culture.

Historiography on the French welfare state is now vast.[11] Mirroring the now-discarded interpretation of French industrial growth as "slow," the generally accepted view on the Third Republic's prewar record on social reform has been that it was "backward": paltry, halting, and failure-ridden; as stodgy and "mired in . . . routine" as the bourgeois Republic itself.[12] The implied standard here, as one might imagine, was Bismarckian Germany with its pioneer status in social welfare.[13] When France did enact legislation, the impetus has thus been attributed to underlying nationalist and imperialist impulses to compete with Germany. In this light, national anxiety in fin de siècle France over the country's perceived low birthrate was channeled into a concern with public health, maternity, and sanitation.[14]

The primary interpretation of French welfare reform, however, has been built around the notion of social defense, whereby reform was enacted in a defensive compromise between big business and ruling elites to preserve social order. The only existing scholarship on the Musée social, that by Sanford Elwitt, falls within this latter category.[15] Although Elwitt's *Third Republic Defended* pinpoints the importance of the parapolitical sphere, his restrictive analytical framework does not explain the collaborative effort of economic elites and the rising professional middle classes to achieve reform, nor does it account for some of the broader implications of this period for public policy in the areas of health, welfare, or housing reform.

Another view, expressed by Judith Stone in *The Search for Social Peace*, widens the interpretive framework of social reform to include coalition building within traditional party formations. This careful reading of legislative debates on factory reform and old-age pensions highlights the role of Radical leaders, often inspired by republican values, as the essential agents in the formation of social policy. It elucidates the mechanics and blockages inherent in parliamentary alliances and offers important insights into why social legislation of the French Third Republic seemed to progress, in the words of Gordon Wright, "at the speed of glacial action"; however, it does not encompass the wider extraparliamentary debate.[16]

Alternatively, reform has been investigated as a technique of industrial management. Such studies emphasize the existence of paternalist practices in industry. They offer a detailed understanding of how reform policies were implemented to achieve specific short-term management goals and how employers and workers reacted to interventionist legislation.[17] Although essential to an assessment of the impact of social reform policy and discourse on the industrial world, such studies do not generally attempt to link industrial reform with public policy. Recent studies have stressed the primacy of scientific innovations and gender biases that had an impact on policy in the areas of public health, child welfare, women's and children's industrial employment, and maternalist policies.[18]

Each of the above interpretations has helped bring the rise of the French welfare state into sharper focus. Yet there is a need to diversify the equation and include the dimension of public debate on welfare. The Musée social provides a focal point for this broader approach to understanding the evolution of French social thought and policy. During the final two decades of the nineteenth century, the push for social reform in France quickly moved beyond the world of industrial enterprise and big business to address larger societal concerns. Lawyers, doctors, university professors, civil servants, reformist labor leaders, cooperative and mutualist activists all participated in republican social reform circles and questioned the relationship of the individual to the state. The results of this broad-based interrogation that reached beyond the social limits of the industrial bourgeoisie and the political limits of the Radical Party were new attitudes toward the law, the role of the working class in the Republic, and the legitimate sphere of government in relation to society.

These changes constitute the legacy of this period, and their practical effects have had sweeping implications for the twentieth century in the areas of public health, urban reform, education, and social welfare. Moreover, these debates called into question the reigning "liberal order of 1900" and led to transformations in liberal thought that were crucial to the establishment of a welfare compromise in France.[19] Whereas a renovation in liberal thought was occurring elsewhere—in England with the New Liberals and the Fabian socialists, and in the United States with the Progressives—no specific term was ever used to describe the similar movement of ideas that evolved in France.[20] I will therefore employ the term *social liberalism* to refer to the transformation in liberal thought that took place in France during the later decades of the nineteenth century and that questioned the liberal orthodoxy of laissez-faire with regard to the role of central government in social policy.

This late-nineteenth-century transformation of French liberal thought was not without precedent, however. To an important degree, the liberal economic and social order ushered in by the Revolution of 1789 had never been fully accepted in France. Some contemporaries rejected the new social and economic order because of the sheer violence of the Revolution, which made them loathe to consider postrevolutionary France as an improvement over the *ancien régime*. Strong attachments to corporatist language and practices persisted in the workplace long after they were supposedly abolished.[21] Catholic social thought also dictated against the full acceptance of a liberal order wherein the individual theoretically severed ties with the organic community of family, parish, and state. Instead, social Catholics, too, strove to make sense of the industrial world of the nineteenth century by relying on older corporatist imagery and structures. The social Catholic tradition thus stood in stark contrast to the basic tenets of liberal thought: it exerted considerable influence on the evolution of a social liberalism in France and on the development of social welfare policy well into the twentieth century.

Part one of this book is devoted to an analysis of the rhetorics of social reform in nineteenth-century France. I employ the term *rhetoric* in its most general sense to refer to that dimension of language which is engaged in the art of persuasion. As an analytical device, the mapping out of rhetorics of reform serves to highlight the underlying social conflicts and political tensions that they both reflected and sometimes helped engender. From the rhetorical devices used in the debate on social reform, patterns emerge that traverse the century—some of which have endured even to the present day—and suggest that public argument obeys a more unified set of parameters than is often supposed. The nineteenth-century reformers cited here all commented on the "social" state of France and were increasingly aware of participating in a form of public argument. As such, their statements and writings were carefully crafted and relied on "common devices of rhetoric: metaphors, invocations of authority, and appeals to audiences," themselves often "creatures of rhetoric." [22] Chapter 1 examines the debate in France on "the social question" and the specific conditions that gave rise to a reformist discourse during the first three-quarters of the nineteenth century that caused a break with the liberal tradition. This discussion is based, in part, on the unique pattern of French industrialization and the changes in traditional social and political arrangements brought about by the French Revolution. Chapter 2 analyzes the Third Republic's first "official" position on the social question, as portrayed at the 1889 Universal Exhibition, and incorporates the problematics of rhetoric and representation into a more traditional approach to social history. It also traces the steps leading to the foundation of the Musée social in the aftermath of the 1889 Exhibition and suggests that the parapolitical sphere was essential to the elaboration of a new language of social reform in the Third Republic.

The second part of this book focuses on the Musée social itself: the institution and the men who comprised it. Chapter 3 details the Musée social membership based on an initial sample of five hundred reformers. What social characteristics did reformers share? Did they make professionally motivated decisions during their involvement with reform efforts? And to what extent were their opinions influenced by religious and political culture? Chapter 4 describes the mechanics of the Musée social's operation and addresses a general problem posed by any institutional history: how can the historian account for the multiple human interactions that occurred within the walls of an institution designed for one purpose but perhaps put to another? This chapter attempts to trace the various social meanings ascribed to the Musée social during its first five years of existence.

Part three of this book examines two case studies of the Musée social's reform activities. Chapter 5 analyzes the Musée's involvement with the French mutualist movement from the end of the nineteenth century until the passage of the 1910 national pension law. The role of mutualism is presented as illustrative of the tensions between state centralization and the liberal republican value of self-help, and of how those tensions influenced the development of social policy in France. Finally, chapter 6 focuses on the shift that occurred among Musée social reformers from a late-nineteenth-century concern for workers' housing to an early-twentieth-century preoccupation with public hygiene, urban planning, and conservationism.

Although the period prior to World War I in France is often portrayed as one of relative stagnation in the realm of social welfare, a closer look reveals that this era was, in fact, one of initial transformation to a more interventionist conception of the state: from private philanthropy to public assistance combined with the action of voluntary associations, and from the benevolent activities of social-minded bourgeois reformers to the acceptance of social rights guaranteed by social law. This history of the Musée social, therefore, brings into focus the people, the ideas, and the organizations that helped move France through a crucial period of transition and that laid the foundations for the rise of the modern French welfare state.

Part One. Rhetorics of Reform

1. The Modern Sphinx: Debating the Social
Question in Nineteenth-Century France

∾

The modern sphinx asks our civilization: how can we grant the impoverished classes more civilization, more happiness, more security; how can we diminish the frightening gap that separates the so-called superior classes from the people? —LOUIS VARLEZ, 1894

This waning century will go down in history as "the century of social questions," not because it has resolved them, but because it was the first to ask them and to understand their importance. —ÉMILE CHEYSSON, 1894

Paris was gearing up for the show of the century. The 1889 Universal Exhibition, a world's fair like no other, would celebrate jointly the centennial of the Revolution, the apparent triumph of French democracy in the Third Republic, and the fruits of the new industrial order. Although France was poised for the festivities, all was not well. Eiffel's tower daily reached higher into the sky, but it also cast a long shadow over a country in the throes of deep political and economic change. Democratic institutions were fragile, threats to their stability abounded, and not everyone cheered the memory of what had been, by all accounts, an extremely violent revolution that scarred French society while catapulting it into the modern era. The Dreyfus Affair soon laid bare the painfully deep fractures that still divided the body politic. Compounded by a serious downturn in industrial growth during the 1880s, France's first great depression, vicious labor confrontations were becoming a regular feature of the industrial landscape. Yet in 1889, under the determined and hopeful leadership of liberal republicans for whom this new day of the French Republic was merely dawning, the Exhibition's show would go on.

From the wings of this world stage under construction, the engineer Émile Cheysson, the former businessman and mayor of Le Havre Jules Siegfried, and a group of their reform-minded friends strategized about mounting their own show at the Exhibition, a "social museum" that would showcase not only the myriad achievements of the industrial age but also its problems.[1] These men were not socialist critics of the regime or malcontents seeking a platform to sell their particular brand of polemic. Instead, Cheysson and his friends were liberal republicans cut from the same conservative cloth as those who currently wielded political power in France. They did have an agenda of their own, a social agenda that added a rhetorical twist to the planned fanfare to the industrial reign of iron. Beneath the electric glow of Eiffel's shrine to industrial achievement, they proposed a controversial idea: that the French Republic offer the world a glimpse of the underbelly of the industrial beast by alluding to the social costs of industrialization and by praising those who had tried to do something about them. Their social museum would do just that. It would not pretend that all was well in paradise, but—fueled in no small measure by social fear—it would focus instead on finding solutions to the dangers and upheavals caused by industrialization. What could be a more fitting centennial tribute to the Revolution's legacy to the Third Republic? With all eyes on Paris as the city preened and polished for the great event, the stage was also being set for French elites to face the republican challenge of a renewed social contract in the age of industry.

From different walks of life and political persuasions, the enthusiasts who rallied in support of Cheysson's social museum shared at least one conviction: social reform had become an urgent priority in fin de siècle France. Avid supporters of industrial growth, they nonetheless shuddered at the evidence of its excesses. Amassed in the margins of a budding new world of factories, trains, cities, and leisure travel for the wealthy were outcast, impoverished workers and their families, victims of overwork, disease, urban squalor, and rural poverty. The social ravages of economic upheaval tarnished the newly minted republican project and threatened to explode the industrial dream. Engineers and professors, publicists and actuaries, doctors and architects, lawyers and students—those who answered Cheysson's call were not among the country's most visible political leaders or well-known intellectuals. They were members of a burgeoning middle class, a faceless crowd in the historical record, often with professional qualifications but lacking secure social or class identities. Ambitious, self-proclaimed experts with pretentions to elite status, they forged and wielded a scientistic language borrowed from their professional fields of endeavor and applied to the analysis of contemporary society.

Equally important, the men and women whose names populate these pages saw themselves as social reformers.[2] An international blossoming of similar reform efforts was underway in each industrializing nation. Networks of exchange, both informal and highly organized, characterized this reform movement, infusing it with a fluidity that echoed results back and forth across the European Continent and the Atlantic Ocean.[3] Though indebted to this international exchange, French reformers also drew upon a wealth of national experience, writing, and debate left to them by their eighteenth- and nineteenth-century predecessors — philanthropists, doctors, social commentators, legislators, and enlightened industrialists — who argued and speculated over the merits and dangers of the industrial era. Well versed in these early debates, late-nineteenth-century reformers continued them. They joined a transgenerational dialogue on the nature of liberal society, on the benefits and drawbacks of public assistance versus private charity, and on the legitimate role of the state in relation to society. They participated in the construction of a public language of social welfare, slowly fashioned in France since the revolutionary era. To understand the sources of this language and to reveal the deeper cultural roots of social reform efforts in France, one must contemplate anew the multifaceted nature of nineteenth-century debate on the "social question."[4]

The Modern Sphinx: Interpreting the Social Question

Omnipresent throughout nineteenth-century public discourse, *the social question* became a catch-all phrase referring to an amalgam of responses to social and economic change in postrevolutionary France. It captured a strong element of bourgeois fear, both of change itself and of the possibility of not being able to understand or harness change; it also embodied fear of workers and of labor militancy. But the social question referred as well to a new form of poverty linked to the advent of the industrial age. It implied far-reaching concerns about social responsibility, the function of a modern elite, citizenship in the Republic, the bonds of civic community, class relations, gender differences, and national identity. As will be seen in this chapter, the rise of social awareness of the lives and working conditions of industrial workers was also at the origin of a "science of *moeurs*," a cataloging of workers' mores, behaviors, and attitudes—characterized by the studies of early sociologist and metallurgical engineer Frédéric Le Play and his disciples—that constituted a first step in nineteenth-century France toward the constitution of a science of society.[5] This rather amorphous term—the social question—would disappear gradually only with the rise of a science of society that offered empirical tools of analysis and intervention. As Léon Gambetta asserted so presciently in 1872, "There is no social remedy because there is no *social question*." Instead, he saw "a series of problems" that would "be resolved one by one and not by a single formula." Indeed, by the century's end, when reformers possessed a sharper assessment of France's social ills, the amalgamated notion of a social question was gradually discarded and was replaced in reform parlance by discrete "social questions," the social issues and problems to which we still commonly allude today.[6]

But when the social question first emerged in nineteenth-century France, it referred primarily to a new experience of life and labor among the working classes. Confronted with the demands of industrialization and urban growth, an increasing number of French workers encountered irregular employment made problematic by alarming levels of poverty. "The industrial era has begun; pauperism is born." Thus, in 1865, did the liberal economist Émile Laurent acknowledge that industrialization had brought in its wake profound changes in the notion and experience of poverty. The general increase in wealth and happiness promised by a generation of political economists and the free pursuit of property, liberty, and industry had given rise instead to a troubling army of indigents, vagabonds, and poverty-stricken workers. These were "the dangerous classes," or "the new poor," a substratum of society where poverty, criminality, and disease were intermingled. Born of industrial wage labor and commonly referred to by the English euphemism "pauperism," this was a different, more permanent form of poverty. Expanding markets, a growing factory system, and a thriving tradition of rural manufacturing not only restructured work but also spawned new forms of fatigue, exploitation, and misery. The face of labor, too, was changing as women and children flooded into the workforce. This human side of the ferment caused by economic growth constituted the social question.[7]

Not confined within elite academies or *sociétés savantes*, the human dimension of the social question was visible to all. Pauperism haunted the public imagination, urban thoroughfares, and factory neighborhoods; it preoccupied citizens from various walks of life, from those who witnessed it through their work in private charities to the industrialists and doctors who took note of the physical and social symptoms that resulted from the new industrial environment. Unprecedented forms of social conflict, such as the Canut silk-worker revolts of the 1830s, erupted in tandem with this new form of poverty, revealing the first stirrings of a new working-class consciousness linked to the condition of proletarianization.[8] The question of how to eradicate pauperism and how to respond to labor unrest only intensified the tenor of public debate on the social question throughout the remainder of the nineteenth century.

As the impact of industrialization and urban growth on workers' lives became more visible to a fraction of French elites, the social question also entered the realm of public debate.[9] It became a Janus-faced phenomenon, rooted in the actual experience of workers but also spawning distinct discourses *about* poverty and the working poor created by contemporary bourgeois observers as they vied with one another for renown in the arenas of public opinion. "The individual is responsible for his impoverishment!" — "Poverty is a moral question, not a social question!" — "The collectivity has a responsibility to investigate and alleviate the material conditions of poverty!" Such conflicting pronouncements *about* poverty seemed to take on a life of their own as, for generation to generation (indeed, from nineteenth-century Europe to twenty-first-century America), platitudes exchanged about the true nature of poverty seemed to deflect attention away from the actual problems at hand, often contributing to stasis and merely comforting those who benefited from the status quo. For the reformers of late-nineteenth-century France, after a century of such debate, the question persisted: How could the social question be solved? This quandary, as if posed by a modern Sphinx, left an enduring riddle. Unresolved, yet omnipresent, the social question brought to the fore a critical debate on the nature of industrial society in France, one that would be pursued far beyond the threshold of the nineteenth century.

The Emergence of the Social Question

The nature of the social question—in both its socioeconomic and discursive dimensions—was tied to the specific patterns of industrialization in nineteenth-century France. French industry did not experience a decisive takeoff as was previously believed; instead, it evolved according to a complex, multirhythmed process of growth, following both regional and industry-specific patterns. A mixed or dual economy best describes what has become known as the French model of industrialization. Based on a concentrated industrial sector (particularly in mining, metallurgy, and the railroads), this model is also characterized by a very gradual shift to an urban economy; a relatively even geographic distribution of the population; and, particularly, the dynamic persistence of dispersed rural industry in combination with subsistence agriculture.[10] The early phases of concentrated manufacturing and large-scale industry in France relied heavily on this mixed economy and a seasonal workforce that could supplement its income through farming or other manufacturing-related activities.[11] The coexistence of old and new forms of work led to the persistence in France of an atomized and craft-oriented working class, marked by small production units and often by workers' ownership of the tools of production, throughout the nineteenth century and even beyond. The familiar contours of a modern working class characterized by the industrial laborer, and of a massive rural exodus toward the cities were late-nineteenth-century phenomena in France.[12]

A Nation Uprooted

These characteristics of French economic development had a profound impact on how the social question was first formulated in the early nineteenth century and subsequently reformulated in the 1880s when industrial capitalism emerged fully. Literature on the social question mirrored this uneven process of industrialization and molded the subsequent language of social reform. One recurrent theme of this literature in France, whether in essays, novels, or political tracts, was the fear of *déracinement*: the uprooting of the peasantry from the countryside, the abandonment of agricultural labor for work in the mechanized factories. Until well into the twentieth century, reformers from across the political spectrum decried this uprooting from the land as a destabilizing factor for the French nation and lauded instead the multiple benefits that would ensue if workers remained close to the land.[13] The deep cultural resonance of this theme—later exploited by the Vichy regime and the French agricultural lobby[14]—is evident throughout the reform literature of nineteenth- and twentieth-century France.

Émile Cheysson's mentor, the early social scientist Frédéric Le Play, for instance, exhorted male workers not to rely exclusively on an industrial wage for their livelihood, encouraging them instead to continue cultivating the land in order to ensure their family's sustenance during the sporadic economic crises of early industrialization. In addition to giving the family a margin of autonomy, Le Play believed that property ownership was essential to establishing the material and moral foundations of paternal authority.[15] A man's secure tie to the land, he argued, would create a sense of continuity between generations and order within the family. Dispossession from the land, however, would undercut the domestic power of the father, causing the family, and thereby society at large, to collapse.

According to the republican historian Jules Michelet, a peasant expropriated from the land had been "expropriated from his own life." Thus, Michelet's portrait of le peuple was premised on the moral value of artisanal and agricultural labor, particularly on the visceral connection he saw between the peasantry and the earth, portrayed as a site of social and economic stability and even of individual health. The introduction of machinery, Michelet claimed, was often dehumanizing and humiliating to workers, who, detached from the land and artisanal workshops, became nothing more than miserable "men-machines." Maintaining a vital connection to the land, on the other hand, would help preserve the coherence of the community. Many of Michelet's contemporaries concurred that rural workers sought employment in the cities only under duress and preferred to remain near their land, their families, and their homes.[16]

Debate on the causes and ramifications of déracinement also focused on the metaphorical uprooting of women. The literature severely criticized the material conditions of women's and children's work, particularly in the textile trades; but ultimately its main concern was to preserve the integrity of the family unit for moral reasons. In his famous treatise L'Ouvrière (1860), the republican statesman Jules Simon detailed, with the pen of a social scientist, the alarming situation of women textile workers. But in a much less objective vein, he also argued in favor of home-based work, asserting that "women were meant to live in their households." Only when a married woman leaves the factory to return home to her family, he claimed, is she restored to her "normal" condition: "Any form of social organization that uproots wives from their husbands and children is a poorly regulated one that does not . . . allow women to be women." [17] Nor, presumably, would such a social system allow men to be men, in yet another veiled reference to how the forces of industrialization might undermine paternal authority. Texts such as these demonstrate how the social question—beginning in the nineteenth century but, as we shall see, carried over into the twentieth century as well—encompassed not only the tangible transformations wrought by the industrialization on urban and rural workers' lives but also the mounting speculations of bourgeois commentators on the consequences of these new forms of labor upon the community, the family, gender relations, and France's traditional focus on rural culture.

Fearing the consequences of detachment from the land for industrial workers, republican housing reformers in turn-of-the-century France extolled the salutary effects of cultivating even a small patch of soil by promoting the *pavillon*—the individual home with a garden—as the ideal type of low-income-worker housing. Tending a garden, reformers believed, would help industrial workers feel a sense of proprietorship in the land, would dissuade them from squandering their weekly pay in the local *cabaret*, and would incite them to adopt habits of thrift and temperance. The abbot Lemire's association, the Ligue du coin de terre, championed worker gardens as an antidote to the alienation of industrial labor and as a means of promoting social peace. Following the lead of English urban visionary Ebenezer Howard, the author of *Tomorrow: A Peaceful Path to Social Reform* (1898)—reissued in 1902 as *Garden Cities of Tomorrow*—city planners in early-twentieth-century France and reform socialists such as Henri Sellier, mayor of Suresnes, proposed the "garden city," where citizens from different social classes would live in harmony with nature and with one another, as an urban model preferable to that of the tentacular industrial city. From the opposite end of the ideological spectrum, Maurice Barrès, who expressed his nationalist regionalism in the novel *Les Déracinés* (1897), chose the theme of uprootedness (*déracinement*) of youth from the land—

particularly from their local regions and traditions—as a leitmotif for his fictional exposé of the disintegration of French national values.

A recurrent, even obsessional theme of reform discourse—the problem of *déracinement* and its corresponding panacea, *la terre*—suggests how the language and concepts generated by the social question in France were tied to a particular pattern of industrialization in which dispersed rural manufacturing, subsistence agriculture, and seasonal factory work long coexisted within a mixed economy. From across political and generational divides, reformers, novelists, and social commentators shared the assumption that the forces of industrialization threatened to upset the equilibrium, considered so essential to France, between its rural and urban cultures. An unsevered tie to the land or even a small garden plot might, however, bear the fruits of social peace and national cohesion that reformers so anxiously sought to cultivate.

Debate on the social question thus drew manifold writers from across the entire ideological spectrum into the fray as they traced the fissures of postrevolutionary French society in moral tracts, realist novels, and social surveys. Beginning in the 1820s they spawned a plethora of texts—pamphlets, books, treatises, doctoral dissertations, laws—that attempted to define, label, dissect, analyze, and remedy the problems of a changing social world.[18] But from its inception in nineteenth-century France, the social question was a multifaceted construct of which no one school of thought and no social group could claim proprietorship. Precisely because of its rhetorical dimension, the social question served many purposes simultaneously; it was a harbor with many ports of entry, receiving fellow travelers from disparate social and ideological lands. Its malleable form captured the imagination of doctors, lawyers, engineers, novelists, and other educated members of a fledgling nation that, in the aftermath of the Revolution, had embarked on a broad-based interrogation of its foundations and its future.

Toward a New Social Order

Early-nineteenth-century debate on the social question probed the meaning and direction of postrevolutionary French society. In this regard, contemporaries often relied on the phrase *la question sociale* as a euphemism to describe the lack of consensus in France on the emerging industrial economy and the new postrevolutionary polity. The social question became "the site where the promise of the new social order or the specter of its demise would ultimately be played out." [19] Indeed, more was at stake than finding a way to mend the strained relations between the social classes. Debate on the social question also raised awareness of related anxieties: the new contours of civil society, the role and limits of the state, the identity and responsibility of elites in an industrializing economy, the changing nature of poverty, the shifting functions of secular and religious institutions, the definition of the public sphere, and the perceived lacunae in liberal political economy as a blueprint for modern social relations. Despite shifting political regimes and a fragmented, even polarized elite, the Revolutionary legacy imparted to nineteenth-century France bore with it a new definition of the individual *qua* citizen as well as the notion of a right to liberty and equal treatment before the law. Even the *petit peuple* had earned a putative new status in the emerging public discourse on the rights and responsibilities incumbent upon the citizens of the postrevolutionary polity. In short, those who engaged in debating the social question were helping to shape a much broader public discourse about the role of the individual and the state in postrevolutionary French society.

Much of the debate turned on interpretations of the essential meaning of the Revolution: Had the basis for social order in France been permanently destroyed? In the aftermath of the Terror, popular petitioners railed against Revolutionary efforts to restructure the family and clamored for "the re-forging of civil society and social trust." [20] In an attempt to weaken paternal authority and dismantle the intricate feudal dependencies that had bound individuals to one another for centuries, had successive Revolutionary governments unraveled the very fabric of civil society? "The destruction of feudal orders and corporations," Pierre Rosanvallon has argued, "left a void from which emerged all of the new tensions of the nineteenth century." Indeed, the 1791 Le Chapelier law abolishing trade corporations had consequences that went far beyond the circumscribed realm of traditional labor and trade arrangements. [21]

Corporate bodies had also formed the basis of the ancien régime's *social* order, providing protection and framing many of the daily relations that linked individuals to one another in rural communities, extended families, and parishes. In the aftermath of the Revolution, however, all intermediary bodies—the *corps intermédiaires* that so preoccupied Tocqueville when he examined American democracy—were suspect and were viewed in France as carrying the seeds of feudal reaction. This conflict—how the introduction of economic and political individualism during the French Revolution also undermined the social stability once provided by feudal corporatism—constituted a formidable obstacle to the reorganization of postrevolutionary society. In light of the suppression of intermediary groups and interests between the individual and the state, upon what foundations could a new civil society be built? Was the public sphere to be composed exclusively of an aggregate of individuals? Did the Revolutionary heritage leave to posterity any notion at all of a collective social entity?

Not only did the need for social bonds remain, but the very forms of incorporation and the idiom of corporatism that were theoretically outlawed in fact survived and even flourished in postrevolutionary France, providing structures for a nascent labor movement and for protection from the vicissitudes of early industrialization.[22] One of the essential historical problems posed by this period in France, therefore, is precisely how the social question was created from within the "vacuum" left by the undoing or even the "negation" of the bonds of prerevolutionary society.[23]

"Looking Backward"

From Saint-Simon to Durkheim, commentators, intellectuals, and writers from across the political spectrum were haunted by what they saw as the breakdown of social bonds in postrevolutionary France. Whether one applauded or abhorred the Revolution, there was broad agreement, in its aftermath, that French society had been cut from its moorings and left adrift in the turbulent waters of individualism and mounting social chaos. It is hardly surprisingly, therefore, that in the aftermath of the French Revolution the nostalgic rhetorical trope of looking backward to a lost world became a prevalent feature of nineteenth-century social discourse. Conservative agrarian patricians who rejected industrialism; social Catholic thinkers such as Félicité Robert de Lamennais, author of Le livre du peuple (1837), and Albert de Mun, founder of the Oeuvre des cercles d'ouvriers catholiques (1871); or even Utopian socialists such as Proudhon and Fourier all shared a tendency to look to the prerevolutionary past to construct their social vision of the future. The perception of social disintegration and moral decline also caused republican-inspired writers in the Romantic tradition, such as Michelet or George Sand, to look back to *ancien régime* society with apparent regret and to idealize a world built around small communities of producers and landowners, protected by a stable social hierarchy.[24] Even Auguste Comte's positivist philosophy, the goal of which was "social reorganization" and the rationalization of industrial society, was developed in response to the perceived social disorder and "intellectual anarchy" of postrevolutionary France.[25]

In like manner, the conservative Frédéric Le Play claimed that only the "impartial study of the past" would allow intellectuals to acknowledge that "social harmony was better established in the parish, in the workshop, and in the family" prior to the Revolution. The Napoleonic Code's legal system of property division, he further contended, had only aggravated this postrevolutionary sense of social instability by subverting the paternal authority of the father. But Le Play did not advocate a simple return to the *ancien régime*. "All free and prosperous nations," he acknowledged, preferred the postrevolutionary "regime of common law" to the "regime of privilege" destroyed in 1789. However, he lamented the penchant of his contemporaries to systematically glorify the French Revolution without recognizing the virtues of *ancien régime* society. Only by midcentury did he feel that it was possible to speak of these virtues "without fear of creating a spirit of reaction" and hence to call other intellectuals to join him in an "impartial study of past facts." [26] Le Play's work in social science, which stemmed largely from this assessment of history and the contingent assumption that the family constituted the bedrock of society, sought to restore social order to postrevolutionary France.

Later in the century acute fear of social breakdown and moral decline led a significant portion of both elite and popular opinion to reject modernity in all of its varied political, economic, and cultural attributes. Nationalists sought refuge in efforts to resurrect a glorious monarchical or imperial past. Republicans, on the other hand, generally looked on the evolution of French society with greater optimism, but even they based much of their social thought on the perceived breakdown of social bonds. The republican reformer Eugène Chevalier tried to rationalize the phenomenon of social disintegration in France as just a temporary obstacle along the path to democracy: "Before we can achieve [our] goal," he explained, "which is the unity of peoples, [and] natural democracy . . . we must traverse a period of social decomposition, perhaps even of bloodshed." [27] Given the tumultuous context of nineteenth-century France, the degree to which the perceived breakdown of social bonds permeated reform discourse across ideological families can hardly be underestimated.

The Debate on Industrialization

Many contemporary observers were convinced, furthermore, that this breakdown of social bonds was a consequence of—and had only been intensified by—the introduction into France of what the Swiss historian and economist Léonard Simonde de Sismondi decried (as early as 1819) as "the new industrial mode." Proponents of "social economy" echoed Sismondi's questioning of the *social* ramifications of industrial development. Beyond the obvious technological and economic changes, critics pointed to new forms of risk and insecurity, the growing separation between work and family life, and even new social and cultural attitudes spawned by industrialization. Looking across the Channel to England, where masses of workers left the land to work in large-scale factories and live in cities or new industrial towns, Sismondi and the social economists issued fervent warnings concerning the new, potentially disruptive social-economic system that they referred to as industrialism. Political economists disagreed, countering that only the unfettered development of a liberal economy would bring about a restored social order through increased national wealth. Was industrialization essentially good or bad for France? This question and the controversy surrounding it formed a crucial subtext of the social question as it was articulated in nineteenth-century France.[28]

Political Economy

From Adam Smith to Jean-Baptiste Say, the classical texts of political economy constituted an initial *corpus* for those philanthropists, doctors, and university professors who were concerned with the effects of industrialization on society. These texts, containing the seeds of liberal optimism, wielded the term *political economy* as a metonymical "Wealth of Nations," replete with promises of happiness and material bounty for all who earned them by the fruits of their labor. Political economy was the science of the production of wealth. It was based on the assumption that, much as there were immutable laws governing nature, there were also laws governing the economy that needed merely to be discovered. A free, self-regulating market was held to balance—as an invisible hand—the egotism of the individual and the general interest of society. This quasi-religious substitution of the "invisible hand" for the "divine hand" linked political economy to a larger cosmology based on the existence of abstract and universal truths, and revealed the fundamental ahistoricism of its approach to economic phenomena. Devoted to the accumulation of wealth as a prerequisite for social prosperity, the optimistic school of political economy constituted one recurrent referent of the nineteenth-century debate on the social question.

In this spirit, between 1816 and 1818 many liberal economists contributed to Henri de Saint-Simon's seven-volume collective work entitled *Industrie*, which portrayed industrialization and industrial producers in a positive light. During this phase of his intellectual life, Saint-Simon argued for a scientific approach to industry and urged the formation of alliances between producers, scientists, engineers, and other intellectuals to preside over the transition from a traditional to a modern industrial society.[29] Ironically invoking the moral authority of the Catholic Church in the title of his *Catechism of Industrialists* (1823–24), Saint-Simon asked his readers to ponder the question, "What is an industrialist?" Contrary to the other useless, parasitic members of the elite, an industrialist, Saint-Simon contended, was a productive element of society. France "would become a lifeless corpse," he proclaimed, if it lost its best scientists, artists, businessmen, craftsmen, and manufacturers; whereas, if it lost its dignitaries, they would be grieved "for purely sentimental reasons."[30] Saint-Simon was not alone in defending industrialization; his disciple Michel Chevalier contended that technical progress such as the development of railroads and communications would ultimately serve the interests of political democracy in France. And in his *Leçons d'économie politique* (1862), Frédéric Passy wrote that industry and machines would raise French civilization to new heights through "intellectual progress, advances in the arts, letters, sciences, [and] morality."[31]

These defenders of industrialization also claimed to be the sole protectors of the individual's freedom to work as proclaimed by the Revolution. To varying degrees, their corresponding social vision implied that individuals, not families, formed the basis of society. Individuals were the masters of their destinies; they alone were responsible for their acts, for their misery as well as their happiness. Destitution was the result of individual will, of refusal or failure to participate in a work ethic that required virtues such as thrift and temperance. Consequently, a fundamental premise of this liberal ethos was that individual thrift, or *prévoyance*—a term implying both the act of putting money aside and the moral imperative to use foresight—provided the answer to eliminating poverty. Any interference of the state, even welfare assistance to the destitute, was considered detrimental to the individual since it created dependencies unsuitable to the free movement of the marketplace. Political economy evolved into an official discourse that dominated French political and intellectual life throughout the period under examination.

Social Economy

During the 1820s and 1830s, however, social economy engendered a reformist counter-discourse on industrialization. Rooted in certain works by Malthus and Sismondi, social economy and its proponents eventually broke with the classical liberal tradition and formed the basis for a critique of industrialization in France.[32] Based on a cautionary, often pessimistic view of industrialization, social economy drew attention to the moral and human dimensions of economic life. Its advocates generally believed that the market should be regulated to diminish human misery. Particularly among late-nineteenth-century reformers, social economy constituted a basic idiom of reform and provided a broad conceptual niche within which conservative republicans and moderate socialists alike could mark their distance from orthodox political economy and embrace common reform efforts. Those who rallied under the banner of social economy helped build the foundations of a progressive reform coalition in fin de siècle France.

Contrary to political economy, social economy was based on an inductive methodology of positive observation; and, as such, it gave rise to a nascent science of society in the work of Frédéric Le Play and his disciples. Often grounded in concrete, case-specific studies, it offered a more historically based analysis of economic crises. Malthus's *Essay on the Principle of Population*, for instance, written in response to the 1817 agricultural depression in England, had been in part an attempt to understand the interaction between the conditions of social life and the economy.

Malthus noted that crime ensued when the untrained agrarian workforce, already impoverished, was not absorbed by extant industry. Sismondi's *Nouveaux principes d'économie politique* (1819) criticized the theories of Adam Smith for having transformed political economy into a speculative system instead of an "experiential science" and for having lost sight of the object of government, which in his opinion was, "or ought to be, the happiness of men united in society." Legislators, in his view, needed to ensure the "protection, education, moral development, and physical comforts" of the people: "In pursuing this sublime end, the science of government represents the loftiest theory of welfare." Evoking the legacy of the French Revolution, Sismondi called for protective legislation not only for women and children but for all workers. The stability of the social order, he warned, might otherwise face imminent danger.[33]

Initially, Sismondi's writings provoked the interest of a diverse group of professors, administrators, doctors, journalists, philanthropists, and engineers who reflected upon the means of continuing the country's project of economic expansion without raising the level of poverty.[34] Inspired by Catholicism, philanthropy, or the secular concerns of public administration and welfare, these men investigated the human costs of industrialization and contributed to the distinctly moral approach of social economists to the mounting debate on the social question. Following in the steps of Sismondi, the social Catholic philanthropist Alban de Villeneuve-Bargemont "launched the first systematic critique of French industrial civilization," while the liberal "moral economist" Adolphe Blanqui publicized his despair at the harsh conditions of life among urban workers. And in 1839 the philanthropist Baron de Gérando posited that a relationship of "reciprocal solidarity," a "mutual obligation," should link members of families, professional corporations, and local governments in an attempt to eliminate human poverty. The intention of Providence, Gérando declared in his book *Le visiteur du pauvre* (1820), was that "society be morally constituted as a family." Consequently, he argued, the wealthy should realize "the dignity" with which they were invested and make themselves useful in the public domain by combating poverty. As Katherine Lynch has argued, these moral economists and social Catholics had the greatest impact on the formation of public policy toward the working-class family during the first half of the nineteenth century.[35]

Although such had not been his intention, Sismondi had laid the foundations for a school of social economy that Charles Gide and Charles Rist, in their *History of Economic Doctrines* (1909), labeled as a precursor of Christian socialism and the German historical school of economics represented by Max Weber and the Verein für Sozialpolitik.[36] Sharing an aversion for money and a distrust of industrial capitalism, proponents of social economy spanned the ideological spectrum from conservative Catholics to socialists. Although Karl Marx criticized social economy as a form of "vulgar economics," the French Christian socialist Constantin Pecqueur praised it as "the art of association and of universal solidarity." In Pecqueur's view, social economy aimed at the "conservation and spiritual perfection of societies," whereas political economy was limited merely to their "material conservation."[37] Although social economy emerged in France as a critique of political economy and as part of the critical discourse on industrialization, it also contributed to a more general reflection on the nature of French society and the need to define the social bonds that existed between individual citizens and the state in the postrevolutionary polity.

Restoring a Moral Community: Responding to the Social Question

Whether they issued from social economy or political economy circles, late-nineteenth-century reformers who contemplated the social question were also heirs to a multiplicity of attempts to resolve it. Among the most important efforts were religious charitable relief, public assistance, liberal works of *prévoyance*, and secular philanthropy.[38] Each of these approaches to reform aspired to diminish impoverishment but to do so in a way that would restore social bonds and a moral community to postrevolutionary France. Each left its mark on the history of social welfare in France and, by combining with one another in unique ways, helped create a shared public culture that is still evident in the French attitude of societal responsibility for the well-being of its citizenry.

Religious Charitable Relief. The Christian-inspired model of charitable relief was forged primarily by the culture of Catholicism with its moral insistence on charity as a means to attain personal salvation and its admonitions to members of the elite to fulfill their basic social duty. This model embodied a vital tradition of social Catholicism that has had a significant and enduring impact on social welfare concepts and practices in France.[39]

Only gradually in the aftermath of the Revolution, did French citizens transfer their expectations of social protection from the church and the king to the secular state. Even then, the Catholic cultural roots of welfare reform in France remained indelible: notions concerning the moral responsibility of the elite; the respect for social hierarchy; the preservation of organic ties between the individual, the family, the parish, and the state; the refusal to accept the individual as the basic unit of society; and the importance of almsgiving and helping the poor remained integral features of the social outlook of French Catholics in the postrevolutionary context. These values, moreover, enabled Catholics to accept more readily an interventionist role for the state in matters of social protection. This was true especially later in the century, following the papal encyclical letters *Rerum novarum* (1891) and *Au milieu des solicitudes* (1892), by which Pope Leo XIII enjoined French Catholics to accept the secular Third Republic despite the growing anticlericalism of the regime. These deeply engrained traditions of Catholic social thought, with roots that went back to the legitimist monarchy, provided a powerful bulwark against the full acceptance of a liberal order in nineteenth- and even twentieth-century France. Protestant charities, such as the Société de la morale chrétienne (1821) or the Société protestante de prévoyance et de secours mutuels (1825), and Jewish philanthropic groups, although attributable to minority religions and formed initially to help their members survive the effects of persecution, also served to establish the deep cultural and religious roots of social welfare reform in France.[40]

Public Welfare Assistance. A radically different model of how to respond to the social question had been inaugurated by the public assistance efforts of the French Revolution. By divesting both the Catholic Church and the monarchy of their historic monopoly on protecting the sick, the poor, and the elderly, Revolutionary committees broke decisively with the past. They devised, instead, a new ethos of public welfare assistance—one based on the rights of the indigent—to be administered by the state. In an interesting transposition of religious language to the secular realm, Revolutionary committees asserted the legitimacy of public assistance by proclaiming the French state's "sacred debt" to protect its citizens and by discrediting the efficiency of Christian charity.[41] Since the Directory attributed a new role to the state as the agent of general societal welfare, some have even concluded that the French *État-providence* was born in the 1790s.[42]

Others, however, have noted that these innovations of the Revolutionary period were disappointing since the state promised so much yet delivered so little, having gone bankrupt almost immediately after formulating the goal of providing universal assistance for its citizenry. Catherine Duprat, moreover, has insisted on the complex weave of factors that linked public assistance—including the local *bureaux de bienfaisance* and the Conseil général des hospices (responsible for the administration of public hospitals, poorhouses, and local welfare bureaus)—to private charities and volunteers, such as the visitors of the poor and *dames de charité*, who could be counted by the thousands in the early nineteenth century. In fact, as early as 1839, Baron de Gérando, in his *De la bienfaisance publique*, deplored the fact that although the French state had created public welfare institutions under the Revolution, during the ensuing forty years it basically abandoned them to private hands.[43]

Liberal Prévoyance. French liberals resisted the notion of the rights of the indigent as posed by the Revolutionary committees.[44] They attempted, instead, to shift public attention toward the establishment of national savings banks, municipal savings funds, and insurance companies or mutual aid societies that promoted individual acts of *prévoyance*.[45] Such was the case of the Caisse d'épargne et de prévoyance (a savings and thrift deposit bank) created by liberal Benjamin Delessert in 1818. Liberals often repeated their belief that the act of saving money for the future constituted an important part of an individual's moral education and preparation for citizenship. They touted the moral dimension of savings, by which individuals accepted responsibility for their own welfare, as the basis for a new social contract. With the Revolutionary interdiction still weighing on mutual aid societies, however, their development as the form of social protection that appealed most to liberals did not increase markedly until the Second Republic, which decreed in 1848 the absolute—albeit short-lived—freedom of association. Two years later, the liberal position on social reform was summarized in an important speech before the Legislative Assembly when Adolphe Thiers expounded the precepts of individual thrift and *prévoyance* as the only valid method for eliminating poverty. Workers who did not adopt such virtues were condemned by Thiers as the "vile multitude," a now-infamous expression revealing his view—and that of the liberal bourgeoisie generally—of an essentially degenerate, vice-ridden working class. Largely as a consequence of the liberal aversion to the notion of a right to public assistance, the dilemma of poverty was met with astonishing inertia throughout the nineteenth century.[46]

Particularly during the Second Empire, the continued attachment of French liberals and republicans to *prévoyance*, self-help, savings, and in-surance—and their corresponding aversion to government entitlements —was rooted in their opposition to despotism and their distrust of the intrusions of central government into both private and public life. As Sud-hir Hazareesingh has argued, these men promoted local liberties, worried about the nefarious effects of decades—even centuries—of a heavy, central administration on civic life and on the model of liberal citizenship they hoped to see prosper one day in France. For this reason, the liberal republicans who came of age during the Second Empire and formed the political opposition—"*les républicains de l'Empire*"—often spoke about the benefits of decentralization and modeled their prescriptions for social reform on the ideals of self-improvement, civic virtue, and individual responsibility that, they felt, had been too often stymied by a history of excessive state centralization and authoritarian, even despotic, political regimes in France.[47]

In addition to the three aforementioned models—religious charities, state assistance, and liberal *prévoyance*—late-nineteenth-century reformers also inherited a strong tradition of secular philanthropy in response to the social question. It, too, has contributed to the composite history of social welfare in France. Secular philanthropies, although sometimes rooted in Christian piety or religious sentiment, distinguished themselves by their pluralistic, neutral, or interconfessional approach to reform.[48] As Catherine Duprat has recently argued, secular philanthropy was rooted firmly within the realm of civil society and found its primary source of legitimation in the Enlightenment notions of reason, justice, virtue, and science.[49] During the two decades preceding the French Revolution, the *philosophes* broke with the traditional almsgiving practices of the Catholic Church. Their Enlightenment ideal of philanthropy purported to serve no ends other than secular ones and aspired to achieve not only a sentiment of benevolence, or *bienfaisance*, but also an act of social utility. Following this ideal, secular philanthropists acted out of patriotic devotion to the principle of social progress as announced by the Enlightenment and proclaimed by the Revolution. Through a proliferation of clubs, associations, benevolent societies—such as the Société philanthropique de Paris (1780) and the Société pour l'instruction élémentaire (1815)—or the international network of the freemasonry, secular philanthropists chose to act within an embryonic public sphere, thereby participating in its formation.[50] They did not, however, act anonymously, as often was the case with Christian charitable donors; instead their gestures were public, done with the intent of inspiring emulation and cultivating social bonds. Secular philanthropy also had implications for the notion and practice of government, since it offered new justifications for legislative intervention. Elites close to the seat of political power, philanthropists intended to influence public policy: to "investigate, denounce, propose, experiment, associate, and militate for the common good."[51] Their example was followed by nineteenth-century moral and social economists, liberal social investigators, and even a handful of noteworthy industrialists.

Industrial Philanthropy

Among the various initiatives in industrial philanthropy that marked nineteenth-century France, none was as pioneering or as influential for future generations of republican reformers as the Société industrielle de Mulhouse (SIM). The earliest association of industrialists in France, the SIM was created in 1825 in an effort to promote industry and industrial welfare among men of diverse social backgrounds. Its history illustrates how, in practice, the various approaches to the social question we have been discussing did not issue in discrete attempts to resolve it; rather, they were intertwined and combined in innovative ways, giving the history of French social welfare its unique cultural texture.

Devoted to the goal of raising industry to the level of a science while simultaneously emancipating the worker through instruction, the SIM was founded by a mixed group of twenty-two young Protestant industrialists, scientists, and artists. Opponents of Charles X's conservative regime, these men shared republican values and a commitment to assure the general welfare of their local community. Further united by youth, religion— particularly the Protestant belief in collective salvation—and a desire to promote industry, the founders of the SIM espoused an "industrial political philosophy" closely linked to Enlightenment humanism, the secular values of freemasonry, and Saint-Simonian thought.[52] Their belief that the prosperity of industry was intimately tied not only to the well-being of the workforce but also to that of the local population inspired them to create schools, daycare services, mutual aid societies, credit unions, hospitals, public baths, worker housing, and funds for protection against industrial accidents. The SIM set up a library, conducted studies, published a monthly bulletin, and awarded prizes for the efforts of local industrialists to initiate reform. Alarmed by the exploitation of children in industrial settings, SIM members even petitioned the government in 1835 to pass legislation regulating the conditions of child labor.[53]

In addition to becoming a bastion of industrial welfare, the SIM was a profoundly liberal organization that exalted the spirit of private enterprise. Concerned with preserving the entrepreneurial freedom of its members, the SIM formed a commission in 1850 to study the problem of industrial accidents. In good liberal fashion, it proposed instituting safety inspections within the Alsatian industrial community on a strictly voluntary basis. Although the SIM leadership argued that improving workshop safety would be good for productivity, even this limited attempt to initiate a friendly inspection was met with strong resistance as an unjustified form of interference with private property (not to mention the fear of stealing production secrets) and as an attempt to limit individual freedom. After considerable lobbying efforts, however, the SIM strategy finally won acceptance, and prizes were awarded to entrepreneurs who installed protective devices to prevent accidents. Ironically, despite the success of these efforts to promote industrial social welfare by private initiative, Alsatian industries were among the first to be subjected to compulsory insurance for industrial accidents since, as a consequence of the Franco-Prussian War, they fell under the jurisdiction of the German Empire when it introduced such legislation in 1884.[54]

These experiments in industrial social welfare, coupled with the unique associational model established by the SIM, greatly contributed to defining the social role of the industrial entrepreneur in nineteenth-century France. The name of textile manufacturer Jean Dollfus, who grew to personify this model of Alsatian industrial philanthropy, was cited regularly by late-nineteenth-century republicans for having inspired their efforts, particularly in housing reform. His famous slogan, "Manufacturers owe more to their workers than a salary," recurred as a reformist mantra to remind industrialists that they had an important social function to play. Later in the century, when republican industrialists felt besieged by mounting class conflict and efforts to regulate industry, some found it comforting to recall the legacy of this active group of Alsatian manufacturers who were once held in high esteem by their community.[55]

Other initiatives in nineteenth-century industrial social welfare were introduced by Catholic industrialists such as Léonce de Chagot at Monceau-les-Mines or Léon Harmel, who, in his *Manuel d'une corporation chrétienne* (1876) and in his Val-des-Bois factory, championed Christian associationist and economic thought, which he referred to as corporatism. Harmel proposed instituting mixed unions, or "industrial families," composed of both employers and employees within a given trade, and favored the formation of a Christian political party that would appeal to workers and industrialists alike. A Catholic *patron*, he professed, "is guided by supernatural motivations, and finds in his belief system a source of continually renewed energy." Nor were workers, in his view, just ordinary men; they were "souls that had been saved by the blood of Jesus Christ." It was this conception of the worker, Harmel claimed, that inspired Christian industrialists with the "noble passion" to engage in philanthropic acts. Later, more inclined toward the emancipation of workers through self-education, Harmel helped organize two Christian Democratic congresses, the first held in Reims in 1893. As the anticlerical tone of the Third Republic sharpened, however, and labor disputes grew more acrid, social Catholic industrial philanthropy appeared ever more flawed as a model for the nations' policy makers.[56] Ultimately, it was the new techniques of social inquiry, practiced from the earliest decades of the nineteenth century, that would have the most far-reaching impact on the formation of social policy in France.

A New Faith: The Scientific Observation of Society

In their search for solutions to the social question, many reformers, as early as the 1820s and 1830s—including philanthropists, doctors, engineers, industrialists, and some government officials—turned to a new secular faith: the scientific scrutiny of industrial society. Privileged observers of the industrial world, these men—of whom the most well-known is Dr. Louis-René Villermé because of his indicting investigation of the textile trades, the *Tableau de l'état physique et moral des ouvriers* (1840) — ventured out into factories, workshops, urban centers, and disease-ridden slums to gather information they hoped would rid France of its inner menace: the impoverishment, ill-health, and discontent of its workers. In response to the visible eruption into the public arena of a new working class and the rise of infectious disease, sometimes of epidemic proportions — such as the cholera outbreaks of 1832 and 1849 that disproportionately afflicted the poor and inhabitants of working-class tenements — self-designated social investigators hoped to apply the results of their fact-finding missions to public policy. Their goal was the informed but circumscribed intervention of the state.[57]

These mounting concerns about urban poverty, infectious disease, welfare, sanitation, and housing led to the rise of public hygiene, an interdisciplinary practice at the crossroads of medicine, public administration, and early social science that radically altered the nature of the relationship between the state and society.[58] Created in 1829, the journal *Annales d'hygiène publique et de médecine légale* became the nexus of the public hygiene movement by publishing studies on the effects of urban and industrial conditions on human health and the social order. Increasingly couched in the language of medicine, public hygiene enticed physicians to turn their attention to the social etiology of disease and other public "disorders" such as poverty. Once doctors, engineers, administrators, and scientists began to apply the findings of physiological medicine to their attempts to prevent contagion and to improve living and working conditions in France's urban and industrial centers, "every aspect of human life and the environment took on a potentially public dimension."[59] Hygienists embodied the optimistic Enlightenment ideals of observation and social intervention in the name of the public good.

But it was the cholera epidemics of 1832 and 1849 that thrust public hygiene onto the center stage of nineteenth-century reform movements. Rather than relying on moralistic invocations of God's wrath to explain the contagion, as did Catholic authorities, public hygienists sought to intervene directly in the afflicted areas by relying on a scientific model of contagion and by compiling voluminous statistics in an effort to influence public policy.[60] From the 1830s on, public health inquiries and investigations into the conditions of the working classes proved essential to the process of building social policy. As in the case of the cholera epidemics, efforts to learn about society were rarely based on abstract interest but were linked instead to specific social needs. In this way, the intervention of outside experts who could guide public officials became "the indispensable first step in measuring the dimensions of a social problem, ascertaining its causes, and . . . deciding upon remedial action."[61]

In France, it was François Guizot, as education minister in 1832, who first took a strong stance in favor of social surveys that would compile comprehensive statistical information on industrial and urban life. His support of the state's sociological function was not disinterested, however; statistical knowledge of contemporary society, Guizot argued, was indispensable to the continued political dominance of the bourgeoisie. The July Monarch Louis Philippe agreed. That same year, after having been closed for nearly three decades, the Académie des sciences morales et politiques was reopened with a mission to place "social science at the service of the July Monarchy."[62] As was true of Villermé's investigation, the social surveys conducted under the aegis of the Académie relied on the active collaboration of doctors and other private citizens, demonstrating an important but often overlooked fact: the search for social expertise required the interpenetration of governmental structures and civil society.[63] Similar fact-finding initiatives, such as those begun in 1833 by the English Manchester Statistical Society, were occurring in all industrializing countries.[64] Cities, factories, and rural sweat shops all became social observatories as investigators probed for information on every imaginable human and social problem. By observing, counting, and categorizing, the new social statisticians hoped to defuse the social question of some of its increasingly manifest virulence.

Yet for all their insistence on fact-finding and statistics that would give objective, concrete scope to the amorphous and threatening social question, early social surveys were also impressionistic and intentionally dramatic. Villermé's report, and others like it, were captivating, written in titillating, graphic prose that involved the reader in a complicitous transgression of the worker's domestic space and succeeded in creating a new reading public for literature addressing such concerns. Posing as a participant-observer, Villermé recounts: "I followed the worker from his workshop to his dwelling place. I entered along with him; I studied him within his family; I shared his meals. I did even more: I saw him in his labor and in his household; I wanted to see him in his pleasures, observe him in his social activities. There, listening to his conversations, sometimes intervening, I became, without his direct assent, a confidant of his joys, his pains, his regrets and his hopes, a witness to his vices and virtues." [65]

Another study of the same period, devoted to the city of Nantes, stressed, once again in terms that were dramatically graphic and nearly tactile, the deplorable and possibly disease-ridden housing conditions of many urban workers: "If you want to know how [the worker] is housed," go "to Manure Street which is almost exclusively inhabited by this class; enter, but keep your head lowered. . . . Go into these alleys where the air is as humid and cold as in a cellar; you must feel your foot slip on the dirty floor and you must be afraid of falling into that muck in order to begin to understand the painful feeling one has when entering into the homes of these miserable workers." [66]

An obsession with the private and domestic lives of workers characterized these studies. Some researchers sought such information in an effort to allay their fears of new social upheavals, believing that the patterns of private life had a necessary impact on public behavior. Thus, they recorded vivid impressions and compiled empirical data, often for the first time, on the material conditions of workers' daily lives: their eating habits, budgets, possessions, homes, and social relations. But this invasion of workers' domestic space may well have constituted the flip side of the bourgeoisie's own privacy fetish as it struggled to assert its identity as a rising dominant class. As suggested by Michelet, members of the bourgeoisie strove to distance themselves from the very social stratum from which many of them had, in fact, arisen.[67]

Although the surveys of the 1830s and 1840s strove to draw attention to the social question by submitting it to rigorous examination, they produced such an abundance of incriminating data that liberals were left in a quandary as to how best to respond. On the one hand, they proposed protective legislation that was ultimately introduced into law. For instance, the conclusions of Villermé's study, which attributed the destitution of the working class family to "moral" as well as economic factors — cyclical unemployment, prostitution, alcoholism, absentee mothers working in factories — were invoked to secure passage in 1841 of France's first piece of industrial legislation limiting the industrial work of children. On the other hand, liberal efforts to respond to the social question during this period were stymied by the increasing gap between rich and poor, the spread of socialist ideas, and the dislocation caused by rapid economic growth. The explosion of the 1848 Revolution and the establishment of the Second Republic shifted the emphasis of the social question back to the extension of political rights, as initially posed by the French Revolution. These tumultuous years, which marked a turning point in the political history of universal (male) suffrage, ushered in a newly formulated demand for social rights as well. The acknowledgment of the right to work became, in 1848, the hallmark of a new form of social democracy that remained legendary despite the actual economic fiasco of the state-sponsored workshops, les ateliers nationaux du travail, and the violence of the June Days that cooled the momentum for reform among the republican bourgeoisie. Only later, under the Second Empire and through the creation of groups such as the Société de statistique de Paris (1860), did liberals resume their quest to raise statistical research to the level of a science that could be more effectively applied to the art of governance.[68]

The Social Economics of Frédéric Le Play

When, at midcentury, Frédéric Le Play began publishing the results of his own social investigations, it became clear that he had elaborated a system for the empirical study of human society more intricate than anything French observers had produced thus far.[69] His monographic method, moreover, was destined to have a broad and enduring international impact even, for instance, on the first director of the U.S. Department of Labor, Carroll D. Wright.[70] Rather than merely undertaking a discrete series of social surveys, Le Play attempted to systematize a general science of society and to institutionalize it by consciously building a network of groups, publications, and disciples.[71] The social question, in his view, was a contemporary problem caused by the "disorganization that reigns . . . in the manufacturing centers of the Western world." The solution would be found "by re-establishing harmonious relations between masters [employers] and workers." [72] An understanding of, and respect for, family life, he argued, would provide the key to attaining social harmony and stability, whether in the workplace or in public life generally. Le Play insisted on the centrality of the family as the basic social unit, on the importance of reinforcing ties between the generations, and on the essential link he saw between the private behavior and the public action of individuals. Although Le Play's portrayal in historical accounts often highlights his anti-revolutionary views, reverence for patriarchal authority, and arcane socio-Christian lexicon, such attributes tend to overshadow his more significant intellectual legacy: that of having established an inductive methodology for social analysis and having laid the groundwork for a "secular model of social action."[73] Le Play's ideas and writings on social economy provided many late-nineteenth-century republican reformers with an empirically based language and model of social reform that they could adapt to their own political designs.

Trained at the École polytechnique in the late 1820s, Le Play was caught in the burgeoning movement that "inclined intellects towards the study of social questions."[74] He became convinced, however, that the solution to France's social ills lay, not in politics, but in the constitution of a science of society. "Instead of endlessly changing our institutions, such as we have been doing fruitlessly since 1789," he argued that it was necessary "to provoke a change in the very core of the nation, to modify . . . our ideas and our mores."[75] Although keenly interested in Saint-Simonian thought and in Auguste Comte's goal of an all-embracing system of sociology, Le Play found both lacking as empirical methods of social analysis. Consequently, from 1829 to 1853, during official missions abroad as an engineer, Le Play set out, often on foot for prolonged periods of time, to observe industrial and artisanal families engaged in local communities of production. Such families, he believed, ensured social harmony, whereas those found in highly urbanized and industrialized areas demonstrated what he viewed as elements of social instability. For Le Play the family was a mirror of society and its transformations. From Russia to the Turkish Empire and throughout the European continent, Le Play recorded the effects of the gradual breakup of the feudal and customary social edifice on laboring families, bearing witness to a veritable archeology of family structures in transition. He sought to create typologies, such as the "stem family," which, according to Le Play, was the family type that demonstrated the most resilience in the face of a changing, industrializing world.[76]

Through monographic studies that centered on family budgets and the domestic organization of workers' households, Le Play sought to find inherent commonalities between local custom, family structure, manufacturing, and the organization of labor. Through detailed notes, compiled year after year, on family earnings, budgets, furniture, clothing, diet, forms of entertainment, and household possessions, Le Play accumulated a wealth of data on standards of living among rural, artisanal, and industrial laboring populations in Europe the likes of which had never before been catalogued. Much like an anthropologist doing fieldwork, Le Play established unhurried human contact with his local collaborators, lived among them, explained the nature of his work, and often compensated them for lost time in the fields or workshops. His studies, which seemed to hold promise as a guide to practical reform measures, earned him a certain notoriety among industrialists as early as the July Monarchy.[77]

Since Le Play's scientific aims predominated in his public activities, he attracted individuals of varying politics, backgrounds, and professions. Courted by Tocqueville as an expert on social issues, Le Play's star rose in the intellectual salons of the capital. His courses at the École des mines further revealed his incisive mind and his original "sociological vision of industrial problems." As yet untainted, thanks to the distance he maintained from politics during this phase of his life, Le Play was asked to be a member of the Second Republic's Luxembourg Commission on Labor and Social Problems, presided over by the socialist Louis Blanc. The republican François Arago also sought Le Play's advice and requested that he present arguments in support of a reformist social policy for the regime.[78] Le Play's role as a consultant to the Second Republic was short-lived, however, and he returned with renewed focus to the elaboration of a system of sociological analysis.

The 1855 publication of his *Les ouvriers européens* (which included more than 300 family monographs) launched Le Play's career as a public figure. Appointed as the commissioner general of the 1855 Universal Exhibition, he thereafter served as an advisor on social policy to Napoléon III. Propelled by this momentum, Le Play founded the Société internationale des études pratiques d'économie sociale (1856) — most commonly referred to as the Société d'économie sociale (SES) — the goal of which was to study, through a series of monographs, the domestic life and moral condition of selected laboring families. The SES started a journal, *Les Ouvriers des deux mondes* (1857) and later *La Réforme sociale* (1881), to bring their findings into the public domain. Following the overwhelming success of the 1855 Universal Exhibition's "Gallery of Domestic Economy," which exhibited, for the first time at a world's fair, low-cost housing, clothing, and furniture destined for the working classes, membership in the s e s grew considerably. By the mid-1860s, its three hundred members arguably represented the "social" component of the French elite.[79]

La réforme sociale en France (1864), a book that analyzed varied aspects of French society, from family life and education to the system of government, consolidated Le Play's reputation for social expertise, and he was thereafter reappointed commissioner general for France's next Universal Exhibition in 1867. Le Play gave heightened visibility to social economy at the fair by introducing a prize competition "to reward individuals, companies, or localities that, through special organizations or institutions, have promoted harmonious relations between co-workers and ensured their material, moral, and intellectual well-being." Documents and reports from the labor delegates invited to the Exhibition were carefully studied by the s e s, and these data constituted the basis for Le Play's conclusions on the role of labor in contemporary industrial societies. He presented these findings in *L'organisation du travail* (1870), a book that expounded his "social catechism," or the six "essential" criteria for achieving peace in the workplace: the existence of a labor agreement between the employer and the worker; a complete agreement on fixing salary levels; the alliance between workshop and home manufacturing; the existence of savings in order to insure the well-being and dignity of the family; the indissoluble union between the family and its dwelling; and the respect for, and protection of, women.[80]

Dismayed by the Second Empire's defeat, the Commune, and the proclamation of the Third Republic, Le Play retired to private life. Exaggerated expectations of the role of the state in contemporary society were, he came to believe, one of the causes of decadence in France. From then on, his hopes for the transformation of French society rested on the private initiative of the nation's elite. This elite, the nation's "social authorities," as he called them, could alone instigate the changes necessary to bring about social peace. Le Play was quick to point out, however, that these "agents of social peace" were not merely designated as such because of their social positions as urban or rural notables. Rather, it was public opinion that conferred the status of social authority upon a man. In the words of one of Le Play's close collaborators, this group "of eminent men, irrespective of their rank in the social order" would constitute "the kernel of a new aristocracy," transcending political divisions and fulfilling the traditional roles of aristocrats as models within their communities. Particularly in the aftermath of the Franco-Prussian War, Le Play was not alone in expressing concern, even alarm, over the current state of France's social and political elite.[81]

Identifying A New Elite for Modern France

One result of this long search for answers to the social question was that many contemporaries began to question the function of an elite in modern society. Representatives of the aristocracy had challenged the ability of the new industrial bourgeoisie to fulfill the role of a true elite, and many of the latter doubted their ability to do so as well. After all, according to traditional canons of elite status in France, how could an industrialist, a railroad magnate, or an engineer genuinely purport to be a respected moral figure, a director of consciences, or even an arbiter of good taste? In an age of anonymous joint-stock companies and factories employing thousands of workers, how could paternalistic employers uphold the traditional image of the benevolent father and protector implied by the term *patron*? The fear that France lacked a well-prepared modern elite preoccupied liberal republicans well into the twentieth century.[82]

The 1870 defeat at the hands of the Prussians put the spotlight on the issue of national leadership in France and propelled Émile Boutmy to create, in 1871, the École libre des sciences politiques. Boutmy acknowledged the threatened status of French elites and hoped to infuse them with a sense of dynamic renewal based on merit and utilitarian criteria, not on staid tradition and the privileges of birth. Le Play himself reacted to the events of 1870 by pointing an accusatory finger at the ruling elite of France. His pamphlet, *La paix sociale après le désastre* (1871), draws a rather bleak portrait of the nation's leadership: "Few are the men of social standing who think and live nobly, who care for public affairs with true devotion. Each day, the number of these good citizens diminishes. Assured of having life's necessities, these men once led simple and dignified existences by voluntarily imposing duties upon themselves that were greater than the formal obligations of an honest man, and by dedicating their surplus of resources and labor to the general well-being. . . . These men embodied the true French elite." Without that elite, Le Play warned, "France has no sure direction [or] continuity in its ideas."[83]

From the earliest years of the Third Republic, contemporaries like the liberal economist Paul Leroy-Beaulieu anxiously observed the emergence of what they perceived to be "two Frances"—one that had attained a degree of economic and cultural integration into the bourgeois republic, and another that was impoverished and remained begrudgingly poised in the margins of the regime. Did elites have a responsibility to address this growing problem? In 1875 Leroy-Beaulieu expressed both his awareness of a distinct working-class world and his perplexity when confronted with its apparent opaqueness. "We are much more familiar," he wrote, "with the peasant than [we are with] the worker," who remains ensconced in "an unknown world to which we have very little access." [84]

Although his comments lent a sense of urgency to efforts to study the industrial world, Leroy-Beaulieu's claims to familiarity with the lives of peasants also placed him in the position of identifying with an older, well-established agrarian elite—of which, however, he was not a part. Betraying his own insecure identity as a member of a new industrial and business elite, he established rhetorical continuity with an apparently more stable elite, whose legitimacy was based in the land, not in the shifting values of capital. Conversely, he invoked the immutable values of the peasantry in contrast to the unknowable, transient, and potentially explosive industrial working class. The unsettling, partially obscured image of the new urban and industrial worker reflected back a similarly unstable self-portrait of a member of a new elite that sought control but often failed to achieve it. The familial model of a community of interests between agrarian elites and the peasantry remained a curiously comforting ideal for a man who, through his high-profile writings and professional life, was thoroughly imbued with the contemporary problems of his century and his social class.

By adopting a social mission, however, members of the industrial bourgeoisie could seek to establish themselves as members of a legitimate elite. Although fitted to a modern industrial era, their ideal of the elite's "social duty" remained partly rooted in the hierarchical vision of an *ancien régime* social order, since one of the traditional cultural and political attributes of the nobility, *noblesse oblige*, had been that of providing protection for the weak. In turn, this ideal of social honor was transposed onto the industrial and economic elite of nineteenth-century France. A recurrent theme of anti-industrialist discourse, for instance, was that employers mercilessly exposed workers, without any form of protection, to the violence of industrial competition and the dangers of new production processes. How could industrialists claim to constitute a true elite if they could not protect their own workers? This theme of social responsibility was particularly powerful in France, where the notion of an elite resonated with the formation of an honor-bound feudal aristocracy.[85]

In his book *L'Ouvrière* (1860), republican statesman, moralist, and reformer Jules Simon adopted similar discursive strategies, but not to condemn industrialism; instead, he sought to promote reform within the industrial world, urging industrialists to seize this opportunity to establish their social legitimacy. To achieve this goal, Simon surmised that it would be necessary to educate not only workers but industrialists as well. The only industrialists who were worthy of bearing the title *patron*, he claimed, were those who heeded the call to reform. "Worthy industrialists" worked not only for their own individual profit but, by striving for industrial betterment, for the honor and growth of national industry as well. The others, those who wanted to make big profits and then just as quickly disappear from the public arena, were merely "adventurers of industry." Not surprisingly, in the area of industrial welfare, Simon had particular praise for the initiatives of the Société industrielle de Mulhouse, whose entrepreneurs he viewed as true captains of industry. Their legacy, Simon claimed, would someday be regarded as having regenerated France's "industrial mores." [86]

By the 1880s the extension of industrial welfare practices within some of the nation's largest industries had developed to such proportions that it became possible to speak of industrial paternalism. In company towns like Le Creusot—with its employer-sponsored schools, housing, health services, daycare centers, accident insurance, and retirement plans—the notion of workers being "protected from the cradle to the grave" increasingly appeared to be a reality. Such protection, however, was not universally appreciated by workers. The scars of the Commune resurfaced as a reminder that attempts at workers' control in the workplace would be severely repressed. It was within this context, especially in the large mining areas, that the severe strike wave of the 1880s occurred. Many workers began to resent the interference of company policy in their private lives and the forced dependency that appeared to be the result of industrial paternalism. Workers also increasingly demanded control of their own mutual aid funds and resented the inability to move freely from one job site to another without losing their accumulated benefits. For instance, workers' loss of control over accident funds has been cited as a decisive factor in the 1884 strike at the Anzin mines. The practices of industrial paternalism were clearly aimed at maintaining a stable work force; they could no longer, however, ensure a docile one.[87]

Some industries began to experiment instead with "neopaternalism," which, by contrast with traditional paternalism, distinguished itself by industrial social-welfare schemes that encouraged the direct participation of labor. The engineer Émile Cheysson explained that compared to older forms of paternalism, neo-paternalism was a more liberal practice, better suited "to the political and social mores of the country." [88] Profit-sharing plans such as those advocated by the Society for Profit Sharing (founded by the Protestant Le Playist Charles Robert) constituted, according to Cheysson, one of the most perfect examples of neopaternalism, since they promoted greater worker involvement in the industries that adopted them. Among the Parisian firms that practiced profit sharing were the Magasins du Louvre, the publisher Armand Colin, and the Chaix printing firm. Housing schemes that allowed workers to design their construction plans, build their own houses, or become home owners through annuity payments were also examples of neopaternalist practices. The Vieille-Montange zinc mines, Saint-Gobain, the Paris Gas Company, and the Eastern and Southern Railroads all experimented with similar strategies. Some firms even allowed workers to participate in the management of their own health and accident funds. Considered to be a new and enlightened form of paternalism, such practices were premised on the idea that workers and employers had a common interest in securing the health and well-being of the entire workforce. One major problem with neopaternalist policies, however, was that they proved to be inadequate as an overall response to the social crisis of the 1880s: generally speaking, only the largest and wealthiest companies could afford to implement them. Those who did so, however, constituted "a vanguard" whose example was all the more significant to the industrial world at large precisely because they represented some of the most powerful companies in strategic sectors of the economy.[89]

By the 1880s, when Émile Cheysson and his friends began strategizing for reform, the social question in France had received no adequate answers. The solutions of the preceding decades had all been fragmentary, ineffectual, or insufficient. Paternalist solutions had proven too costly for most industries and touched only a small fraction of workers. Socialists were attempting to develop their own answers to the social question by organizing political parties, congresses, trade unions, producer and consumer cooperatives, newspapers, and mutual aid societies in the margins of, and in opposition to, the bourgeois republic. Social critics, despite presenting their ideas to the public and often capturing the attention of the highest government circles, never garnered sufficient political support to achieve more than a few pieces of protective legislation covering women's and children's labor. Responding to the disruptions posed by industrial labor to traditional gender arrangements proved to be a more consensual terrain than any other reform issue.

Yet, as Cheysson noted, fin de siècle reformers had at least infused the social question with a sense of urgency. The defeat of 1870, a devastating smallpox epidemic, and the violence of the Commune reignited the fear of social, moral, and even physical degradation that had plagued French elites for decades. In the climate of heightened nationalism that followed, many observers of the changing social world were called to action by the need to consolidate the regime of the Third Republic and strengthen its foundations. By the mid-1880s the political climate had thus taken a decisively republican turn.

The liberal generation of the Third Republic's founding fathers had achieved several important political and cultural goals that included resounding legislative victories and a surge of new policy choices reflecting republican values: the right of association, the freedom of the press, a new divorce law, and a civilizing mission promoted by Jules Ferry to further France's imperialist goals.[90] But it was the establishment of the compulsory and secular primary schools of the Third Republic (1881–82) that played the most critical role in defining and diffusing republican attitudes toward the social question. Civic education was introduced into the official curriculum in 1881 because the formation of the citizen was considered to be a Revolutionary heritage and "one of the primary needs of a republican society."[91] Personal hygiene and the notions of thrift and savings were highlighted in these lessons as being among the goals of a civic education in which private virtues and public comportment were intimately linked. Principles of self-reliance, or *le gouvernement de soi-même*, as it was sometimes referred to in the civics textbooks, were used to propagate the notion that self-control and individual autonomy were necessary to ensure the success of a liberal republic. Education was a tool with which to govern. If a citizen, in turn, could learn to govern himself (*se gouverner*), then France would theoretically no longer be tempted by authoritarian regimes.

To preserve their fundamental freedoms, France's young future citizens or the "wives of future citizens" needed to learn the moral as well as the political foundations of the Republic. "Ignorance of these matters," the republican Paul Bert proclaimed in one of his civics textbooks, was only "suitable to a despotic regime," one that was "in flagrant contradiction with a reign of liberty, discussion, and free election."[92] The basic message of these civics texts was that the citizens of a republic needed to rely first and foremost on themselves. With regard to the social question, these texts promoted the liberal ideal of *prévoyance*, thrift, foresight, and moral rectitude as a basic value of republican fraternity and solidarity. Schoolbooks from the early 1880s also promoted mutualism as a concrete example of *prévoyance*, and some schools even established mutual aid societies for their students. The term *solidarity* appears frequently in these texts, long before Léon Bourgeois elaborated his theory of solidarism. The Republic had an important role to play in ensuring the general welfare, but so did the individual: "Far from expecting everything from the state," one text explained, "a man should count only on himself." "If, however, he did not save money and act with foresight, or if he preferred the immediate gratification of his desires, then he alone is responsible for his downfall, and for that of his family as well."[93] The transformation of private mores was considered by liberal republicans to be tantamount to the formation of a responsible citizenship: "It is not enough to be in a republic," intoned Jules Simon, "if one does not have the austerity of republican mores."[94]

Yet despite education and the invocation of republican values, poverty persisted and loomed large as a disquieting indictment of the new Republic. Poverty reminded republicans, who considered themselves the legitimate standard-bearers of the Revolutionary tradition, that their inherited social mission had been left largely unaccomplished. Within this new political context, traditional charity—linked to a framework of Christian ethics and a model of hierarchical social relations—was increasingly incompatible with the needs of a secular republic. Private philanthropy, whether of a secular or confessional type, was viewed as a laudable but ultimately ineffective response to the needs of the working poor. The social question, posed in terms of republican and secular values, rose higher on the policy agenda of the Third Republic.

Despite growing public attention to the social question during the final decades of the century, the vast majority of laboring men and women in the nation's industrial sector were experiencing unprecedented levels of risk and insecurity in their lives and jobs. The great economic depression of the 1880s was forcing an end to the traditional multivalence of the French countryside and marking the beginning of the country's "second industrial revolution." It was also becoming evident that French industrialists had reached only a miniscule percentage of workers through their programs of industrial paternalism. Despite mounting sociological evidence to the contrary, however, the rhetorical strength of the argument that industrial employers, as members of a new, socially responsible elite, could provide sufficient social welfare coverage for the nation's workers endured well into the twentieth century.

In other quarters, the economic depression of the 1880s fueled criticism of the reigning liberal orthodoxy's apparent incapacity to explain, or even respond to, some of the country's most serious problems. Charles Gide, the economist and figurehead of the French cooperative movement, was convinced that if the banner of liberalism continued to be upheld by the nation's most prestigious institutions, publishing houses, economic associations, and journals, it was merely one consequence of the country's tumultuous past.[95] In 1887, as a direct response to what he saw as a changing climate of opinion in France, Gide created a new journal, the *Revue d'économie politique*. Representing a "new school" of social economy, Gide's *Revue* served as a rallying point for reaction against the orthodox liberal school and as a mouthpiece for those who advocated a more active role for government in social policy.[96]

Many other voices joined the chorus of critics who felt that the time had come to rethink the basic tenets of orthodox liberalism. To accomplish this goal, they drew upon the wealth of debate from earlier in the century. Commonly shared representations of society were undergoing profound transformations and had an impact on how the social question was being redefined. Darwin's theory of evolution had undermined the idea that immutable laws governed nature; hence, by transference from the biological to the social body, Pasteur's scientific theories and the model of contagion — "the solidarity of microbes" — implied the interdependence of social groups and the need for public policy to address the common good.[97] Faced with recent cycles of economic recession, some contemporaries — particularly Catholics and socialists — demanded the intervention of the state to end the unregulated chaos of industrial production, which they held to be the cause of economic and social strife. The prevailing anarchy, Gide explained, was the result of liberalism carried to an extreme, as reflected "in a distorting mirror." The Republic had brought in its wake the implicit promise of social mobility: citizens were better educated, and workers were more aware of their problems and rights; consequently, labor strikes were on the rise. These combined factors induced a broad range of contemporaries to begin questioning the beneficent action of liberal orthodoxy's "invisible hand."[98]

Some of these critics emerged from the Le Playist school, which had offered the "first breath of dissent" by demanding that an ethical dimension be maintained within industrial relations. This movement of "public piety," as the Orleanist and liberal Catholic count d'Haussonville described it, was a "very modern sentiment," distinct from charity. These were the "men of progress," who followed what Eugène Chevalier described in 1882 as "the generous principles of solidarity."[99] Although the early warnings and prescriptions of social commentators such as Sismondi, Villeneuve-Bargemont, Morgues, Blanqui, and Gérando had been ignored by liberal economists for many years, their writings regained relevance to republican reformers and social economists during the final decades of the century.

Increasingly conscious of the importance of the votes of industrial workers, the republican government's attitude toward them began to change. In 1883 the minister of commerce, Waldeck-Rousseau, and the ministry's director of the Bureau des associations professionnelles, Joseph Barberet, a former baker, launched a comprehensive industrial survey, the results of which were used to support the passage of the 1884 law authorizing labor associations. By 1885 the government was actively monitoring the labor situation and officially keeping strike statistics.[100] A fraction of republican politicians attempted to forge an alliance with representatives of labor in an effort to restrain the violence and repression of industrial conflicts. These *républicains de gouvernement*, the majority of whom were Radicals, hoped to break the autocracy of the industrial world by extending republican rights to workers. They also wanted the state to intervene by monitoring labor relations within the factory.

By 1886, when Joseph Barberet published his seven-volume study of labor monographs, the scope of social investigation in France was beginning to have an impact on public policy.[101] However, since France was still a largely rural country marked by a stalemate compromise between small landowners and the bourgeoisie, the political impetus within Parliament for urban and industrial reform was never very great.[102] Often operating within a political void, republican reformers therefore turned to extraparliamentary institutions to carry forward their initiatives and to mobilize public opinion.

The 1880s left France with a mixed legacy of social reform that included a strong but limited tradition of enlightened paternalism, a contested liberal tradition, a centralized state, a largely agrarian social structure, industrial concentration in select segments of the economy, a historic ambivalence of elites toward rapid industrial growth, and a tradition of criticizing industrialism. The final decades of the nineteenth century also introduced new sociological methods that would have a more direct impact on policy formation. In France, as well as in the industrial world at large, the political rhetoric of liberalism was put in temporary abeyance while the social rights of republican citizenship occupied the center stage of public discourse. A new variant of liberalism would emerge. Could the social sciences serve as a guide for public policy and action? The final decades of the nineteenth century would be marked by a struggle for control over the powerful vocabulary and metaphors of the social sciences as applied to public policy. By the late 1880s, the stage was set for a new language of social rights and responsibilities to emerge in modern France.

2. Inventing a Social Museum

～

Exhibition: Nineteenth Century subject of delirium.

—GUSTAVE FLAUBERT, *Dictionnaire des idées reçues*

Despite the false starts and failures of the preceding decades, liberal republicans such as Émile Cheysson and Jules Siegfried, the former businessman and mayor of Le Havre, seized upon the sociopolitical context of the late 1880s as a propitious moment to realize their vision of a new social contract for republican France. The 1889 Universal Exhibition held in Paris provided them with just such an opportunity. It served both as a catalyst and as a national stage for introducing their reform ideas to the public. Convinced that lasting solutions to France's social problems could be found only through the scientific study of industrial society, these men also used the 1889 Universal Exhibition to launch their concept of a "social museum"—which, in 1894, after several metamorphoses, became the Musée social.[1]

According to a nineteenth-century usage of the term *musée*, this novel museum embodied an important pedagogical mission. It would oversee a vast sociological survey of modern France, the findings of which, its promoters believed, would serve as a guide to the achievement of practical social reform for the Republic. But several years were required for these ideals to congeal and for reformers to build networks and decide on the best institutional support for their museum. This chapter traces how the idea of a social museum evolved over a six-year period, from its most embryonic form during the planning stages of the 1889 Universal Exhibition to the official inauguration of the Musée social in 1895.

The public, museological, and pedagogical functions of the 1889 Universal Exhibition, particularly as seen in its social economy section, a smaller exhibit devoted primarily to the role of labor within the industrial republic, provided direct inspiration for republican reformers to create the Musée social. The story of the Musée social's genesis serves as an analytical prism through which we can interpret a series of late-nineteenth-century reform initiatives—the successes as well as the failures—and how they inform us about the aspirations of middle-class reformers who observed contemporary social strife and thought they could, or should, contribute to its resolution. Taking a broader view, the steps leading from the 1889 Exhibition to the creation of the Musée social reveal the dense historical fabric of the early Third Republic: the political struggles and social movements of the period; the impact of the developing social sciences; and the crisis of liberalism that heralded a long debate on the legitimate role of the state in industrial society.

Another important feature of the process that led to the invention of the Musée social was the redrawing of boundaries between the public and the private spheres of life during the late nineteenth century. Situated at the crossroads of public and private interests, "the invention of the social," as Jacques Donzelot has termed it, constitutes one of the lasting legacies of this period for modern France. As successive republican governments took social politics more seriously, the social question not only moved onto center stage, but it became a matter of government regulation. However, if in the late 1880s and early 1890s republican reformers conspired to build a new institution whose primary function was to study industrial society and propose practical solutions to the social question, it was because, in their view, none of the existing government agencies, political groups, or private philanthropies of the early Third Republic was adequate to the task. Through what institutional channels, then, did they propose to address and remedy the social question? After examining various options for their Musée social, Jules Siegfried, Émile Cheysson, and their colleagues opted for a hybrid solution—a privately endowed foundation with public utility status—as the most flexible and dynamic structure to give shape to their vision of reform. Through their focus on the scientific study of industrial society, civic involvement, and the search for innovative institutional structures through which to remedy the social question, the Musée social and its founders were operating, as Madeleine Rebérioux aptly put it, "at the center of a social field under construction."[2]

Finally, by incorporating into this study an analysis of the rhetoric of republican reform, for which the 1889 Universal Exhibition became an official testing ground, I hope to demonstrate how reformers framed their arguments for social reform and presented them to the public for its approbation. Throughout the chapter, I argue that it was during this period, rather than during the Revolution of 1848, that France built the lasting foundations of a social republic.[3]

Industrial Culture at the 1889 Universal Exhibition

By 1889 the universal exhibition as a cultural form had become one of the great rituals for celebrating the industrializing world. Secular high masses devoted to industrial culture and society, exhibitions mobilized extraordinary material and human resources and transformed urban landscapes in France, England, and the United States. The industrial imagination was placed prominently on display as visitors from around the world congregated to contemplate the new thresholds of modernity.[4]

The shapes and language of industrialization were self-consciously presented at these exhibitions as harbingers of a dawning age of mass culture and production. This was particularly true of the 1889 Universal Exhibition held in Paris, where the Machine Palace[5] elegantly displayed ordinary factory machines as if they were precious objects and where the Eiffel Tower rose in tribute to the new sociocultural status of the engineer. The 1889 Exhibition's message was clear: industry had emerged as the matrix of modern life and culture. Indeed, modern technology did more than supply the gears, motors, and locomotives of industrial change; it gave rise to architectural forms that were feats of engineering in iron and glass. The constructions could inspire a new aesthetic, evoke a feeling of awe or national pride, and impart a message of confidence to the throngs of visitors who pressed their way from the Trocadéro Palace to the Champs de Mars, and along the Quai d'Orsay to the Esplanade des Invalides. In 1889 this unprecedented flourish of material wealth seemed to announce the beginning of a new modern era, as if the Exhibition itself were setting the stage for the upcoming millennium.

Much like a series of carefully positioned mirrors, however, the 1889 Universal Exhibition reflected a multitude of images highlighting the mutations and changing forms of life and culture in nineteenth-century industrial society. Although some images were relatively accurate, others, as if reflected in a fun-house hall of mirrors, represented distorted or contradictory impressions of the new industrial world. Many contemporaries found this sensation of change unsettling, not thrilling. In turn, the commonly shared but often exaggerated perception of rapid cultural and economic change that occurred in fin de siècle France introduced an element of uncertainty and conflict into representational forms ranging from literature and the plastic arts to public festivals such as the universal exhibitions.

The celebration of industrial life at the 1889 Universal Exhibition did not, therefore, go unchallenged. Although its hymn to modernity and progress was well orchestrated, the 1889 Universal Exhibition could barely conceal underlying tensions and conflicts that threatened its success and, at times, its very existence. One element of uncertainty and conflict stemmed from the uncomfortable juxtaposition of the Exhibition with the centennial celebration of the French Revolution. Despite official pronouncements attempting to dissociate the two events, the convergence of the Revolution's anniversary and the first universal exhibition planned entirely by a French republic was greeted with a cacophony of public reactions, ranging from exaltation to outrage. As will be discussed, the convergence of these two events, although conflict-ridden and perhaps merely coincidental, had a lasting impact on French political culture. In particular, as this chapter will demonstrate, the conjunction of the two major themes of the 1889 Universal Exhibition—the celebration of industrial culture and society, and the centennial of the French Revolution—served to generate a specifically republican rhetoric of social reform that marked the beginnings of an official social welfare policy in modern France.

The rhetoric of reform is most evident in the social economy section, one of ten official groups constituting the 1889 Exhibition. This section included the only displays at the fair devoted to the social question, including industrial welfare schemes, the problem of labor management, and certain features of working-class life and culture. Although resolutely pro-industrial, the social economy section also set out to inscribe the Republic within the social and political heritage of the French Revolution. The rhetoric of social reform that ensued was therefore part of "a historically conditioned discourse," dependent both on the republican ideal of finishing the work of the Revolution and on defending the benefits of industrial society.[6] This rhetoric of reform helped determine the ideological parameters for a reexamination of the Republic's social contract in fin de siècle France and set the stage for the rise of the modern French welfare state.

Mass Culture and National Unity at the Fair

To an unprecedented extent, the 1889 Universal Exhibition was geared toward a mass audience. Its displays of machinery, agricultural and manufactured products, architectural models, and colonial wares were part of a grandiose *leçon de choses* that often focused on the material culture of everyday life. Indeed, the physical incarnations of modernity at the fair were intended to be accessible to all: artisans, farmers, industrial workers, bourgeois *rentiers*, and foreign dignitaries alike could presumably understand and revel in the fruits of such material progress. The 1889 Exhibition generated new, popular symbols of the Republic, industrial progress, and national grandeur, including the Eiffel Tower, which today has outlived acerbic controversy about its aesthetic value to become a symbolic, even mythological amalgam of all that is "French." In 1889, however, the traditional allegorical figures carved into exhibition statuary to commemorate the ancient origins of the Republic no longer held much meaning for the general public; such classical references constituted "a nearly obsolete rhetoric," argues Pascal Ory. On the other hand, visitors could readily grasp the meaning of the multicolored, electrically illuminated fountain, with its operator stationed inside a glass booth like a demystified Wizard of Oz, manipulating huge levers to produce the desired effect. "What better way to plead the cause of democracy as the predictable culmination of the progress of the Enlightenment" than to offer visitors a nightly spectacle of illuminated fountains shooting water triumphantly twenty meters into the air? Consonant with the image of republican France as a democratizing polity, and in sharp contrast to a restricted, aristocratic model of high culture, the 1889 Universal Exhibition celebrated the new symbols and context of a mass culture derived from the evolving conditions of industrial and urban life. Its organizers transformed this extraordinary public forum into a pedagogic instrument, soliciting all members of an idealized and harmonious republican family to participate in the benefits of industrial society.[7]

One general function of nineteenth-century exhibitions was to consecrate the existence of an expanding and all-embracing industrial culture. In his book on the Chicago World's Fair of 1893, Alan Tractenberg has argued that these exhibitions sought "to display the fruits of production as universal culture." [8] Accordingly, and as part of an Enlightenment heritage, the exhibitions served a museological function and attempted to give order to the modern world by establishing categories, hierarchies, and types of putative universal value.[9] Yet the universal topos adopted by the exhibitions was not universally accepted. Speculation and controversy arose over the nature of progress and competition, the definition of industrial society, and the place of nation-states in an imperial and industrial world order. This became particularly evident when, during the 1889 Universal Exhibition, two socialist congresses convened and articulated very different objectives. As Walter Benjamin's percipient eye captured so well, these celebrations of "universal" material progress belied an anxiety concerning the extinction of an old order and the doubt that the new industrial utopia could fulfill its promise of a more egalitarian society.[10] Indeed, upon closer examination, nineteenth-century expositions did not always impart a clear message of confidence in the future.

The years and months prior to the 1889 Universal Exhibition had posed a number of domestic threats to the stability of the regime. One of its greatest trials came from General Boulanger, whose successful and broad-based protest movement revived apprehensions of a coup d'état, a specter that haunted a country whose political history had been punctuated by such attempts.[11] The founding fathers of the Republic did not take this challenge to the regime lightly; some even contemplated exile.[12] In the face of the Boulangist threat, the Universal Exhibition of 1889 emerged as an opportunity to rally support for the fledgling Republic. The Exhibition also offered to boost confidence in the economy, given the protracted economic depression of the 1880s. At the very least, the Exhibition would help France believe in herself again. As Georges Berger, the general director of the Exhibition, indicated to Jules Simon in 1888: "Everything seems to be going badly, but there is one thing that is still going extraordinarily well, for France and the rest of the world: the Exhibition." [13]

Despite the optimistic, celebratory tone in which the exhibition catalogues were written, the actual consolidation of the Republic had not gone unchallenged. The official documents and the carefully organized events surrounding the Exhibition were therefore intended to create an aura of consensus and to consolidate the regime.[14] In 1889, however, despite attempts to present the world with a vision of national unity and progress, plans for the Exhibition were nearly shattered by the proposed centennial celebration of the French Revolution.

Inscribing the Revolutionary Heritage

Since the 1889 Universal Exhibition was the first in France to be completely planned and executed under a republican regime, the government hoped it would provide a forum for legitimizing the country's Revolutionary heritage by firmly inscribing that heritage within the history of the Republic. In this light, the 1889 Exhibition and the centennial commemoration were perceived by the public as being "inextricably linked." Passions soon flared throughout the international community, however, at the mere mention of celebrating the violent downfall of the French monarchy. All monarchs immediately said: "It is a celebration of 1793, and we cannot possibly allow our subjects to take part in it." When several monarchs and heads of state threatened to cancel their visits to the Exhibition, it was a cruel reminder to the young Republic that the continental powers still regarded the Third Republic as a renegade regime and the inheritor of an unpardonable regicide.[15]

But international dissent was not the only cause for alarm: the centennial commemoration also generated considerable debate in domestic political circles. Dissension even occurred within the ranks of French republicans over the legacy of the Revolution, both among elites and intellectuals and between the bourgeoisie and the laboring classes. The divided legacy over conflicting interpretations of the Revolution—the liberal revolution of 1789 versus the radical revolution of 1793—still split republicans who claimed to be the legitimate heirs of an entire ideological tradition. Plans for the centennial commemoration also exacerbated historic tensions between the city of Paris and the central government, and the recent socialist municipal electoral victories succeeded in compounding the problem by pitting socialists against conservative republicans. Dissent arose as well at the opposite end of the political spectrum when some conservatives and monarchists banded together to launch a countercentennial movement. In an attempt to galvanize opinion around a moderate version of the Revolutionary past, republican forefather Jules Simon argued that it was necessary to "protest on this and every other occasion against the confusion which has developed between 89 and 93." [16]

To avert a brewing domestic and diplomatic crisis, the republican government strictly circumscribed plans for the centennial celebration. To safeguard the success of the 1889 Exhibition, it formally banned meetings of a religious or political nature and excluded all Revolutionary memorabilia and statuary from the fairgrounds. But references to the Revolution did not disappear quite so easily. By curtailing its initial plans for the centennial, the government of the Third Republic opted to present the world with a "modern" image of France: one united by the fruits of material progress, not torn apart by ideological divisions. Despite these efforts to obviate France's conflict-laden historical memory, traces of the centennial commemoration persisted at the fair both in exposition statuary and in the texts of inaugural speeches. Pascal Ory suggests that visitors to the Exhibition had no trouble recognizing the double significance of the Eiffel Tower: it was both the symbol of industrial progress and "the true commemorative monument of 1789." The Eiffel Tower was "the gateway to the modern world." "Mathematics and materialism" had made it possible to construct a tower that reached upward to "a sky where there was perhaps no God, but where at least there was electricity." [17]

Despite attempts to downplay the French Revolution, it remained the primary historical referent at the 1889 Universal Exhibition. Organizers credited the events of 1789 not only with ushering in a long list of political and social freedoms but also with the "emancipation of trade and industry." [18] According to their perspective on history, the abrogation of the Le Chapelier Law in 1791 put an end to a series of abuses and obstacles and led to the development of a free market. As a result, they portrayed the French Revolution as one of the historical "motors" of industrialization, and all of the material wealth on display at the Exhibition as one of its consequences.

"The Revolution of 1789 begins a new era. . . . Liberated from arbitrary shackles, fertilized by the free growth of human activity, French production enters the path of uninterrupted progress that will be hers throughout the nineteenth century." [19] Embedded within this rhetorical account, whereby the French Revolution also becomes the matrix of the nation's economic growth, lies the repeated refrain of the linear progression of history. Characterized as "uninterrupted," nineteenth-century French economic development is explained as a force unleashed by the Revolution itself. In tautological fashion, the notion of an inevitable progression of history is used to justify the end result: an industrial republic. According to this narrative, which formed an essential subtext of the republican rhetoric of reform, all social and industrial progress is rooted in the Revolution, and its development is evidenced by history.

First and foremost, the 1889 Exhibition was set up as an official public defense of the fruits of industrial progress since the Revolution. In addition to sounding the clarions of the future society, the organizers of the Exhibition promoted it as a gigantic cultural and historical retrospective demonstrating all that had been accomplished in the century gone by. Even the popular Galerie des machines was more of a retrospective than an exhibit turned toward the future. Incorporated into the physical presentation of the machines and technical achievements was the familiar narrative that stressed the evolution of industrial development as a linear, historical progression. The Galerie des machines served to illustrate the march of modernity: an entire way of life was being implicitly defended in each of its displays. If production was becoming more mechanized, it was all for the sake of creating a more modern and even a more democratic society. Portrayed in this manner, the itinerary of industrial development appeared reinforced by the very logic of history, which, since the French Revolution, had entered into the modern, secular age of progress and science. Despite momentary setbacks in French political history, the primary historical narrative of the 1889 Exhibition stressed the overall march of humanity since the Enlightenment as being one of inevitable progress.

But this retrospective rhetoric was also introspective: to what extent had the French Revolution been left unfinished? Also, how had such material wealth been generated? To many visitors, the answer seemed obvious enough: the fairgrounds, in all their material splendor, stood not only as a testimony to the forces of economic development and the accumulation of capital but also to the monumental achievements of labor. Émile Cheysson imagined that the visitor who was exhausted with admiration — "as if crushed under the weight of this artistic and industrial grandeur" —

would naturally be led to wonder about the workers who were responsible for building such magnificent displays: "Here is a new world of iron and industry surging forth," he wrote. "What will become of its actors?"[20] Although it might seem imprudent for a republican gala celebration of national productivity to occur without acknowledging the labor force that made it possible, references to the industrial worker remained largely a subtext of the official exhibition discourse.

The social question, or the role of labor in the Republic, was not initially a planned feature of the 1889 Exhibition.[21] Decided almost as an afterthought, and urged by private citizens who were not on the government planning committee, a new section on social economy was authorized only in 1887 to figure in the Universal Exhibition. Four men, belonging to overlapping social reform networks, were responsible for this turn of events: two followers of Frédéric Le Play, Émile Cheysson and Charles Robert, who was also known to French reformers as the chief promoter of profit-sharing; Etienne Lami, the author of the official French report on the 1885 Exhibition held in Anvers; and Jules Siegfried, whose actions in the area of social policy as mayor of Le Havre had already earned him a position of certain stature in reform circles.[22] These men did not want the 1889 Exhibition to run the risk of suggesting the separate existence of "two Frances"—one that clearly benefited from the regime of material abundance, and one that merely toiled and made sacrifices. They saw the social economy section as an opportunity to present the public with an image of social and political harmony within the Republic. But at the same time, they thought it would be a mistake for the government to ignore the question of the social costs of industrialization. These issues, they felt, should be addressed in the social economy exhibit.

Social economists such as Cheysson and Siegfried recognized that there had been excesses and imbalances created by rapid industrialization. In a country with a resurgent socialist movement and increasingly sharp labor disputes, they hoped, moreover, that the social economy exhibit would convey the political message that workers were not the forgotten members of the larger republican family. A possible panacea to France's growing social ills, social economy was portrayed as an integral part of republican ideology, even as a repository of the Revolutionary values of social justice and fraternal cooperation between classes.

Focused on labor and the social relations of industrial production, the social economy section, although small in size, was rich in rhetoric. It did not highlight the political dimension of the Revolutionary heritage, but rather its social legacy to the Third Republic. One hundred years earlier, Revolutionary committees had posed the problems of social welfare, education, and aid to the indigent and the elderly.[23] If republicans were to pick up the banner and finish the work of the Revolution, they would have to address these social concerns. Moreover, as a polity based on universal (male) suffrage, the Third Republic could no longer avoid the problem of poverty or the concern that it might be an endemic feature of industrialization.

Although the social economy section addressed the social question, it also fit within a global rhetorical strategy of the 1889 Universal Exhibition to defend industrial society. As seen in the preceding chapter, nineteenth-century reformers of all persuasions had participated in a long debate concerning the relative benefits and drawbacks of industrial expansion. The promoters of the social economy exhibit came down clearly on one side of this debate. Although decidedly in favor of industrialization and economic growth as a precondition for a stable regime that aspired to improve the material conditions of its citizens' lives, they were also conscious of having inherited a social mission from their Revolutionary predecessors. Vigorously affirming their political identities as republicans, they relied on references to the Republic's Revolutionary heritage to justify their call for reform. If the industrialization of France was going to succeed, they argued, the Third Republic was going to have to reexamine its social policy. Certain reforms aimed at improving low-cost housing and insuring workers against the risks of accident, illness, and old age were urgently needed. At first these reformers hoped to use the social economy exhibit to convince industrialists to take independent action and improve social welfare services in their own factories. If this did not occur, they warned, the state would have to intervene, and social legislation would have to be enacted. The social economy section, therefore, presented an official commentary on the debate over the pros and cons of industrial progress. Reformers used the 1889 Universal Exhibition as a public platform from which to argue their case.

The "Social Mechanics" of the Industrial World

The language of social reform used in both the planning stages and in the social economy catalogue is of particular importance to the overall legitimization strategy pursued by exhibit organizers. By drawing on the semantic prestige and legitimacy of science and technology, promoters of the social economy section borrowed vocabulary and analogies from the world of applied science to help forge a more technical and scientific discourse on society. Thus, reformers frequently depicted society as a highly complex machine with delicate gears that could only be tinkered with by trained experts who, in this new metaphorical landscape, were typically engineers or industrial advisors. Technical vocabulary, with greater emphasis on statistics and mathematical equations, conferred new legitimacy on the claims of self-taught social scientists and reformers, who identified with a positivist worldview that emphasized empiricism over theoretical speculation and who had been influenced by developments in the scientific world, from the physiological demonstrations of Claude Bernard and the evolutionism of Darwin to the biological experiments of Pasteur. Their vision of society, much like the language they used, was based on the acceptance of a basic social paradigm in which applied science and technology would trace the path to progress and modernity and eventually to social peace.

Whereas the imposing Galerie des machines, the iron frame of which was designed by Gustave Eiffel, stood as a monument to the materials, machinery, and motors of the Industrial Revolution, the nearby social economy exhibit provided a perfect counterpoint by highlighting the "social mechanics" of the industrial world. This phrase, a translation of *outillage social*, was coined by Émile Cheysson to explain the contents and function of the social economy exhibit: "Side by side with the manual and mechanical tools offered to the gaze of visitors . . . it would be suitable to the democratic orientation of our mores to also display what one might call the 'social mechanics' of the workshops, that is to say the means to improve the welfare of workers and to ensure harmonious industrial relations with their employers." [24] In like manner, Cheysson exhorted engineers to supplement their finely honed technical skills with an equally fine understanding of the workings of contemporary society. "In the fields of chemistry, medicine, law, or mechanics, no one would do without the help of specialists," he argued. So why should it be any different with regard to the social relations of production? In an attempt to encourage engineers to apply their technical expertise to social relations in the workplace, Cheysson asked members of the Society of Civil Engineers in Paris if they thought "social mechanics would be easier to regulate than those of a machine made of iron or copper." He assured them that to assume so would be an error, since behind each machine "there was a man, with his complexity, his passions, and his interests."[25] The quest for a science of society, one that approached the complexities of social and industrial life with the precision of a scientist or an engineer, appeared increasingly to be a goal befitting a secular republic. Cast into the semantic mold of industrial progress and Revolutionary values, the language of social reform could thereby gain even wider public acceptance and legitimacy.

Another important dimension of the attempt to transfer a scientific discourse to the realm of politics and society was the claim of rising above ideological conflict. The adoption of a mechanistic, rational, and seemingly objective language with which to speak about otherwise conflictual social problems gave republican reformers a powerful tool with which to advance their goals. Strengthened by this empirical approach, they cloaked their agenda for social reform in the authority conferred on it by science and garnered support for their ideas as part of the pursuit of the general interest of society. Republican reformers thereby hoped to supersede the ideological debates that had divided France since the Revolution and to argue that the republican state and its developing social policy would represent the superior interests of the nation.

Each of these different discursive elements — the defense of industrialization, the Republic's Revolutionary heritage, and a more scientific approach to the understanding of industrial society — combined to produce a distinctly republican rhetoric of social reform. This rhetoric was intended to help republicans continue the interrupted social mission of the Revolution and to justify making social policy part of the normal business of government. As demonstrated in the social economy exhibit, organizers maintained that industrialization did not inevitably increase levels of poverty, that the Third Republic was not turning a deaf ear to workers, and that social reform was necessary in order to attain social peace. This process of bringing public policy into a forum designed for a mass audience was a constituent part of the modernity on display at the fair. In 1889 social policy was not yet an integrated function of government (the Conseil supérieur du travail, for instance, was founded in 1891), and it was still unclear whether social policy fell under the purview of industrialists or of the state. Was the factory a private space, protected from regulation, or a public space that could be regulated? Until this juncture in the Republic, social legislation had been piecemeal, and no official attempt had been made to define a coherent social policy. For these reasons I contend that a republican rhetoric of reform, one that argued for the development of social welfare policy in France, was first articulated publicly at the 1889 social economy exhibit.

The creation in 1887 of a special section devoted to social economy was, however, clearly a politically motivated decision that set ideological parameters on future government involvement in social politics. When the Radical minister of commerce and industry, Edouard Lockroy, tried to incorporate a socialist contingent into the new section, the idea was adamantly rejected by the Exhibition's organizing committee and the project almost abandoned. A conservative republican, the Exhibition's general director, George Berger, was acutely aware of the symbolic dimension of a social economy exhibit; if approved, it would quickly evolve into a public platform for the articulation of the Third Republic's emerging social policy. Since it would be perceived as such, Berger did not want to include socialists who were vociferous critics of the social costs of industrialization. When Benoît Malon refused to play the role of a token socialist in a bourgeois exhibit, the *Revue socialiste* railed against Berger for giving over the exhibit to the disciples of Le Play, "the most fearsome clerical-monarchist-economist enemies of the Republic and its emancipatory ideas."[26] Since the basic political premise of the 1889 Exhibition was to promote industrialization while consolidating the Republic, moderate and conservative republicans rejected their proposed socialist partners. This early exclusion of even moderate socialists from the social economy section indicates that any attempt to treat the sensitive questions of labor relations and social politics was far from consensual, even on the center-left of the political spectrum. From its very inception, the social economy section was intended to be an important vehicle of conservative republican ideology.

Located on the Esplanade des Invalides, just a few steps away from the main display of the French Ministry of War, the social economy exhibit was thus officially promoted by the government as the Exposition's monument to social peace, since its primary goal was to suggest ways to regulate and reduce social conflict within the Republic. The irony of this physical layout with its militaristic subtext was not lost on Émile Melchior de Vogüé, an aristocrat preoccupied with the social question, who quipped: "He who says peace presupposes a former state of war . . . another mode of the struggle for life." [27] Indeed, Vogüé had pointed to one of the great silences of the exhibit, the absence of any reference to labor unrest. Although trade unions had been legalized in 1884, the exhibit recognized only those that promoted class harmony. Reminiscent of the earlier barring of socialists from the exhibit, this omission of any explicit reference to labor unrest implied that organizers wanted to avoid any potential image of conflict that could tarnish their presentation to the public of an organic industrial family. As was true of the Exhibition generally, the social economy section proposed a carefully molded vision of industrializing France. Designed, in part, to reconcile the working classes with the Third Republic, the exhibit proffered the social wares of the enlightened industrialists: employer-owned daycare centers, housing and old-age pension plans, and a variety of organizations promoting mutual aid and self-help for workers. This social economy exhibit would give rise, five years later, to the creation of the Musée social, whose founders hoped to showcase similar reform initiatives on a more permanent basis.

The theme of France's national and military grandeur also prompted fair organizers to situate the social economy exhibit directly across from the colonial exhibit, the Exhibition's monument to French imperial expansion under the Third Republic. Commenting on this curious spatial juxtaposition, Cheysson remarked, "By a contrast which, although not planned, is nevertheless striking, the social economy exhibit was installed directly across from Annam, Cambodia, and Tonkin. Along one axis of the esplanade, there was the Orient, frozen in the immobility of forty thousand years; whereas, along the other, there was the West, burgeoning with the problems of the modern world." By characterizing social reform as inherently modern and progressive, in sharp contrast to the ancient, immobile world of the Orient, Cheysson suggested that human societies evolved according to a hierarchical order of complexity. Such rhetorical mirroring of metropole and colonial empire became a common feature of an imperialist discursive strategy to define civilization itself as an evolutionary hierarchy with complex Western industrial societies at its pinnacle.[28] To a more prescient observer, however, the proximity of the colonial and the social economy exhibits might have suggested yet another implicit ethnographic logic: the observation and comparison of cultures so distinct from the dominant model of the French bourgeoisie that they both seemed to warrant the status of curiosities. The analogy between the two exhibits was further reinforced by their similar physical layouts (see figures 1 and 2). Covering half of the total area space of the esplanade, the displays of the colonial exhibit included ornate national-style palaces representing Algeria, Tunisia, Annam, Tonkin, Cochin China, and India; an entire reconstructed African village; a *souk* (marketplace) replete with indigenous merchants; and a life-size simulation of a typical animated Arab street, lined with palm and coconut trees. Women appeared alongside men merely as secondary actors in simulated displays of street merchants, traditional dance, and the material culture of domestic life. The official catalog concluded that "the illusion was complete, visitors could imagine themselves on the other side of the Mediterranean." Here, the imagined empire was construed as more true to life, more perfectly represented, than the imperfect reality it sought to emulate. At the 1889 Exhibition the public encountered an idealized version of imperial rule that had a lasting impact on French popular representations of the colonial world.[29]

In mirrored fashion, on display as part of the social economy exhibit was the Workers' Housing Street, composed of four full-scale models of low-cost housing, some of which were decorated with domestic furnishings typical of a working-class household and, in one case, adorned with workers themselves, dressed in their traditional blue overalls and accompanied by their "hard-working families." [30] The social economy exhibit presented the public with clean object lessons of a microcosmic social utopia, not the sensational, tactile world of odors, humidity, filth, and darkness that reformers so obsessively detailed in their written descriptions of visits to the slums during their discovery of pauperism. Instead, visitors who strolled down the exhibit alleys could participate in a continuum of displays that spatially and discursively linked orderly workers

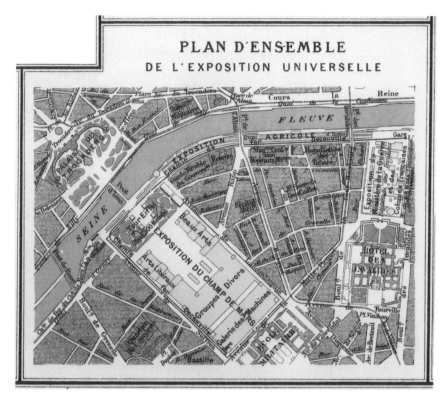

PLAN D'ENSEMBLE

DE L'EXPOSITION UNIVERSELLE

Figure 1. General layout of 1889 Universal Exhibition, Champs de
Mars. Ministère du commerce de l'industrie et des colonies, Exposition
universelle internationale de 1889. Bibliothèque nationale, Paris.

in model housing to the exotica of African dancers and the amusement of
donkey rides across the street. Both the social economy and the colonial
exhibits provided commentaries on the hegemonic bourgeois republican
order by offering the public carefully planned visual demonstrations of the
moral and material progress of industrialization, on the one hand, and of
colonialism, on the other.

The Social Economy Exhibit

Occupying one-quarter of the total space of the Esplanade des Invalides,
the social economy section included two main exhibits devoted to
working-class culture: the "Cité sociale," conceived as a grandiose

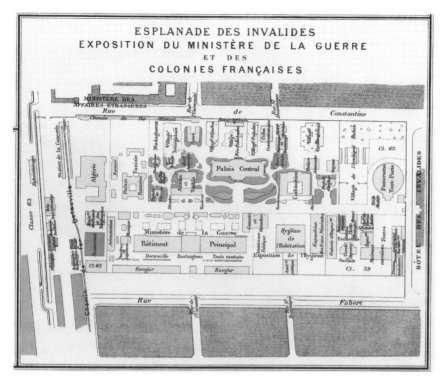

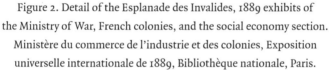

Figure 2. Detail of the Esplanade des Invalides, 1889 exhibits of
the Ministry of War, French colonies, and the social economy section.
Ministère du commerce de l'industrie et des colonies, Exposition
universelle internationale de 1889, Bibliothèque nationale, Paris.

workers' village, and the "Galerie de l'économie sociale," which displayed
documents on recent industrial experiments in social welfare. Among
other displays, the Cité sociale featured a *fourneau économique*, set up by
the Société philanthropique, that offered meals for 10 centimes each and
a Temperance Café, sponsored by the Women's Christian Temperance
Union of Chicago, where tea was served.[31] Two private insurance companies, the New York and the Urbaine, also figured prominently in the
Cité sociale, as did a pavilion devoted to Charles Robert's Society for
Profit-Sharing, with displays on 131 French companies with profit-sharing
schemes, including the Bon Marché and the Familistère de Guise. A pyra-
mid built in honor of the English cooperative movement and a section
devoted to gymnastic societies combined the themes of social economy

with those of worker sociability and leisure activities. Finally, a temple was constructed to honor the Maison Leclaire, the first company in France to practice profit-sharing, and its founder Jean Leclaire, a house painter who, a forerunner of mutualism, also created the Mutual Aid Society of Housing Painters in 1838.

Although they were inheritors of a philanthropic tradition, the planners of the social economy exhibit ultimately rejected it as a model for social welfare; goodwill and charitable sentiment, they now argued, were insufficient for achieving social harmony. Moreover, in the political, social, and religious context of late-nineteenth-century France, they considered charity to be incompatible with the needs of a secular republic since it was linked to the Catholic Church, a framework of Christian ethics, and a model of rigid hierarchical social relations. A republican rhetoric of reform that stressed self-help was therefore needed. Although personally involved in a myriad of charitable efforts, liberal reformers increasingly viewed philanthropy as an ineffective response to the needs of the working poor. Goodwill might be the motor of reform, but, they concluded, technique must be its rudder. The English Central Cooperative Board, whose banner proclaimed "Self Help by Mutual Help," best summarized the Cité sociale's overall social philosophy. The model working-class housing built by the chocolate magnate Menier or the mining company of Anzin also illustrated this approach by displaying housing plans based on long-term employer loans to personnel for the construction of individual homes or the acquisition of property. By promising a limited degree of direct worker involvement and autonomy, this type of housing scheme suggested an alternative, more liberal strategy for labor management and social reform.[32]

An exhibit on workingmen's clubs featured discussion circles, libraries, trade-related evening courses, and groups promoting leisure activities for male workers.[33] In his report on this part of the exhibit, Étienne Lami affirmed that workers needed places in which to meet and socialize other than local bars and *cafés concerts*. By the same token, the bourgeois promoters of social economy sought places where they might be in contact with workers on an occasional basis. Such mixed social spaces, Lami admitted, were practically nonexistent in late-nineteenth-century France: there was no place where "practical socialists, philanthropic entrepreneurs, and good-willed men" could engage in discussions with "reasonable workers." Confronted with the exacerbation of social tensions and the recognition of economic, spatial, and cultural barriers separating the social classes, reformers promoted workingmen's clubs as a means of facilitating interclass relations.[34]

Republican reformers also saw the workingmen's clubs as a potential vehicle for civic education, all the more necessary in a regime of universal (male) suffrage. One such club, located in Le Havre, was the Cercle Franklin (named after Benjamin Franklin), sponsored by Jules Siegfried and operated by workers. An impressive brick structure built in 1875 with a gymnasium, a reading room, a library, and an evening school for laborers, the Cercle Franklin adopted a cultural and educational mission, offering classes, concerts, and Sunday afternoon lectures organized by the Ligue de l'enseignement. During the inaugural ceremonies, Siegfried affirmed that the Cercle Franklin would "serve no political party or church," but would attempt, instead, to develop "the moral independence that forms the true citizen." On the same occasion, Jules Simon stressed the need for civic education in France as a means of bridging the gap between a political regime that proclaimed civic liberties and a social order that still belied them.[35] For its achievements, particularly its propagation of popular libraries, the Cercle Franklin was awarded a gold medal at the 1889 Exhibition. In contrast, the social Catholic Albert de Mun's workingmen's group, the Oeuvre des cercles d'ouvriers catholiques, was denied a spot at the exhibit, since it was deemed too political and militant in nature. In 1874 De Mun had called on its members to engage in a life-or-death struggle against the Revolution. His proposal was rejected because the Cité sociale only promoted those forms of associational life and leisure activities for workers that would simultaneously reinforce republican and secular notions of civic education.

The attention bourgeois reformers paid to workingmen's clubs in this part of the exhibit also implicitly defined the notion of leisure as being primarily a male preserve. Their gender-specific notion of leisure activities was linked, moreover, to an even more pervasive bourgeois idealization of the worker as being male. This general omission of women from the mise-en-scène of labor was part of a broader romanticized vision of the working class in which social relations reproduced, in miniature, the structures of bourgeois life itself. After all, if bourgeois models of society and culture were hegemonic in fin de siècle France, they also predominated in the republican reformers' visions of an ideal society and influenced their prescriptions for social reform. One implied message of this part of the exhibit, therefore, was that just as women in a perfect bourgeois family stayed at home, relegated to the domestic sphere, working-class women should refrain from seeking employment in industrial factories. This truncated representation of working-class life carried with it yet another key subliminal message: the omission of women laborers was an important rhetorical component in the projection of industrialization as a beneficial force for the Third Republic. As long as women stayed at home, the exhibit implied, industrialization could proceed without inflicting harm on the family and therefore on the stability of society generally. The absence of women workers, socialists, and labor unrest from depictions of working-class life constituted another significant unspoken theme of the overall social economy exhibit.

The Gallery of Social Economy, on the other hand, was reserved for a more sober, methodical demonstration of social welfare experiments, primarily in industrial settings. This more austere display consisted mainly of diagrams, wall murals, charts, books, and brochures. Whenever possible, the wooden stands mounted by industrial exhibitors incorporated banners, models of handwork, insignia, and other visual elements, such as miniature models of worker housing or a daycare center. Organizers sought to leave a lasting impression on even the most hurried spectator: "The international public gathered in Paris had to be made aware of the interest of each exhibit, but not by explaining them as in lectures, but by putting them in direct physical contact with the evidence, in a museum of documents, charts, drawings, graphs, tables and mural legends (see figure 3). Thus, through the observer's eyes, these documents could reach straight to the soul of often ignorant visitors, who are approached, as it were, through the concrete experience of life in order to bring them to intellectual reflection." [36] This "museum of documents" was assembled to pay tribute to the industrialists who had experimented successfully with social programs and to underscore the resulting harmony and stability of their workforce. One graph represented the curve of employment stability at the Creusot mines, a company where 1,491 of the workers had more than thirty years of service. To illustrate the same point pictorially, some stands boasted photographs of long-term employees and other members of the same family who had worked side by side for generations. Striking

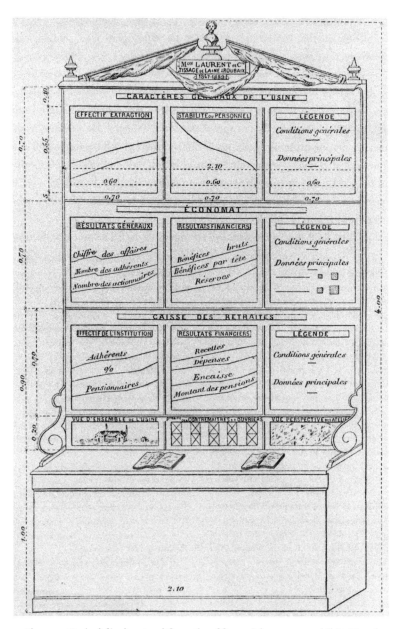

Figure 3. Typical display stand from the 1889 social economy exhibit. Picard ed., Ministère du commerce, de l'industrie et des colonies. Exposition universelle internationale de 1889 à Paris. *Rapports du jury international. Groupe de l'economie social*, 2:353. CEDIAS-Musée social, Paris.

a nationalistic note, these results were portrayed in stark contrast to the German metallurgical factories of Krupp, Herde, and Bochum where, according to an 1873 survey, the worker turnover rate exceeded 75 percent during the year.[37]

At the conclusion of the fair, the Anzin mining company received an award for its model worker housing; the Baccarat crystal works, for its professional training schools and medical service; and Le Bon Marché department store, for its employee profit-sharing program. These "enlightened" industrialists of republican France had had the foresight to experiment with social welfare policies and could serve as models for the country as a whole. This part of the exhibit was a demonstration of liberalism with a social conscience.

Liberalism and the Rhetorics of Reform

The section on social economy had been forged on the basis of a narrowly defined liberalism that exalted employer-sponsored initiatives and excluded the state from the arena of social welfare. Indeed, the two main approaches to social reform presented by the exhibit were private employer initiatives and associational life as illustrated by the workingmen's circles. These two distinct means of addressing the social question functioned quite differently, since one stressed neo-paternalistic practices, whereas the other promoted worker self-help and autonomy. The first emphasized the importance of maintaining a stable workforce; the second highlighted the goals of republican civic education and interclass communication. One implied that social reform could be achieved by reforming the workplace, whereas the other suggested that social peace would be attained by fostering voluntary associations and the integration of workers within the Republic and the municipality.

Shifting governmental alliances during the planning stages of the Exhibition only accentuated the failure of exhibit organizers to develop a clearer stance on the best means to achieve social and industrial reform. On the surface, however, there seemed to be agreement in at least one respect: whether they were Catholics or Protestants, disciples of Le Play and members of the Société d'économie sociale, or secular republicans and members of the Ligue de l'enseignement, the social economy exhibit demonstrated that a fraction of the nation's elite was reacting to the palpable atmosphere of social crisis in fin de siècle France. In the words of Melchior de Vogüé, the exhibit revealed that there had been "a recent and serious awakening of consciousness among the entrepreneurial elite concerning their social duty. These intelligent men have understood that in order to safeguard their threatened positions, they must be willing to give up something." [38] Although the organizers of the social economy exhibit usually masked their internal dissension with the language of republican defense, a close reading of the official two-volume report reveals some very real conflicts and divergent opinions concerning the social question.

The height of disagreement and irony was reached by the exhibit's section XVI, which was devoted to the achievements of state intervention. This section, added at the last minute in August 1888 by the left-leaning Floquet government, drew protests from Georges Berger and other liberals, who perceived the addition merely as an irritating example of political strong-arming.[39] In response, and as a provocation to the government, the judges of section XVI, including the ultra-liberal Yves Guyot, awarded the section's main prize to the militant antistatist League for the Defense of Liberty and Property. The French branch of an English group devoted to the ideas of Herbert Spencer, this group's stated purpose was precisely to struggle against all forms of government interventionism, most particularly the spread of socialism. Interestingly, whereas many French liberals, such as Léon Say, both admired the league and expressed great pleasure at this scintillating symbolic affront to the government, in England this extreme group was shunned by British New Liberals, who considered it to be composed of "administrative nihilists" who were "hopelessly out of step with the times."[40]

In retaliation, from the left wing of the republican political spectrum, the engineer Alfred Picard, a Radical and admirer of Gambetta, vehemently protested against the "liberal leagues," which, he claimed, had used section XVI merely as a platform to support their own ideological views. Picard subsequently took advantage of his position as the author of the official report on the social economy exhibit to assert that liberal groups such as the League for the Defense of Liberty and Property were powerless to stop the progress of government intervention or even of state socialism. In a show of support for the interventionist role of local government, Picard lauded the innovations of municipal socialism in the areas of public service, transportation, water, gas, and electricity. His report reminded readers of the positions taken by Sismondi when, early in the century, he had distanced himself from the orthodox liberal school of Adam Smith and called for government intervention to assist the weak and the poor. By rhetorically aligning himself with Sismondi, Picard placed his argument within the legitimating matrix of the social economist critique of industrialization.[41]

Although the social economy exhibit constituted the first attempt by the Third Republic to address the social question in a quasi-official manner, there was no consensus among its organizers about how to resolve labor problems. But as Cheysson concluded, if the nineteenth century was to be called "the century of social questions," it was not because those questions had been resolved, but because their importance had finally been understood.[42] The 1889 Exhibition, in fact, helped to legitimate social economy by giving it an official forum as well as the approval of the republican establishment. The Exhibition also provided a unique opportunity for industrialists, members of the liberal professions, and an international audience to meet and join in common cause. The conferences and congresses organized concomitantly with the 1889 Universal Exhibition gave further impetus to the whole French social reform movement by mobilizing public opinion and multiplying opportunities for exchange.[43] Several key parapolitical groups of the late nineteenth and early twentieth centuries, such as the Société française des habitations à bon marché, were founded at congresses held during the 1889 Exhibition.

As the final decade of the century approached, the general public's interest in social reform was heightened by the growing attention in Parliament to social and labor issues. If, however, the 1890s marked the rise of an explicitly republican social reform movement in France, it was also quite clearly a marriage of convenience: the Republic needed to harness the burgeoning social question just as much as the reform movement needed the Republic as a political and cultural referent to legitimate its concerns.

The Idea of a Social Museum

No sooner were plans underway for the 1889 social economy exhibit, than its organizers began envisaging how to transform it into a museum that would be open to the public on a regular basis. Convinced of the importance of public opinion in the formation of social policy, the organizers of the social economy section had taken pains to craft an exhibit that embodied a social pedagogy. As members of a self-conscious elite in a young liberal democracy, their plans to establish both the exhibit and a museum were linked with a larger political project to persuade the public of the moral and social leadership not only of this new industrial elite but also of the Third Republic.[44]

The idea of creating a permanent social museum emanated from the basic museological function of the universal exhibitions themselves. By extending the Encyclopedic tradition into a visual public realm, exhibitions became temporary outdoor museums for collecting, classifying, and displaying the physical results of modern technical, commercial, and social knowledge. Many contemporaries felt that such demonstrations of material and commercial culture warranted a more permanent form of display. As general commissioner of the 1867 Universal Exhibition, Le Play had questioned the efficacy of exhibitions, which, he charged, had grown to unmanageable sizes and were ill suited as forums for learning and exchange. The temporary nature of most exhibitions, moreover, did not allow visitors the time needed to make useful contacts that would someday result in technical or social change: "Exhibitions go by, just as [do] industrial crises and bouts of curiosity." As a result, Le Play, like Proudhon before him, proposed the creation of permanent exhibits or museums to display international goods as well as the customs of social life.[45] In Le Play's museum, international products would be displayed to the general public, not as neutral or isolated objects, but in relation to the social customs of their milieu, almost anthropologically. The interrelatedness of social custom, family life, and the conditions of production would be highlighted in this curiously modern and sociologically grounded conception of the meaning of material culture. Although he never realized his project, Le Play was convinced that such a museum would truly have a social mission. When Émile Cheysson first proposed his plan to establish a museum of social economy, he was therefore extrapolating on Le Play's original idea.

Le Play's proposal for a permanent museum suggests, moreover, that the function of a museum in nineteenth-century France went beyond that of a place for the preservation of old objects of value.[46] Although today the term *museum* is often used in casual metaphor as an organizational form inherently disconnected from the present, in its etymological sense a *mouseion*, or museum, had a more active and educational connotation. It is this broader definition of a museum that informed the late-eighteenth and nineteenth-century use of the term in France. Thus, museums were often built, not merely for the preservation and exposition of valuable cultural artifacts, but as places where a general public could enter freely and receive self-guided instruction on a variety of topics. Initiatives in museum building during the Revolutionary period tended to transform the function of the museum from that of a *cabinet de curiosités* to that of an institution vested with an educational and civic mission. Some museum directors, during the latter half of the nineteenth century, went so far as to imbue their educational mission with a quasi-religious fervor, referring to their museums as "temples of self-improvement."[47]

To this pedagogical end a wide variety of museums, pitched to topical interests or tastes more than to the established *beaux arts*, emerged in France during the second half of the nineteenth century: military museums, museums of the industrial arts, museums of commerce or of education. Such institutions, particularly those that focused on the new industrial world, were inherently likely to attract a more socially diverse public. In conjunction with the Musée des arts décoratifs, founded in Paris in 1877, the Conservatoire national des arts et métiers presented displays on all branches of the trades: mechanics, construction, metallurgy, agriculture, and textiles. But not all museums of trade and commerce conceived of their subjects in glowing lights. Fernand Pelloutier, whose career and ideas had a decisive influence on the *bourses du travail* (labor exchanges and union headquarters) in France, envisioned the creation of *musées du travail* that would serve a militant purpose: to demonstrate to workers that, despite reforms, their cycle of impoverishment persisted.[48] Universal exhibitions had previously spawned museums, as in the case of the Educational Museum of South Kensington, created following the Universal Exhibition of 1851. None of the above mentioned museums, however, were monuments to a world gone by; on the contrary, they heralded the arrival of a new age. When the French government initially expressed interest in creating a museum of social economy, it was intended to serve as a guidepost to the social problems of the contemporary industrial world.

From the outset, the planners of the social economy exhibit were preoccupied with issues similar to those of museum building. As we have seen, they confronted the problematics of display and of how to render appealing a subject—social economy—that was rather abstract and not particularly entertaining for a mass audience. By contemplating how they would present their industrial welfare displays to the general public, organizers were already engaging in attempts to define the social question within an explicitly public realm. When they made decisions about how to place items on display, they were crafting a form of public argument through the means of a visual language. Cheysson commented at length on this problem:

> If we only had had to consider a public of economists, men of leisure and learning, the installation of such an exhibit would have been limited to setting out on tables the documents that govern those institutions, i.e., statutes, statistical and administrative records. But the problem became all the more complex, once the target was the man on the street and the goal was to interest the hurried visitor who would not stop to leaf through the documentation. . . . These passers-by had to be captivated by an outside show, their attention held: they had to be forced into looking and thinking.
>
> That is precisely where the special difficulty of this new kind of exhibition lay. No need to enhance the contents of a furniture, gun, or machine exhibit; but how, then, to emphasize the importance of [social welfare] institutions? How to materialize immaterial things? How to display abstractions? [49]

Cheysson hoped to attract a mass audience to the social economy exhibit, and he later claimed to have been successful: "The far end of the Esplanade des Invalides, where the social economy exhibit was set up was among the [displays that were] most frequented and studied, not only by men of science and professionals, but also by the crowd, the workers." [50] The exhibit was intended to demonstrate the potential force of industrial social welfare and associational life to improve social and industrial relations, but at a second level, it was also aimed at convincing the visitor *qua* citizen of his new participatory role in the Third Republic. Visitors saw how industrial welfare schemes operated and realized, moreover, that their approbation was necessary for these schemes to function smoothly.

Expanding on Michel Foucault's theories of power and knowledge, Tony Bennett defined what he termed an "exhibitionary complex," as "a technology of vision" that sought "to organize a voluntarily self-regulating citizenry" by allowing the people "to know and thence to regulate themselves; to become, in seeing themselves from the side of power, both the subjects and the objects of knowledge." Similarly, the social economy exhibit sought to incorporate viewers into the problematics of display in a politically poignant manner. Organizers aspired to convince a mass public of its own important role in achieving harmony in the workplace and within the Republic. If social reform were to succeed, citizen involvement would be necessary. The displays, therefore, were much more than exhibits devoted to benign objects or documents; they were also carefully conceived lessons in civic training that argued for social reform by instituting a "new pedagogic relationship between the state and the people." [51]

But the organizers of the social economy exhibit were more ambitious still. They hoped that their exhibit and subsequent museum would amass information on industrial society in the service of more scientific goals. The logical first step toward arriving at a science of society was to decompose the social question analytically by labeling, categorizing, and dividing it into its constituent parts. In this spirit, the social economy section had been divided into sixteen categories corresponding to the "principal chapters of social science." [52] These headings were based, in part, on the results of a survey sent out by exhibit organizers to industrialists throughout France. Respondents were asked detailed questions about their employees, the average length of employment, social welfare practices, and industrial relations in general. It was designed to be, in the words of Georges Berger, a "cahier de doléances" of the industrial world. Leon Say expected the results of this industrial survey to become a scientific monument, an equivalent of Descartes' *Discours de la méthode* for social science.[53]

References to the social discontent preceding the French Revolution and to the Cartesian method of rational thought were both part of a rhetorical legitimization strategy. They implied, on the one hand, that in a republic, and as part of the Revolutionary tradition of 1789, public consultation would be an integral part of policy formation; and, on the other hand, that the rational, systematic study of society would provide the answers sought by reformers. Exhibit organizers further hoped that this method would instill confidence in the public by suggesting that the complex problems facing industrial society would one day be fully understood. In the long run, these scientific methods would help defuse the volatile atmosphere brewing in some industrial sectors and reduce the fear (their own as well as that projected onto the general public) of social conflict. The social economy exhibit had been designed to demonstrate that the same scientific spirit that culminated in the majestic material realizations at the fair would also lead the Third Republic to social peace.

Rival Plans: A State-Sponsored or a Private Museum?

Although the Musée social was eventually created as a private foundation in 1894, this solution was only reached after a frustrating series of failures on the part of reformers to garner enough support for a state-sponsored museum. At first, everyone seemed convinced that a state-sponsored museum was the logical way to proceed. Prior to the Exhibition's closing, the idea of creating a state-sponsored social museum was favorably examined by the government. In pursuit of this goal, many exhibitors agreed to donate their displays, and several members of the social economy jury founded an Association du Musée d'économie sociale, under the presidency of Léon Say.[54]

When the Exhibition closed, however, the donated objects became a vagabond collection, first deposited in the warehouses of the Palais des arts libéraux on the Champ de Mars and then moved to the former stables of the Quai d'Orsay, where the Ministry of Public Works gave them temporary shelter in less-than-favorable conditions. Thanks to the efforts of several association members, the displays on profit-sharing and professional associations were more adequately preserved. Housed by the Paris Chambres syndicales de l'industrie et du bâtiment, these objects were incorporated into a small museum-library that opened to the public on March 20, 1892. Another portion of the original exhibit, composed of printed matter, was entrusted to Émile Boutmy and integrated into the library of the École libre des sciences politiques. Most of the documents, however, were left to rot in the stables while successive plans to obtain permanent shelter for them never materialized.[55]

The government channeled its efforts to found a state-sponsored museum through the Conseil supérieur du travail (CST). Created in January 1891 under the auspices of the Ministry of Commerce, the CST included among its first members Jules Siegfried and Léon Say. A few months later the CST founded the Office du travail, hoping that the creation of a museum devoted to the world of labor would crown its second year of activity.[56]

Although the CST wanted to use the new museum to popularize social economy, it was also in pursuit of a more political goal: it hoped to influence the pending debate in Parliament on industrial accidents. Since the CST favored methods of preventing industrial accidents through private initiative without recourse to compulsory legislation, it aspired to build a museum that would bolster its views. Analogous museums, entirely devoted to the prevention of industrial accidents, already existed in Vienna and Winterthur, Switzerland. After visiting the museum in Vienna, Cheysson suggested incorporating a similar display within the French museum; and Engel-Dollfus, the grandson of the Alsatian industrialist Engel-Gros, quickly responded to the call by contributing model safety devices of this type.[57] Therefore, the CST's proposed museum would adopt a pedagogical as well as a political dimension, one designed to influence public opinion but also to convince industrialists to take initiatives that would prevent industrial accidents and thus preclude government interference.

Giving a slightly more populist twist to their original plans, CST members, after a frustrating search for a permanent home for their museum, finally settled on the Conservatoire national des arts et métiers (CNAM).[58] Located in a working-class neighborhood, the CNAM was justified as a site for the proposed social museum since it was frequented by artisans, employees, and workers who attended evening courses in the trades. In fact, as the newspaper Le Petit Havre reported in January 1893, "more than 6,000 persons visited [the CNAM] weekly," and this "museum of the tools and products of labor" was centrally located "in one of the capital's most populous neighborhoods." [59] Those who considered the CNAM to be a favorable location for the social economy museum clearly had an eye on this potential audience, even planning to hire guides for workers who visited the collections on Sundays, their day of leisure. Promoters saw much to be gained by adding a social economy perspective to the school's technical course offerings: the CNAM would become "a teaching museum" with public lectures and night classes for workers, artisans, employees, and engineers. Such a "school of social economy" would encourage interaction among the social classes and help popularize savings funds, mutual aid societies, cooperatives, and associations to improve the standard of living of workers and bring harmony to industrial relations. In the words of Jules Simon, the CNAM would become a veritable "Sorbonne de l'ouvrier."[60]

Despite these various initiatives, the project for a museum of social economy ran up against a wall of inertia and opposition that satisfied none of its promoters. Even when Siegfried, as the minister of commerce in 1892 and 1893, submitted two separate bills to obtain financing for the museum, his efforts were in vain. Although included in the 1894 fiscal year budget, the requested allocation of 40,000 francs credit for the installation of the museum was never granted by the Chamber of Deputies. This defeat came in spite of the appointment by Siegfried of his friends Charles Robert and Émile Cheysson to the Conseil de perfectionnement des arts et métiers to hasten the realization of his project.[61]

It was more than fiscal conservatism, and not simply indifference to the project that prompted the Chamber of Deputies' refusal to grant the necessary credits. The chief snag seems to have been the lack of a clear mandate or a political consensus on the function and goals of a museum of social economy. For one thing, the concept of a museum that could influence public opinion and parliamentary debates on the issue of industrial accidents was quickly losing ground. Although the museum promoters wanted industrialists to experiment with social welfare schemes in their own factories, the tide of parliamentary opinion was quickly turning in another direction. Although it was rejected in the Senate, a bill was passed by the Chamber of Deputies on June 10, 1893, that would have enacted compulsory accident insurance. Then, on June 29, 1894, a parliamentary majority voted into law mandatory retirement funds for miners, marking the introduction of compulsory legislation into the French labor code. This was precisely the type of state regulation that proponents of a social economy museum had been initially trying to avoid. It represented "a breach," Cheysson remarked; he feared "that it shall soon widen."[62] If Parliament had refused to finance this first project for a museum of social economy, it was precisely because its organizers intended to promote private initiatives in reform, not government mandated ones.

In the end, however, the state did accept legal responsibility for the vagabond collection of objects and displays. It granted a limited form of financing for the CNAM museum, and the Association du Musée d'économie sociale was dissolved. Toward the end of 1894, after nearly four years of negotiations, Cheysson could muster little enthusiasm, however, for the small, embryonic version of a state-sponsored museum that, he claimed, "was inaugurated without fanfare" in the Vaucanson gallery of the CNAM. Although containing the best-preserved displays from the 1889 social economy exhibit, this museum was far from the dynamic ideal that had germinated in the minds of its organizers.[63] Faced with these obstacles, the promoters of the social economy museum therefore decided to take a completely different path toward the realization of their project.

Toward a Privately Sponsored Museum

Faced with the multiple deceptions encountered during the CNAM project and despite the long French tradition of state-sponsored cultural and educational institutions, the friends of the museum turned to a private source of financing: the count Aldebert de Chambrun, who quickly became their new benefactor.[64]

Born in 1821, the count de Chambrun was a direct descendant of Lafayette, the son of an army officer, the grandson of a field marshal in the armies of Louis XVI, and a member of an old, established line of nobility from the Lozère department. A chameleon of political life, Chambrun adapted himself to every regime. Ahead of his time, he used "advertising" techniques as early as the Second Empire to fashion a public image and promote his political career. On one occasion he distributed throughout his region *images d'Épinal* of himself and his wife performing charitable gestures.[65] A *sous-préfet* of Toulon in 1850, a deputy at the Corps législatif under the Second Empire, and an Orleanist senator in 1876, Chambrun also authored an 1874 monarchist brochure entitled *De l'institution d'une régence.* By 1889, however, he agreed to support the Republic, since it was, as he wrote, the "legal government of my country." Afflicted with the permanent loss of his eyesight after a long illness, Chambrun had withdrawn from active political life since 1879 and concentrated instead on his passion for music, charity, and the arts.[66] Original and enigmatic, Chambrun was well suited to realize an ambitious work of social betterment, not merely the sort of philanthropic gesture to which the traditions of his social background would have predisposed him.

If, toward the end of his life, Chambrun placed his trust in the pro-

Figure 4. Comte Aldebert de Chambrun (1821–1899).
CEDIAS-Musée social, Paris.

moters of a museum of social economy, it was in large part because of his growing passion for the development of sociology and his personal experiences in the industrial world. Having become the heir to the Baccarat Crystal Works through his marriage to Marie-Jeanne Godard-Desmarest, Chambrun had first-hand knowledge of the firm's long tradition of enlightened paternalism, legendary in reformist circles for its worker housing, free medical assistance, and retirement fund.[67] Chambrun's "conversion" to social economy, however, occurred later, during what he described as "a night fraught with illness," probably in 1891, the year of his wife's death. At that time, Chambrun began referring to social economy as "sociology," and his philanthropic ideas were reoriented toward the principles of self-help. From his villa in Nice, he organized a

Figure 5. Émile Cheysson (1836–1910).
CEDIAS-Musée social, Paris.

group of *agrégés*, professors, and private tutors to read to him and instruct him in subjects as diverse as social economy, socialism, history, and the Koran. "Socialism," Chambrun wrote, "the true name of which is Charity, has become my very first subject of study." [68]

One visiting instructor, the economist André Liesse, who taught social economy at the École spéciale d'architecture in Paris, explained to Chambrun the functioning of the Society for Profit-Sharing and organized a meeting with its president, Charles Robert, who eventually became one of the count's closest friends and advisers. Chambrun had also personally known Frédéric Le Play and was well disposed toward his disciples in social economy. In 1891 Chambrun met Jules Siegfried and Émile Cheysson, who "strongly inclined the count's preoccupations toward social reform"

Figure 6. Jules Siegfried (1837–1922). CEDIAS-Musée social, Paris.

and suggested that he help create a social museum in Paris that would be of a more dynamic nature than a simple exhibition.[69] The regular correspondence that ensued between Chambrun, Siegfried, Cheysson, and Léon Say convinced Chambrun to become the financial benefactor of the newly conceived social museum. From that point on, Chambrun began to refer to the "Musée social" in his letters, although the precise nature of the institution had not yet been settled.

Although his introduction into the circle of social economy promoters was somewhat fortuitous, Chambrun was not merely an aging, lonely millionaire searching for a new hobby. He developed a serious interest in social economy and was careful to surround himself with well-chosen advisers. In 1893 Chambrun published two volumes of "sociological conclusions" based on his own experience of the industrial world.[70] He called for new social and professional relations in the factory since current practices, he believed, belonged to a by-gone age. He admonished social reformers, however, against relying too exclusively on industrialists to initiate these reforms. Most of them, he claimed, had led existences that were far too insular; they were anathema to interference and suspicious of change. Chambrun no longer believed in the "industrial wellspring" that promised a surge of benevolent action on the part of industrialists. Industrial social welfare alone, he concluded, could not provide an adequate answer to France's contemporary social crisis; it was too imbued with the old ways of thinking associated with private charity and public assistance. Chambrun preferred what he referred to as the "free socialism" of associational life, of profit-sharing, and of limited state intervention. Industrial relations in France, he wrote, lagged far behind the new political and social framework of the Third Republic: "The factory has remained at the stage of personal, autocratic, and arbitrary government; it must evolve and elevate itself to the level of a free, representative, democratic government."[71]

In Chambrun's view, an industrial factory was much more than a site for producing cast iron, cloth, or cotton; it was a new social entity that embodied the "realization of the human condition." For this reason, he proposed that workers be given a voice in factory management at Baccarat and at the five other companies awarded gold medals at the 1889 social economy exhibit—the mining companies of Anzin, Blanzy, and Creusot; the Bon Marché department store; and the Mame publishing house. To this end, he favored the creation of industrial councils—conseils patronaux—composed of representatives of both industry and labor. These "lower chambers" of the "new parliamentarianism," according to Chambrun, would eventually be elected by the universal suffrage of workers. Since they have gained the right to vote, workers should also become associates of the industrial world. "As I have already said, after receiving his political rights, the citizen, independent and proud, armed with the ballot of free suffrage, will demand his social rights: the worker no longer wants to be, no longer should be, a salaried employee, but an associate."[72]

His efforts, however, were in vain. With the exception of the Mame publishing house, each company he approached, including his own, Baccarat, rejected his proposals for reform. Chambrun's profound disappointment at the refusal of his industrial peers to innovate led him to turn, as a last resort, to the group of social reformers, whom he first described as a rather nebulous array of "theoreticians, publicists, journalists, philanthropists, politicians with no mandate, a few engineers, and few financiers," who operated in the interstices of the worlds of industry, parliament, and philanthropy.[73] Moreover, this abrupt change of heart led Chambrun to take some extraordinary actions that had important financial benefits for his new social economist friends. He removed the names of the Baccarat administrators from his will and eventually, to the great consternation of his family, made the Musée social the sole heir to his fortune.[74]

Chambrun's personal experience, coupled with years of reflection and study, reoriented his philanthropic works in the direction of republican social reform. He hesitated, nevertheless, between a form of activity directed toward education or toward research and policy implementation. At first, Chambrun chose education, pursuing the idea of establishing a chair of social economy at the Sorbonne and of creating a private institute of sociology. In 1893 Chambrun endowed a chair of social economy at the Sorbonne for Alfred Espinas, thereby introducing sociology into the French academy, a bastion of conservatism that sorely lacked any focus on contemporary social issues. Chambrun, however, eventually abandoned the idea of establishing an independent institute of sociology, despite the protestations of his assistant and confidante Jeanne Weill, who wrote under the name of Dick May. As a result, Weill abruptly ended her collaboration with Chambrun on the Musée social project and directed her efforts instead to the creation, in 1895, of the Collège libre des sciences sociales.[75]

Finally, on May 19, 1894, in a private meeting at the Parisian home of the count de Chambrun, the Musée social was born. The new foundation, which was granted public service status three months later, gave itself a triple mission: to reinforce the networks of associational life; to inspire an enlightened elite to actively pursue solutions to the social question; and to assemble a broad-based documentation on social movements in France and abroad.[76] Its vocation as a center for consultation and independent research instilled the foundation with a spirit of public service. Addressing its message to a wide audience—the general public as well as specialists—the Musée social incorporated a civic, a pedagogic, and even a scientific mission into its activities. Not content to study contemporary industrial society in the isolation of a laboratory, founders would regularly invite public scrutiny of the results of their work. Through lectures, task groups, publications, and meetings, they would encourage dialogue, exchange, and the dissemination of information to workers, employers, and all interested parties. This pedagogical link with the public helps us understand the broader social and political implications of the Musée social's creation. Unlike a closed intellectual *salon* for the philosophical contemplation of the modern world, the Musée social would operate within an open public realm, its founders being convinced that the social question could be successfully resolved only with the direct involvement of civil society.

According to its founders, Chambrun's Musée social was even closer to their initial intentions than had been the idea of a state-sponsored museum. Cheysson, for one, was convinced that the spontaneity of the social reform movement in France corresponded to a deep social need that could not be channeled by government. To the contrary, the republican regime, he felt, should capture this wellspring of civic energy, be attentive, and learn from it. The growing number of mutual aid societies, retirement funds, and producer cooperatives offered ample testimony to the vitality of this movement. In a similar vein, Chambrun decided to keep the title "Museum," which was "easily acceptable to everyone," instead of "Institute," which reminded him of "a capital, a centrality, a seat of government" — to which he even added: "I was going to say a form of tyranny: Death to tyrants!" [77] An independent foundation, therefore, situated at a privileged crossroads between the public and the private sectors, with the intention of opening its doors to a more diverse public than could be found in the parliamentary hemicycle, the Musée social attracted individuals from a broad sociopolitical spectrum to join the debate on finding practical solutions to the social question.

The Inauguration of the Musée social

On March 25, 1895, the Musée social officially opened its doors to the public with elaborate ceremonies befitting a bourgeois inaugural rite. The dinner banquet for 300 guests at the Hôtel Continental in Paris attested to the new museum's wealth and wide approbation among republican elites. The presence of foreign dignitaries signified the foundation's international scope, and its domestic renown was suggested by the presence of high government officials, including one of the founding fathers of the Third Republic, Jules Simon; the premier, Alexandre Ribot; and the minister of commerce and industry, André Lebon. A broad cross section of republican elites and members of the liberal professions were also in attendance: deputies and senators, members of the Institut de France, industrialists, university officials and professors, doctors, high civil servants, and members of government agencies. These were the future collaborators the Musée social hoped to enlist to generate a national momentum of support for republican social reform efforts.[78]

During the inaugural festivities, the Musée social was widely promoted as a private foundation created in the national interest. Jules Simon declared: "There will be three monuments in Paris: the Bibliothèque nationale, upon the door of which one could write: 'Here one learns'; the Musée du Louvre, upon the door of which one could inscribe 'Here one admires'; and your Musée social for which I propose this inscription: 'Here one loves.'"[79] Obviously, the task incumbent upon the Musée social was much larger than private philanthropy. By virtue of its high-level government support and its quasi-official status as a public-utility foundation, the Musée social was symbolically assigned a larger role in the republican theater of action: defending the ideal of a social republic.[80] As such, it had inherited the symbolic charge first attributed to the social economy exhibit in 1889: to articulate the Third Republic's social mission to the general public. Elevated above the arena of fragile and divisive political alliances and defined in terms of the national interest, the idea of forging a social republic drew broad support from across the spectrum of republican opinion. The Musée social, in turn, reaped the benefits of a heightened awareness that social politics would be the pivotal point of the Republic's success or failure.

Léon Bourgeois, the president of the parliamentary Commission d'assurance et de prévoyance sociales and future Radical premier, was scheduled to give the closing speech at the inaugural banquet. Unable to attend for health reasons, Bourgeois sent a telegram praising the Musée social for its efforts to situate the social question in a new realm beyond the traditional reaches of divisive politics. The propagator of solidarism hoped that by "removing the observation of social facts from the arena of partisan political passions," the Musée social might help instill in politics "the serenity and good faith that are the conditions of any science," thereby contributing to the establishment of "social peace."[81]

The powerful ideals embodied by the notions of social science, social peace, and the collaboration of capital and labor—all attributed to the Musée social—help explain the institution's early and widespread prestige. The apparent enthusiasm with which so many rushed to the Musée social's side served, however, to mask the lurking fear—rarely acknowledged on such official occasions—that the battle for a social republic may already have been lost. Armand Peugeot, officially representing the French *patronat* at the inaugural ceremonies, was the only speaker to voice these misgivings. He deplored the gloomy spectacle offered by "the fierce struggle between labor and capital" that gave rise to "appalling strikes that hurt workers as much as they do industrial employers." This leads one to wonder, he concluded, if "such antagonisms will ever disappear and if there exists a potential for conciliation."[82]

If the Musée social's paternity can be traced to the extended republican family, it might also be suggested that it was an offspring of the divorce between the moderate republic and the working classes. Flying in the face of the language of social peace were some harsh realities. Since the army had intervened during the 1886 Decazeville strike, more than 10 percent of strikes in France during the next four years and 15 percent in 1890 had involved police or army action. The rise in the use of military force against labor had culminated in the 1891 massacre in Fourmies where, to the horror of everyone involved, twelve people including four young adolescents were gunned down by police following a mildly raucous demonstration on Labor Day (May 1). As Michelle Perrot concluded, this "first great massacre of the Third Republic finalized the split between the moderates and the working class and hastened the rise of socialism."[83] Workers increasingly tended to identify the regime as a conservative bourgeois republic set on a quasi-militaristic course of imposing law and order in defiance of basic republican rights. Fractures, even among supporters of the Republic, could be traced along class lines. Workers felt betrayed by the Republic, and republican elites, in turn, felt beleaguered both as defenders of a fragile political regime and as guardians of a bourgeois social order. Given this context, a sense of urgency fueled the government's support of the new Musée social as a republican foundation devoted to "the material and moral betterment of workers." Within this highly contested setting, the Musée social was quickly elevated by government officials to the level of a republican symbol of social peace.

The social question slowly gained a foothold within the structures of government, and the process by which this took place had been initiated by a collaboration between members of civil society and the state. The Conseil supérieur du travail, for instance, enabled private citizens and government officials to collaborate on government policy affecting the world of labor. And when its members created the Office du travail in 1891, they set in motion a logic that led to the establishment in 1906 of an independent Ministry of Labor. The government's support of the Musée social represented a similar impulse. Whereas the Office du travail was a small statistical research bureau generally invisible to the public, the Musée social was seen as a showcase for explaining and displaying the Republic's social wares. Thus, the Musée social was symbolically invested with the mission of embodying the Republic's ideal of social peace at a time when most republicans considered it good strategy and some believed that such a goal was still attainable.

If the Musée social hoped to build the foundations of a social republic, its strength and uniqueness lay with its independent and private status: its creators wanted France to become a social republic of private initiative.[84] In his speech at the Musée's inaugural ceremonies, Alexandre Ribot stressed that Chambrun's endowment represented more than simply a generous gift by a social-minded aristocrat whose "soul was rejuvenated by its contact with democracy." The Republic, he explained, actively sought the support of private initiative, and in this regard, the Musée social was exemplary. Although Ribot believed that by passing long overdue social laws, the Parliament could advance the cause of social justice, he also warned that the state had only limited influence on society; it was unable to instill the sense of respect, fraternity, and solidarity needed to avert social violence and hatred. A proliferation of private initiatives, associations, and groupings of all sorts, with multiple points of contact in civil society, was necessary, he stressed, to impart the moral message of a liberal democracy. This task would be incumbent upon the social-reform movement emerging in France. The inauguration of the Musée social, therefore, provided an occasion for republican elites to ponder the larger political task that lay ahead: to define the nature of liberal democracy in France.[85]

Officially inaugurated in 1895, the Musée social emerged as the result of a six-year gestation period during which several different projects were elaborated: a government-sponsored museum at the CNAM; the introduction of social economy into the Sorbonne; the creation of an independent school of sociology; and, finally, a private foundation devoted to research and the practical study of social reform. Through these various designs appear the developing outlines of a broader republican reform movement in formation. Moderate and conservative republican elites intended to institutionalize the domain of social reform, seizing this opportunity to endow the Third Republic with a social platform while simultaneously wresting it away from the growing labor and socialist movements. Etched behind the often nebulous contours of social economy lay the foundations of a science of society that republicans hoped to apply to a more efficient management of competing social groups within a torn, industrializing economy.

By voluntarily situating itself at the heart of an extraparliamentary network of activity, the Musée social effectively offered a new context and institutional framework within which the social question could be examined. Not affiliated with any single political group, and theoretically excluding discussions of an explicitly political or religious nature, the Musée social intended to attract individuals from divergent professional, political, religious, and social backgrounds. In the words of former premier Charles Dupuy, the Musée social constituted a unique milieu that would help foster the growth of a new language and practice of social reform in France.[86]

Part Two. Networking for Reform

3. A Genealogy of Republican Reform

~

In order to realize the general principles of solidarity, men of progress
propose a variety of solutions. —EUGÈNE CHEVALIER, 1882

In their quest for social peace, a new industrial order, and a better balance between the interests of labor and capital, the men who founded the
Musée social were not alone. Through their participation in international
networks of exchange—both formal and informal—devoted to resolving
the social question, these men became the French interpreters of a movement of reform that touched each industrial nation at the end of the nineteenth century. Their search for a new synthesis of ideas and strategies
for social reform required that they be open to collaboration across social, political, and even national borders. Whatever the national context,
whether in France, England, the United States, or Germany, one finds a
common initiative among reformers: to rethink the relationship between
the individual and the state in industrial society.

Social reformers of this era in France—whether socialists, conservatives, Catholics, Protestants, workers, members of a liberal profession,
or traditional social elites—came from quite diverse social and political
backgrounds. Yet they often found themselves—sometimes confusedly
and despite earlier, antagonistic ideological positions—on similar terrain: the search for practical answers to the social upheaval provoked by
the new industrial economy. In France, the Musée social constituted a
sort of microcosm of this phenomenon. The Musée, moreover, reached
beyond its national borders to establish networks of foreign correspondents among like-minded reformers and to send study missions abroad
to assess economic developments and reform initiatives in other indus-

trial countries. Émile Cheysson compared this international dimension of social reform during the late nineteenth century to a network of "electric cables" linking the entire industrial world and transmitting similar solutions to countries of nonetheless very different political traditions.[1] A wealth of exchange ensued among industrial nations as reformers from an array of political and professional backgrounds avidly gathered to read each other's reports, meet at international congresses and exhibitions, and visit sites of social betterment and experimentation abroad.[2]

To underscore the process by which individuals from divergent national, political, religious, and social backgrounds could at least converse about, if not agree upon, solutions to the social question, we might borrow the image of a "community of discourse," the contours of which proved to be remarkably similar in France, England, and the United States during this period. To suggest that New Liberals, as they were called in England, or American Progressives at the turn of the century belonged to a similar community of discourse is an attempt to recognize that each of these movements relied on a panoply of political and cultural languages to express its views on reform and make them intelligible to the broadest possible public. Much like in France, these reformist movements in England and the United States cannot be explained solely by reference to a political party or even to a specific political ideology. Rather, they represent an amalgam of discourses and sociopolitical strategies from liberal democracy to social Christianity, and from socialism to a new ethos of professional expertise among the rising middle classes. In the American case, to justify a regulatory role for government, the Progressives relied on the traditional rhetorical terminology of "social bonds" and "duties," as borrowed from the Social Gospel and ordained by Protestant pastors from their pulpits. But they also wielded a modern vocabulary of efficiency and expertise that appealed to a middle-class social constituency and that reinforced both their rational discourse on society and their own legitimacy as "experts." The Progressive movement thus reveals itself to have been an ensemble of old and new ideas, tools of intervention, and social discourses, rather than one single or unified political ideology. The same could be said for England, where alongside the spiritual descendants of Bentham and Mill, conservative idealists, positivists, social Fabians, and Christian socialists all contributed to a trenchant critique of industrial society.[3]

One shared characteristic of this reformist reflex—particularly in France, England, and the United States—was the renewal of liberal thought. Confronted with a fundamentally new world, rife with social problems that threatened the very foundations of industrial progress, liberal thinkers such as J. A. Hobson, L. T. Hobhouse, or T. H. Green in England; John Dewey in the United States; Célestin Bouglé, Alfred Fouillée, or even Émile Durkheim in France began to question the desirability of a free and self-regulated market and of a society composed of individuals who appeared to be as separate from one another as atomized units. At first the writings of these men were primarily of a philosophical, epistemological, and moral nature. Progressively, however, by seeking to define the specificity of "the social" as something qualitatively different from an aggregate of individuals, they contributed to a radical reformulation of the social thought and practice of their time. James Kloppenberg has described how the commonality of their thought forged an "intellectual community" among thinkers who, without knowing one another, asked very similar philosophical and political questions between 1870 and 1920, thus finding themselves to be "neighbors in a territory of new ideas." Classical liberalism was transformed by each of these thinkers, who, although defending individual freedoms and, most often, private property, also contested the excesses of industrial capitalism.[4]

British New Liberals began the unorthodox process of tempering liberal individualism by insisting on concepts of justice and the rights and duties of citizens living in society. They sought to clear a famous "third path" between socialism and liberalism that was intended to correct the excesses of laissez-faire liberalism yet prevent the collectivist domination of society by the state. However, no specific term ever designated the like-minded reform movement that emerged in France. Recently, terms such as "social liberalism," "liberal sociology," "progressives," or even "neo-liberalism" (despite its very different contemporary resonance) have been proposed to describe this intellectual and ideological phenomenon and to better situate it within the context of the history of political ideas. But during the latter part of the nineteenth century, the French never adopted a specific term to designate this new liberalism. For one thing, at the universities and the Institut de France, classical political economy still reigned. But there was also resistance among republicans, who, having only recently attained political power, preferred to give priority to the defense of individual liberties—such as the freedom of expression, of the press, and of assembly—rather than to label themselves as critics of classical liberalism. Solidarism, to be discussed later in this chapter, as elaborated by Alfred Fouillée and Léon Bourgeois, was the sole doctrine—thanks in part to the electoral successes of the Radical party—to succeed in capturing the importance of this renewal of liberal thought in France. Nevertheless, despite the absence of a precise political label, the phenomenon of a new liberalism (or social liberalism, as I also refer to it) did exist in France and, as we shall see, extended well beyond the limits of the Radical party, even to the point of violating traditional ideological divisions on the French political landscape.[5]

Because of its refusal to conform to the conventional political categories of its day, the Musée social can help us perceive this transformation of liberal thought in fin de siècle France. Its search to improve the moral and material conditions of workers reflected a new awareness, in France and abroad, that the amelioration of the individual was as much a consequence of his social and physical surroundings as it was of his own individual will. Like the New Liberals and the Progressives, Musée social reformers became convinced that the best way to protect individual freedoms was to ensure a minimum level of organized social protection through a combination of private initiative, associational life, and the intervention of municipal and state governments. This chapter, therefore, traces the contours and foundations of a new liberalism in France by examining the social origins and political affiliations of individual Musée social members as well as the major religious, ideological, and socio-professional networks that linked them. By including both the formal and informal networks that operated in the margins of political power, we see how the forces that ultimately gave rise to l'État-providence were more intricately rooted within the cultural fabric of France than is usually recognized in studies centered on more traditional political institutions such as the Parliament. The men featured here devoted a major portion of their public lives to the cause of social reform by exerting influence within broad-based professional, academic, religious, and public health networks. The title of this chapter, "A Genealogy of Republican Reform," is intended, moreover, to convey the idea that these Musée social reformers often inherited—and then altered—traditions of reform and social thought that were in place much earlier in the century and that informed their language and practice of social reform as well as their questioning of classical liberalism.

Since the Musée social was a foundation that espoused political and religious neutrality, its membership—which included nearly five hundred individuals between 1894 and 1914—represents a diverse cross section of republican reform circles. Most of the individuals referred to here never held political office or were known to the general public. Their names, with few notable exceptions, do not appear in histories of the Third Republic. Yet these men contributed in significant ways to the ongoing debate on the social question at a time when the terms of that debate were still largely being defined outside of Parliament. They penned innumerable tracts and brochures and gave hundreds of public speeches on the social question but never wrote a single book that attempted to theorize or analyze the global problem of welfare reform in France. They were most often the practitioners of social economy, the intellectuals of a middle class that was not supposed to have intellectuals. The social reform groups they represented were rooted in the heart of French civil society during the early decades of the Third Republic.

Networking for Reform: The Role of Parapolitical Groups

A hybrid institution that was part private and part public, the Musée social purposefully situated itself within a parapolitical sphere, in the margins of government, industry, philanthropy, and traditional political formations. As such, it was both the product of preexisting reform networks and the initiator of new ones. These networks often intersected with other types of political, regional, familial, or religious alliances. They were rarely conceived, however, with a precise policy goal in mind, as might be the case today of single-issue pressure groups. The Musée social refused to adopt a specific reformist platform. Instead, it chose the "research section" as its basic organizational unit, a choice that allowed the Musée to mold its policy recommendations according to the results of its own ongoing investigations. As will be discussed further in chapter 4, these research sections were collaborative structures that invited the participation of politicians, professionals, representatives of reform groups, and other members of civil society in a demonstration of the Musée's commitment to open dialogue among experts as well as its reliance on outside networks of exchange. Through its research sections—such as the section on legal affairs or that devoted to urban and rural hygiene—the Musée social embraced a protean structure that allowed it to adapt and transform according to its chosen subjects of research and to the social and political realities of the day.[6]

Given the Musée social's unique approach to reform, one might ask why its members chose to join forces within the interstices of power rather than through more institutionalized political channels. The answer to this question is complex. Potential members of the Musée were to a certain degree self-designated, since their previous affiliation with a reform group usually qualified them for membership. In turn, since reform groups were open to a greater degree of sociological diversity than that found in the established political institutions of their day, they allowed for broader participation of the general public in social reform debates. Moreover, a personal "investment" in reform groups such as the Musée social often served broader strategies of social and professional promotion: to bolster a flagging political or administrative career; to open doors for aspiring members of a new republican elite; to consolidate or redefine a professional identity. But part of the answer also resides in cultural factors such as religion, the individual's sense of responsibility to society, the social and moral duties of republican elites, the meaning and experience of community—local, national, sociological, professional—as well as the general attitudes that reformers had developed toward the state, such as its rightful role in modern society as a protector of the weak or as the guarantor of security and republican rights.[7]

Independent reform groups and voluntary associations were constitutive elements of the parapolitical space in which the Musée social operated. As such, these groups formed a loose network within which the Musée parlayed its vision of reform into action. It is important to note that membership in voluntary civic associations in France was historically linked to the cultural construction of bourgeois identity itself, particularly for men. For one thing, the bourgeois club or circle arose in contradistinction to the traditions of the aristocratic *salon*. Whereas the former provided a horizontal structure more conducive to a society with democratic aspirations, the latter embodied a vertical construct defined by social hierarchy. Voluntary clubs and *cercles* were therefore symbolic of a much larger social and cultural project: creating a new world of signifiers distinctive to the emerging bourgeois order, one that would eventually replace the hegemonic cultural model of the aristocracy. Accordingly, voluntary associations helped the bourgeoisie assert its distinctive identity as a class and even became "the primary context of expression for [its] aspirations to the general leadership of nineteenth-century society."[8]

Since the early nineteenth century, the French bourgeoisie had relied on voluntary associations and the informal networks they engendered to heighten its economic visibility through local chambers of commerce or national groups such as the Société pour l'encouragement de l'industrie nationale. By virtue of their activities in such groups, men often developed local public personas and honed skills such as public speaking, a tool of even greater civic value once universal (male) suffrage was introduced. These groups also reinforced the political and cultural stature of their members. Some associations were academic, scholarly, or professional in nature, such as the Académie royale de médecine. Others were religious: the Protestant bourgeoisie's tradition of voluntary societies developed, beginning in the seventeenth century, as a response to social and economic needs born of their experience of persecution and flight. Jewish integration into French public life had also been facilitated by secular philanthropies. By the end of the nineteenth century, what appeared to be an informal proliferation of networks and clubs, spanning a diverse spectrum of the French middle class, had in fact become an entrenched male path to prominence. By legitimating the bourgeoisie and structuring the public sphere, this configuration of networks and clubs constituted an "associational trajectory" that often led men from local public life to national policy-making circles.[9] The Musée social was shaped by groups and networks that functioned in a similar manner.

The nineteenth-century traditions of both republicanism and liberalism in France further reinforced the impulse of reformers to create or join groups formed outside of state agencies. At different points during the earlier part of the century, French liberals and republicans had been forced to organize either clandestinely under a repressive political regime, or along the periphery of an official political culture in which their oppositional views were merely tolerated. Instead of establishing a political party apparatus, these men frequently developed their ideas within an interlocking network of clubs that met under the guise of philanthropic organizations, sociétés savantes, Masonic lodges, or public lecture groups. Such was the case, during the Bourbon Restoration, of the Société de la morale chrétienne (1821), a philanthropic society organized in "tacit opposition to the regime" that became one of the pillars of the liberal and Protestant communities.[10] At other times they adopted political forums for their meetings that were informal, yet organized overtly in public spaces with the intent of being seen and heard, as was true of the famous banquets that led to the revolution of February 1848 or the long litany of republican banquets that became a venerable tradition throughout the century. The press, moreover, accentuated this general phenomenon by forming a critical echo chamber for republican and liberal political organizations of the parapolitical sphere.

But it is also important to point out that voluntary associations were open to a mixed public, not merely a bourgeois one. If the members of the Musée social and other reform groups of late-nineteenth-century France chose to operate through voluntary societies, it is because they could thus act within the public sphere of civil society where diverse opinions could be formed and expressed. Voluntary societies embodied what Tocqueville described as the "power" and "spirit of association" by providing a structure for exchange between individuals of divergent backgrounds. As was true for the Musée social, these groups generally attempted to avoid polemics involving religious or political issues. They served instead "as bridges across the troubled waters which separated men of rival sect and party" and facilitated a heterogeneous membership.[11] By respecting the bourgeois principles of public order, respectability, and virtue, they also set themselves up as models to be emulated by the working class.

But voluntary societies erected another type of bridge as well: that between the private and public sectors. Despite shifts in political fortune during the first three decades of the Third Republic, the apolitical, objectivist, and scientific pretensions of most reform groups facilitated long-term collaboration among civil servants working within government agencies (themselves charged with upholding an apolitical standard of service to the state) and the mixed recruits of private or semi-private reform associations.[12] As a vehicle for republican reform efforts, these networks of voluntary associations helped define a new and more effective public space for the construction of social politics in France.

In addition to its primary commitment to the development of a republican civic culture, the Musée social was identified with four main overlapping networks of religious and ideological influence: the Le Playist school of social science, social Catholicism, social Protestantism, and Solidarism. Each of these networks was built on moral and empirical foundations that influenced both the language and practice of republican social reform. In their appeals to specific audiences, members of these networks interpreted the social problems of the modern world in terms informed by older cultural and religious traditions. As such, they helped popularize the issues of social reform that had, earlier in the century, mainly preoccupied elites. They served as essential conduits—providing ideas, terminology, and personnel—for the social reform movement that arose along with the advent of the Third Republic. Composed of groups that linked political, philanthropic, and industrial circles, these networks operated primarily outside of government. Many were international in scope, published journals or newspapers, held congresses, and formed associational structures; others functioned as *sociétés savantes* and pressure groups. Together, they helped channel and strengthen the broad critique of liberalism that marked late-nineteenth-century French political life.

The Disciples of Le Play. Having previously discussed the foundations of Le Playist social science, it is important here to recall the legacy of Frédéric Le Play and the men who continued and transformed his social thought. Even before the establishment of the Société d'économie sociale (1857), Le Play had stressed that the scientific observation of societies was a prerequisite for achieving social peace. He saw social reform as an experimental science subject to rules of methodology, testing, and inductive reasoning. Accordingly, when the violence of the Paris Commune rattled the newly proclaimed republic to its core, Le Play's disciples responded by creating a network of reform-oriented groups throughout France—the Unions de la paix sociale (1874)—in an effort to apply the master's scientific theories to the real world and bring about a lasting social peace.

But not all of Le Play's disciples were in agreement on the ultimate goals of social science. Should it aspire, as some claimed, to attain the status of a pure science? Or should it focus instead on the practical aims of social reform and policy formation? After several years of tempered discord among

Le Play's disciples, a split defined two factions, one proclaiming the goals of reform, the other those of science. In 1881 the first group founded a journal, La Réforme sociale, and solicited contributors from the reform-minded Unions de la paix sociale and the Société d'économie sociale. Those who rallied around La Réforme sociale sought to achieve practical social reform through industrial social welfare projects, low-cost housing, savings, and mutual credit funds. In 1885 the second faction founded a rival journal, La Science sociale, which, as its name implies, pursued a purely scientific methodology for the study of modern societies and was much less interested in reform.[13]

Representatives of both factions of the Le Playist school of thought were present at the Musée social, particularly during its early years, when nearly twenty percent of its members were affiliated with the Société d'économie sociale and contributed to the journals La Réforme sociale and La Science sociale.[14] These preexisting Le Playist networks fed directly into the Musée social and help to explain its general approach to reform, particularly its use of the monographic method of social research. By 1896 the influence of Le Playist social methodology was so widespread in French reform circles that one commentator proclaimed: "It is no longer possible, in the second half of the nineteenth century, to study any category of social education, including the socialist categories, without going back to the principles of action established by Le Play's Réforme [sociale]."[15]

Figuring most prominently among the Le Playist group at the Musée social were Émile Cheysson; Georges Picot, housing reformer and administrator of the Société philanthropique; Eugène Rostand, academician and founder of a people's credit union in Marseilles; and two professors at the École libre des sciences politiques, Robert Pinot and Paul de Rousiers. Their sociologically informed approach to social reform had considerable influence on experiments in low-cost housing, public assistance, and popular credit banks as well as on the analysis of the industrial world. Their shared methodology and outlook enabled them to forge working relationships with the Office du travail, where other Musée members, such as the engineer Arthur Fontaine and statisticians Pierre du Maroussem and Lucien March, exercised leadership.

Given the institution's conscious attempt to avoid the strong ideological connotations still attached to Le Play's name — due to his collaboration with Napoleon III and his earlier condemnation of the French Revolution—explicit references to Le Play are almost nonexistent in the Musée social's publications. Le Play's method of social inquiry, however, was omnipresent at the Musée and supplied reformers with the basis of their vocabulary and their cognitive tools of social analysis.[16] After initially limiting their research to the monographic study of workers' families, a model set forth by Le Play in his *Ouvriers européens* (1855), his followers branched out to study larger-scale social and economic phenomena. Thus, the Société d'économie sociale initiated research studies on local and regional industrial production (1883), the industrial crisis in Paris and the provinces (1884), and low-cost housing in France and abroad (1887), the latter under the direction of Georges Picot and Émile Cheysson.[17] Studies such as these, the results of which were published in *La Réforme sociale*, constituted research models for the first generation of Musée social reformers.

Social Catholicism. Social Catholics at the Musée social were the inheritors of an even older tradition. Having responded to the plight of workers during the earliest years of industrialization in France, social Catholics were, as a rule, vociferous in their calls for government intervention to resolve the social question. The "social" dimension of this strand of Catholic thought is rooted historically within the traditions of the legitimist monarchy, which claimed the protection of the poor to be one of the divinely ordained functions of the state.[18] Throughout the nineteenth century, French social Catholicism represented a multifaceted attempt to analyze the problems of the contemporary world in relation to church doctrine. Despite its varied and sometimes adversarial supporters—ranging from those who attempted to dissociate politics from religion, to those who dreamt of establishing a Catholic political party—social Catholicism emerged from a common rejection of economic liberalism, individualism, and the social consequences of the industrial revolution. At the Musée social, the representatives of this tradition were equally eclectic in their prescriptions for reform: they included the liberal Orleanist Count d'Haussonville, the militant corporatist Albert de Mun, and the democratic champion of worker gardens, Abbot Lemire.[19]

Although transformed radically by Pope Leo XIII's encyclical letters, *Rerum novarum* (1891) and *Au milieu des solicitudes* (1892), relations between French Catholics and the "godless" Third Republic remained strained and often antagonistic.[20] Along with his call for French Catholics to accept the

Republic and work within its legal institutions, the pope also admonished the regime for perpetuating social inequities that were, in his view, only aggravated by economic liberalism. By proclaiming that the state had a duty to ensure distributive justice and to protect the weak, the pope's provocative encyclical letters helped move the social question into the spotlight of the French political stage. His call for state intervention at the precise moment when Radicals, socialists, and moderate republicans were beginning to struggle over this issue guaranteed that the social question in France would continue to be defined at least in part by the social Catholic tradition.

Social Catholic groups remained relatively weak during their period of adaptation to the new, albeit short-lived sociopolitical doctrine of the church and to the political culture of a secular, even anticlerical republic. The pope's encyclical letters, nevertheless, served as a catalyst for a flurry of new Christian democratic initiatives—including the creation of journals, newspapers, trade unions, youth groups, and cooperatives—that sought to attract Catholic workers by distinguishing themselves from traditional Catholics who clung to nationalist and hierarchical views of French society. Such was the case of Marc Sangnier, founder of *Le Sillon* (1894), whose attempts to woo workers and reconcile church doctrine with the goals of a democratic republic were condemned by the Vatican in 1910.[21]

The rise of a more democratic strand of social Catholicism in fin de siècle France was also, in large part, a response to the Dreyfus Affair and the virulent anti-Semitism of the extreme right Catholic milieu represented by the Assumptionist congregation and its newspaper *La Croix*.[22] However, confirming their internal fragmentation and hence overall weakness, other Catholic groups, such as the political party Action libérale populaire (1902), founded by Jacques Piou, attempted to rally the full spectrum of Catholic opinion—liberals, social Catholics, and *ralliés*—in an alliance to defend religious freedoms. Particularly in the aftermath of the 1902 elections that brought victory to the Bloc des Gauches, reactions to secularist politics and the increasing anticlericalism of the Radical republic proved to be a litmus test for French Catholics, who did not always agree among themselves about the best plan of action. The journal *Action populaire* (1902), founded by two Jesuit priests, Henri Leroy and Gustave Desbuquois, stands as evidence of this difficulty. Leroy, in an editorial diatribe, described the new journal as an anti-Dreyfus, antisocialist group that would appeal to popular suffrage in order to save France from "the horde of savages that Freemasons, Free-thinkers, and Anarchists had unleashed upon the Republic." Yet far from being the mere mouthpiece of a Catholic political party, *Action populaire* opened its columns to an array of social doctrines and published articles and brochures, most of which were far less ideologically charged, offering practical information to its readers on the benefits of all forms of associational life, trade unions, cooperatives, and mutualism as well as general economic and parliamentary news.[23]

The Musée's librarian, Étienne Martin Saint-Léon; its labor investigator, Léon de Seilhac; Émile Cheysson; Georges Picot; the law professors, Georges Blondel, Maurice Dufourmantelle, and Raoul Jay; and the deputy from Ardeche, Hyacinthe de Gailhard-Bancel, contributed to *Action populaire* and were involved with the yearly national congresses known as the Semaines sociales, once described as "a sort of migratory popular university for social research" intended for Catholic youth and workers.[24] Begun in Lyon in 1904, these week-long meetings rotated every year from one city to the next, enabling economists, lawyers, sociologists, students, and local reformers to meet and discuss contemporary social problems from a Catholic perspective. This same group of Musée social reformers also contributed to the journal *Association catholique* (also entitled *Revue des questions sociales et ouvrières*), which, although originally created in 1876 as the journal of Albert de Mun's Cercles ouvriers, joined forces with *Action populaire* and was renamed *Le Mouvement social* in 1909.[25] Members of the journal's new editorial staff, including Léon de Seilhac, considered themselves to be the precursors of a new Catholic movement that promoted independent trade unions, voluntary associations, and social legislation.

The overriding impact of social Catholicism on the republican reform movement at the Musée social, however, was its support of government intervention in social affairs. To close the widening gap between the social classes and redress economic inequalities, social Catholics called for a just intervention of the state. They considered it to be the legitimate function of the state to protect workers, pass legislation, and act in a providential role. Social Catholic intellectuals and jurists were among the first to teach interventionist theories in their classrooms, in direct defiance of the reigning school of liberal political economy.

A prominent social Catholic, Raoul Jay, was a professor at the Paris Faculty of Law who lobbied actively for industrial legislation through his teachings, writings, and participation in groups and associations such as the Association internationale pour la protection légale des travailleurs (1900) and the Union d'études des catholiques sociaux (1902). His courses at the Paris Faculty of Law served as one of the few forums in French academe to offer a dispassionate examination of the German insurance laws adopted by Bismark in 1883–89. Abbot Lemire commented that Jay's courses demonstrated "what is true in practice, deeply human, and profoundly fair in the German law." Also a contributor to *Action populaire*, Jay was on the editorial board of *Le Mouvement social* and contributed to Marc Sangnier's *L'Éveil démocratique*. Jay took an early and forceful stand in favor of compulsory insurance protection for workers; his phrase, "Workers' pension insurance will be mandatory, or it will not be at all!" was echoed for years in parliamentary debates and in the press.[26]

Musée social member Georges Blondel participated, too, in several of these overlapping social Catholic networks. A law professor at the University of Lille, Blondel was an active Le Playist, a regular participant in the Semaines sociales, a member of the Association nationale pour la protection légale des travailleurs, and a specialist on Germany and Austria. He was particularly concerned about the social responsibilities incumbent on the new elite of modern society. Democracy, he proclaimed, had been the most important achievement of the nineteenth century, but it was the task of the twentieth century to introduce more justice into a world riven by economic and social inequalities. Illustrating, once again, a pervasive concern of late-nineteenth-century reformers, Blondel blamed class conflict on the nation's elite: "The ruling classes in France have demonstrated a deplorable form of short-sightedness, by not attempting to ease the inevitable rise of the popular classes, by displaying awkward suspicion towards them, and by not seeking to better integrate them into society. The masses have only received guidance from those who flattered them; in such conditions, how could they have been expected to adopt mores conducive to a democracy?" Blondel accused the French elite of being "superficial," "spineless and lethargic," and of having shrugged off their responsibilities as privileged members of society. If France had avoided another recent major social uprising, he surmised, it was only because there were so many small landowners in the country who resisted revolutionary theories. If the popular classes become the prey of socialist ideas, he concluded, "we have only ourselves to blame." From a social Catholic perspective, Blondel called for educational reform and exhorted republican elites to join in efforts to defend the social and economic interests of the working classes.[27]

The social Catholic tradition had a strong impact on the rethinking of the liberal order at the turn of the century and as such contributed to the emergence of social liberalism in France. It exerted its influence in Parliament as well as in the parapolitical networks we have been discussing. At a time when government intervention was shunned by most liberals, social Catholicism offered an explanatory model that enabled social policy questions to be framed in a new humanist language, one that was not incompatible with the secular republic. Although the secular and anticlerical roots of the republican tradition are well known, the important religious and moral bases of that same republican tradition need not remain lost in the shadows of positivist historiography. Until at least 1848, religious imagery was commonly used to celebrate the Revolutionary tradition as the advent of a new Christian order of greater justice on earth.[28] Claude Nicolet has also commented on the "abundance of religious metaphors" that sought to portray the 1789 Revolution as an epiphany, an incarnation, or even an act of Providence.[29] In a similar manner, religious culture played an important role in shaping a republican language of social reform and translating it to a broad public.[30]

Although its intellectual influences were primarily secular—from contractual legal philosophy and Darwinian evolutionism to the Pasteurian revolution—the republican language of social reform in fin de siècle France also bore the marks of religious culture. Metaphors borrowed from Christian ethics and religious teachings were invoked repeatedly by both Catholic and Protestant reformers to interpret the social and economic upheavals caused by industrialization and urban growth as well as to formulate prescriptions for change. The use of religious language was therefore not always synonymous with a political project to restore an *ancien régime* society, nor was it reserved for antirepublican ideological battles. To the contrary, the use of Christian religious rhetoric often neatly dovetailed with the republican project to define a new social contract.

Social Protestantism. The impact of Christian ethics, language, and religious teachings on many republican reformers is also evident in the

French Protestant community. Steven Hause has called for renewed attention to the role of puritanical austerity and Christian moral values in interpreting how Protestants helped define the political culture of French republicanism during the nineteenth century.[31] Indeed, the Protestant reformers associated with the Musée social turned consistently to religious referents and metaphors to explain their involvement in republican reform efforts and to justify their underlying critique of liberal political economy.

Social Protestantism, also commonly referred to as social Christianity, a religiously inspired movement that called for the construction of a more balanced socioeconomic order was the second prominent religious influence on the Musée social's reform activities. The achievement of a more just world was seen by social Protestants as part of the gradual realization of God's kingdom on earth. Social Christian doctrine did not stress the importance of individual acts of charity; instead, its goal was to achieve social or collective salvation. At the Musée social, this religious network intersected with the cooperative movement, solidarism, popular education, municipal reform, mutualism, and freemasonry.

Married to the daughter of an eminent Protestant pastor, the first president of the Musée social, Jules Siegfried, became a symbol of this social Protestant movement in republican reform circles.[32] He widely acknowledged the influence of religion on his social thought and reform efforts: his book, La misère, and his unpublished personal diary are liberally scattered with references to Christian charity.[33] He and many prominent Musée members—such as French cooperative activist Charles Gide; father of the French profit-sharing movement, Charles Robert; the engineer Édouard Gruner; director of Public Assistance Henri Monod; and Radical deputy and solidarist Paul Guieysse—were all active in the social Protestant movement, which gained momentum along with the advent of the Third Republic and contributed to the development of republican social thought. Other Protestants affiliated with the Musée social were the liberal economist Paul Leroy-Beaulieu and member of the Conseil d'État, Henri Hébrard de Villeneuve.

Although only a minority of the approximately one million Protestants who resided in France in the 1880s were actively affiliated with social Protestantism, its intersecting networks constituted one of the most important channels that initially brought reformers to the Musée social.[34] The

Protestant theological premise that God would make his will manifest in the secular world did not lead Protestants to reject scientific discoveries such as Darwinian evolutionism as did many Catholics of this period. Instead, Protestants readily accepted the social metaphors that reformers borrowed from the biological sciences to speak about transformations in contemporary society. The idea that God was working out his divine plan on earth implied an organic view of society consistent with the republican language of reform. As Charles Gide liked to remind his audiences, the foundation of Church doctrine was "solidarity."[35]

Protestants were drawn into the reform networks that coalesced at the Musée social for a variety of reasons, many of which had to do with the general context of political life in the early Third Republic. For one thing, during those years new possibilities existed for the involvement of Protestants in public life.[36] They were able to fill a void created by the Catholic Church's discrediting of the Republic prior to *Rerum novarum* (1891) and the progressive dissociation, during that period, of the Catholic Church with public affairs in general. Protestant intellectuals figured prominently at the crossroads of major cultural and intellectual trends such as romanticism, positivism, and spiritualism. They were also at the forefront of educational reform, shared a long tradition of political liberalism, and placed great importance on freedom of thought and conscience.[37] Moreover, as a minority group, Protestants were victims of the animosity of the far right. Much like Jews during the same period, Protestant Musée social members Paul Guieysse and Henri Monod and their families came under vicious attack by the notorious anti-Semitic writer Édouard Drumont, who blamed a Judeo-Protestant-Freemason conspiracy for ruining the country.[38] It is hardly surprising that Protestant reformers often became active Dreyfusards and, as in the case of Guieysse, were founding members of the Ligue des droits de l'homme. Freemasonry, another network in which social Protestants figured prominently, also undergirded many republican reform efforts and ministerial cabinets of the early Third Republic.[39]

Another factor that explains the close collaboration of Protestants and the republican reform circles at the Musée social is that in late-nineteenth-century France the social Protestant movement made a direct appeal to attract workers who were also being solicited by socialists and social Catholics. The Association protestante pour l'étude pratique des questions sociales was founded in 1888 with that explicit goal. Two hundred and eighty people gathered in Nîmes for the first meeting of this new association, whose president was the Christian socialist preacher Tommy Fallot and whose vice president was Charles Gide. Along with Gide, Jules Siegfried and Charles Robert were also present at this initial meeting. The founding declaration of the association was labeled by Fallot as "The French Language Charter of Social Protestantism." The insistence on the charter's being written in the French language was a discrete reference to the much larger international network of social Protestantism—also referred to as the Social Gospel or Christian socialism—that influenced the foundation of settlement houses and worker cooperatives in England and the United States.[40]

References to socialism were not absent from the French network. The opening address at the Association protestante's first meeting, given by Tommy Fallot, was entitled "Protestantism and Socialism." In his speech, Fallot concluded that the "duty of Protestantism" was to "hasten the coming of a kind of socialism," which he referred to as "universalist individualism."[41] The Association protestante also opened an essay contest that same year, inviting contestants to write submissions on the relationship between socialism and the teachings of Jesus. In preparation, contestants were urged to read Karl Marx's *Das Kapital* and Lassalle's *Capital et travail*.[42]

Despite its overtures to workers, however, the Association protestante succeeded in attracting only an elite group among the Protestant bourgeoisie. As Charles Gide later explained, the Association protestante was "too Christian for the workers" and "too social for the bourgeoisie." It evolved along "a path lined by two walls," as Gide described it, with "worried onlookers watch[ing] from the right and defiant ones from the left."[43] Nevertheless, the Association protestante's president, Tommy Fallot, pursued his social ministry in the working-class neighborhoods of northern Paris at the Église de la Chapelle du Nord, where he preached a version of nonviolent socialism. The grandson of Alsatian industrialist Daniel Legrand, who was the first in France to call for international labor legislation, Fallot also earned a devoted following among the Protestant bourgeoisie. Julie Siegfried, the wife of Jules, who became a moving force in French social feminism at the turn of the century, kept Fallot's book *Le Christianisme social* on her nightstand and referred regularly to his writings.[44] Gide, who supported Fallot's efforts, continued to use the Association protestante as a platform for encouraging members of the Protestant bourgeoisie to study social problems and calling for the creation of more libraries containing books on social economy that would remind them of their social mission.[45]

The Association protestante also tried to enlist Protestant pastors into the social economy movement and, to the extent that it was successful, recruited support for the type of republican reform effort sponsored by the Musée social. The *Revue de théologie pratique et d'études sociales* (which became the *Revue du Christianisme social* in 1896), was created specifically to spark interest in a social ministry in France.[46] Charles Gide's talk during the 1888 congress, "Du rôle pratique du pasteur," exhorted pastors to abandon charity, since it would never alleviate poverty. Instead, he urged them to look for the economic and social causes of poverty and turn to preventive measures such as mutual aid societies, credit cooperatives, and low-cost housing. If they studied social problems, Gide maintained, they would discover that the current social order defended by orthodox political economy was in "profound disagreement with God's plan." Gide viewed profit-sharing as a form of industrial solidarity and argued that Protestant entrepreneurs had a moral duty to implement such programs in their industries and businesses. He suggested that the only global remedy to social problems lay with state and municipal governments, which alone possessed sufficient resources and the means to organize public services.[47] The social programs espoused by Gide and other social Protestants were liberal and eclectic, ranging from profit-sharing schemes and social legislation to cooperatives and low-cost housing.

Although as a general doctrine social Protestantism inspired the work of some prominent Third Republican reformers, it did not offer a specific program for social action. As a result, much like the Musée social itself, social Protestants followed different paths to achieve reform. Jules Siegfried promoted housing reform at the Association protestante's third congress, held in Montbéliard in 1890, and explained to the audience that his activism was rooted in a social ethic inspired by his faith. Protestants were generally receptive to his message since they had had a tradition of involvement in housing reform since the early part of the century. The Société protestante de prévoyance et de secours mutuels (1825), for instance, specifically helped women and children of the Protestant faith acquire affordable housing. Throughout his parliamentary career, Siegfried continued to publicly acknowledge the influence of the Protestant social ethic on his work in housing reform.[48]

Social Protestantism merged with the efforts of many Musée social members because of its general reassessment of the tenets of classical political economy. As such, it contributed to the advent of social liberalism in France and reinforced the logic of republican social reform. Although in the earlier part of the nineteenth century the liberal Protestant bourgeoisie had firmly supported orthodox political economy as applied to the worlds of industry and finance, by the end of the century a new social philosophy had taken hold. The division of labor, uncontrolled prices, and rising unemployment characteristic of nineteenth-century industrialization were perceived by many Protestants as having created more conflict than harmony. Moreover, since the idea of collective salvation implied that the work of individuals should benefit the community as a whole, social Protestants often turned to cooperatives and profit-sharing as economic correctives to the excesses of the free market. Gide's École de Nîmes became a powerful force in the French cooperative movement and was the catalyst behind the creation of the Chambre consultative des associations ouvrières de production de France in 1885. Their journal, L'Émancipation, became the official publication of the Ligue française pour le relèvement de la moralité publique in 1892. Social Christianity rejected laissez-faire capitalism and proposed that a more just socioeconomic order could be achieved through a process of moral as well as social reform.[49] Social Protestantism, therefore, emerged as the liberal Protestant bourgeoisie's response to the problems of modern industrial society.

Solidarism. Finally, in addition to the Le Playist, social Catholic, and social Protestant influences on reform, the fourth major social doctrine that defined republican reformism at the Musée social was solidarism. In many ways, solidarism provided an ideological umbrella that unified the diverse approaches of republican social reform discussed above. Even before being adopted as the official social philosophy of the Radical party in 1908, solidarism triumphed in France, gaining wide currency as one of the primary theoretical structures of a revitalized liberalism that sought to "outbid the socialists." Popularized as a social doctrine by moderate Radical Léon Bourgeois in 1895, solidarism had massive appeal that reached across traditional divisions within French society. Protestants, Catholics,

Le Playists, freemasons, social liberals, Radicals, and reformist social-ists alike could identify with its fundamental premise that society was an entity composed of interlocking relationships linking generations, indi-viduals, and groups. This theory portrayed French society—and by exten-sion the Republic—as an interdependent whole, or, as Debora Silverman has so succinctly put it, "an organic model of unity in diversity."[50]

The educational reforms of the early 1880s guaranteeing free, secular, and compulsory primary schooling seemed to justify solidarism de facto by inaugurating a new role for the state as an agent of "reparative justice." Republicans, Bourgeois argued, shared the "moral duty of solidarity" be-tween rich and poor that, in the final analysis, is a feeling or a conviction that "no one is strong enough to do without the help of others." Without this sense of solidarity, "the political revolution that was France's glorious invention one hundred years ago, will not be fully realized." Bourgeois re-ferred to social solidarity among citizens as the "cooperative republic."[51] Although he did not invent something entirely new when he published his first series of articles on solidarism in 1895, Bourgeois did have an ear tuned to the pulse of the young republic and offered it a much-needed articulation of modern social relations.[52]

Later that same year, Léon Bourgeois, then prime minister, invoked solidarism in a letter he wrote for the Musée social's inauguration. Soli-darism, he proclaimed, provided the overarching social philosophy that could unite the disparate strands of this nascent republican reform move-ment. Indeed, its organicist imagery attracted the secular left as well as the conservative right. "It was precisely this eclectic character," suggests J. E. S. Hayward, "that gave the idea of solidarity its ephemeral popularity and potent political influence."[53] Solidarism, however, was hotly debated by orthodox liberals entrenched in the nation's most august intellectual academy, the Institut de France.[54] Even liberals who questioned ortho-dox political economy, such as Émile Cheysson and the economist Émile Levasseur, had difficulty accepting solidarism at first, primarily because it attempted to translate what they considered to be the moral basis of so-cial reform into a legal framework. By positing that each citizen had a so-cial debt toward the community, solidarism sought to rationalize claims for the social rights of citizens and to serve as a theoretical justification for the development of social law. Its premise that society functioned as a contractual series of reciprocal rights and duties later served to justify claims that the state must guarantee a modicum of social justice to its members. Accordingly, the state would become the guarantor of the public good and the general interest. At first, this conception of an interventionist state worried many liberals, even at the Musée social. Solidarism, however, should not be assimilated to government interventionism: private initiative and the individual continued to play a crucial role in its model of social reform. As Levasseur came to acknowledge in 1909, "Intervention is necessary; the debate bears upon its applications and its limits."[55]

Solidarism, furthermore, provided a convenient explanatory model for social reformers who touted the benefits of mutual aid funds and consumer or producer cooperatives. Its proponents argued that the inequalities of industrial society would be lessened through the action of voluntary associations, but that the state had an essential role to play in overseeing and guaranteeing basic social justice. "In contrast to ideologies and practices of laissez-faire," Ellen Furlough argues, "the goals of solidarism were to be achieved not only by governmental aid, but also through a myriad of associations and institutions which would overlap and form a web of voluntary solidarity."[56] At the Musée social, solidarism provided a rationale and philosophical underpinning for social liberalism and the call for a hybrid state, one that combined the virtues of individual initiative with the protective guarantees of social law.

Political and Social Diversity at the Musée social

In addition to understanding the main ideological underpinnings of reform at the Musée social, it is important to examine the political and social backgrounds of its members. Although, as will be discussed in greater detail in the following chapter, the official portrait of the Musée social's directors was that of the conservative republic, industrial welfare, and social peace, the institution itself embodied a far more composite membership. In fact, the diversity of the individuals who assembled there forces us to reexamine and broaden current interpretations of social reform that explain it primarily as a political phenomenon, a technique of industrial management, or a strategy of class defense.[57] Such approaches cannot fully account for the mixed nature of the Musée's membership, the common denominator of which proves to have been less attributable to political ideology or social origin than to the will to elaborate a new language of expertise in social affairs.

Although the degree of actual involvement with the institution varied greatly over time from one individual to the next, analysis of the Musée social membership lists for the years 1896, 1906, and 1911 confirms that the foundation attracted a heterogeneous array of reformers and demonstrates the permeability that existed between various reform groups and networks of fin de siècle France.[58] It is precisely the sociopolitical and professional diversity of the Musée's membership that shaped the institution's unique character as a think tank of republican social reform. Its composite membership, moreover, gave rise to what may be called a strategic elite, an alliance of men formed essentially by a cross section of conservative and progressive republicans. But even this portrait does not do justice to another dynamic that we see at work within the Musée social: the renewal of elites. These reformers are not merely a collection of old and new notables, but a portrait of ambition, change, and permeability among social and political groupings. It is within this context that Christian Topalov has suggested the term "field of reform" (*champ réformateur*) to describe the dynamic mixture of professional itineraries and sociopolitical aims that gave rise to institutions such as the Musée social in fin de siècle France.[59]

Political Origins

The political diversity of the Musée social was particularly striking for a republican institution of this period. Beginning with the count de Chambrun, the Musée incorporated a reserve of former monarchists who, in the aftermath of *Rerum novarum*, decided to support the Third Republic. These men, who also shared an active commitment to philanthropic or social endeavors, included Albert de Mun, the founder of the Oeuvres des cercles d'ouvriers catholiques; the prince d'Arenberg, the president of the Société philanthropique; and the count d'Haussonville, a member of the Institut de France known for his books on the Parisian laboring classes.[60] The majority of Musée social members, however, were conservative or moderate republicans, some of whom—such as Jules Méline, Émile Loubet, Paul Deschanel, René Waldeck-Rousseau—were players in the highest theater of republican politics; or others, such as Alexandre Ribot, Victor Lour-ties, Jean Audiffed, and Émile Chevalier. Radical republicans also figured prominently at the Musée, particularly those who achieved national re-nown for their contributions to policy debates on retirement pensions and public hygiene. These Radicals included Léon Bourgeois and Paul Guieysse; deputies Louis Ricard, Raoul Bompard, and Charles Beauquier; and senator Paul Strauss, elected from the department of the Seine from 1897 until 1936.

Socialists, on the other hand, were rare at the Musée, revealing a per-sistent exclusionary practice first noted during the 1889 Universal Exhi-bition. At first the absence of socialists was explained by their distrust of an institution whose board member, Georges Picot, had in 1895 de-clared "war on all forms of socialism."[61] But gradually, as will be exam-ined in greater detail in chapter 4, relations between the Musée and the socialist movement improved. By virtue of its day-to-day activities and the nonpartisan actions of its staff members, the Musée social convinced a good number of prominent socialists that, as an institution, it harbored no hidden political agenda to undermine their cause. Contributors to the Musée's publications, such as Jean Bourdeau, who proved to be a critical but well-informed observer of the socialist movement through his regular chronicles in the *Revue politique et parlementaire* or the *Revue des deux mondes*, helped legitimize socialism as a viable feature of French political life.[62]

Among the socialists who eventually created ties with the Musée social was the pivotal figure Alexandre Millerand—the first socialist to partici-pate in a "bourgeois" government—as well as those who situated their so-cialist convictions within the larger republican tradition and attempted to build bridges with the reform community. Another socialist at the Musée social was Jean-Baptiste Dumay, the former *communard* from Le Creusot who became a municipal councilor of Paris in 1887 and was a deputy from the department of the Seine from 1889 to 1893. A *possibiliste* and *alleman-iste* socialist, Dumay went on to become the assistant director of the Paris Bourse du travail when it reopened in 1896.[63] In 1906 Dumay sat on the Musée social committee on labor associations alongside Émile Cheysson, his former ideological nemesis from the 1870s in Le Creusot, where Cheys-son briefly directed the mines. Another member of this same committee in 1906 was Achille Daudé-Bancel, a leader of the cooperative movement and a *libre penseur* who was close to both Fernard Pelloutier and Charles Gide.[64]

The social question also drew together the socialist network of Albert Thomas and Musée social members Arthur Fontaine and Lucien March, a statistician, both of whom were directors of the Office du travail.[65] In many instances, it was the Musée's library that proved to be the site of multiple contacts among intellectuals close to anarchist and socialist circles such as Georges Sorel and Jean Grave. Others, including Jean Jaurès, were introduced to the Musée social through its meeting hall, which was widely used for public conferences. In the end, the Musée's quest for solutions to the social question was linked to no preestablished political doctrine other than a broadly defined republicanism.

The Association internationale pour la protection légale des travailleurs, founded during the 1900 Universal Exhibition, was emblematic of the permeability of the various networks that intersected at the Musée social. The association, which sought the unification of international labor legislation, united reformers from diverse political and social tendencies: only "intransigent liberals" were excluded. More than thirty Musée social members belonged to this group, including the liberal jurist Charles Lyon-Caen, Léon de Seilhac, Raoul Jay, Étienne Martin Saint-Léon, Arthur Fontaine, Charles Gide, Émile Cheysson, Jules Siegfried, Édouard Gruner, Albert de Mun, Alexandre Millerand, and the baron Flaminius Raiberti, a Radical deputy from the department of the Alpes-Maritimes. As part of this reform-minded endeavor, these men joined forces with socialists Édouard Vaillant and Hubert Lagardelle, editor of the journal *Mouvement socialiste*.[66]

Social Origins

The social origins of the Musée social members were equally diverse. No single social group predominated, and even within a given social category, the language and practice of social reform varied to such an extent that it is impossible to conclude that the Musée social was the tool of a consensual and class-based political strategy.[67] The members of the aristocracy, both old and new, at the Musée represented a broad spectrum of interests, from agricultural unions to the preservation of national monuments and municipal parks, to industrial labor unions and the socialist movement, as was the case of Léon de Seilhac. Many of them represented the interests of the agricultural world: the count Louis de Vogüé, the marquis Eugène-Melchior de Vogüé, the count Imbart de la Tour, the viscount de Lapparent, and the count Stanislas de Rougé were all members of the Société nationale d'agriculture, the Société des agriculteurs de France, the Société d'économie sociale, and the agricultural section of the Musée social. Others, primarily concerned with urban planning and aesthetics, joined the Musée in 1908 to participate in its newly created section on urban and rural hygiene.[68] This was the case of the count d'Andigné, a former army officer who became a municipal councilor of Paris; the baron Flaminius Raiberti; and the baron Robert de Rothschild.

The commercial and industrial bourgeoisie were represented at the Musée social by Jean Audiffred, the son of a wealthy textile merchant from Roanne; René Bérenger, the son and grandson of lawyers and political figures; Eugène d'Eichtal, the descendant of a Saint-Simonian disciple and a family of bankers and industrialists; Ernest Glasson, who belonged to a bourgeois dynasty of judges and parliamentarians from the *ancien régime*; and Georges Risler, who was born into a family of industrialists from Mulhouse.[69] The petite bourgeoisie also figured among the Musée membership. Achille Daudé-Bancel, for instance, was a pharmacist; and Léopold Bellan had been the accountant for a clothier in the Sentier quarter of Paris before opening his own cloth business as well as a fabric manufacturing firm in the Vosges.

Finally, a segment of the Musée membership was of working-class origin and was recruited primarily from among those who occupied administrative positions in the government, those who held political office, or those who were activists in the cooperative movement or in reformist trade unions. Such was the case of Joseph Barberet, a former syndicalist who entered the civil service at the ministry of the interior, where he first directed the bureau of professional associations and then its mutualism service. Edmond Briat, the secretary of the Union of Precision Instrument Workers, became a member of the Conseil supérieur du travail before joining the Musée social; and Pierre Coupat entered the Musée as the secretary of the Federation of Mechanics Workers.[70]

In 1896 the Musée's section on labor associations—whose president was Charles Robert and whose vice president was George Breton, the assistant director of the Office du travail—was dominated by members of producer or consumer cooperatives. The section also included Raphaël Barré, the director of the Banque coopérative des associations ouvrières de production; Louis Favaron, manager of the "Carpenters of Paris" workers' association; and Henry Buisson, a housepainter, union-member, and co-operator, who founded "Le Travail," a cooperative society that offered welfare benefits and profit-sharing even to its seasonal workers. Buisson declared his interest in "contributing to a better organization of labor while at the same time enhancing the self-esteem of workers" and explained that cooperators and Musée social reformers shared a common faith in the ideal of solidarity as the solution to the social question. He also directed a cooperative bank financed by an anonymous disciple of Fourier, which offered credit to producer cooperatives and became the first worker to direct the Union coopérative des sociétés françaises de consommation, where he succeeded Charles Robert. These men were among the French cooperative movement's most politically conservative and financially successful members.[71] Émile Ladousse, president of the Chambre consultative des associations ouvrières de production, thus declared: "We are not utopian thinkers, but simple men, workers. We strive to put into practice, in the social realm, the theories proposed by great thinkers, and we are content if we see them gradually have an effect upon our lives." [72] Ladousse also directed a producer cooperative of upholstery workers in Paris that received a prize at the 1900 Universal Exhibition for its commercial success. These skilled workers, who sold cloth, dye, rugs, furniture, and upholstery, were in competition with the growing department stores for a middle-class clientele. Cooperative ventures such as these also entered in direct conflict with the small shopkeepers and their increasingly politicized defense leagues, a phenomenon that prompted them to seek the support of reformers.[73]

The Musée social, therefore, incorporated workers who were the potential leaders of a reformist labor movement, those who were open to collaborating with government bureaus and who supported the alliance of economic and social pursuits for the betterment of the working class. The Musée social served, for instance, as the French home for the International Cooperative Alliance, created in 1895. But this perspective did not exclude other approaches to reform: Léon de Seilhac remained convinced that the best way to defend the economic interests of the working class was not cooperation but the development of labor unions, which he considered to be the foundation of a true industrial democracy.[74] Along with a diversity of social origin, there was at the Musée social a corresponding variety of reformist practice, characterized, nonetheless, by a willingness to work with the state—although not under its complete administrative control—and by the concern for reinforcing the social and industrial structures that would enable dialogue between partners of divergent political and economic interests.

Socioprofessional Networks

As fruitful as an analysis of the social, religious, and ideological origins of Musée social members is an examination of the different sociopolitical groups that met there—in particular the representatives of industry, politics, the civil service, the university, and the liberal professions. This approach sheds new light on the type of reform activity practiced at the Musée, the networks generated there, and the contributions of each group to the new representations and language of social reform developed during the early Third Republic.

The Industrial World. Contrary to the notion that the Musée social constituted a lobby of industrialists and businessmen, industrialists were, in fact, poorly represented at the Musée (representing 9.6 percent of the members in 1896 and only 1.5 percent in 1911) and were practically absent by World War I. If industrialists generally abstained from joining the Musée social, their absence, on one level, reflected deep-seated misgivings that reformers were simply meddling in their affairs. But it was also, certainly, a response to the decidedly greater interventionist tone of government policy, particularly after 1892, with the introduction of mandatory labor inspections in French factories.[75] Among the rare industrialists at the Musée, we find Alfred Engel, who was the president of the Société Belfortaine des habitations à bon marché, as well as Eugène Motte, the major cotton manufacturer from Tourcoing, who entered the Musée in 1906 after losing his seat in the Chamber of Deputies to Jules Guesde.[76] These industrialists were atypical of their socioprofessional group since none of them joined as industrialists per se, but as reform activists—usually in profit-sharing or neo-paternalist low-income-housing ventures—or as businessmen with political aspirations.

Instead, industry was represented at the Musée social by men who may be labeled "industrial advocates." These new delegates of the industrial world were typically engineers, lawyers, and representatives of employer interest groups—such as the Comité des forges, the Groupe des chambres syndicales de l'industrie du bâtiment, the Comité central des houillères, or the Caisse d'assurances mutuelles des forges de France. Industrial advocates were sometimes employed directly by the companies themselves—particularly in the case of old-style, family-owned businesses that experimented in profit-sharing—to act as interlocutors with government, policy, and reform circles. This was the case of F. Dubois, the associate director of the Chaix printing firm; of Auguste Lalance, an administrator of the Edison Company; and of M. Rose from the Baccarat crystal works. Others included engineers, such as Émile Cheysson; lawyers, such as Albert Gigot; or Le Playist social scientists, such as Robert Pinot—all of whom worked in close relation with the heavy, concentrated industrial sectors most directly affected by the problem of industrial accidents—the railroads, the mines, and the iron and steel industries. In these newer industries that were increasingly technical and capitalized by groups of investors that had little direct contact with the factories, owners relied more and more on the expertise of administrators and engineers. At a time when the notion of a managerial elite was still a new concept, engineers—who represented a rising socioprofessional group of the new industrial age—were often seen as substitutes for absentee owners.[77]

Coming mainly from middle-class backgrounds, engineers often found themselves in a difficult position: although hired to defend the owners' interests, engineers had prolonged day-to-day contact with workers and therefore frequently found themselves in the role of mediators. Professionally, they were just beginning to gain social and economic prominence toward the end of the century. Engineers and other similar industrial experts formed a new-style elite that, at least initially, helped mobilize support to prevent government regulation of industry. In the early 1890s, when many reformers still believed that changes in society could be initiated by reforms within the factory itself and that industrialists could be leaders in improving their industries, the Musée social sought to rally men who promoted the self-regulation of the industrial world. The careers of Édouard Gruner and Albert Gigot illustrate the profile of this type of industrial advocate, and the multiple networks on which they relied support their ideas.

Édouard Gruner (1848–1933), the scion of an old family from the Protestant bourgeoisie of Bern, was the son of a prominent civil engineer who was both the assistant director of the École des mines and the vice president of the Conseil des mines. The younger Gruner, in turn, became a civil engineer in 1873 and developed a keen interest in the problem of industrial accidents. Thanks to family connections, he was appointed the following year as the assistant director of a factory in Châtillon-sur-Seine and, in 1876, as director of the Neuves-Maisons mining factory. Then, in 1889, after several technical study missions abroad in Germany, Austria, Russia, Algeria, and Spain, Gruner was named secretary general of the newly formed Comité central des houillères, a coal mining interest group. That same year, during the 1889 Universal Exhibition, Gruner founded the Comité permanent du Congrès des accidents du travail, a group that promoted industry-based regulation of accident insurance. The Comité permanent included Oscar Linder, Maurice Bellom, Léon Say, and Jules Simon and constituted one of the earliest networks that contributed to the formation of the Musée social.[78]

When Gruner was first brought into the Musée in November of 1894, he served on the board of directors and presided over a research section on social insurance and another that focused on employer-sponsored social welfare. At the Musée social, he was also an industrial advocate, representing several employer interest groups in business, coal mining, and steel production. Gruner was, for instance, the president of the Houillères de la Haute-Loire, the Aciéries de Paris et d'Outreau, the Société de l'industrie minérale, and the Société d'encouragement pour l'industrie nationale. No other reformer at the Musée compiled such an impressive portfolio of industrial connections.

Reinforced by his role as an "industrial ambassador,"[79] Gruner also used his leadership role within the Protestant community to implore Protestant industrialists to organize themselves rather than passively await the day when government regulation would force its way into their factories. As the president of the Fédération protestante and of the Société des missions évangéliques, he addressed the congress of the Association protestante held in Nîmes in 1891 with a talk entitled "The Responsibility for Accidents from a Christian Point of View." Identifying with the mission of social responsibility among Christians, he asked the audience to stop and reflect upon the problem of whether or not the state should be involved in the business of organizing accident insurance. Wasn't this proposition, he queried, simply a way of washing one's hands of a sacred social duty incumbent on the Christian elite? He implored the members of his audience to ask themselves whether there was "a more anti-Christian solution" than that which allows "the employer to consider himself released from his duties of charity and welfare at the cost of a few francs paid to the state?" He further queried whether there was a solution "more destructive to the feelings of fraternity which bind — in France to an uncommon degree — employers to workers?" Instead, Gruner urged the industrialists in the audience to imitate their Alsatian ancestors and organize their own cooperative forms of industrial inspection. If they followed the German example, he warned, their workers might turn to an intransigent form of socialism. Appealing to their sense of moral responsibility, Gruner entreated the industrialists of the region to study problems such as work-related illnesses and to organize themselves to prevent industrial accidents. Recognizing, however, that only the largest industries were able to afford such insurance, he suggested that local industrial entrepreneurs demonstrate their social responsibility as Christian employers by banding together and forming regional mutual insurance funds.[80]

We can begin to see how, through his appeals to the Protestant community, a civil engineer like Édouard Gruner became an industrial advocate and how he relied on his multiple parapolitical networks — political, social, and religious — to garner support for his ideas and projects. The Musée social, as the nexus of so many parapolitical groups and networks, was precisely the type of milieu in which he liked to operate. The problem of industrial accidents mobilized reformers, whose preoccupations were both technical and political, thus creating the possibility of a new dialogue on social reform that occurred in the interstices of the worlds of industry and politics. Concerned with preserving entrepreneurial freedoms, these reformers also contributed to a concerted effort to fortify the public image of industrialists, who increasingly felt beleaguered by a political class that, in the name of republican rights, was making incursions into the once-private industrial citadel.

The divergent interests of Parliament, which in the early 1890s was veering decisively toward increased government regulation of industry, and industrial entrepreneurs, who sought to preserve their economic freedoms, underscores the equally divergent paths of political versus economic elite formation in fin de siècle France. As Christophe Charle has noted, along with the advent of the Third Republic, there had been an important shift in the sociological modes of recruitment between political elites on the one hand, and economic elites on the other.[81] The typical configuration of elite formation in nineteenth-century France had given rise to a relatively endogamous political and economic class, based on family-financed firms and marital strategies to consolidate bourgeois dynasties. However, the concurrent arrival of the Third Republic's political triumph and France's second phase of industrialization tended to undermine the apparent unity of that old elite. Moreover, the foundations of the nation's political class were altered by universal (male) suffrage, which tended to broaden the sociological base in the Parliament. At approximately the same time, the economic requirements of more concentrated forms of capital and unified production sites were making family-owned firms more difficult to operate in certain sectors of the economy. As a result, particularly in the aftermath of the 1898 law on industrial accidents but also as a general response to increased labor militancy and the economic crisis of the fin de siècle, industrialists often turned to more combative forms of business unionism to defend their interests.

This was the case of Robert Pinot, the Musée social's first administrative director, who, after resigning from his position at the Musée in 1897, went to work as an industrial advocate for the Union des industries métallurgiques et minières in 1900 and then for the Comité des forges in 1904. Given this changing configuration, industrialists seemed more inclined to call on new elites or lobbyists such as Pinot to represent their interests to the government and the public. Part of a broader reaction of "economic rearmament," this new form of employer syndicalism proved to be an important ingredient of the nationalist impulse embedded within belle époque France.[82]

In a similar manner, Gruner's fellow board member at the Musée social, Albert Gigot (1835–1913) became involved in the problem of industrial accidents. The son of a civil engineer and a liberal Catholic who joined Le Play's Société d'économie sociale in 1863, Gigot was a lawyer who crowned his career by entering the Conseil d'État and the Cour de Cassation. After a brief stint as the police prefect of Paris, he sat on the board of several industrial firms and was appointed as the administrative director of the Forges d'Alais. He quickly made a name for himself as a liberal defender of industrial property rights and a specialist in the area of accident insurance. His opposition to compulsory legislation to prevent industrial accidents led him to launch a campaign in favor of creating and expanding corporate insurance funds. Once discussion on worker compensation opened in Parliament in the 1890s, Gigot's career soared to new heights. He was appointed manager of three privately run combined funds in the mining, textile, and sugar industries that had been designed to stave off all mandatory government schemes for accident insurance. Despite the contrary direction taken in Parliament, where the idea of compulsory accident insurance was quickly gaining ground, Gigot continued to study comparative labor legislation and remained convinced that what he referred to as "the German model" should not be adopted in France. At the Musée social, Gigot also presided over the research section on legal affairs until his death in 1913.[83]

Political and Administrative Networks. Although the existence of a parliamentary network was crucial to the Musée's work in public policy, the number of members involved in national political life was small, a fact that is not too surprising, since most Musée members believed that public policies could best be discussed and planned outside the confines of government. In 1896 only four deputies participated actively in the Musée's work—Jules Siegfried, Jean Audiffred, Paul Guieysse, and Louis Ricard—but these men shared one important characteristic: they had all been members of the same parliamentary committee on insurance and social welfare, the Commission d'assurance et de prévoyance sociales, since its creation in 1894. Because this committee was directly involved in social policy formation of the Third Republic, it provided the Musée social with a direct conduit into the inner circles of national political debate. This small but efficient parliamentary network served to disseminate the ideas and proposals that issued from the Musée social—such as those on social insurance, retirement pensions, and mutualism—in an attempt to influence the direction of national policy.[84]

Musée social members also took on leadership roles in the government administration. Georges Breton worked within the Ministry of Commerce as the assistant director of labor and industry; Georges Paulet headed the ministry's main office on social insurance, the Bureau des caisses d'épargne de retraite, des assurances et de la coopération. Assigned the task of implementing the 1898 industrial compensation law, Paulet was named as the director of social insurance, first at the Ministry of Commerce and then at the Ministry of Labor.[85] Hubert Brice, who was the bureau chief and then the director of retirement pensions at the Ministry of Labor, was also an active member of the Musée social from 1896 until 1914.

If the membership lists in 1911 reveal a new orientation among the political and administrative representatives at the Musée social, it is primarily due to the creation in 1908 of the Musée's new research section on urban and rural hygiene. This section attracted men such as the deputies Charles Beauquier, founder of the Société française pour la protection des paysages de France, and Jules Lemire, creator of the Ligue du coin de terre et du foyer. Other members of the new section included the senators Auguste Calvet, who presided over the Amis des arbres association, and Paul Strauss, the president of the Ligue contre la mortalité infantile, as well as the "physician-legislator" Henri Marmottan, a deputy and founding member of the Association médicale-humanitaire. As we shall see in chapter 6, the parapolitical networks they represented linked environmental concerns with those of housing, urban planning, public health, and even certain forms of cultural nationalism that flourished in regionalist circles.[86]

But from both a political and an administrative perspective, the novelty of this section was that it boasted the presence within its ranks of several influential Paris municipal officials. Particularly prominent were Léopold Bellan, president of the Paris municipal council; Ambroise Rendu, a municipal councilor and member of its hygiene bureau; Louis Bonnier, who directed the architectural services of the city (a bureau that also dealt with roads, parks and walkways); the engineer Pierre Colmet Daâge, who directed the municipal water services; and Paul Juillerat, the administrative bureau chief of public hygiene services for the city of Paris.[87] Such a concentration of technical expertise and political influence at the level of the municipal government enabled the Musée social to become an important vehicle for developing new ideas and projects in the areas of public hygiene and urbanism, the echoes of which were heard far beyond Paris and the borders of the metropole.[88]

The World of Academe. The representatives of academe at the Musée social were usually law professors, although there were also several engineers who taught at the École polytechnique and the École des mines. Others were professors of social economy at the Conservatoire national des arts et métiers, such as Léopold Mabilleau, André Liesse, and Émile Levasseur, who was better known as a professor at the Collège de France. These professors came to the Musée social through their common interest in analyzing the contemporary social and economic world. University professors from the humanities or other intellectuals from the nation's cultural elite — such as prominent novelists, the literary avant-garde, or painters — were notably absent from these republican reform networks. However, once the Dreyfus Affair and its raging debates provoked a mobilization of intellectuals, fracturing the *mandarinat* of the narrow academic establishment, a greater number of professors increasingly adopted new public roles as critics of the contemporary world. But it is significant that, much like the political world itself, the academic networks of republican social reform at the Musée social were dominated by men who were trained as lawyers, since the terms in which the social question was debated in the early twentieth century would increasingly be defined by the language of jurisprudence and the law.[89]

The professors who presided over the Musée social's research section on legal affairs in 1896, however, were not members of the regular university system. Instead, they taught primarily at the École libre des sciences politiques and were affiliated with the Le Playist Société d'économie sociale and liberal circles of political economy. This group included several founding members of the École libre: in addition to Émile Boutmy, there were Gabriel Alix and Ernest Glasson, both of whom were lawyers. Others, although trained as lawyers, did not practice law: André Liesse, Charles Lyon-Caen, Louis Renault, Georges Paulet, André Siegfried, and the economist Paul Beauregard, who founded the journal *Monde économique* in 1891 and who contributed regularly to the *Revue internationale de sociologie*. Although the vast majority of these men did not support the idea of active state intervention in social policy, they nonetheless pushed for a redefinition of the liberal canon, particularly in the area of labor and industrial affairs. Glasson, for instance, who was a member of the Institut de France and the dean of the Paris Faculty of Law in 1899, professed that the Napoleonic Code was insufficient as a means of regulating the problems of contemporary labor; instead, he argued for a separate legal code to monitor the world of labor.[90] Although they were liberals, these men were all involved, in one way or another, with the reformist school of social economy. Furthermore, they all accepted the premise that social reform was linked to the general economic prosperity of the nation.

By 1911, however, the university professors at the Musée social no longer came primarily from the École libre des sciences politiques, and their attitudes toward government intervention had drastically changed.[91] These men were economists such as Paul Cauwès and Charles Gide, the founders of the *Revue d'économie politique*, or Raoul Jay, a member of the Union d'études des catholiques sociaux—all of whom argued for greater state regulation of the industrial world. At the Paris Institut Catholique, Adéodat Boissard, one of the founders of the Semaines sociales and an editor of the social Catholic journal *Le Mouvement social*, was also part of this network.

If these various members of academe joined the Musée social, it was in large part due to the flagrant absence from the university curriculum of any subjects that dealt with contemporary social problems.[92] In an attempt to rectify this situation, Alfred Espinas had been brought in to teach social economy at the Sorbonne at the behest of Ernest Lavisse and thanks to a private endowment by the count de Chambrun, who, nevertheless, was unhappy with the choice of Espinas. "He teaches the old-style political economy," Chambrun complained. Fernand Faure, director of the *Revue politique et parlementaire*, also led a campaign to introduce the discipline of sociology into the curriculum of the nation's law schools.[93]

It was not until the final years of the century that Émile Durkheim, after mobilizing his own networks of support, succeeded in penetrating the fortress of the academy and establishing the study of sociology as a legitimate discipline. Whereas the disciples of Le Play failed to graft themselves onto the world of academe, Durkheimians flourished there and eventually overshadowed the Le Playist school of thought as an historic source of the French sociological tradition.[94] Instead, the disciples of Le Play influenced government research bureaus, early think tanks such as the Musée social, and employer interest groups.

Other university professors at the Musée social, such as Georges Blondel at the University of Lille or Édouard Fuster at the Collège de France, undertook research projects to gain a better understanding of the laboring populations of Germany and Austria. They contributed to an accumulation of empirical knowledge about contemporary societies that became a fundamental component of the new public discourse on social policy.

The Medical Profession. Doctors entered the Musée social in significant numbers only after 1908, when public health concerns became a main target of the institution's reform efforts. This tendency was partly the result of the increased prestige of the medical sciences, which, having benefited from the discoveries of Pasteur, had drastically improved their efficiency and become of momentous importance to public policy. As excitement grew around the implications of Pasteur's discoveries, doctors and public figures alike helped popularize what Robert Nye has termed the "medical mode of social analysis." The language of social reform became inflected with the accents of a scientific and a specifically medical authority. But as several studies have recently suggested, the force with which the biological model of social analysis took hold in France at the turn of the century was as much fueled by the ideals of secular progress as it was by the fear of national degeneracy.[95]

In 1896 only Dr. Henri Napias had joined the Musée social as a delegate for the Société de médecine publique et d'hygiène professionnelle. He was, at that time, already at the height of an exceptional career, built jointly on experience in medicine and public administration, since in 1898 he was appointed as the director of public assistance. Each of the doctors who entered the Musée in the following years followed a similar path: they combined the practice of clinical medicine with an involvement in public health reform. For nearly twenty years, as the president of the Comité supérieur d'hygiène publique, Dr. Paul Brouardel amassed an impressive series of statistical data in epidemiology and worked with Henri Monod to prepare for the passage of the 1902 law that defined the legal foundations of public health in France. This legislative victory was not unrelated to the fact that in 1902 forty senators and nearly ten percent of the deputies in the Chamber of Deputies were also physicians, a phenomenon that in itself further testifies to the improved social status of the medical profession at the turn of the century. Brouardel was also a coroner, the director of the *Annales d'hygiène et de médecine légale*, the president of the Société de médecine légale, and a court-certified expert in public health.[96] Although the Musée membership included only two "deputy-physicians" — Drs. Henri Marmottan and Adolphe Pinard — others had been pressuring Parliament for decades to reform the nation's public health administration.[97] They originated new models of social intervention — as in the case of tuberculosis prevention and other examples of public hygiene measures, such as salubrious housing inspection — that required the close collaboration of the public and the private sectors.

The career of Dr. Albert Calmette was also devoted to propagating the ideals of public hygiene. After serving as the director of the Pasteur Institute in Lille, he founded the Pasteur Institute in Algiers and dedicated his life to the prevention of tuberculosis. Working both with Édouard Fuster and the social Catholic activist Abbot Lemire, Calmette chaired a congress on worker gardens in 1906, during which he proposed that the military terrains encircling French cities that were once medieval fortresses be reserved for the use of poor families. Léon Bourgeois persuaded him to accept the vice presidency of the National Defense Committee Against Tuberculosis; he was inducted into the Academy of Medicine and was appointed as the assistant director of the Pasteur Institute of Paris.

Also a member of the Musée social was Louis Landouzy, dean of the Paris Faculty of Medicine, who became the vice president of the Musée's section on urban and rural hygiene in 1911. In addition, he was the president of the Central French Association Against Tuberculosis, opened a people's sanatorium in Bligny, and directed the "Léon Bourgeois" antituberculosis dispensary. Similarly, Dr. Maurice Letulle entered the Musée's hygiene section in 1908 when he was a professor at the Paris Faculty of Medicine and a member of the Conseil d'hygiène et de salubrité for the department of the Seine. As an administrative official, Letulle was particularly interested in popularizing the basic notions of hygiene and the prevention of contagious diseases and work-related illnesses.[98] Other physicians came from the city's sanitation inspection corps: Drs. Frédéric Bordas and A.-J. Martin were both general inspectors with the city's bureau of technical hygiene services; Dr. Henri Thierry was the general inspector of housing conditions for the Paris prefecture. The careers of these individual men and the collective portrait of their colleagues at the Musée social demonstrate the growing interest and expertise of physicians in the area of public welfare.

Architects and Urban Planners. As was true for the physicians, the architects—who numbered more than twenty—all joined the Musée social in 1908 when the section on urban and rural hygiene was created. These architects were generally young and shared an interest in hygiene, housing, and early city planning. Their concern with the social function of architecture represented a departure from the beaux-arts traditions of the profession, which was more imbued with matters of aesthetics, form, and composition. Indeed, the rapidly changing character of modern cities had enticed the Musée social architects to shift their focus away from individual buildings and toward the placement of buildings within a larger urban and even suburban fabric. The city, in their view, comprised an increasingly complex web of urban elements such as landscaped walkways, boulevards, and parks.

Some architects and planners at the Musée social had first been interested in civic architecture and the construction of public-use buildings such as schools and municipal swimming pools. The Musée social provided these men with a unique place within which to congregate, one located outside of the established, even entrenched architectural circles of early-twentieth-century France. As a new professional group, these architects and urban planners used the Musée social as a professional springboard from which to launch and diversify their professional lives. Membership in the hygiene section enabled them to connect with an array of individuals who approached urban problems as complex issues demanding collaborative expertise. The networks they established there helped them consolidate their professional identities and status, and served as a catalyst for the creation of the Société française des architectes urbanistes (1911) and the École des hautes études urbaines (1919). Many of these architects played an active role in the municipal reform movement. Thus, Alfred Agache, Raoul de Clermont, and Augustin Rey were all members of the Association générale des hygiénistes et techniciens municipaux; while others, such as civic architect Louis Bonnier or the *polytechnicien* and landscape architect Jean-Claude Forestier, worked for the architectural services of the city of Paris.[99]

The contributions made by these architects to the early stages of the urban planning movement has begun to receive scholarly attention.[100] The very nature of their multidisciplinary approach to the city required the elaboration of concepts and techniques that encouraged collaboration among architects and engineers as well as political and administrative personnel. This particularly modern form of knowledge—one that is both technical and social, urban, and hygienic—found a congenial home in the Musée social. The men who activated these networks found the Musée to be equally well suited to their strategies of urban intervention and their concerns for professional legitimization.

In conclusion, this analysis of the Musée social membership suggests that well beyond the limits of the Radical party and its official doctrine of solidarism there were multiple cultural discourses and rhetorics, deeply anchored in French society, that contributed to the renewal of liberal thought at turn of the last century. To better understand the reformist milieu at the Musée social and the international dimensions of its concerns, we once again turn to the idea of a community of discourse. The existence of a broad-based community of reform discourse in France explains better than does the study of specific political groups or ideologies the extent to which liberalism was being reassessed and the goals of republican social reform were gaining momentum. Protestants, social Catholics, socialists, and conservative or Radical republicans all contributed—with their respective experiences, rhetorics, and analyses—to formulating a new collective social ethic for the Third Republic. In the long run, it was this community of discourse, so deeply rooted in the cultural, political, and religious traditions of nineteenth-century France, that enabled reformers to articulate their criticisms of industrial society to such a broad public and to contribute to the elaboration of republican social policy.

Another conclusion of this study is that reformism in France needs to be understood within the context of the rising professional middle classes and the advent of early social science. Engineers, lawyers, doctors, university professors, architects, civil servants, and reformist labor leaders all played crucial roles in shaping debates in public policy, social medicine, welfare, retirement, and housing reform. Social science generated information that cast new light on the dilemmas facing contemporary French society. In order to appreciate the diversity of the republican reform networks in France during the late-nineteenth and early-twentieth centuries, however, it has also been necessary to temporarily set aside the analysis of traditional political institutions such as the Parliament and to adopt a new lens through which we can more clearly discern the contours of civil society. Since the Musée social was situated in a parapolitical realm and both integrated and was traversed by so many social reform networks, it is perhaps the institution of the early Third Republic that allows us to best recognize the diverse public that supported the new ideas of social, moral, and legal responsibility and that fueled early social welfare debates.

When faced initially with the social question, reformers at the Musée social eschewed narrow theoretical approaches and opted to open their doors and encourage dialogue between partners of very different social and ideological backgrounds. Being among the first in France to take the notion of public opinion seriously, they created a new space within which to define and debate the social question. In this sense, the Musée social helped render this dialogue between dissimilar parties both possible and respectable. By contributing to the renewal of liberal thought in France, they helped to prepare the way for the rise of the État-providence.

Indeed, one common thread that unites the disparate elements of the Musée social is the institution's thorough questioning of the hegemonic liberal credo of late-nineteenth-century France. Since the advent of the Third Republic, transformations in liberal thought had important consequences for the evolution of public assistance, public medicine, the economy, and the law; but these transformations also pointed to the emergence of a new attitude on the part of a significant fraction of French elites toward the role of the state in modern society. Progressively, the state became more interventionist and played a greater regulatory role in society. Even the Musée social members who were closest to the school of classical political economy recognized that those who did not accept this new role for the state were simply not realistic. At the same time, however, partisans of a new liberalism at the Musée social fought to preserve private initiative as a crucial springboard of a thriving society and economy. In the end, as shall be demonstrated in subsequent chapters, Musée reformers wanted a hybrid state, one that would integrate the public and private sectors and create an alliance between entrepreneurial freedom and the protection of republican rights. Gradually, the notion of social law would replace that of social duty in the vocabulary of Musée social reformers.

Along with questioning of the tenets of classical liberalism, Musée members demonstrated their willingness to collaborate with a wide array of partners, to create interdisciplinary teams for research and study and to practice the general principles of social science—the study of social facts, the method of direct observation, and the gathering of social statistics. In the end, they sought more scientific and objective foundations—not ideologies or dogmas—on which to build social policy. Sorely aware of the lack of cognitive tools for understanding contemporary society, the Musée social remained open to all schools of thought and areas of experimentation. Its members were not theoreticians, but rather practitioners of social reform who believed that French society could be shaped and transformed by the policies they sought to build. The history of the Musée social and its reform networks invites us, therefore, to rethink this founding period of the Third Republic, not as one of "institutionalization" or of "consolidation" of state structures, but rather as a period of exceptional social and political fluidity.

4. A Laboratory of Social Reform

⁓

According to the wishes of the comte de Chambrun . . . the Musée social should be above all the home of the people, [and of] civic associations, which are the vital organs of its collective and conscious life, the instrument of its education and its progress. —LÉOPOLD MABILLEAU, 1919

A research institute and a public service organization, the Musée social quickly became the country's largest nongovernmental agency to focus on the social dimensions of industrial life. Its research sections and consultation services analyzed all types of experiments in social welfare, both in France and abroad, irrespective of their ideological bent or whether they were sponsored by private enterprise, voluntary civic groups, or the government. The Musée social disseminated the results of its studies by publishing bulletins on a regular basis and distributing them to government offices, civic and labor groups, and the general public. Its innovative publicity machine used newspaper accounts, posters, and public meetings featuring well-known political personalities to advertise the Musée's research initiatives and reform efforts. Its institutional structure reflected this dual preoccupation with social research and civic pedagogy.

The Internal Structure of the Musée social

From 1894 until 1900, the Musée social operated according to a two-tier organizational design. A seven-member board of directors appointed by the comte de Chambrun made all major policy and budgetary decisions, while a salaried administrative staff oversaw day-to-day operations. Following Chambrun's death in 1899, a third tier was added to this basic ar-

Figure 7. Facade of the Musée social, 5 rue Las Cases.
CEDIAS-Musée social, Paris.

rangement: the Grand Conseil, an advisory board composed of sixty members who determined general policy at biannual meetings. Of these three administrative levels, the Grand Conseil fulfilled the most symbolic function, whereas the administrative staff had the most direct contact with the users of the Musée social's facilities and left the greatest impact on its operations. Its board of directors gave social and political legitimacy to the Musée and was responsible for conceptualizing its unique structure and mode of functioning.

The Board of Directors. Beginning in the fall of 1894, the men who would form the Musée social's first board of directors met weekly in the *salon* of the Siegfried family home at the rond-point des Champs Elysées in

Paris.[1] From there, they rapidly transferred their permanent headquarters to Chambrun's renovated *hôtel particulier* on the rue Las Cases in preparation for the Musée's official opening to the public in March of 1895. In addition to president Jules Siegfried, vice presidents Émile Cheysson and Charles Robert, and secretary-treasurer Édouard Gruner, the board included Georges Picot, perpetual secretary of the Académie des sciences morales et politiques and a director of the Compagnie des chemins de fer du Midi; Albert Gigot, a former police prefect of Paris, director-administrator of the Forges d'Alais and of the accident insurance fund of the Comité des forges; and Émile Boutmy, a member of the Institut de France and the founding director of the École libre des sciences politiques. These men planned and centralized the institution's activities, decided how to allocate funds for research and publications, solicited new members and outside collaborators, and represented the Musée in official circles.

Only a few members of the board, particularly its president Jules Siegfried, were actively involved with the Musée's routine administration and services. Most remained aloof from the daily life of the institution, limiting their involvement to board meetings and lending their names to Musée letterhead. Collectively, however, these men of the *haute bourgeoisie* represented an imposing human frontispiece for an institution that sought immediate legitimation from the conservative republic. In this sense their strategy was successful, since the members of the board embodied many of the most salient attributes of the Opportunist regime. They were in the twilight of successful careers in business, industry, education, and government and had demonstrated their commitment to the Republic as well as to the renovation of French elites. Their strong professional ties to the Chamber of Deputies and the Senate, the powerful Conseil d'État, the high civil service, the Institut de France, big business, and industry revealed their stature within the regime and served the Musée social's designs to have a broad yet direct influence on the major centers of decision making in fin de siècle France. Accustomed to straddling the public and private sectors, Musée board members carefully preserved their powerful links to government and public institutions as well as to industry and business, a choice that marked their reform initiatives as well. The board also incarnated the religious proclivities of the secular republic; a majority of its membership was Protestant, although it also featured figureheads from the world of Catholic philanthropies.

The range of influence, moreover, extended beyond these official circles into the vast network of parapolitical associations that was proliferating in France at the turn of the century. With the notable exception of Émile Boutmy—whose inclusion in the board seems to have been largely intended to calm his misgivings about the Musée's potential competition with his École libre des sciences politiques—the members of the board participated in an impressive and diverse array of such groups, including the precursors of employer unions such as the Comité des forges and the Comité central des houillères; the pro-natalist Oeuvre de l'allaitement maternel pour femmes enceintes and the Alliance nationale pour l'accroissement de la population française; the low-cost housing group Société française des habitations à bon marché; the Le Playist Société d'économie sociale; and the Office central des oeuvres de bienfaisance (OCOB), which strove to coordinate private charities.[2] Musée board members also figured prominently within many *conseils supérieurs*—the consultative bodies that worked in tandem with government as a way of involving private citizens in policy formation—such as the Conseil supérieur de l'assistance publique or the Conseil supérieur des habitations à bon marché, for which Émile Cheysson, who never held political office, authored annual activity reports for a period of fifteen years.[3] Therefore, beyond the most obvious socioeconomic contours of the Musée social's board of directors, which were those of the *haute bourgeoisie*, what distinguished these men from other representatives of that same elite was their attempt to grapple with the social question by devoting a portion of their public lives to its resolution.

From the perspective of the sheer number of his parapolitical affiliations, Cheysson was the most notable figure among the Musée social's board members: by one tally, he had lent his name, as an honorary officer, to over one hundred associations. Although he could not possibly have been active in every organization to which he belonged, Cheysson's willingness to accumulate so many honorific titles was part of a larger strategy to achieve social legitimization on the part of reformers whose public status had heretofore gone unrecognized. By adopting Le Play's notion of "social duty," Cheysson and his colleagues at the Musée social called for a renewed code of social ethics among the nation's elite, particularly among the new industrial bourgeoisie who would lead the nation in reform efforts. According to Cheysson, "If everyone in France fulfilled his duty, there would be no social question."[4]

The initial reputation of the Musée social, therefore, was based largely on the prestige of its board members and their close ties to the republican establishment. When the Musée social figured as a tourist site on the official map of Paris distributed for the 1900 Universal Exhibition, it was because the republican regime had entrusted the Musée with the role of announcing to the world that the Third Republic was making an effort to improve the lot of workers. At a time when the Opportunist republic was being challenged to take a position on the social question, the Musée social provided some members of the republican establishment with a convenient way of publicly asserting their intention of pursuing reform efforts, however symbolic those intentions may have been.

Although the board's initial composition was periodically altered by deaths or resignations, it never substantially changed in character. When Émile Boutmy resigned in 1897, he was replaced by Jean-Honoré Audiffred, a deputy from the Loire department who was also a member of the commission of the National Retirement Fund and the parliamentary commission on social insurance. Appointed as the board's vice president after Cheysson's death in 1909, Eugène Tisserand was a member of the Academy of Sciences, an honorary councilor at the Cour des comptes, a member of the Société d'encouragement à l'industrie nationale, and a three-time president of the Société nationale d'agriculteurs de France. Siegfried remained the president until his death in 1922, and Gruner maintained his position as secretary-treasurer until 1914.[5] Between the years 1894 and 1914, there was great continuity in the composition of the board of directors, and its members continued to uphold the Musée social's powerful political and social status within government circles of the early Third Republic.

The Administration. The salaried administrative staff of the Musée social, charged with overseeing daily operations, originally included seven individuals, none of whom was as socially prominent as were the members of the board. These men, nevertheless, were crucial to the success of the institution since they organized its library, archives, and consultation services, and ensured the open-minded exchange with the public that became the Musée's trademark. Of particular significance were Robert Pinot, Charles Salomon, Léon Marie, and Léon de Seilhac.[6]

Pinot, a key collaborator of the Le Playist publication *La Science sociale*, was brought in as the first administrative director in 1894 and entrusted with overseeing "the sound and rapid organization of the Musée." Charles Salomon, a Protestant and friend of Jean Jaurès, was hired as the Musée's first administrative secretary.[7] Despite having no prior experience in politics or industry, Salomon held a law degree, had traveled widely, and was considered to be extremely knowledgeable about contemporary Europe. Thanks to his excellent command of the Russian language, Salomon established ties between the Musée and the Russian intellectual community, most notably with Leon Tolstoy, who followed the Musée social's activities and publications with great interest.[8] From 1896 to 1900, Léon Marie was kept on a regular retainer as the Musée social's actuarial expert, a gesture demonstrating the institution's conviction that insurance techniques would be necessary for the success of many social reform schemes.[9] Finally, Léon de Seilhac, the other key figure of the Musée's first administrative staff, was placed in charge of the Musée's industrial and labor service.

Robert Pinot, however, resigned abruptly from his position as administrative director in 1897, following a disagreement with Chambrun and the board over the future direction of the Musée. In a letter to Jules Siegfried, Pinot indicated that, in his view, the Musée social had not lived up to its own standards as an impartial research institute, one that had been "founded in an essentially philanthropic" spirit. The Musée needed to preserve its scientific means of action and maintain its distance from politics, which, Pinot added, must never be placed in doubt; only then could it "disarm workers' suspicions, bring closer together people of different opinions and social backgrounds, enlighten public opinion, and facilitate the impartial study of facts." What Pinot disliked most, however, was his lack of autonomy as director. He let it be known that his wings had been clipped and that he no longer wished to work under such conditions. Pinot's resignation, however, did not unduly alarm the board or Chambrun.[10] Rather, it underscored a basic philosophical disagreement between Pinot, who, as a member of the Le Playist *La Science sociale* group, was committed first and foremost to developing a science of society that was detached from politics, and the Musée directors, who were increasingly embroiled in efforts to achieve pragmatic social reform.

It is not surprising, then, that when looking for Pinot's successor, the board first turned to two men who, although *polytechniciens* and mining engineers influenced by Le Playist social science, did not shun practical efforts to achieve social reform: Arthur Fontaine, who had organized the statistical section of the Office du travail and went on to become its director, and Maurice Bellom, a professor at the École des mines and a specialist in social insurance and industrial legislation.[11] Preferring to pursue their chosen career paths, both Fontaine and Bellom, however, declined the offer.

The Musée directors then made a somewhat surprising choice. In 1897 they appointed Léopold Mabilleau as the Musée social's second administrative director. A graduate of the École normale supérieure and a former member of the École française de Rome, a classics scholar and a professor of philosophy at the Faculty of Letters at Caen, Mabilleau had experience neither with Le Playist social science nor with the industrial world. His strong academic credentials, however, weighed in his favor, as did his reputation as an outstanding orator. Convinced that the Musée social needed a more activist voice in the public debate on social reform, board members evidently felt that Mabilleau's skills were of more value than those of a more technical social scientist. Whereas Pinot had primarily seen himself as a man of science working in the background to effect change and to perfect the tools for a science of society, Mabilleau stepped in as an activist director who was willing to adopt a more interventionist public role. Indeed, partly because of his public-speaking skills and the position of visibility afforded him by the Musée social, Mabilleau rose quickly to national prominence as a spokesman for the mutualist movement.[12]

These men of the Musée's administrative staff were pivotal figures since they dealt most directly with the public. They were held, moreover, to higher standards of objectivity and political nonpartisanship not only in their work but also in their public lives outside of the Musée. Unlike the Musée's board members, several of whom were involved in politics, the administrative staff was formally advised not to accept any political role that might compromise the image of institutional neutrality that the Musée hoped to preserve. When Mabilleau's name was advertised in 1898 as a member of the organizing committee of the Grand cercle républicain, he immediately requested that it be withdrawn. The board expressed satisfaction with Mabilleau's decision, approving of his "attitude which coincides with the strict political neutrality that the Musée must uphold." Mabilleau even asked the board's permission before giving a public lecture on the topic of mutualism at the Grand cercle républicain. On another occasion, in 1901, when Mabilleau's name circulated as a potential candidate for a legislative seat from the district of Castelnaudary, the board informed him that they considered any active participation in political life to be incompatible with the direction of the Musée. Furthermore, when Mabilleau was hired, it was stipulated that he should devote his time exclusively to the foundation, thereby forgoing his scholarly career and transforming himself into a public militant for the causes espoused by the Musée social.[13]

The Grand Conseil. The Musée social's 1894 by-laws stipulated that after the death of Chambrun a sixty-member Grand Conseil would be established with automatic membership reserved for honorary presidents, members of the board of directors, and representatives from fourteen specified institutions and reform groups.[14] Members of the Grand Conseil included senators; deputies; members of the Académie des sciences morales et politiques and the Conseil supérieur du travail; employers who had instituted social-welfare programs; workers who were particularly active in reform groups; representatives of voluntary associations, trade or agricultural unions, cooperatives, and mutual societies; and journalists and writers known for their studies of contemporary social problems. The Grand Conseil functioned merely as an advisory board, but its composition was broad-based and symbolized on yet another level the Musée's desire to showcase its political connections and to forge an influential network of parapolitical social-reform groups. The Conseil met only once a year to approve the annual budget, oversee major financial decisions, review publication proposals, and encourage the Musée to orient its work in particular areas such as economic and rural development, or public health and worker housing.

The Conseil also counted in its membership an impressive array of national dignitaries and economic power brokers. The two honorary presidents of the Musée's first Grand Conseil were president of the Republic Émile Loubet and former premier Léon Bourgeois. Thereafter, nearly every former president of the Republic became an honorary president of the Musée social's Grand Conseil. In 1900 it included politicians such as Paul Deschanel, Jules Méline, and Raymond Poincaré; businessmen such as Léon Aucoc and Eugène d'Eichtal, respectively president and vice president of the board of the Compagnie des chemins de fer du Midi; industrialists, including Alfred Engel and Auguste Lalance; jurists such as René Bérenger and Charles Lyon-Caen, both of whom taught at the Faculty of Law; and members of the Parisian social and philanthropic elite, including the prince d'Arenberg, the count d'Haussonville, and the marquis de Vogüé. One-third of the Grand Conseil was composed of high-ranking civil servants, including Arthur Fontaine; Henri Hébrard de Villeneuve; Henri Monod, the director of the Assistance publique; and Georges Paulet, the head of the Office of Savings, Pensions, Social Insurance, and Cooperation at the Ministry of Commerce. Representatives of labor groups, such as Henry Buisson, a member of the Chambre consultative des associations ouvrières de production, who directed a bank for producer cooperatives, and Louis Favaron, the director of the "Carpenters of Paris"; professors such as Émile Levasseur and the vice rector of the Academy of Paris, Louis Liard; and medical authorities such as the dean of the Faculty of Medicine, Paul Brouardel, also a member of the Conseil supérieur de l'assistance publique, comprised the remaining members. By associating figures of such high social and economic status with those who represented a cross section of professional categories, the Musée social was able to maintain its privileged links to government, state-sponsored social welfare agencies, institutions of higher learning, industry, and the voluntary reform organizations operating in France.[15]

The Musée social's Resources and Services

The Musée social hoped to generate a well-informed dialogue among the general public, social reform groups, government, business, and industry, particularly since the social stratification of nineteenth-century French society virtually precluded interaction among them. Musée social reformers believed that their mission involved helping French civil society adjust to a new republican political framework by encouraging cooperation among heterogeneous social and political groups. The Musée's resources and public services—research sections, library, consultation services, publications, and public lecture series—also fit within its more scientific mission to serve as an impartial guide to understanding industrial society. Through these varied channels, the Musée social maintained its active link with the public and influenced the various agencies of government that contributed to social policy formation in fin de siècle France.

The Research Sections. Beginning in March of 1896, when the research sections (*sections d'études scientifiques*) of the Musée social officially opened, eighty-eight volunteer experts—including doctors, lawyers, professors, actuaries, and reformist labor representatives, each of whom had been solicited by the board of directors—gathered to take part in them. Forming the infrastructure of the Musée's think tank on social reform, the research sections gathered a wealth of information on contemporary social issues, developed a reservoir of expertise that proved valuable to the government, and attracted international interest. Throughout the period under examination it was the second of these missions—providing services to the government—that proved to be the most problematic since at times the Musée's desire to serve as a catalyst for practical reform conflicted with its more disinterested scientific mission.

At first, seven research sections were created, each presided over by a Musée social board member: (1) agriculture; (2) labor and cooperative associations; (3) social insurance; (4) employer-sponsored social welfare services; (5) study missions and surveys; (6) legal affairs; and (7) relations with social reform groups outside the Musée. The number and focus of the research sections shifted according to the tenor of public debate. By the turn of the century, for instance, the section on employer-sponsored social welfare services had been abandoned, since the general public no longer believed that entrepreneurial forms of welfare could resolve the country's pressing social problems. In 1908 the section on urban and rural hygiene was added, the workings of which will be addressed in chapter 6. And in 1916, after years of postponement, the Musée social created a women's section that was active particularly during the interwar years, promoting civic and professional equality for women.[16] All research sections met as semiautonomous entities and established their own research agendas, with the exception of the women's section, which, in the beginning, was forbidden to address political matters such as citizenship rights and suffrage—an interdiction that can be interpreted both as an extension of the Musée's general policy of leaving politics in the cloakroom and as a manifestation of continuing seated resistance to women's full participation in political life. Board approval was required of all sections, however, for the funding of research missions abroad and the publication of project results.

The way in which the sections disseminated the conclusions of their studies was a potentially thorny issue. The Musée's official position was that it would publicly endorse the conclusions reached by its sections only if they had been formally solicited to interpret specific legal or technical points. If, however, their conclusions involved statements of a philosophical or political nature, the Musée preferred to shroud itself in the cloak of institutional neutrality and "merely record [the results] in documentary fashion," representing the opinions of the section but not those of the institution as a whole. The sections, therefore, merely issued documentary reports or commentary on parliamentary bills and, after 1902, published the minutes of their meetings in the Musée's *Annales*. In keeping with the documentary aura surrounding the Musée's work, these minutes were reproduced as "scientific documents" that had been "faithfully recorded." Nor did the Musée want to be perceived as authoring legislative bills. Its sections could communicate their findings to the public or the appropriate government ministry, but it was not within the institutional mission of the Musée social to "submit counterproposals to the government." Instead, the board felt the Musée should limit itself to publishing the objective findings of its investigations and allow others the task of deciding whether or not to transform the data into an amendment or a parliamentary bill.[17]

Musée members were therefore free in theory to make use of the conclusions reached by the various sections as they saw fit, provided that they did not mention the Musée social by name. Although politicians such as Jules Siegfried or Jean-Honoré Audiffred regularly submitted bills to the Parliament that had either been generated or discussed at length within a research section, the Musée itself remained a silent partner in the enterprise, preferring to have a more discreet influence on policy making. Other members, such as Picot and Cheysson, branched out and relied on the vast parapolitical network centralized at the Musée social for support. Under the aegis of the Société française des habitations à bon marché, Picot devoted much of his time to writing and revising various versions of the French housing laws of November 30, 1894; April 2, 1906; and

April 10, 1908. Cheysson, in turn, became particularly committed to the issues of work-related accidents and social insurance. According to Louis Rivière, "Each time a new project was submitted to Parliament either by the government or by a deputy, Mr. Cheysson had it examined within one or another of the associations to which he belonged."[18] These men, moreover, were periodically called on to testify before parliamentary subcommittees in their area of expertise. Thus, despite its aversion to direct involvement in partisan politics, the Musée social functioned as an informal think tank, regularly scrutinizing the details of ongoing legislative and policy debates within its sections. Because of its reputation for indirect input into policy formation, the Musée social was commonly referred to as "the antechamber of the Chamber."

The Musée's quest for information on industrial society was also international in scope. In this spirit, networks of foreign delegates were established and special investigators sent abroad to gather independent, firsthand information on economic developments and social reform measures in countries as diverse as England, Germany, Italy, Belgium, Spain, Russia, the United States, New Zealand, Argentina, Morocco, Algeria, and Tunisia. These research projects were quite exceptional in their day, as was the conviction that statistical data currently available through official government channels were insufficient to adequately inform public opinion and parliamentary debate. The Musée social did not see itself in competition with the research efforts sponsored by the Office du travail. To the contrary, the two institutions often collaborated and shared investigators. However, because of its independent status and generous financing by the count de Chambrun (who earmarked 50,000 francs in 1895 for investigations abroad), the Musée social could set its own research agenda and undertake detailed, anthropologically informed studies abroad that were not within the scope of the Office du travail.

In a manner reminiscent of Le Play's fieldwork, Musée researchers were required to speak the language of the target county fluently in order to conduct interviews, attend meetings, and participate in homestay arrangements with local families. Research teams were also conceived as training schools to provide experience to promising young men in the techniques of social investigation. In 1895 Paul de Rousiers headed the Musée's first mission abroad to England, which, as will be discussed later in greater detail, focused on the political and economic organization of

English workers. He reported the results of this mission in his book *Le trade-unionisme en Angleterre*, published in 1896 by Armand Colin, the first volume in a series entitled "La Bibliothèque du Musée social."[19]

Inspired by the methods of Le Playist monographic studies, the Musée's second mission in 1895, led by Georges Blondel to Germany, concentrated on peasant response to the current agricultural crises of overproduction, competition, speculation, and debt. This mission focused primarily on the effect of Bismarckian insurance laws on the peasantry and on the organization of agricultural credit. Although Blondel and his team consulted a voluminous documentation and met with dignitaries such as Dr. Bödiker, the president of the Imperial Insurance Office, they also gathered as much firsthand information as possible through interviews and long-term stays in small villages. In their conclusions, they predicted that German farming districts would overcome the agricultural crisis, not because of individual will or government intervention, but because of the strength of groups, families, and associations that formed the basis of rural society in Germany. A second volume in the Musée social's book series, *Études sur les populations rurales de l'Allemagne et la crise agraire*, was published in the aftermath of this mission.[20]

The Musée social continued to sponsor international research by establishing a network of approximately twenty-five salaried correspondents in France and abroad who kept the Musée abreast of current events and social or economic developments in their respective countries. These foreign correspondents included William Willoughby, an expert investigator at the U.S. Department of Labor who went on to head the Institute for Government Research (1916), a direct precursor of the Brookings Institution; William Howe Tolman, a social engineer who founded the American Institute of Social Service, modeled on the Musée social, in New York; Tjeenk Willink, an engineer who reported on Dutch parliamentary debates; Louis Varlez, a lawyer at the Appellate Court of Ghent who become an active member of the League of Nations and the International Labor Bureau; Victor Muller, a lawyer from Liège, Belgium; and Albert Stanley, an English worker and secretary of the Midland Miners Federation who became a Member of Parliament. A testimony to its international influence, the Musée social inspired the creation of a *Museo social* (1911) in Buenos Aires as well as a *Museo sociale* (1910) in Milan under the auspices of the *Società Umanitaria* (1894).[21]

At a time when such information was not readily available, these foreign correspondents wrote regular reports, sent brochures and news clippings, and chronicled parliamentary debates on the formation of economic and social policy in their countries. Victor Muller, who wrote a detailed account of the socialist cooperative Le Vooruit for the Musée, also sent regular bibliographies of recently published works on the social question in Belgium, as well as summaries of discussions underway in Parliament on a pending labor union bill.[22] The Musée's foreign correspondents also contributed fresh, eye-witness accounts of social and labor movements. Albert Stanley, who attended the International Miners' Congress in London (1897) for the Musée social, was asked to provide, not "a dry report," but "a personal diary of an English miner's leader" from his own "personal and genuine experience."[23] Such efforts contributed to the original documentation made available to users of the Musée social's library and readers of its publications. Both Stanley and Muller eventually resigned from their positions—as Robert Pinot had done, although from a different ideological perspective—due to what they perceived to be the Musée's increased involvement with official policy and political circles, and its seemingly weakened commitment to independent scientific research.[24] Standing as evidence, of the Musée social's deep commitment to gathering an eclectic and nonpartisan information base, nevertheless, was its library. The true cornerstone of the Musée's documentation center, the library opened its doors to the public in 1896.

The Library. A specialized research library on contemporary social and industrial questions simply did not exist anywhere in the world, according to William Willoughby. Having made several trips to France, Belgium, and Germany to investigate social and industrial conditions for the U.S. Department of Labor, Willoughby praised the Musée's innovative cataloging system and enumerated the wealth of resources in its library: French and foreign government publications relating to industry and labor; parliamentary reports; official investigations; reports from international bureaus of statistics, mine and factory inspections, and arbitration-board deliberations; reports from labor organizations, cooperative societies, and mutual-aid funds; reports and proceedings of congresses on social problems; publications of economic and statistical associations; as well as books and periodicals available in many languages on current labor and social conditions throughout the industrializing world. A reserve of factual data on experiments in social reform, industrial conditions, and the welfare of labor, the Musée's archives featured dossiers of association by-laws, first-hand reports on labor strikes, and newspaper clippings and pamphlets from around the world on contemporary social and economic problems.[25]

From its inception, the Musée social also collected a startling array of books, brochures, charts, posters, and other materials—from across the political and ideological spectrum—often in the form of gifts or purchases from individuals and organizations wishing to contribute to the Musée's project of building a social laboratory. The anarchist Jean Grave, who for thirty years ensured the publication of Pierre Kropotkine's *Révolté* (1879) and later his own anarchist newspaper *Temps nouveaux* (1895), donated a major portion of his personal library to the Musée social.[26] In 1897 the Musée purchased an important archive from the former Communard and member of the Workers' International Jules Martinet, including newspapers, brochures, political and labor congress proceedings, and books authored by all the major socialist figures of the day—Jules Clément, Benoît Malon, Paul Lafargue, Jules Guesde, Paul Brousse, Paul Strauss—as well as those by a myriad of lesser-known, and thereby all the more interesting, figures of the socialist world.[27] The militant anarchist Paul Delesalle—who after being a regular contributor to *Temps nouveaux* and *Voix du peuple* (1900) opened his own bookshop in Paris specializing in socialist and labor publications—sold boxes of rare pamphlets to the Musée social on anarchism, antimilitarism, revolutionary trade-unionism, and socialist agricultural movements.[28] Among the pamphlets obtained by Delesalle for the Musée's rich and varied collection were Kropotkine's *L'esprit de révolte*; René Chaughi's *La femme esclave*; and Elisée Reclus's *Un anarchiste sur l'anarchie*, translated into English (see figure 8). Finally, one of only fifty extant copies of Max Nettlau's *Life of Michael Bakounine* was donated to the Musée social by its author in 1899.[29] The astonishing diversity of the Musée's library holdings attests to its open-minded conception of social research as well as to the equally surprising support the institution received, particularly among anarchists, who undoubtedly appreciated the Musée's autonomy and claims of independence from the state. Certainly, this was not the type of documentation one would expect to find in an institution founded by some of the more conservative liberal republicans of their day.

Figure 8. René Chaughi's *La femme esclave*; Elisée Reclus's *An Anarchist on Anarchy*; and Peter Kropotkine's *L'esprit de révolte*. Anarchist pamphlets purchased by the Musée social from Paul Delesalle in November 1906. CEDIAS-Musée social, Paris.

As director of its labor service, Léon de Seilhac played a critical role in helping the Musée social to achieve its nondoctrinaire approach to the acquisition of materials and to accumulate the most current and practical information available, regardless of ideological orientation. Accumulating precious tracts, flyers, notebooks, pamphlets, and posters—documents "that seemed trivial to most librarians"—Seilhac was single-handedly responsible for amassing much of the Musée social's impressive archive on the French working class and its different forms of political organization.[30] Whether he went to observe strike proceedings or to attend a labor conference, Seilhac remained on the lookout for revealing material to bring back for the Musée social's collection. He developed an extensive international network of trust and exchange in the world of labor that had a significant impact on the institution's acquisitions. Thus, for instance, the Musée social procured one of the most complete collections of publications by the American Knights of Labor available anywhere. In 1896 Albert Métin, a professor at the École coloniale and the translator of Beatrice and Sydney Webb's writings into French, wrote in the *Revue*

blanche: "I do not think that there exist many collections on the French socialist movement of the Commune that have the breadth of the one compiled by Léon de Seilhac for the Musée social. One can find there some of
the most rare pamphlets, such as Jules Guesde's famous *Catéchisme socialiste,* which formed the basis for Émile Pouget's *Variations guesdistes.*" [31] On
one occasion, in 1898, the board of directors even complained to director
Léopold Mabilleau that the Musée was receiving more socialist journals
than those expressing an opposing view.[32] This open acquisitions policy
helps explain how a bourgeois reform institution such as the Musée social
became such a valuable resource for historians of France seeking documentation on socialism and syndicalism for the period before 1914.

The Musée's library attempted to be international in scope by purchas-
ing the full documentary series published by the British Commission of
Labour, subscribing to press-clipping services in England, and setting out
to acquire a complete bibliography on the history of the social question in
England. The directors of labor bureaus from several American states sent
copies of their official publications to the Musée social, and the general
secretary of the Feminist Exhibit at the Chicago Columbian Exhibition,
Mrs. Pegard, donated the sixteen wall murals from their display. Foreign
correspondents, such as Willoughby in the United States, Bödicker in Germany, and Luigi Luzzatti in Italy, regularly sent copies or lists of major
social and statistical publications from their respective countries; and a
Mr. Raffalowich was asked to send the Russian equivalent of the *Journal officiel* on a regular basis. As early as 1896, Willoughby claimed that, given the
wealth of material available there, the Musée social had become a genuine
"international bureau of labor." [33]

Although the Musée's library quickly became one of Europe's largest
centers of social documentation, the rapid acquisition of such diverse material posed serious challenges to the library staff and led to the establishment of new cataloging practices. The new cataloging system was based
on the following basic categories of Le Playist social science: social statistics and generalities; the family; property; work; the life of the worker "in
normal times" and "in times of crisis." [34] Musée reformers considered
this system to be more than a simple organizational tool, since the classification of social "facts" was crucial to the Musée's scientific work. Reformers felt that social phenomena, if adequately broken down, could be
understood and would even reveal their underlying interrelatedness. The

process of classification, therefore, was viewed as an integral step toward gaining knowledge and establishing a practical guide to social science.

A place of quiet contemplation furnished with leather table tops and stuffed chairs, the Musée's library was the physical prolongation of the bourgeois *salon*. It was divided into two main rooms, named in honor of the Musée social's honorary presidents and figureheads: the Léon Say reading room featured recent issues of French and foreign newspapers and journals on social economy, labor, and the conditions of industrial life; and the Jules Simon study room contained research tools such as thematic card catalogues that integrated books with brochures and other archival materials. William Willoughby insisted that it was *"more than a library"*: it was "a laboratory in the broadest sense of the word." "Every facility for research is also provided in the way of a private desk, stationery, etc., since the library is devised not so much for casual consultation as it is for prolonged and detailed investigations. The staff, moreover, is always at the disposition of the public to answer queries or give assistance and advice." [35] Although not interested in theoretical solutions to social problems, its organizers recollected that the Musée social did attract its share of self-appointed prophets and social soothsayers: "There was a time . . . when those who thought they had found the way to fit a square peg into a round hole or the ideal solution to the social question considered the Musée social the perfect place to confide their wild imaginings. Particularly at the approach of a heat wave, the Musée's personnel greeted a great number of rather foolish philanthropists." [36]

The Musée's administrative staff further contributed to the library's resources by soliciting documentation from a wide variety of reform groups and private social services, cataloging them, and making them available to the public for consultation. Archival dossiers, constituting the "table of contents" of the Musée's activities, were created in five categories: (1) labor; (2) social education and the protection of children; (3) voluntary insurance initiatives; (4) public assistance; and (5) questions of general interest. A category on feminism was also established soon thereafter. Practical information, Musée reformers explained, would be better suited to the general public and more accessible to workers.

At Chambrun's insistence, the library remained open on Saturdays and Sundays, when workers could visit. Its broad-minded acquisitions policy was also intended to attract a diverse public. "The Musée social," Cheysson proclaimed, would "exclude no one."[37] A library card was issued to anyone on simple proof of identity. Jean Grave's request in December 1896 for six library cards for himself and five anarchist friends was therefore not out of the ordinary. Although Grave may have been a "reasonable anarchist" who promised not to disturb any meetings at the Musée social, merely one year before this request a rash of anarchist bombings had wreaked havoc in Paris, killing the president of the Republic, Sadi Carnot.[38] It is as noteworthy that the directors of the Musée social found Grave and his friends to be acceptable participants, as it is that these anarchists chose to associate with the Musée social.

One documented instance of the library's influence concerns Father Desbuquois, a founder of the social Catholic journal *Action populaire*. While in Paris studying theology at the Institut catholique, Desbuquois began frequenting the library of the Musée social and, much to the apparent dismay of his superiors, devoted the better portion of his days studying "social ideas." Through his personal contacts with Léon de Seilhac and Raoul Jay, a professor at the Institut catholique, Desbuquois began to gain a better understanding of changes in the contemporary world of labor, a fact that led him, for instance, to promote independent trade unions. In 1903, while working at the Musée social's library, Desbuquois stumbled across a socialist almanac—the *Almanach socialiste illustré pour 1902*—and suddenly "he had the idea to create something analogous as a means of popularizing the social Christian perspective." He apparently got to work immediately, using the socialist almanac as a model, and worked feverishly to produce the *Annuaire-Almanach de l'Action populaire* (1904), a 400-page "practical encyclopedia" with articles signed by the most important names in the French social Catholic movement, including Musée labor director, Léon de Seilhac; librarian, Étienne Martin Saint-Léon; and several other Musée social members.[39]

Although global readership figures do exist for the first four years of its operation (see table 1), we do not have a sociological breakdown of those who used the library. It is impossible to know just how many workers crossed sociogeographic barriers and made the trip to the Musée's library in the aristocratic *beaux quartiers* of the seventh arrondissement, but one can ponder how off-putting such a solemn setting (described as a "milieu of luxury" and a "cozy nest")[40] may have been for them. A letter received in 1897 from the secretary of the Paris Bourse du travail, Baumé, praised the

TABLE I.

THE MUSÉE SOCIAL LIBRARY, 1895–99

	1895	1896	1897	1898	1899
Volumes	6,289	9,178	11,570	14,380	15,149
Readers	—	991	2,289	2,611	3,023
Volumes consulted	—	2,692	5,881	6,469	6,480

Figures from Le Musée social: Organisations et services, 23.

work of the Musée but lamented the fact that its headquarters were located so far from the Parisian working-class neighborhoods. Commenting that at least it was possible to work there without being bothered by disturbances in the street, another user of the library surmised that its organizers had chosen the aristocratic neighborhood near the Hôtel des Invalides to avoid "the disturbance of vagrants" and "the heckling, that annoying but singular public display" that seemed to characterize the participation of young intellectuals of the Latin Quarter at public conferences. "The only barriers that exist was this intended distance." At the rue Las Cases, he concluded, "the public is greeted and informed." [41]

Finally, the Musée social hoped to complete its function as a social laboratory by establishing consultation and advisory services for the general public. Through these services, as well as through its publications and lecture series, the Musée attempted to disseminate its information on social reform as widely as possible.

The Consultation and Advisory Services. Public consultation and advisory services at the Musée social offered free advice on legal or other technical matters, including an industrial and labor service, an agricultural service, a publications service, and a mutualism and cooperative service.[42] Designed to respond to the specific needs of individuals or groups, these consultations with the public, in Cheysson's words, "answer[ed] a true need of our democracy" and helped the Musée social fulfill its mission of civic pedagogy. "Wherever a public information bureau opened" in the areas of low-cost housing, mutualism, cooperatives, or prison reforms, "requests for information streamed in." "There is a great *élan* in this country" for initiatives in social reform. Cheysson stipulated, however, that limits should be placed on the Musée's willingness to respond to certain politically motivated requests. When imagining, for instance, what the appropriate response should be if an anarchist approached the Musée's industrial and labor service for information on how to make explosive bombs, Cheysson quipped that such a request should logically be denied since the Musée was limited by its statutes to serve only those "whose objectives and results are to improve the material and moral conditions of workers." "Dynamite," he reasoned bemusedly, "would therefore be excluded."[43]

Even before the Musée social officially opened its doors, requests for information came pouring in from employers and workers, including the champagne manufacturers Moët & Chandon, the Mutual Society of Gien, and the newspaper *La Coopération*. General inquiries were handled by the Musée's administrative staff, but if too technical in nature, they gave rise to more formal consultations—usually in writing—by the Musée's legal consultant or actuarial counselor.[44] These technical consultations quickly became one of the institution's most appreciated services. By 1900 the Musée had given more than 1,200 written consultations in the following areas: cooperatives (258), insurance (188), mutualism (142), agricultural unions (107), old-age retirement pension funds (79), workers' housing (58), popular and agricultural credit (56), labor unions (50), bibliography (50), profit sharing (27), employer-sponsored welfare institutions (15), and alcoholism (10). Cooperatives, insurance, mutualism, and agricultural unions—all of which fell under the category of voluntary associations—clearly rose to the top of the public's inquiry list. The rarity of requests concerning employer-sponsored social services and profit-sharing stands as further indication that by 1900 the Musée's public no longer looked to industrial *patronage* as a solution to the social question. In addition to these written consultations, the staff gave daily verbal consultations on a daily basis to visitors who came seeking their advice. By 1900 the Musée social recorded having given over 3,299 verbal consultations.[45]

One function of the Musée's industrial and labor service was to act as an information source for workers and employers on such practical matters as workshop rules, trade union business, apprenticeships, the setting up of retirement funds, or the application of industrial legislation. The service proposed model by-laws, guidelines, and concrete advice based on the experiences of others. Workers at *La Solidarité des travailleurs de Bagnères-de-Bigorre*, for instance, wrote in 1900 to express their appreciation for the Musée's consultation service and to complain about how difficult it had been previously for them to obtain information on setting up social services for their members. Such information was only available in large cities, and even there, they complained, "we grope around in the dark." "We think we've created something new in Marseilles, but we proceed by trial and error . . . whereas in Lille, a similar project already exists and is thriving." "The experiences of the North," they concluded, "don't benefit the South." This was precisely one reason for the existence of the Musée's consultation service: to analyze the successes and failures of voluntary social welfare programs throughout the country—be they organized by employers, trade unions, bourses du travail, mutual aid societies, producer and consumer cooperatives, or savings institutions—and to establish guidelines to encourage new initiatives. Modeled after the one at the Musée social, the *Solidarité des travailleurs de Bagnères-de-Bigorre* created its own labor information service so that its members could study why "some associations prospered, while others declined and disappeared."[46]

Publications. Reports and surveys resulting from the Musée's research sections and consultation services were made available to the public through an array of publications. Initially, the board of directors envisioned publishing a newsletter that would appear only at irregular intervals, but given the difficulty of obtaining reliable current information on social problems in France and abroad, the Musée social decided to edit its own monthly publication (initially called *Circulaires*, and after 1902, the *Annales* and *Mémoires et documents* series). Once again, by declaring that its *Circulaires* would not be "dogmatic or polemical, but above all, a documentary information sheet," the Musée affirmed its intention of observing the rule of impartiality so often invoked to describe its work.[47]

Reformers hoped that the objective and practical nature of these publications would be useful to specialized journals, the government, and private reform groups alike. Generally sold by subscription, the Musée social's monthly bulletins were also sent free of charge or at a reduced rate to workers' associations, unions, cooperatives, and labor exchanges. Whenever possible, the Musée preferred to practice an exchange of journals with these groups. In 1895, when 7,000 copies of the first edition of the Musée's bulletin were printed, the overwhelming majority of them were sent to unions and voluntary associations: employer unions received 1,399 copies; labor unions, 1,927; mixed unions, 173; agricultural unions, 200; labor exchanges, 34; consumer cooperatives, 1,200; credit cooperatives,

100; producer cooperatives, 120; and mutual-aid societies, 1,048. The remaining 800 copies were sent to the press, government-affiliated institutions, parliamentary committees, universities, and the Musée's network of foreign correspondents. By distributing its publications so widely, the Musée hoped to stimulate widespread civic interest in social reform.

By 1896, the Musée social began receiving letters from the Cercle social in the 12th arrondissement of Paris and the Bourse du travail in Niort, thanking the Musée for the informative and impartial nature of its publications. The Fedération des bourses du travail, located in Paris, also gave its approval to "the orientation and research of the Musée." Paul Argyriadès, a wealthy Greek socialist who had migrated to Paris after the Commune and who, after completing law school, became the director of the *Almanach de la question sociale* and *La Question sociale* expressed his "satisfaction in finding at the Musée documents that had been acquired in a spirit of complete impartiality." [48] The nonpartisanship of the Musée's publications and its general operations helped to overcome the initial reluctance of many representatives of labor to work with the foundation.

The Public Lecture Series

In 1895 Jules Siegfried envisioned a lecture series that would be familial in nature, where discussions would freely ensue, "while drinking a glass of beer and smoking a cigar." Although public lectures constituted another important way for the Musée social to reach a wide, nonspecialized audience, this portrayal of the ideal public lecture reveals it to be an inherently masculine form of sociability, particularly if one takes—as does Maurice Agulhon—the cigar to have been a defining feature of a gendered social space in nineteenth-century upper- and middle-class circles.[49] Police reports reveal that women did attend at least some of the public lectures held at the Musée social, but the fact that their presence was even recorded attests to its being an anomaly.

Inaugurated by Paul de Rousiers in January 1896, the Musée social's public lecture series was directed toward workers and students as well as specialists. Posters widely advertised the first lecture, and 300 invitations were sent to workers who had been recommended by Charles Robert and his Society for Profit-Sharing. The 1896 lecture series was, by all accounts, a resounding success, attended by nearly 2,500 individuals. Documentary in nature and oriented toward the practical resolution of specific social problems, the lectures did not engage in theoretical speculation. Among the speakers were social investigators who had gone abroad on study missions for the Musée as well as other Musée members, collaborators, or guests who addressed economic and social themes of contemporary importance. Personalities from the world of politics or social science were invited as ticket-drawers to preside over the lectures and say a few words in conclusion.[50]

To promote the growing network of voluntary associations in France, the Musée social also reserved its meeting hall for groups, such as the International Cooperative Alliance, the International Association for the Legal Protection of Workers, Congress on Social Education, and the Congress on Social Hygiene, that had difficulty finding adequate or affordable places to hold meetings and congresses. Several groups maintained their headquarters at the rue Las Cases, including the Institut des actuaires; the Alliance d'hygiène sociale; the Fédération nationale de la mutualité française; and a mutual aid society, La Femme prévoyante. The problem of procuring a suitable space for meetings proved, however, to be such a major concern of French associations that the Musée social received a deluge of requests, eventually forcing it to curtail this service in 1900.[51]

Although the precise influence of an institution such as the Musée social is difficult to measure, the nature of its structure, its outreach activities, and the collaborators it recruited clearly reflect the Musée's intention to build bridges between government agencies, the legislature, representatives of business and industry, and the multiform network of voluntary reform associations in France. The Musée social recognized the importance of forming public opinion particularly in a democratic regime founded on universal (male) suffrage. It also attempted to exercise an indirect influence on public debate and policy formation, and went to great lengths to maintain its image as a nonpartisan player in this game. As we have seen, the Musée's independent status enhanced its credibility as a research institute among a diverse cross section of the French public. The men who founded this institution and the administrative staff that worked there were committed to social action taken by voluntary associations as well as by the government. United by a reformist temperament that sought to accommodate the dominant liberalism of the day, they pushed to instigate reforms that would instill a moral and social dimension to public policy.

The Social Meanings of a Reform Institution

When the Musée social first appeared on the political horizon during the final decade of the nineteenth century, its goal of achieving social reform was considered provocative, albeit for different reasons, by those on both the left and the right of the political spectrum. On the one hand, merely for raising the social question, the Musée social was condemned by some liberals as having capitulated to a socialist-inspired critique of industrial society. On the other hand, the institution was rejected by some representatives of labor who denounced the institution's class designs on reform policy. Once the Musée social opened its doors to the public, however, its mode of operation could be judged less in ideological terms and more on its concrete achievements. By the turn of the century, thanks to the actual functioning of its services and the commitment of its salaried administrative staff to the disinterested pursuit of social knowledge, the Musée social earned an international reputation as an unbiased center for the study of the industrial world.

Given the potentially volatile atmosphere in which it operated, the Musée social's founders carefully etched out a parapolitical space where politics and religion were officially left in the cloakroom and where the rhetoric of objective social inquiry was adopted as an acceptable common language by all its members. Social problems, its founders contended, should be approached in the detached spirit of a secular faith that would lead to a science of society and promote an impartial understanding of the industrial world. Politics had proven too divisive, arbitrary, and unstable as a foundation for reform. "Simply put, those who use the Musée will find a competent and reliable guide, not a dogmatic or indoctrinating master who serves a particular ideological system." [52] The Musée social thus presented a public face that was not inflammatory or polemical. It sought to avoid the turbulent political waters inside and outside of Parliament by suggesting that attempts to resolve the social question should supersede the passions of partisan politics and religion.

In keeping with this spirit of institutional neutrality—and as an explicit rejection of politics and religious wars—the Musée social never took a public stand on the Dreyfus Affair. Nor, interestingly, did the fiery polemic leave a direct trace within the institution's publications or archives. On one occasion in 1898, however, the comte de Chambrun made it clear that he would not tolerate anti-Semitism on his staff. With characteristic verve, he dismissed André Fleury, a young researcher, because, in Chambrun's words: "He is an anti-Semite. At the end of the nineteenth century, to return to wars of cult and race—to the ghetto! . . . I am taking away his research mission scheduled for next year in England."[53] Beyond its walls, individual Musée members were free to adopt both public and conflicting positions on the Dreyfus Affair. Whereas, the comte de Vogüé did not hide his anti-Semitic views, Paul Guieysse, a founding member of the Ligue des droits de l'homme, Jules Siegfried, Paul Leroy-Beaulieu, Charles Gide, and Arthur Fontaine expressed early and vigorous support for a revision of Dreyfus's trial.[54]

The social question, therefore, was presented at the Musée social not as a volatile issue that threatened to shatter the republican consensus if not defused, but instead as an inert collection of "social facts" that could be assembled, examined, dissected, and studied with cool detachment in much the same way, it was claimed, as one could study the past. The Musée's founders rendered the social question as unthreatening as possible, implying with positivist conviction that its resolution was imminent. Thus the rhetorical stance of objectivity espoused by Musée reformers postulated a neutral distance between the observer and the observed, between the subject and the object of study. Yet the Musée's official aura of neutrality often created deep contradictions for an institution that claimed to promote an objective science of society while simultaneously aspiring to influence the very political process from which it sought shelter.

To begin with, the conservative republicans who founded the Musée social, despite their commitment to the sociological study of industrial society, shared certain common expectations of their mission that seemed, at times, to color the Musée's ideological orientation. Their main hope was that reform efforts would ensure social peace and contribute to the further consolidation of the liberal republic. But they also fully expected that the scientific basis of their studies of industrial society would produce results that conformed to their own conservative political views. The applicability of a scientific or rational model of inquiry, they believed, would corroborate their vision of the world as members of a bourgeois elite that had achieved hegemony in large part due to the progress of science, trade, and industrial technology. As a result, the founders of the Musée social tended to rely on their own experience of social and economic ascendancy as a universal model for social progress. To them, economic development was a prerequisite to social betterment. Therefore, property ownership and the accumulation of savings could never be construed solely as examples of individualistic, self-interested behavior. Instead, these acts of proprietorship were closely linked in their minds to the achievement of a model of civic republicanism in which individuals first needed a material stake in the polity before they could work toward its success and conservation.

For these same reasons, they felt justified in wielding a rhetoric claiming that all members of the industrial community—workers and employers alike—shared common interests. Members of this industrial and business bourgeoisie saw themselves as productive elements of society, as working people who had succeeded. These convictions led the Musée's board of directors to believe, for instance, that objective sociological analysis would prove socialism to be an untenable system, since it erroneously posited an inherent conflict of interest between labor and capital. As we have seen, biology and evolutionary theories provided republican reformers with a powerful paradigm that further reinforced their preconceived notion of solidarity between the social classes as well as their claims that material progress would ensure social mobility. Finally, as liberal republicans, they directed their calls for reform first to civic society—to the parapolitical network of voluntary associations and agencies of public opinion that were prospering in fin de siècle France.

But reliance on social inquiry did not always confirm the expectations of the Musée social's founding fathers. At times their commitment to the unbiased study of industrial society served as an open invitation to interpret social data freely and apply them to a variety of ends. Instead of placating workers and encouraging them to come to the table of social peace, the social data generated by the Musée investigators sometimes merely reinforced a socialist or a labor perspective on reform. Such results even confounded the expectations of many socialists, anarchists, and labor radicals who initially had expressed ideological hostility toward the Musée social as a bourgeois institution that could not possibly represent their interests.

From its inception, therefore, the Musée meant different things to different audiences. Although we may be able to discern a certain unity of vision among its founding members, the Musée social did not promote a doctrinaire approach to social reform, nor could it control all the uses to which its resources were put. Rather, the Musée tolerated a diversity of opinion concerning reform plans even if, at times, the results seemed to give rise to a cacophony of voices all struggling to define and resolve the social question.

What, then, was the essential meaning of the Musée social in fin de siècle France? This question is not an easy one to answer. Open to individuals from every walk of life, the Musée social, in fact, served multiple purposes as a site of encounter, discussion, controversy, and sometimes merely as a *lieu de passage*. Part of the fabric of civil society, the Musée social was not a neutral space, but rather participated in "an arena of contested meaning."[55] As such, operating within the realm of public exchange and seeking to promote dialogue as well as all forms of associational life, the Musée often escaped the narrow definition initially conceived by its founders. At the same time, despite its much-touted vocation as a public-interest institution, the Musée social occasionally drew lines of exclusion along the perimeter of its circle of potential collaborators. Although its library and services were open to the public, membership remained restricted, requiring approval by the board of directors. Other limitations were the result of self-exclusion, both on the left and the right of the political spectrum, in reaction to the fact that, as we shall see, despite their declarations to the contrary, certain prominent Musée social board members were clearly not disinterested observers of the debate on the social question. Consequently, contemporary observers of the Musée social were quick to judge the institution as a whole based on the activities of a few of its most outspoken members, often leading to conflicting proclamations about the Musée's "true" intentions.

The Campaign to Eradicate Socialism

When Émile Cheysson took the high road of the international congress circuit, he crusaded for the institutional neutrality of the Musée social; but when he took the low road of popular public lectures, his words were hardly neutral. In 1895—the same year that the Musée social opened its doors to the public—Cheysson embarked upon a vociferous, antisocialist campaign with other Musée members such as Georges Picot, Albert Gigot, Anatole Leroy-Beaulieu, and Eugène Rostand. These men engaged in verbal sparring matches with young socialist supporters in the Latin Quarter and in provincial cities throughout the country.[56] Partially in response to recent socialist electoral gains, they uncharacteristically donned militant cloaks and took to the streets, descending into the arena of public debate to rebut Jean Jaurès, Paul Brousse, Jules Guesde, and other speakers invited by the revolutionary socialist student group's Latin Quarter conference series. As the reformist socialist Louis Dubreuilh noted in *La Petite République socialiste*, "Messrs. Leroy-Beaulieu, Picot, Gigot and other economists of like ilk have sworn to save society. To accomplish this commendable but lofty goal, these gentlemen have decided to engage in battle with the barbarian collectivists over the souls of our youth."[57] Their participation in a cycle of antisocialist debates organized by the French branch of Herbert Spencer's Defense League for Liberty and Property (hereafter, Defense League) was designed to counter the growing force of organized socialism in France. As Georges Picot declared unabashedly in a letter to Jules Simon in February 1895: "I've embarked upon a tough campaign against socialism; it is my design to eliminate it this winter . . ."![58]

As part of their antisocialist campaign strategy, Picot and several of his fellow Musée social board members used new tactics to promote the political goals of conservative republicanism. Both socialists and Radicals, Picot observed, had gained ground by increasing the number of public conferences they gave and by distributing political pamphlets of all sorts: "We must, in similar fashion, go out and spread the good word."[59] Even Léon Say went on the road as a traveling salesman of the Republic to refute chimerical socialist utopias. By organizing local public meetings and circulating propaganda brochures, they hoped to enlist the ranks of the nation's youth in their cause and even to establish a new conservative political party.

Although most of these conservative reformers were not politicians campaigning for office, they spoke with the inflections of social crusaders and articulated a broad political vision to the public.[60] In 1892, as a member of the political group Union libérale républicaine, Picot had asserted his ideological affinity with Adolphe Thiers's earlier proclaimed notion of a conservative republic. If he took to the streets to combat socialism, it was because he had resolved to defend liberal republican political culture and to distance himself from the radical Revolutionary tradition—a position, moreover, that was generally shared by the Musée social's founding members. Picot and his colleagues believed that the nineteenth-century tradition of liberal republicanism—that was rooted in the events of 1789 and the Estates General—had been thwarted by the Jacobin insistence on egalitarianism, centralization, and the state-sanctioned use of violence during the Terror, at the expense of individual and regional liberties. Socialism and Radicalism, Picot believed, were the contemporary political embodiment of what had gone wrong in France since 1793. Socialists and Radicals, he professed, represented a tradition anathema to that of the true "liberal republic."[61]

A historian of the Estates General and the descendant of a family of renowned liberals, Picot also saw himself as a member of the "enlightened Third Estate."[62] He exhorted his youthful audience not to confuse fraternity and generosity with socialism. He warned against the excesses of individualism and urged them to resist the "cult of the self" that had crowned the literary reputation of writer Maurice Barrès and that was gaining popularity among young intellectuals in turn-of-the-century France. Instead, Picot professed that French youth needed to adopt a sense of social responsibility toward their less fortunate fellow citizens and to involve themselves in voluntary works of social betterment. As an administrator of the Société philanthropique, founded in 1785, Picot saw his own social commitments as being rooted in the prerevolutionary spirit of liberal resistance to an absolutist state. He presented himself, moreover, as a modern symbol of that spirit since his Société philanthropique did not promote the techniques of Christian charity, considered outdated, but rather promoted the values of *prévoyance* and self-help, considered progressive at the time. Picot's leadership role in the Office central des oeuvres de bienfaisance (OCOB) reinforced this departure from traditional philanthropy. A coalition of secular charitable institutions, OCOB stood as an affront to older practices of charity and almsgiving, which Picot decried as harmful to the poor. Instead, he promoted a more rationalized approach to private charity, one based on the medical model of public hygiene and disease prevention. "We join forces," proclaimed Picot, "to fight epidemics: we should also join forces to fight poverty, which is also an epidemic." Therefore, when Georges Picot, and several fellow Musée social members took to the streets to lecture against socialism, their discourse was imbued with a complex political and ideological agenda combining conservative republicanism with social reform, destined to educate the nation's youth and offer them an alternative to the temptations of utopian thought.

Their decision to join forces with the Defense League's confrontational tactics in the Latin Quarter was in blatant contradiction, however, with the intended educational methods and impartial goals of the Musée social. Jeanne Weill, who observed these early meetings, foresaw that their polemical style would be the cause of their failure: the debates, which frequently degenerated into shouting matches, were "drowned in noise," and no dialogue took place. "The Defense League," she declared, "was completely in error." [63] Consequently, many observers of these public skirmishes began to identify the Musée social with the small handful of individuals who had embarked upon this antisocialist crusade. For years to come, this reputation stuck. Since the Musée social was inaugurated in March of 1895—at the height of the Defense League's antisocialist campaign—its pretension to be a purely disinterested center for social change was challenged by many. In certain quarters, the Musée social became known as an antisocialist propaganda machine—a legacy that, in combination with its Le Playist affiliations, has swayed much of the historiography on the institution until the present day.

In the *Revue socialiste*, the reformist socialist Georges Renard expressed serious reservations about the Musée social, which he saw as being dominated by liberal political economists and excluding socialists and Radical socialists.[64] Although not doubting the comte de Chambrun's sincerity about working toward the moral and material betterment of workers, Renard did question the Musée's true institutional independence, and he criticized its claim to eliminate political discussion from its agenda. Renard argued that since the 1889 Exhibition, the social economy group that founded the Musée social had been dominated by orthodox liberal economists. He identified Émile Cheysson as the embodiment of this position, particularly since Cheysson had criticized the 1893 bill, passed by the Chamber of Deputies, on accident compensation and obligatory insurance. Renard concluded that the Musée social would serve merely as a front for the liberal war against government intervention in industrial affairs. "We thus stand forewarned: The new institution is conceived in a spirit of hostility to state intervention in economic matters and to the transformation of the laws and customs regulating property." Renard also expressed concern about the criteria that would be used to select the Musée's "future lecturers and the young men who will be sent out on missions." Socialists and Radical-socialists "seem to be excluded," he observed: "We would have preferred more breadth."[65]

In this assessment, Renard was not entirely wrong. Georges Picot, after all, had explicitly linked the 1889 social economy exhibit with the fight against socialism.[66] But contrary to Renard's initial impression, the members of the Musée social revealed that, in fact, they did support limited forms of government intervention in social policy, a position that remained anathema, however, to orthodox liberals. No one at the Musée social agreed with the liberal economist Yves Guyot, who declared at the 1897 Congress on Labor Legislation: "All of these [social] laws are police laws that pave the way for a police state." Even Cheysson proclaimed at the 1900 International Congress on Industrial Accidents and Social Insurance that he was not intransigent and did not deny to the state a role in social policy, as long as it remained within its proper sphere, which was to encourage private initiative and not to supplant it. Acceptance of this fluctuating line, which sought to define the legitimate scope of state intervention in social affairs, distinguished the members of the Musée social from the traditional liberal community. Although Renard was correct in pinpointing Cheysson as one of the Musée spokesmen who remained closest to the positions of liberal political economy, Cheysson's views cannot be attributed to the institution as a whole.[67]

Despite the strong perception—reinforced by the activities of the Defense League—that the Musée social was intended primarily as an antisocialist and antilabor front for the conservative republican bourgeoisie, Musée members were actually divided on how to respond to the changing political landscape of late-nineteenth-century France. There was, in fact, no consensus at the Musée social on how to interpret the rise of socialism or on what the legitimate role of the state should be in social politics. According to Jules Siegfried, social reform implied a reordering of traditional liberal principles that would allow for greater state involvement in social policy. Although never giving explicit political backing to municipal socialism, Siegfried's campaigns for municipal autonomy and for a more activist role for local government, as well as his concern with developing civic pride through municipal institutions, were not far removed from those of English liberals or Fabian socialists, both of whom he admired. His colleague Paul Deschanel was equally supportive of what he termed "reasonable socialism," which, in his view, embodied all forms of voluntary association, but particularly trade associations and mutual aid societies.[68] The comte de Chambrun, well-read in the German socialist tradition, also expressed an interest in what he termed the "free socialism" of voluntary association, profit-sharing, and limited state intervention. He claimed to accept even "state socialism" and "revolutionary socialism," as long as their proponents did not resort to violence. Each of these schools of thought, Chambrun felt, deserved representation in Parliament.[69]

Socialism as a Rhetorical Device

Most Musée social reformers, however, shared a renunciation of what they often referred to as "state socialism." Rarely used in reference to any precise form of socialist thought or practice, the term *state socialism* was wielded in reformist discourse as a rhetorical device, evoked polemically with certain specific purposes in mind. One the one hand, when reformers decried the evils of state socialism, their primary audience was most often other liberals, and their main concern was to criticize reform schemes imposed by the state, the bête noire of intransigent liberalism. On the other hand, once they had distanced themselves from state socialism and rhetorically established their bona fide credentials as liberals, Musée reformers were then free to use the term *socialism* in other, more creative ways—as we have just seen, referring to mutual aid societies as a form of "reasonable socialism" or profit-sharing and limited government intervention as "free socialism"—in order to articulate what they believed ought to be the state's legitimate role in republican political culture. Their remarks about socialism, therefore, said more about how they defined themselves as liberal republicans than about their actual political views of socialist proposals. Often it was not socialism at all that was the central issue at hand, but rather an embattled determination on the part of French liberals to advocate a new social discourse for themselves and for the Third Republic at the turn of the century.

Evidence to support such an approach to reform discourse can be found in the conservative posturing of Émile Cheysson. He invoked the specter of state socialism when arguing for limits on government intervention in housing policy. First identifying himself as a liberal and a determined adversary of "state socialism," Cheysson revealed that his primary interest was not to discredit socialism but to convince the liberal community of the urgency of supporting private efforts to achieve housing reform. He then qualified his initial criticisms of state socialism by adding that it was also necessary to acknowledge the enormous role played by the state in modern society: "We need to have it with us rather than against us."[70] If the state, however, were to begin building worker housing instead of merely promoting favorable conditions for its construction, this, Cheysson claimed, would be a disaster. It would be tantamount to an entire amalgam of evils that he delineated as "state socialism, the socialism of the *État-providence*, the socialism of a *paterfamilias* state." These conflated forms of state "paternalism," he argued, constituted "a poison for our republican institutions and a constant danger for a popular government: it perverts patriotic sentiment."[71]

Cheysson's comments implied that authoritarian paternalism in all its forms—from employer paternalism to state-sponsored social welfare—did not allow enough room for individual initiative. These old solutions to reform, in his view, needed to be modified in order to embrace the political mores of a liberal republic. The state should not be an authoritarian father but should grant more freedom to its citizens, who were more emancipated and proud of their independence. Their new status should be respected even if at first they were merely given "the illusion" and then only "progressively the reality of their liberty."[72] In the arena of social reform politics, Cheysson ended up calling for an intermediary role for the state, one that would supplement "the deficiencies, the failures and sometimes the ill will of private initiative." This new role for government, he termed "state liberalism."[73]

Paul Deschanel, too, argued that republicans needed to remain vigilant, since the risk of new oppressive forms of government still loomed large in fin de siècle France. For that reason, he did not want socialists—or republicans for that matter—to rely exclusively on the state or on self-proclaimed demagogues, "eternal exploiter[s] of ignorance and misery, . . . eternal artisan[s] of deception." Workers were suffering, he recognized, but in a republic they were also sovereign and needed moral and political education based on self-reliance.[74] These Musée social reformers tended to speak about the rise of socialism—and state socialism in particular—as a short-term aberration in a country not yet confident in the institutions of a liberal democracy or as yet another result of the havoc wrought on French society by the process of industrialization.

In like manner, to Georges Picot socialism was akin to a populist reflex to seek refuge in the arms of the state when the progress of liberal democracy appeared too slow or uncertain. In his first public lecture for the Defense League, Picot proclaimed that although Germany had defeated France militarily in 1870, it had thereafter "surrendered" to the "idolatry of the state," which, in his view, was the latest religion of those nations that had abdicated freedom and returned an authoritarian power to the altar. "Socialism," he concluded, "is the *césarisme* of weak democracies." State socialism, and diatribes against it such as this one, fit within a larger anti-German nationalist discourse used commonly among republican reformers as a code-word for the Bismarckian social insurance laws of the 1880s. According to Picot, the brand of state socialism that had emerged full-blown from the German universities brought in its wake "the abandonment of individual will." The French, he maintained, would never tolerate the German regime of "collective servitude," a view echoed by an audience member who shouted out: "We are not slaves!" Only young people who were languid and discouraged, Picot concluded, would embrace state socialism.[75]

Picot's nationalist anti-German rhetoric and his apprehension about the languorous state of French youth were also expressed in gendered terms that revealed his fears of France's national decline. In a thinly veiled allusion to the German bureaucracy, Picot claimed that no ideas of lasting value had ever been generated by civil servants. "Sterility," he concluded, "is the effect of this system." In a discursive sense, Picot's comment drew upon nationalist rhetoric used to promote natalism and colonialism, two revanchist stratagems whereby the French were called upon to avenge the loss of Alsace-Lorraine to Germany. References to vital energy—in a Barrèsian sense of the term—were common in this masculinist procolonial and pro-natalist discourse. Energetic, intrepid young men, not passive, neurasthenic civil servants, were needed to reverse the trend of a declining birthrate and to expand imperial territory. France needed industrious and dynamic young men to be "missionaries of social peace" and to promote voluntary associations, cooperative societies, and people's banks.[76] Such real men would provide a new elite for modern France: they would one day supplant the docile, ineffectual civil servants in the colonies and rejuvenate a vital liberal republic at home.

Closing his talk with a reference to Herbert Spencer, Picot surmised that state socialism—that "pseudo-science"—would be definitively proven wrong by the laws of nature. Human nature and evolution itself would resist it; civilization would ultimately destroy it. Experimental science, he claimed, had revealed the inherent laws governing human society: "The progress of the natural and physical sciences is one of the factors of social progress." Alongside the progress of science and biological evolution, he explained, there had been a concomitant spread of "civilization." Citing Gustave Le Bon's Les lois psychologiques de l'évolution des peuples, Picot asserted that "as the races move up the ladder of civilization, their members tend to differentiate themselves more and more." Human society was becoming more refined and individualistic—"the great achievements of every civilization have been accomplished by an elite group of men"—whereas the concept of class struggle harked back to a primitive form of animal society.[77] According to this logic, socialism would inevitably be destroyed by the progress of human society itself.

In like manner, Émile Cheysson also predicted that social research conducted abroad would help debunk the socialist, collectivist ideal at home. Speaking as a self-proclaimed expert at the Museum of Natural History on the goals and methods of colonial sociology, Cheysson urged travelers—or "scientific missionaries," as he called them—to undertake monographic studies inspired by Le Play and advised them to bring back information on "primitive peoples" who lived in communal fashion. His invocation, however, was not simply a matter of adding to the growing body of knowledge in comparative sociology. Such research would have political relevance at home since, he speculated, French socialists would finally be unmasked as the "primitive people" they truly were. They would be proven to be nothing more than visionaries who looked to the outdated, "primitive" past to find their vision of the future.[78] Concepts of race, civilization, and scientific progress were, therefore, all embedded within the antisocialist discourse of many liberal reformers. Added to their discursive arsenal, these concepts were used to strengthen the underlying claim that liberal reform, not socialism, represented the true path of social progress.

Of primary interest here is how a new discourse on social reform— that of a handful of liberal republicans affiliated with the Musée social—

evolved within a larger rhetorical framework. By relying on commonly understood references to nationalism, natalism, colonialism, or the republican tradition, these liberal reformers struggled to position themselves within the larger political debate on the social question. If the argument for limited state intervention in social policy was often framed by antisocialist rhetoric, it was done in an effort to more emphatically define a new liberal position on social reform, one that struck a middle ground between traditional liberal thought on the right and socialism on the left and that may be labeled "social liberalism."

Not surprisingly, this stance drew criticism on the right from many orthodox liberals who saw the Musée social as the primary vehicle for the articulation of this new social liberal discourse, which was akin, in their minds, to creeping socialism. Consequently, Jules Fleury declared in 1898, that the Musée social was nothing less than "a social evil." [79] Vilfredo Pareto concurred by announcing in the Journal des économistes that the entire realm of social economy amounted to nothing more than some "vague and cloudy conceptions, nothing but utopia, mysticism, and mush fit for a dog's dinner"! Yves Guyot added his voice to the chorus of critics by concluding that the Musée social was characterized by "a spirit of clerical, employer and governmental socialism." Charles Robert responded confidently to these provocations by affirming simply that the Musée social embodied "the benefits of the experimental method, guided by the spirit of the law." "It serves the cause of progress," he declared. "Social evil lies elsewhere." [80] Clearly, the Musée social created a political stir within the reigning heights of political economy. Since the Musée's founding members came from the ranks of the republican liberal bourgeoisie, they appeared to be ideological traitors: the very existence of the Musée social amounted to an open critique of the liberal order and as a statement of its incapacity to respond to the social question.

Interclass Collaboration

The interaction between Musée reformers and representatives of the labor movement during the final years of the nineteenth century constituted a privileged moment of dialogue between the social classes. Drawn together by a mutual fascination for the world of labor and the "disinterested" techniques of early social science, reform-minded elites and labor leaders engaged in a brief phase of intellectual collaboration through the innovative social observatories provided by both the Musée social and the Office du travail. The parameters of a new industrial order, conceived as a form of partnership between the forces of labor and capital, were traced by bourgeois reformers, reformist labor leaders, and members of the French cooperative and mutualist movements. Interestingly, from an opposing perspective, those who did not accept the premises of this new industrial order—the socialist, anarchist, and Marxist theoreticians who promoted the abolition of wage labor—used the new pool of social and economic data generated by the industrial surveys of the Musée social and the Office du travail with a different goal in mind: to underscore fundamental class antagonisms. Georges Sorel, after having been initially seduced by the rich holdings of the Musée social library, denounced the foundation for trying to conceal its class-based position.[81] He continued, nevertheless, to consult the library regularly, as did Lenin and later Trotsky during their Paris sojourns. Since the postulate of a community of interest between labor and capital permeated the Musée social's discourse on reform, the foundation attracted the active participation of the more moderate elements of the labor movement, including reformist labor organizations such as Auguste Keufer's Syndicat du livre, whose goal was the defense of the economic interests of its workers.

If one Musée social reformer commanded particular respect in the world of labor and contributed to a better understanding of the industrial world, it was without question Léon de Seilhac (1861–1920). Born to an aristocratic family from the Corrèze department, Seilhac, whose grandfather was a captain of the French army during the American War of Independence, came to Paris after the Commune and began collecting data on the socialist movement. Reportedly considered "the black sheep of the family" for having abandoned his family estate in Corrèze in order to frequent Parisian cafés—where he apparently delighted in engaging workers in conversation—his name has been dropped from several family genealogies.[82] This was the unusual man who directed the Musée social's industrial and labor consultation service; participated in its section on missions and surveys; had extensive contacts in the worlds of labor, socialism, and social Catholicism; and managed to earn the admiration of individuals as different as Émile Boutmy, Fernand Pelloutier, Édouard Vaillant, and the historian of socialism, Paul Louis. His rigorous documentary work and the breadth of his knowledge on the international socialist and syndicalist movements initially brought Seilhac to the attention of the Musée social. The author of *Le monde socialiste: Groupes et programmes; Syndicats, fédérations, et bourses du travail;* and *Congrès ouvriers*—among other titles devoted to the social movements of his day—Léon de Seilhac should be included among the first historians of French socialism.[83] As Louis Dubreuilh noted in *La Petite République socialiste*, had Seilhac not written his account of socialist and labor congresses, French socialists themselves would have had no reference works documenting their own history. His books, Dubreuilh suggested, would help preserve the memory of organized socialism in France and be useful for the education of future generations of socialists.[84] Thanks in part to the significance of Seilhac's work, the socialist movement became a serious object of historical inquiry, thus further legitimating it as a political force in the early Third Republic.[85]

As director of the Musée's industrial and labor service, Seilhac believed that a "constant observation [of the social world] was needed." His service, therefore, monitored social and economic conditions with the intent of foreseeing crises before they broke out. Once a conflict arose, however, he sent out an investigator to study its causes, evolution, and results: "It is easy to uncover the buried dimension of a strike, that which stewed beneath the surface long before exploding, and whose official motives are not always the real ones."[86] Seilhac viewed strikes as legitimate social phenomena that could be studied as one might study illnesses or movements of the population. If there was, indeed, a science of society to be ascertained through the careful observation of social phenomena, perhaps strikes too could be dissected and their underlying laws or causality revealed.

In November 1895, Seilhac conducted a study of the causes and results of the glassworkers' strike in Carmaux. He expanded his investigation to include a history of the glassmaking and mining industry and published, in 1897, a separate volume on the social history of the Carmaux strike and the creation of the *Verrerie d'Albi*. In this study, Seilhac demonstrated a favorable opinion of trade unions—"a necessary institution in the present state of large-scale industry"—and applauded the glassworkers' practical resolution to establish a producers' cooperative, a decision made in November of 1895, when the striking workers accepted 100,000 francs from a wealthy philanthropist to set up a workers' cooperative in

Albi, thereby ending the five-month strike. Seilhac concluded his study on an optimistic note: "Despite itself, the revolution will have given birth to creative and healthy forms of labor organization, whose success will be the source of our joy." Seilhac's personal research on strike activity culminated in 1903 with the publication of Les grèves, a historical overview of industrial strikes in France.[87]

Seilhac's concern with labor disputes was mirrored by his attempts to develop professional trade unions. As early as 1895, largely at his instigation, the Musée social sent representatives to all national and international labor congresses, including the trade-union congress in Cardiff and the famous 1895 congress in Limoges when the Confédération général du travail (CGT) was founded. Seilhac also published, in 1902, an important historical survey of the various forms of professional trade association in France entitled Syndicats ouvriers, fédérations, bourses du travail. Recognized for their objective reporting on labor issues, Seilhac and his collaborators were invited regularly to attend labor congresses. At the tenth National Corporative Congress, held at Rennes in 1898, a Parisian worker declared to his colleagues: "We can speak freely. The only foreigner in our midst is the delegate from the Musée social, and there is nothing that we will say that he doesn't already know as well as we do."[88] Thus, Seilhac's firsthand knowledge of the issues about which he wrote, his unbiased journalist style, and the objective reporting of his fact-finding missions greatly improved how the Musée social was viewed by the world of labor.

The Musée's Mission to England

In another attempt to build bridges with the world of labor and deepen its understanding of the industrial world, the Musée social, in 1895, sent its first team of researchers on a two-month mission to study the British trade-union movement. Led by Le Playist social scientist Paul de Rousiers, the team attended labor congresses and met with British reformers such as Sidney Webb as well as with industrialists and workers. They returned with rich sociological data and filled with admiration for the British trade union movement.[89] The stronger and better organized the union, they now believed, the more it would serve the cause of the moral betterment of workers and contribute to the rational organization of the industrial labor market. The moderation and strength of English trade unions became a model for reformers at the Musée social.

On his return, Rousiers gave a series of public lectures at the Musée social and the Paris Bourse du travail, highlighting the implications of his study. Not only did he find the existence of trade unions to be perfectly normal, given the growing size of contemporary factories, but he approved of their development and urged French employers to accept and encourage their growth if they hoped to encourage greater harmony in industrial relations. In light of their mission to England, Rousiers and his colleagues began to focus on unions as a key factor in normalizing industrial relations rather than as vehicles for class conflict. Rousiers concluded that industrial relations in France must be transformed and the "abnormal" state of warfare between labor and capital ended: "A strike indicates a state of war, and this state of war, which cannot last forever, must be replaced by a peaceful and normal state. This normal state implies the representation of the interests of workers not as individuals but as a group; it means the replacement of an individual labor market by a collective market." [90]

Musée researchers were also convinced that British trade unions helped moralize the work force and promote a progressive civic pedagogy. One member of the research team, Octave Festy, noted more occurrences of alcoholism and domestic violence among nonunion workers. Unions helped develop a spirit of solidarity and mutual aid among their members. "Instead of feeling isolated as before," he claimed, "[the worker] understands that he is now somebody in the world and that he has social importance." [91] Rousiers concluded that union leaders cultivated a public image that transformed them into role models of temperance and respectability for other workers. Thus, he disagreed with those reformers who perceived industrialization as the cause of moral collapse in contemporary society. Instead, he argued that the increased mechanization of production actually raised the intellectual level of workers.[92] Musée investigators found that it was precisely in the most mechanized professions that a new labor elite was emerging. Trade unions, therefore, could serve as potential vehicles for the acculturation of middle-class values. The Musée team cited, among others, the case of Mr. Pickard, a former miner and president of the Miners' Federation, who had been elected as a Member of Parliament. Union work fostered leadership skills and served as legitimating structures; Rousiers maintained that it was virtually impossible for an English worker to enter politics without first having risen up through a union. In keeping with republican ideology, the trade union would ensure the "social education of labor," much like the nation's primary schools would inculcate the basic values of citizenship.[93]

Although Rousiers's language remained moralistic, it introduced the basic terms of a new discourse on labor that stressed the equal and permanent representation of workers' interests in an industrial democracy. The country's elite, he felt, had an important role to play in this process:

> We must not be afraid of strong organizations that can defend themselves, demand their rights and make themselves respected. The danger does not lie with them. It resides with the weak, with those who live under a form of tyranny or who believe they do, but do not know how to defend themselves because they are incapable of it.
>
> The answer lies in the elevation and thus in the improvement of the worker and in the spirit of justice among the members of the non-working class. It is this elevation of the worker that will prod him along that wide avenue of social justice that leads to social peace.[94]

The Musée social's mission to England demonstrated both the institution's interest in the development of independent labor organizations and its continued commitment to applying the tools of social science to reform.

Léon de Seilhac was equally convinced of the importance of independent trade unions. "The emancipation of workers," he declared, "can only come from workers themselves. Its organizational basis lies in the union." But most French trade unions, he lamented, were mere "skeletons" of what they could be. To achieve independence, they needed to have a firm financial foundation. Arthur Fontaine agreed. According to a study he conducted in 1894 for the Office du travail, French unions lagged far behind their English counterparts in terms of the social services offered to union members.[95] Seilhac and Fontaine recommended that French unions adopt the British tradition of high union dues in order to provide long-term services to their members and fulfill their educational role. In turn, members of the Musée's section on labor associations began a campaign to modify the 1884 law that had legalized unions in France. They

hoped to lift restrictions that prevented unions from engaging in financial and business operations. According to the 1884 legislation, French
unions were forbidden from owning or renting property other than that
needed for their professional meetings. Based on their observations of English unions, which were wealthier and therefore less inclined, reformers
thought, to waste their savings on strikes, Musée members proposed that
French unions be legally authorized to invest in property and to engage
in limited commercial ventures, similar to those authorized for cooperatives. Of course, these men believed that increased financial worth would
have a tendency to pacify unions and transform them into more equal economic and social partners. "Landed property possesses in and of itself a
calming virtue that quickly transforms its owner into a defender of public
order." [96] The strong endorsement of French trade unions by bourgeois
reformers such as Seilhac, Rousiers, Fontaine, and others at the Musée social contributed to an emergent model of industrial democracy whereby
trade associations would be regarded as stable partners in the new industrial order.

The Model of Industrial Democracy

The model of industrial democracy, in which the organization of labor was
viewed as an essential ingredient toward preparing for industrial peace,
not class warfare, provided another common discursive terrain for social
Catholics, reformist socialists, and social liberals at the Musée social.[97]
Raoul Jay, a professor at the Institut catholique and the Paris Faculty of
Letters, expressed a modern social Catholic analysis of industrial relations by calling for an end to the laissez-faire economic and social policies
dominant in late-nineteenth-century France. Rather than creating conditions favorable for industry and commerce, Jay argued that liberal policies had destroyed organized labor relations. "The industrial world," he
suggested, "seems to be tired of anarchy. It endures the pain of constant
struggle generated by the unlimited freedom of competition. It is in search
of a new organization of the labor market and is beginning to realize that
this will only be possible through the development of professional trade
associations." Jay referred to Beatrice and Sydney Webbs's book, *Industrial Democracy*, as well as to Rousiers's study on English trade-unionism as
models of research in this area. He further argued that the new conditions

of industrial production made it senseless to even conceive of labor contracts or negotiations on an individual basis. Workers were paid according to a category of labor, and therefore they must negotiate for their collective interests: "That is the inevitable result of the industrial and commercial growth that is occurring before our eyes." [98] Moreover, Jay's analysis led him to abandon the traditional social Catholic ideal of "mixed unions" or "yellow unions" — such as those promoted by Albert de Mun — in favor of independent labor unions.

Social Catholics had traditionally supported a corporate trade union structure to which both employers and employees belonged, as if they were members of one harmonious industrial family. Social Catholics at the Musée social, however, promoted modern, independent trade unions with separate entities representing labor and management. Current transformations in industrial labor, they believed, had only increased the workers' feelings of forced dependency and heightened their frustration. Modern trade unions, they believed, were needed to enhance individual autonomy and personal self-esteem among workers. According to this view, the model of industrial democracy whereby employers and employees organized separately and negotiated for their respective interests represented the best way to structure the labor market. This position represented an innovation in social Catholic thought. Raoul Jay, therefore, became a prominent spokesman of the reformist coalition that pushed for stronger institutions of collective bargaining and labor conciliation boards in France. Reformist socialist Alexandre Millerand also collaborated with the Musée social toward this goal. He too felt that the first essential step toward securing the basis of an industrial democracy in France was to fortify the legal and institutional structures of labor.

The Cooperative Movement

Since the Musée social ultimately sought the reconciliation of labor and capital, it also gave institutional support to the French cooperative movement. Preference was given to moderate cooperatives, however, rather than to their socialist variants premised on a total transformation of the economic structure. Producer cooperatives, in particular, offered their members a concrete demonstration of the identity of interests between labor and capital. This ideal partnership embodied the precise message that social liberals hoped to convey. Reformers at the Musée social also promoted producer and consumer cooperatives as models of civic republicanism. According to this view, cooperatives were vehicles of bourgeois and republican "acculturation" that promoted the internalization of new habits and values associated with "a new industrial morality" such as savings, thrift, and upward social mobility. Consumer and producer cooperatives, they argued, could help workers identify with, and participate in, the goals of economic growth but also provide them with practical experience in management and long-range planning. As such, cooperatives were practical training schools that would mold their members into model worker-citizens of the liberal republic. Reformers argued that in every respect, cooperatives and profit-sharing were more beneficial to workers than the vague promises of revolutionary socialism.[99]

The Musée social demonstrated its support for producer and consumer cooperatives by hosting both the ninth National Cooperative Congress and the second congress of the International Cooperative Alliance (ICA) at the rue Las Cases from October 25 to November 1, 1896 (see figure 9).[100] A week-long series of activities—"La Semaine coopérative"—was organized at the Musée in honor of the international cooperative movement. Events included public meetings, speakers, an essay contest, dinners, drinks, and general fanfare to attract the press and promote the cause of cooperation. Chambrun financed the publication of a brochure detailing the week's events and donated 3,800 francs specifically for the organization of the ICA's Paris Congress. In 1896, when the ICA convened in Paris, the French national section of the ICA was dominated by Musée social members. Although the principle of political and religious neutrality was common to both the ICA and the Musée social, the Musée's public support for the cooperative movement at that particular juncture amounted to taking a political stance, since cooperators were being threatened by the Senate and were under increasing attack by the small business lobby. That same year, the vote of a patent tax on cooperatives, which had previously been exempted from such taxation, was under discussion in the Senate. The shopkeepers' movement had successfully gained votes in the Senate in favor of such a tax on cooperatives. Members of cooperatives argued that price increases would simply be passed along to the consumer. They claimed that the Senate was blind to the larger social value of cooperatives, which were not just ordinary commercial operations: they were also edu-

Figure 9. Second Congress of the International Cooperative
Alliance (ICA) held at the rue Las Cases, October 25 to
November 1, 1896. CEDIAS-Musée social, Paris.

cational entities that required a moral commitment on the part of their
members. Cooperatives, supporters argued, were schools of republican
virtue and, as such, should have a special legal status.[101]

During the Semaine coopérative organized at the Musée social,
speakers attacked conservative senators as members of "the ignorant
minority" who were bending to the pressures exerted on them by shopkeepers and blocking social reform. When some senators likened cooperatives to collectivism, Jules Siegfried retorted that greed, not socialism, was the real social enemy. Not only should citizens be able to buy
goods wherever they pleased, but cooperatives should be given special
treatment since they taught good habits by preventing the temptation of
buying on credit. Speakers at the Musée said that some shopkeepers took
advantage of workers by allowing them to buy on credit in time of need
and then exploiting their dependence by charging higher prices or selling them poor-quality merchandise. To put an end to these practices of
exploitation and to strengthen the movement as a whole, Frédéric Clavel, president of the Cooperative Union, called for greater participation of
bourgeois honorary members in cooperatives: "Nothing would contrib-

ute more to the disappearance of distrust and prejudice existing between the different social classes, than regular contact between the bourgeoisie and workers, meeting side by side in the same associations, discussing together their common interests and learning to know each other better and to hold each other in greater esteem." This theme of interclass cooperation continued to be a recurrent refrain among republican reformers throughout this period. By orchestrating an entire week of activities based on these themes, the Musée social hoped to generate a movement of public support for the nation's cooperative organizations. Explaining that newspaper coverage would influence public opinion in this crucial area, Jules Siegfried invited the press and made a formal appeal for their collaboration: "We ask the Press from every country to take up or to continue to defend the great cause of social progress."[102]

An elaborate banquet for 230 guests, an organ concert, and a reception at Chambrun's Parisian home to conclude the conference was followed by the inauguration of a statue in honor of the profit-sharing pioneer and mutualist Jean Leclaire in the square des Epinettes in the 17th arrondissement of Paris. George Jacob Holyoake referred to the dinner as "The Banquet of a Thousand and One Nights." Set in a gallery "where the electric light beamed forth from chandeliers and was reflected in abundant mirrors," the event was intended to marry the riches of the new world and the refinements of the old in a tribute to the goals of justice and social peace. Siegfried raised a toast to all apostles of democracy, founders of social welfare institutions, educators of the people, and arbiters of social peace, who though divided by nationality and religion were united by cooperation. Merely one year after its official opening to the public, the Musée social, by the neatly orchestrated events of La Semaine coopérative, succeeded in drawing public attention to the social value of cooperation and, in a radical departure from its earlier policy of strict neutrality, intervened for the first time as an institution to take a public stance in political debate. This type of institutional involvement in social politics would only increase throughout the period before World War I.[103]

Reactions to the Musée social

During the first few years of operation, the Musée social attracted representatives of the world of labor who were familiar with the institution's services, publications, and manner of operating. Although before the Musée's opening to the public, socialist Georges Renard had expressed reservations concerning the conservative ideological leanings of the Musée's board of directors, he still urged the readership of the *Revue socialiste* to reserve its judgment and predicted that at least the Musée social would be useful as an information bureau for the general public and as a "philanthropic laboratory for the ruling class." [104] By making such a recommendation, Renard implicitly recognized the need for such an independent social research institution in fin de siècle France.

Even the comte de Chambrun emerged as a widely admired figure among prominent socialists. His book *Aux montagnes d'Auvergne* was favorably reviewed by Paul Lagarde in the *Revue socialiste* and by Fernand Pelloutier in the *Démocratie de l'Ouest* and the *Avenir social*. Although not inspiring unlimited confidence, Chambrun's ideas for profit-sharing, cooperation, or the creation of "industrial parliaments" composed of workers and foremen in each factory were praised as constituting "the first step, the necessary apprenticeship, the direct path to socialism." [105] In an obituary article, socialist Louis Dubreuilh praised Chambrun for having had the courage to rise above his aristocratic roots and devote his fortune to the betterment of workers' lives. Thanks to the vast documentation accumulated at the Musée social on the industrial world, Chambrun's foundation, he claimed, would continue to serve the socialist cause. On a monthly or almost weekly basis, he wrote, this laboratory produces documents that are "imbued . . . with a broad-minded spirit of impartiality." Even if most often "the political efforts of the proletariat are unrecognized or misrepresented," its economic efforts "are always appreciated and highlighted with an undeniable sense of goodwill. . . . The Musée social has helped us more than its directors probably realize. . . . That is why we have the right to declare that for us, Monsieur de Chambrun will not have passed through this world in vain. This benevolent aristocrat, this ultra-rich plutocrat, will have contributed—perhaps despite himself, but at least efficiently so—to furthering the cause of *la Sociale*." [106]

Gradually, over the course of the first five years of its operation, the Musée social began to win the confidence of certain sectors of the world of labor. This change from the initial reticence expressed at its foundation was a testimony to the Musée administrators, investigators, and chroniclers who strove to bolster the foundation's objectivist rhetoric with their impartial work. Significant social and ideological differences separated bourgeois reformers from the representatives of labor with whom they hoped to establish a dialogue, but the need for an institution providing sociological and economic data on the industrial world was so great that these differences diminished within the Musée social. Its insistence on the primacy of social research during these years was responsible for its acceptance in so many different circles. Thus, the Musée acquired multiple social meanings. As demonstrated, for instance, through Rousier's study of English trade unions, or Seilhac's studies of strikes, investigators approached their work primarily in a spirit of nonpartisan social analysis, not as a moralistic device for inculcating a counterrevolutionary ideology. Therefore, the founding fathers' initial intent to form a conservative nucleus for social thought and action never became the Musée's primary identity. As Pierre Mille commented in 1899, after attending an evening lecture at the rue Las Cases: "The Musée social has become a true museum. Everyone goes there and everyone is welcomed."

Musée social members had moved beyond the neo-paternalist prescriptions for reform they once touted at the 1889 social economy exhibit. By 1900 they widely agreed that the mechanisms for attaining social peace needed to be moved beyond the walls of the factory and into the public arena of national policy. Nor were professional trade unions looked upon as adversaries, but as necessary partners in a new industrial order. By the early years of the twentieth century, the Musée reformers, almost without exception, promoted the position that only the organized collective interests of industrial partners—through labor or business unionism—could bring about the nation's desired goal of social peace. In this regard, the Musée social's work contributed to a new configuration for industrial relations in modern France. In light of their research at home and abroad, the ideal of an identity of interests between labor and capital—which had been present in productivist-oriented reform discourse in one form or another since the earliest days of industrial development—was infused with new political and social meaning. Recast as "industrial democracy," this ideal was no longer based on the vague notions of preindustrial nostalgia. Instead, confronted with the results of their own investigations, the Musée social reformers were compelled to incorporate the political and economic realities of industrial capitalism and a liberal democracy into their prescriptions for reform.

But, as we shall see in the following two chapters, the Musée social's focus on strengthening trade unions proved to be rather short-lived. By the turn of the century, Musée social reformers had shifted their strategies for public intervention. First, in light of the fact that discussions of social policy—particularly those on social insurance—had moved to the forefront of parliamentary debate, Musée social members activated their networks to lend support to the mutualist cause in an effort to influence the future configuration of national retirement pensions. Second, their efforts to improve public hygiene culminated in a very modern, protracted battle to preserve park spaces in Paris and to enforce the goals of long-term urban planning as a means of preventing urban congestion and irrational growth. Although as a research institution, the Musée social continued to function along similar lines and to provide the same services, its role in public debate during the first decade of the twentieth century would become decidedly more political.

Part Three. Implementing Reform

5. Voluntary Associations and the Republican Ideal

~

The more I see of free countries, the more I believe their pervasive liberty to be founded on the existence of longstanding associations. Without small, voluntary societies, no nation is free. —GEORGES PICOT, 1895

From its inception, the Musée social lent its full support to all forms of associational life in France. Gradually, however, without eschewing its commitment to this broad spectrum of voluntary groups, the Musée leadership sharpened the focus of its patronage to concentrate on mutual aid societies, a change reflected in the 1897 appointment of Léopold Mabilleau as the institution's new director. Serving first as a meeting ground for the mutualist reform network and then as an active agent of mutualist propaganda, the Musée social quickly earned a reputation as a key lobby group for mutualists in both parliamentary and extraparliamentary circles. Strategically placed in government, business, and mutualist circles, Musée reformers became influential players in the social policy debates of the early twentieth century.

Founded to provide aid to workers and their families in the event of illness, injury, accident, old age, maternity, or death, mutual aid societies evolved as a practical response to the needs of labor. Although these societies had existed since the *ancien régime,* it was only toward the end of the nineteenth century that republican reformers worked to strengthen their organizational and legal foundations. Promoting mutual aid societies as the ideal conduits for involving workers in voluntary schemes of social protection and insurance, the Musée social took on a prominent role as an advocate of the mutualist cause in France. Its president, Jules Siegfried, headed the mutualist group in the Parliament, and its members spearheaded the creation, in 1902, of the Fédération nationale de la mutualité française (FNMF), a national mutualist alliance still in existence today. By the turn of the century, French mutualists and their allies occupied a pivotal position during the protracted social insurance debates in Parliament that culminated in 1910 with the hard-won vote inaugurating France's first national pension law.[1] Situated within the context of these debates, this chapter analyses the Musée social's role in the evolution of French mutualism and demonstrates how mutualists influenced social policy formation during the early Third Republic.

Since Tocqueville's famous essay on democracy in America, it has become commonplace to assume that French associational life was depleted, if not destroyed, in the aftermath of the Revolutionary banishment of *corps intermédiaires* as legislated by the 1791 Le Chapelier law. Although labor and social historians have insisted on the central role of trade associations, unions, and political organizations in the formation and identity of the French working class, the history of other types of voluntary associations and their role in the formation of republican political culture has until recently received only scant attention by scholars. Such is the case of the *sociétés de secours mutuels*, or mutual aid societies, which constitute the oldest and largest but, paradoxically, the least well known social movement in France. Yet by one calculation, fin de siècle mutualists outnumbered *syndicalistes* — trade unionists — by sixteen to one: whereas at its creation in 1895 the Confédération national du travail counted fewer than 100,000 members, the aggregate membership of French mutual aid societies for that same year was 1,600,000, rising to nearly two million members by the end of 1898.[2] The Musée social's involvement with promoting mutual aid societies in France constitutes but one part of a larger history of mutualism that is now being written.[3]

The Emblem of a Reformist Republic

Late-nineteenth-century reformers invested much hope in mutualism as an alternative and complementary framework for the organization of labor. The vision of mutualists as independent workers cooperating voluntarily toward their collective betterment gratified republican reformers since this goal so closely mirrored their own ideal of the true foundations of a liberal democracy. If French liberals admired the friendly societies of England or the voluntary associations of the United States that had so impressed Tocqueville in the 1830s, it was because these small-scale initiatives were launched by a local, active citizenry and provided a counterweight to the encroaching powers of the state.[4] This vision undergirded much of the liberal republican enthusiasm in France for all forms of voluntary association, but particularly for mutual aid societies. By virtue of the exchange of services and the collective sharing of risks among their members, such groups embodied a vivid demonstration of the social bonds existing within a republic. To many republicans, mutual aid societies symbolized the regeneration of civic life they valued so highly in postrevolutionary France.

In this spirit, mutualism was promoted energetically by two successive presidents of the Third Republic, Félix Faure (1895–99) and Émile Loubet (1899–1906)—who, in 1902, referred to himself "the first Mutualist of France"—as well as by highly visible politicians such as the Radical premier Léon Bourgeois; the vice president of the Chamber of Deputies, Paul Deschanel; and Senator Victor Lourties. Presiding over mutualist banquets such as the spectacular one for 20,000 mutualists held at the 1900 Universal Exposition in Paris, these men praised mutualism for combining the values of individual independence with the spirit of fraternity, the very principles on which the Republic claimed to be founded. Against a backdrop of rising class tensions and the growing appeal of socialism and revolutionary syndicalism among workers, moderate republican reformers turned to mutualism as the vehicle of an alternative social outlook, one based on the principles of self-help, class harmony, and pragmatism.[5]

The convergence of interests between mutualists and republican reformers at the Musée social was cemented by the doctrine of solidarism, which stressed the interconnectedness of generations and the mutual debts linking individuals to one another and to the state. Solidarism provided a theoretical complement to the practical activities of mutual aid societies. In turn, mutualism embodied the organicist imagery of a harmonious society that appeared to obey the laws of biological interdependency. Léon Bourgeois, the chief proponent of solidarism, even predicted that mutualism bore the seeds of a total transformation of social life. The Third Republic itself, he proclaimed, would become "a great overarching mutual aid society," where individuals who were "equally imbued with the spirit of public service" would voluntarily help one another as "members of the same family who had been definitively appeased and reconciled."[6] At the turn of the century, mutualism had clearly become an emblem of the reformist republic's quest for social peace.

French Mutualism in Historical Perspective

In a quasi-naturalist vein, liberal republicans of the late nineteenth century often invoked the medieval roots of mutualism, arguing that the deep-seated history of mutualism in France made it an intrinsic, organic part of French labor and society. Léopold Mabilleau and Étienne Martin Saint-Léon linked contemporary mutualism to its medieval antecedents in the books they authored, reminding readers that although French guilds and the compagnonnage had been organized during the Middle Ages to protect members of a particular trade and to exercise control over the labor market, they also played an important social function by providing financial assistance to workers temporarily incapacitated or in need of credit. Unlike revolutionary syndicalism or state socialism, which they considered to be imported movements of "foreign" origin, mutualism was a French "indigenous" response to the needs of labor. It had evolved naturally over the ages from the local corporative customs of France and its people.[7]

Despite the French Revolution's abolition of guilds and coalitions, mutualism survived, often clandestinely, as a collective form of labor solidarity. Tolerated by authorities for its pragmatic influence on workers, mutualism revived under the Napoleonic Empire and continued to develop under the Bourbon Restoration and the July Monarchy.[8] Despite the patronage they received from liberal philanthropists, however, most of these benevolent societies lacked sufficient funds, were poorly managed, and almost always failed to provide services that required transgenerational calculations, such as retirement pensions.

The sociopolitical context changed dramatically during the Second Empire, when Napoléon III officially legalized mutualism through the decree-law of March 26, 1852. Mutual aid societies, he proclaimed, should "henceforth be considered public instruments of social betterment." Yet by introducing a new type of mutual association—the sociétés approuvées, or approved societies—Napoléon III asserted even greater control over the movement and attempted to undermine any potential political role it may have played. Unlike earlier mutual aid societies, which operated as single-trade groups and as such anticipated the demands of labor unions, Napoléon III's approved societies were organized on a strictly local geographical basis. His imperial-style mutualism removed the management of mutual aid funds from the control of its members by placing them instead into the hands of local notables inducted as honorary members into each approved society and entrusted with the mission of upholding the social order. Although officially promoted as efforts at social betterment, these measures, seen from the perspective of the Second Empire's liberal financial elite, served mainly to link French mutual aid societies to the growing network of state-sponsored financial institutions, such as the national savings banks and the national retirement fund, and were part of a disguised long-term borrowing strategy to fortify the national treasury. Under the Second Empire, therefore, mutual aid societies remained a far cry from the ideal of self-help promulgated by the friendly societies in England. In fact, in 1859 the French translator of British mutualist Samuel Smile's book *Self-Help* complained that the term "self-help" was nearly impossible to translate into French, since the practice barely existed in France.[9]

This "imperial" chapter in the history of French mutualism left a lasting mark on its future development: its putative collusion with the Second Empire was at the root of a breach with the nascent labor movement, especially in the aftermath of the Commune. The differences between the two movements, largely ideological in nature, also resulted from the dissimilar sociological composition of their memberships. Mutualism appears to have recruited members largely among the growing middle classes: petite bourgeoisie, small shopkeepers, state employees, and civil servants. In 1894 the socialist deputy Antoine Jourde echoed the commonly shared sentiment that mutualism was not truly a "working man's" movement. "Until now," he claimed, mutualism "only concerned an elite among the working population." Léon Bourgeois concurred, in 1902, that France's total mutualist tally of 3,500,000 members included only 500,000 manual laborers. Despite the absence of conclusive sociological data that could explain this phenomenon, the dissociation that ensued between the two movements was real, and its effects endured well into the twentieth century.[10]

With the establishment of the Third Republic, however, French mutualists found a new lease on life. Fourteen years after the official recognition of trade unions by the Waldeck-Rousseau law of 1884, mutual aid societies, in turn, received their republican birth certificates through the passage of a law on April 1, 1898, later known as the "Mutualist Charter." [11] Henceforth, mutual aid societies could legally proclaim their existence without prior government authorization and could band together to form mutualist unions on a local, regional, or national level. By allowing them to pool their resources, the 1898 law enabled mutualist unions to undertake long-term financial operations that had been infeasible previously. Moreover, the 1898 Mutualist Charter created provisions for the establishment of a Conseil supérieur de la mutualité to advise the government on mutualist affairs. The 1898 Mutualist Charter thus ended the excessively restrictive phase of mutualist regulation inaugurated by the Second Empire. It also opened a long phase of active involvement of the mutualist movement in the formation of national social policy in France.

Mutualism and the Musée social

The Musée social's earliest research activities reflected the Third Republic's growing interest in mutualism. Its researchers published case studies on mutual aid societies in France and abroad and gathered membership statistics in order to assess the vitality of the movement.[12] Many Musée reformers—and perhaps foremost among them the comte de Chambrun, who designated 100,000 francs specifically for this purpose—emphasized the need to develop mutualism among women workers in the Paris sewing, retail, and wholesale trades. Prior to the 1913 law instituting maternity leave in France, Fernand Engerand actively promoted mutual societies that would enable working women to stay home for four weeks following childbirth.[13] Others, such as Émile Cheysson, stressed the important social role of women in the development of rural mutual aid societies, which were lacking in France. Mutualism, he felt, was particularly beneficial to the entire family unit and not simply to the individual worker.

But women were more reluctant to join mutual aid societies, primarily because of their lower wages but also because mutual aid societies were traditionally preserves of male culture and sociability. Moreover, when women did join mutual societies, they were often charged higher dues than men since women—particularly when multiple pregnancies were taken into account—were considered more prone to "illness." [14] Cheysson acknowledged that woman had been long looked upon by mutualists as "*une éternelle malade*," and consequently often refused entry into male-dominated societies. Between 1881 and 1891, however, the number of women in mutual aid societies had grown significantly—by two-thirds of its previous rate, representing an increase of 120,000 individuals. Of the 11,355 mutual aid societies in France in 1898, 2,741 of them were gender-mixed, and 411 of them were composed exclusively of women. But that same year, the total number of women covered by French mutual aid societies was estimated at 300,000, a paltry figure when compared to the total mutualist tally of nearly two million members. [15] In light of these numbers, reformers at the Musée social identified women workers as a particularly vulnerable group whose urgent health concerns should be met and who needed mutual aid societies specifically designed for them.

In another study for the Musée social on the English settlement house Toynbee Hall, Joseph Guérin argued that if English reformers had lent strong support to friendly societies, it was because these societies often had a beneficial effect on trade unions by urging them to act as "instruments of help and moral support for the working class" rather than primarily as tools of class warfare. [16] Republican reformers hoped that mutual aid societies would have a similar effect on French syndicalism. The Musée social, however, took steps not to appear to promote mutual aid societies at the expense of unions. Its legal section conducted a survey on trade associations since the advent of the 1884 law and concluded that, since mutual societies and unions did not generally offer the same services, they would not be in direct competition for members. [17] Although a few unions, such as the Paris Masons and Plumbers Union, offered accident insurance to their members, most concentrated their demands on wage levels, the length of the workday, and labor conditions. In point of fact, however, most workers could simply not afford to pay dues to two organizations.

Musée social reformers participated actively in framing the Third Republic's new official attitude toward mutualism. The 1898 Mutualist Charter had involved the collaboration of Jules Siegfried, Léon Bourgeois, Joseph Barberet, Émile Cheysson, Victor Lourties, and others affiliated with the Musée social. The reformist coalition that helped legitimate mutualism by representing its interests in government was initially formed in extraparliamentary groups such as the Musée social and the Ligue nationale de la prévoyance et de la mutualité. Extraparliamentary groups were important to this process because their membership was mixed and brought together mutualists, economists, politicians, lawyers, and high-ranking members of the civil service. Nor were the personnel of parapolitical groups subjected to the shifting political alliances that resulted in the chronic instability of ministries and government appointments. Thus, Musée social members were able to study bills or government projects relating to mutualism and to develop strategies for action without being dependent on the fragile balance of parliamentary politics.[18] Furthermore, the politicians within the Musée social actively represented mutualist interests in Parliament, facilitating hearings with subcommittees and giving mutualists a voice in social policy debates.

Musée reformers also collaborated within the most important parliamentary committee to deal with the elaboration of social legislation during the early Third Republic: the Commission d'assurance et de prévoyance sociales (CAPS), created in January 1894. "The goal of CAPS," as stated by its first president Léon Bourgeois, was "to lay the foundations for a system of *prévoyance*."[19] After Bourgeois, this committee—which presented the 1898 Mutualist Charter and the 1910 pension law to Parliament—was successively presided over by Jules Siegfried and Alexandre Millerand. Nearly one-third of the CAPS membership also joined the Musée social. Such was the case of Jean-Honoré Audiffred (1840–1917), who, as a protégé of Gambetta and a member of the republican left, had a long political career as a deputy and senator from the Loire department. An early member of the Musée social, Audiffred served on its board of directors and was the vice president of its research section on social insurance. In addition to his participation in CAPS, he was also a member of the Ligue nationale de la prévoyance et de la mutualité, the Institut des actuaires français, and the Conseil supérieur de la mutualité. Audiffred was a typical member of the reformist network that linked several parapolitical organizations to government advisory boards and parliamentary subcommittees during this period.[20]

Musée reformers were encouraged in their efforts to support mutualism because membership figures had nearly doubled since the advent of the Third Republic (see table 2). This steady growth sparked the interest, and sometimes the concern, of political figures. As Musée social direc-

TABLE 2.

FRENCH MUTUALIST MEMBERSHIP FIGURES

Year	Societies	Membership
1852	2,500	271,000
1870	5,800	825,000–913,000
1898	11,355	1,900,000
1902	15,000	3,000,000–3,750,000
1914	—	5,300,000

Source: Dreyfus, *Mutualité*, 38.

tor Léopold Mabilleau later remarked, the expansion of mutualism was "too rapid and too remarkable not to have aroused some degree of concern among politicians who do not like to witness the creation of such formidable groupings outside of ordinary party structures." [21]

The renewed dynamism of the mutualist movement also created an opportunity for conservative republicans, Radicals, and reformist socialists to meet on common ground. Despite their political differences in other realms, Léon Bourgeois, Joseph Barberet, Jules Siegfried, Émile Cheysson, Paul Guieysse, and Alexandre Millerand collaborated and worked within their respective spheres of influence to promote mutualism. From his office at the Ministry of the Interior, Barberet tabulated the most recent figures on mutualism, while Bourgeois used his high political profile to publicize them. Siegfried headed the mutualist lobby in Parliament, while Cheysson used his influence in parapolitical circles to promote rigorous financial controls in mutual aid societies. During the heated debates preceding the 1910 vote of a national pension law, the Radical Paul Guieysse and the reform socialist Alexandre Millerand attempted to reconcile mutualists to the inevitability of compulsory pension legislation while continuing to support them as principal agents for providing these services to French workers.

It had taken twenty-seven years, however, for mutualism to be fully embraced by the institutions of the Third Republic; consequently, mutualists at first accepted the government's sudden interest in their well-being only reluctantly. Within this context, reformers at the Musée social, particularly Léopold Mabilleau, became key interlocutors of both the mutualist movement and the government. The reasons for the Third Republic's early

Voluntary Associations ~ 201

interest in mutualism were clear enough. As Émile Cheysson explained, "Mutualism brings peace to its members; it regulates and organizes their lives; it reconciles them with the social order, of which they become solid supporters." Some mutualists, such as Dergas, a founding member of the mutual aid society Les prévoyants de l'avenir, concurred wholeheartedly: "We have succeeded in transforming yesterday's discontented worker into [today's] defender of social peace; we have made a capitalist out of him who once had nothing. We have served the interests both of the state and of social peace." [22] But in the ensuing pension debates, a majority of FNMF members steadfastly resisted the government's overtures to enlist their movement in compulsory social insurance schemes for providing retirement pensions. Despite these grave tensions, throughout the social policy debates of the early twentieth century, reformers and mutualists alike continued to insist on the moral as well as the economic benefits of mutualism.

The Advent of Republican Social Policy

When the Musée social came into existence in 1894, reformers were well aware that in comparison to its European neighbors, France appeared to be alarmingly slow in developing a consistent attitude toward social policy. Bismarck had enacted national health insurance in 1883, workmen's compensation in 1884, and old-age insurance in 1889. Compulsory national social protection was thereby granted to 18 million German workers — including those in Alsace and Lorraine. Belgium had adopted a system of state-subsidized voluntary insurance based on mutual aid societies. Both Victorian England, which boasted 11.5 million friendly society members, and Italy, which had a remarkable network of local credit and insurance institutions, had also opted for voluntary systems of social insurance. When, in 1902, Léon Bourgeois pointed out that a single American provident society (and not the largest among them) possessed capital funds equivalent to 320 million francs — a sum that represented the total national wealth of all French mutual aid societies combined — he drew the inevitable conclusion that France lagged far behind in the area of organized social protection for workers. Bourgeois and Cheysson explained this state of affairs as the accumulated result of decades of prohibitive legislation under the empires and monarchies of the nineteenth century, which had left scars upon civil society and the development of associational life in France.[23]

The Third Republic assumed responsibility for navigating the troubled political waters surrounding social reform and overcoming obstacles inherited from the sometimes violent social conflicts of the nineteenth century. France had to find a viable form of national social protection, one that would address the needs of workers, be financially solvent, and reconcile the liberal founding principles of the Republic with the demands of the state-guaranteed insurance funds. Édouard Fuster recognized that although each industrial nation faced a similar set of concerns, their solutions might differ markedly: "Obviously, those countries which have 'fallen behind' endeavor to find national solutions that are cautious and that carefully integrate pre-existing institutions and administrative traditions with the country's financial situation and vision of its future. Nations clearly do not march to the same drummer, let alone down the same path."[24] By the turn of the century, reformers in France agreed that something had to be done to protect workers from the vicissitudes of industrial life. Increasingly, some measure of government intervention in social policy was viewed as inevitable: social liberals—including reformist socialists, solidarists, Radicals, and more conservative republicans—all acknowledged that the state had an important role to play in such matters. Dividing lines were drawn, however, over the extent of government involvement, the notion of mandatory as opposed to voluntary insurance, and the agencies that would be designated to administer the new social policies.

Until World War I, the precise role to be played by the state formed the crux of all social policy debate in France. With regard to retirement pensions, the question boiled down to one of *obligation*: should legislators require compulsory forms of social protection for workers or merely rely on the wellsprings of voluntary initiative? Any attempt to answer this question invoked larger issues of social philosophy concerning the relationship of the individual to the state. Although orthodox liberals theoretically proscribed state interference in such matters, social liberals were more inclined to accept a limited degree of government intervention. But as Cheysson pointed out, there was no clear dividing line between the two schools of thought: "Thus far no one has found the methods, instruments, or surveyors to trace this boundary with precision."[25] The problem of industrial accidents, addressed below, proved to be a critical litmus test of this fluctuating boundary of government intervention in the social policy.

Industrial Accidents and Social Insurance

A symbol of the dangers of modern life, the issue of industrial accidents provoked the Third Republic's first major social policy debate and introduced a new conceptual era in legislative reform. Industrialization had ushered in a new form of society that was perceived in fin de siècle France as inherently dangerous. The daily press capitalized on this fear by featuring gruesome accounts of industrial accidents, most frequently connected with work in the mines or railroad construction. At the forefront of public attention, miners and railroad employees were the among the first new industrial workers to be targeted as beneficiaries of workers' compensation. In his 1894 introductory lecture on labor issues at the École libre des sciences politiques, Cheysson professed that an industrial worker's chances of incurring serious injury were seven times greater than that of the general mortality rate. The Belgian lawyer and Musée social correspondent Louis Varlez agreed that "the insecurity of the worker has never been as grave as it is today." [26] Although accidents may have represented some of the most visible and dramatic risks of industrial life, there were other risks as well, including illness, unemployment, and destitution. Each industrial nation faced similar problems, and the reformers who met in international congresses to address these issues sought solutions compatible with their national sociopolitical realities.

Before rising to the level of national policy debate, the question of industrial accidents had been addressed, in limited manner, by the private sector, particularly by the textile entrepreneurs of Alsace and by the nation's mining companies.[27] But the first Congress on Industrial Accidents, organized during the 1889 Universal Exhibition, definitively moved the problem of industrial accidents out of private hands and onto a public, international stage. By involving international experts, industrialists, legislators, doctors, reformers, and engineers, the 1889 Congress provided a new forum for private individuals and government representatives to exchange views and collaborate on policy initiatives. Maurice Bellom and Édouard Gruner, both mining engineers and future members of the

Musée social, participated actively in the work of the Congress through its executive council, the Comité permanent des congrès internationaux et accidents du travail, a group that was founded at the 1889 Exhibition and that continued to meet regularly in its aftermath. Two years later, in a decision announcing a key conceptual change in the debate, the 1891 Congress on Industrial Accidents voted to add the term "social insurance" to its official title. This step, according to Louis Varlez, was far from merely symbolic; it revealed "both the deep bond that unites all forms of insurance and the need to resolve the question of industrial accidents through insurance." [28] Henceforth, the question of industrial accident legislation was placed under the broader rubric of the debate on social insurance. Each ensuing congress was organized by reformers who saw themselves as members of an "avant-garde" and as "pioneers of public opinion" in social policy.[29] When Parliament passed France's first worker compensation law on April 9, 1898, the successful legislative outcome was largely the result of extensive lobbying efforts by extraparliamentary groups such as the Comité permanent during the preparatory phases of the debate. As noted by Émile Cheysson, the problem of industrial accidents "was ripe for lawmakers who, in a way, were left with the simple task of writing into law the progress that had been achieved outside of Parliament." [30]

The major innovation of the 1898 workers' compensation law was that, in the event of an industrial accident, the presumption of fault would heretofore lie with the employer—the *chef d'entreprise*—not the worker, as had previously been the case when liability was determined according to the Napoleonic civil code. But the 1898 law was even more innovative than this break with the traditions of civil law would indicate. In fact, the 1898 workers' compensation law enabled legislators to deftly sidestep the entire issue of "fault" by introducing instead the new juridical notion of professional risk. *Risque professionnel*, according to Émile Cheysson's "canonical definition," recognized that the risk of accidental injury was inherent to all industrial work and was, therefore, "independent of the fault of [particular] workers or employers." In this way, professional risk was also portrayed as a societal risk, something of concern to everyone in France, since society at large benefited from the fruits of industrial labor. Industrial accidents were construed, therefore, as general risks that should be recognized as such by the legislature and dealt with through insurance. In this way, the 1898 law set up a situation in which industrial employers were held responsible for the safety of their workers but could protect themselves and their firms through insurance. At the eleventh hour, legislators, particularly those in the Senate who were concerned with preserving the private juridical nature of industrial property, forced a compromise that retained the notion of *risque professionnel*, but refused to mandate that employers obtain accident insurance. Still, legislators on both sides felt vindicated, since the rationale of *risque professionnel* created a very strong incentive for industrial employers to contract some type of accident insurance either through a mutual aid society, a private insurance company, or the state fund. Employers remained implicitly liable for all industrial accidents except those caused by worker negligence, but the choice of how to contract accident insurance to protect their workers was left up to them.[31]

The global effect of the 1898 compensation law was to recast the social question in an entirely new light. "We have definitively left the field of private law for that of public law," Raoul Jay proclaimed; the 1898 law is "a truly 'social' reform." [32] François Ewald has coined the term "logique assurantielle" (a form of social reasoning based on actuarial calculations) to describe the process by which insurance would find broad applications in social policy far beyond the realm of industrial accidents. The 1898 workers' compensation law introduced a new way of thinking about industrial society itself and, in the long run, paved the way for the universal social welfare coverage of the post-1945 period in France.[33] Individual *prévoyance*, once espoused by liberal reformers, had been replaced by the goal of generalized social insurance.

"Once we've taken care of those who have been injured on the job" and other crises in the "life of the modern worker," explained Édouard Fuster, "we are inevitably drawn to the related problems of those who stopped work because of illness, chronic disability, or old age." Life itself, especially for workers, was filled with risks that could interrupt employment indefinitely and throw an entire family into utter destitution in a matter of weeks. New terms and attitudes accompanied those unpredictable events in life that were once traditionally referred to as misfortunes. Illness, death, old age, or even maternity, Fuster explained, all fit into this new category of social risks. They are "risks that are undoubtedly poorly understood from a statistical viewpoint, risks that require extensive and heavy coverage." But, he quickly added, "How great the temptation is to insure these risks as well, by substituting the certainty of a legally guaranteed stipend for the uncertainty of almsgiving." [34] The mere fact of contracting an insurance policy or contributing to an insurance fund could therefore "guarantee" an individual's right to receive aid without directly involving the state. Social insurance appealed to liberals as a solution, since it adroitly avoided the problem of social rights guaranteed by law.

Professional risk, and the social insurance contracted to protect one from its nefarious consequences, was predicated on the notion that in industrial society—or so the argument went—everyone was equally at risk of accident or misfortune. Based on the general laws of probability, which were admittedly sketchy, it was a convenient form of theoretical equality. Although an adversary of the 1898 law, even Léon Say understood its broad implications. "What is professional risk?" he queried. "It's the risk of life itself." [35] Since social insurance embodied the notion of shared risk, it laid the groundwork for the socialization of responsibility in France. What started as a simple technique of calculation and probability generated the basis for a universal system of welfare coverage. Insurance revolutionized social thought by providing a new paradigm of social reform: "We have ended up seeing insurance," Fuster asserted, as "the great agent of social renovation." Louis Varlez coined the term "integral insurance" to describe this new attitude toward social reform. [36]

Within this context, the technical skills of actuaries and statisticians were suddenly of critical national importance. Just as Cheysson had spoken previously of the social role of the engineer, reformers began exalting the social role of the actuary. Reliable statistics on which to base social policy calculations such as those needed to establish a national pension plan were "utterly lacking," deplored the deputy Jean Audiffred before the parliamentary committee on social insurance. [37] Cheysson elaborated on this dilemma: "Lawmakers are in dire need of a statistical base upon which to build their edifice. Without that solid foundation, the latter is at risk of merely floating in the air or of crumbling to the ground. Never before has this need been more acutely felt than since the day social laws began knocking at the door of Parliament. But, likewise, never before has one taken notice of how infrequently this need is satisfied, or of the great lacunae existing in the official statistics." [38] The technical problems faced by Parliament in the elaboration of social policy were very similar to those faced by private insurance companies and mutual aid societies. In the eyes of many social liberals, in fact, there seemed to be no clear dividing line to mark where mutualism left off and private insurance began. "In place of the defenseless individual, [mutualism] substitutes the collectivity, functioning according to the immutable laws of probability." [39] For Cheysson, mutualism was, simply put, the best form of social insurance.

By the early years of the twentieth century, the notion of social insurance had decisively moved French social reform into a new conceptual era. The protective legislation of the nineteenth century, which targeted specific subgroups of the working population, was being absorbed within the new parameters of a voluntary social contract. Social liberals who had first-hand contact with the industrial world no longer contested the fact that all workers needed to be protected against illness, old age, and accidents. But as Cheysson noted, the way in which this insurance should be administered—by the state or by voluntary, independent institutions such as mutual aid societies "is the question that creates dissension and divides us into several schools of thought." [40] Social Catholic and Musée social librarian Étienne Martin Saint-Léon was quick to underscore the rift caused by this debate: "Rarely," he remarked, "has there been such a deep split between the economic and the social Catholic schools of thought." [41] An examination of the Musée social's role in the quest to organize national pensions for workers and peasants in France, based not exclusively on the state but also on mutualism, highlights the tensions that were inherent in this debate for social liberals.

The Musée social and the Debate on Retirement Pensions

After workers' compensation, the next protracted debate on social policy in the French Parliament concerned retirement pensions. Reminiscent of earlier polemics, the issue of government intervention in the pending pension law was a thorny one. Should retirement pensions be a state-guaranteed entitlement? Should they be administered by a national pension fund, by mutual aid societies, or by both? For mutualist sympathizers, the crucial issue centered on whether or not mutual aid societies would ever be numerous and strong enough to become the exclusive, or at least the privileged, agents for administering the proposed national pension plan. Supporters argued that mutualism could provide the law with a preexistent, decentralized organizational structure and with the allegiance of its expanding membership. However, even on the eve of the dual passage of the Mutualist Charter and the workers' compensation law— passed within nearly one week of each other in 1898—Émile Cheysson voiced concern that the mutual aid societies might not yet be up to the task. They were, in his words, "hardly abundant, poorly managed," and, most pessimistically, had enlisted "relatively few members."[42]

The Musée social reacted to these early debates on retirement pensions by organizing a vigorous campaign to strengthen, and even restructure, French mutualism. It quickly established a mutualism service under the direction of Félix Raison and, in an effort to disseminate information to the public, published the text of the 1898 Mutualist Charter along with the complete record of the parliamentary debates.[43] Since the Mutualist Charter was often difficult to interpret for those not familiar with the new legal terminology, that is to say, for the people most directly affected by the law—mutualists themselves—the Musée social acted as an information bureau, publishing the jurisprudence established within the nation's court system and placing its legal counsel at the service of mutualists.[44] Its objective was to facilitate the creation of mutualist unions across the nation and to advise mutualists on the technical aspects of setting up retirement and illness funds. Initially, the Musée was overwhelmed with requests on how to create mutualist unions and start pension plans and other insurance funds.[45] In response, its social insurance section invited a select group of lawyers, economists, high civil servants, mutualists, actuaries, and representatives of the nation's insurance companies to meet at the Musée on a regular basis. Based on its findings, members often made recommendations for legislative bills or proposals, which were then submitted by Jules Siegfried to the Parliament or the appropriate ministerial office. As early as April 1896, the social insurance section had requested funding from the Musée's board to have Léon Marie, president of the French Actuarial Institute—also located at Musée social—draw up insurance rate tables that could be distributed freely among mutual aid societies. Groups such as the Ligue nationale de la prévoyance et de la mutualité also requested the Musée's technical assistance to set up probability tables for old-age and invalidity insurance.[46] Because of the multiple technical services it rendered, Léon Bourgeois referred to the Musée social as "the council of scientific advisers to national mutualism."[47]

Despite these early efforts, Musée reformers remained concerned that

Figure 10. Léopold Mabilleau (1853–1941).
CEDIAS-Musée social, Paris.

French mutual aid societies were not taking advantage of the 1898 Mutualist Charter's provision allowing them to form unions.[48] They therefore undertook new, more aggressive measures to bolster French mutualism. Léopold Mabilleau, the newly appointed director of the Musée social, was designated to lead this crusade.[49] Although a young scholar in classics and philosophy with a solid academic reputation, Mabilleau was a neophyte to the mutualist movement.[50] Thanks to his strategic position at the Musée social, however, doors opened easily; Mabilleau quickly assumed the presidency of the Leclaire Mutual Aid Society and accepted a newly endowed chair in social insurance at the Conservatoire national des arts et métiers. His rapid accession to notoriety within mutualist circles makes it clear that Mabilleau was being groomed to fulfill a public and a political role as the "champion of mutualist unions." [51]

After delivering more than a hundred lectures throughout the country, Mabilleau soon became a familiar, if not always welcomed name in mutualist circles. His first public lecture as an official mutualist, given in 1898 at the Musée social—"L'Avenir de la Mutualité"—was presided over and symbolically endorsed by the French premier, Charles Dupuy.[52] Mabilleau pushed for a greater role for mutualism in the proposed national pension plan, and he was lauded for having helped create thirty-one new mutualist unions in France.[53] By June 1902, when the Musée's mutualism service published the nation's first statistical chart on mutualist unions, there were forty-four unions located in thirty-two different departments.[54] Although the mutualist momentum seemed to be growing, Musée reformers remained concerned that this progress was not sufficient.

In view of the imminent parliamentary debate on retirement pensions, mutualists felt the need to meet and consolidate their positions regarding the proposed legislation.[55] The first National Congress on Retirement Pensions was therefore convened at the Musée social from April 11 to 14, 1901, under Mabilleau's presidency. At the time of this congress, when the director of the Musée was being introduced as an official spokesman for the movement, French mutualists were overwhelmingly favorable to a liberal and strictly voluntary solution to the problem of national pensions. However, given the political tenor of parliamentary debate, particularly after 1902 in a chamber dominated by Radical-socialist coalitions that favored compulsory national pensions, Mabilleau would later have to assume the difficult task of guiding mutualists along a gradual path of acceptance of a more state-directed pension plan.[56]

On December 20, 1901, Mabilleau received his highest official mutualist accolade at a banquet, presided over by Léon Bourgeois, for 150 mutualist guests at the Palais d'Orsay. On behalf of the government, "the gold medal of Mutualism" was bestowed on Mabilleau, and Paul Deschanel expressed his gratitude to him for having contributed to the cause of social progress.[57] A republican banquet was always a highly charged political and symbolical affair. This one became an occasion for the Musée social, government representatives, and other mutualist leaders to strategically regroup and launch a concerted campaign to promote mutualism as a vehicle for national pensions. In his banquet speech, Léon Bourgeois could not have been more explicit: "Hasten to develop mutualism, because our society can no longer wait; the problem has been posed in such a way that retirement pensions will become law, no matter what; if you do not want to be excluded, organize now and move speedily into action so that with regard to this long-awaited and much needed public service, you will be able to say: 'We want to take charge of it, and we are ready.'"[58] A few months later, as if in response to this call, the French delegation at the 1902 International Congress on Social Insurance declared that French mutualists were ready to federate into a single, more powerful organization and to assume "responsibility for the heaviest of social enterprises" as the chief agent for administering national pensions. The group that made this declaration included Musée social members Émile Cheysson; Édouard Fuster; and G. Jouanny, a paper manufacturer, the vice president of the Paris Chamber of Commerce, and the secretary general of the Mutualité industrielle.[59]

Shortly thereafter, on November 10, 1902, representatives of seventy-nine departmental and regional mutualist unions met at the Musée social and voted to create the Fédération nationale de la mutualité française (FNMF). The creation of the FNMF made clear that the groundwork had been laid for a much larger plan: the institutional base for incorporating the voluntarist mutualist network into any new equation for social welfare policy on pensions now existed.[60] Clearly, the FNMF had been created to generate a strong, decentralized national network that could serve as the political arm of the mutualist movement.[61] It even aspired to provide the infrastructure for regional social insurance funds that would administer a national system of social welfare protection. As Bourgeois declared: "il faut que les mutualistes se mutualisent."[62]

From the outset, the FNMF's activities were intertwined with those of the Musée social, where it maintained its headquarters. Mabilleau served as the FNMF president until 1921, and the chief editor of the FNMF's publication *Mutualité nouvelle* was Henri Barrau, the general secretary of the Musée social.[63] Cheysson and Audiffred were the FNMF's honorary vice presidents, while its honorary president was Émile Loubet, the current president of the French Republic.[64] The Musée social and its reformist network offered mutualists a national platform, high political visibility, and a conduit to the inner circles of national policy making.

As soon as the parliamentary debates on pension policy began, tensions surfaced between reformers and mutualists over the role of the state. Léon Bourgeois had sent shock waves through the mutualist community when he took advantage of Mabilleau's 1901 banquet to announce his position in the debate. Bourgeois had been unequivocal: in order to be successful, a national retirement policy had to be made compulsory. "After many years of thought and study," he said, "I have come to the conclusion that retirement pensions will not be successfully organized if the principle of obligation is not written into the law. But do not misunderstand me, there is only one thing, in my opinion, that can be made obligatory, and that is the act itself of *prévoyance*." [65] The position he announced was a difficult one for most mutualists to accept. On the one hand, Bourgeois called for compulsory insurance, which was anathema to the traditional mutualist cause of voluntary contribution. On the other hand, he attempted to assuage the mutualists in the audience by proclaiming the following conciliatory motto: "Unity of purpose, diversity of means." This motto, he explained, was the solidarist compromise position. Although Bourgeois argued in favor of a government mandate on pensions, he also supported the liberal cause of maintaining the freedom of choice for obtaining that insurance. According to his scheme, therefore, mutualism could still conceivably serve as the essential agent of the long-awaited national pension law. Bourgeois's idea slowly made its way forward as the compromise political platform that would eventually, albeit reluctantly, be accepted by the mutualists themselves. Many social liberals and mutualists continued to balk for several more years, however, at the idea of compulsory insurance.

Since pension policy was being hotly debated in the national political arena, Musée reformers were soon pressed to take a clear stand on the question of government intervention. Although they had subscribed to the broad outlines of a voluntarist, liberal approach to reform, on this issue, the Musée membership was internally divided. Social Catholics, solidarists, Radicals, and reformist socialists promoted government intervention and compulsory insurance; but the liberal economists, financiers, and members of business and industrialist interest groups rejected compulsory insurance as yet a new form of taxation.[66] Until at least 1904, when CAPS finally decided to introduce a compulsory version of the pension bill to Parliament, there was also a crucial middle group on the committee, composed of influential Musée social members who hesitated, momentarily torn between their multiple allegiances. Jules Siegfried fell into this latter category. During the early parliamentary debates, Siegfried had argued in favor of adopting the Belgian model of subsidized voluntary insurance schemes. He expressed this position, including his misgivings on the issue, in his 1902 electoral platform as a Democratic Republican candidate for the Chamber of Deputies: "I consider that workers' pensions can no longer be delayed. If obligation is absolutely necessary to attain this goal, I will vote for obligation. But prior to resorting to this extreme measure, it would be wise to experiment with the system which has worked so well in Belgium, one that uses mutual aid societies as intermediaries, and that grants them significant state subsidies." [67]

Even the "compulsory camp" at the Musée social wanted to integrate the mutualist network into the pension law. Compulsory insurance, they believed, was necessary to achieve comprehensive coverage and a broad financial base for social programs, but they did not discount mutualism as an essential agent for administering the new pensions. To the contrary, the principles of mutualism and compulsory insurance were not, in their view, necessarily in conflict. But because of such roundabout rhetoric, the debate grew more elaborate, intractable, and often confusing to the public. Social liberals found themselves with their backs to the wall. In the end, they were forced to decide whether they were more on the "social" or on the "liberal" side of the debate. Whereas they had preached the benefits of self-help and voluntary insurance for years, when put to the test by the demands of policy making, many of them crossed the line and began to admit the advantages of government intervention. Despite disagreement on details, the majority of Musée reformers who were actively involved in the pension debates—either within Parliament or in parapolitical forums—continued to voice the concerns of mutualists. When the debate was narrowed down to the question of state intervention, however, the Musée's membership remained fundamentally divided. A rich confrontation of ideas on this point ensued within the extraparliamentary sphere.

A *"National" Solution Must Be a "French" Solution.* A particular image of France and national identity permeated the debates on the legitimate role of the state in social policy. Those who were opposed to compulsory or state-administered insurance often equated the word *obligation* with a

"German" or an "anti-French" solution that was in contradiction with the true national French spirit and culture. According to this view, although France had a strong, centralized state, its vitality belonged to the decentralized regions. In this light, mutualism embodied the regionalist diversity of twentieth-century France: "Just as it would be unthinkable, in our pleasant country of France, to substitute for the wonderful variety of our regional cultures, one homogenous culture imposed by the reigning order, one should not rule out . . . the diverse and flexible structures of *prévoyance*, in order to promote one single form imposed by *obligation*." [68] Similarly, the Society of Industrialists and Businessmen of France declared in 1905, "We ask that the problem of pensions not be resolved 'the German way,' but rather 'the French way.' " [69]

Many social liberals, such as Siegfried, avoided engaging in anti-German nationalist rhetoric by proposing the Belgian model as a preferable alternative for France. Accordingly, the Musée social organized two missions (1901, 1902), led by Georges Salaun, to study the goals, operation, and results of the Belgian pension system. [70] In a public lecture on his findings, Salaun explained that the Belgian system was a voluntary yet subsidized regime, boasting 430,000 individual pension funds. The results of this study, Cheysson proclaimed, "ought to be brought to the attention of French mutualists, whose Federation was just formed at the Musée social, but also to that of our legislators since they are about to pronounce themselves on the organization of workers' pensions." [71]

Not only did Cheysson believe that the German state-run approach to social policy was incompatible with the institutions of free government and therefore inappropriate for France, but he also intended to use the FNMF as a vehicle to promote his personal views on social reform. He argued that a nation must respect its own unique traditions, what Le Play had previously referred to "its essential constitution." In France, Cheysson considered that essential tradition to be one of decentralization, not the Jacobin model of centralized egalitarianism. [72] A state-organized form of social insurance may have corresponded to the German "militarist" culture, he claimed, but it was profoundly repugnant to French liberals and would only create or reinforce bad statist habits reminiscent of the authoritarian Second Empire. Government-administered social programs would also, in his view, overburden the bureaucracy and drain the economy. [73] It would cause workers to become dependent on state aid and take away their incentive for individual initiative and social betterment: "Today's provident man will be tomorrow's public welfare recipient."[74] Rather than reverting to a "German" model of state management of funds that would bring in its wake the old specter of state socialism, Cheysson proposed that mutual aid societies and private insurance companies join forces.[75] According to this scheme, mutual aid societies would serve as a link between the insured party and the insurance company itself. Cheysson maintained this position until his death in 1909.

The Interventionists. Not everyone at the Musée social was opposed to compulsory insurance, however. Social Catholics, for instance, had no reservations about calling for state intervention. Étienne Martin Saint-Léon developed this position in his review of a book entitled *Les Caisses de retraites ouvrières*, whose author, J. Lefort, argued that compulsory insurance would destroy the conscientious duty of employers to take care of their workers. Paternalist ideas such as these, Martin Saint-Léon retorted, were entirely outdated and showed that the author had no idea what the new industrial order implied. Martin Saint-Léon believed that social insurance must be compulsory, especially since the mutualist movement everywhere, including in Italy, had reached a plateau and would never, in his opinion, be strong enough to assume the burden of administering retirement pensions: "The solution to the problem of workers' retirement pensions will not be found through piecemeal forms of encouragement that try to foster a hypothetical awakening of the spirit of *prévoyance*. Only in an immediate and comprehensive manner, through the combined action of the law, or if possible through the law alone, will a solution be found."[76] Other prominent social Catholics at the Musée social such as Raoul Jay, Hyacinthe de Gailhard-Bancel, Albert de Mun, Adéodat Boissard, and Léon de Seilhac took similar positions in the debate.[77] Their opinions were channeled through the Association internationale pour la protection légale des travailleurs, social Catholic publications such as the *Association Catholique*, and organizations such as the Action populaire and the Semaines sociales.

Other interventionists, however, were not social Catholics. Paul Guieysse, the official reporter of the legislative bill on pensions that emanated from the CAPS and became law in 1910, endorsed a compulsory pension law early in the debate. In 1901 he openly regretted that mutualists did not produce better results, but despite government subsidies and legal advantages to help them grow, mutual aid societies, in Guieysse's opinion, could simply not handle national pensions alone.[78] Louis Varlez, the Musée's correspondent in Belgium, criticized his country's voluntaristic pension system for being too expensive and called it detrimental to the mutualist ideal because so many independent worker initiatives had failed and had lost the savings of "those who believed." He concluded that the government had a responsibility to protect the general welfare of its citizens, even those who did not want to help themselves: "The state has the right and the duty to intervene in this question of social hygiene in order to coax the stubborn in the direction of the general interest."[79]

The Converts. The Musée social's tradition of independent research also contributed to a broad reevaluation of the terms of the debate.[80] The conclusions of these studies were responsible for the conversion of several prominent social liberals at the Musée social to the interventionist cause. These "converts" fell into three main categories: those who ended up admiring the German system for offering universal coverage, those who concluded that French industrialists were simply not responding to the call to provide insurance for their workers, and those who grew critical of the Belgian system for its lack of dynamic growth. These conclusions were reached respectively by Édouard Fuster, Maurice Bellom, and Jules Siegfried. The results of their independent investigations, coupled with the sociopolitical pressures surrounding the pension issue, persuaded them to support the compromise position first announced by Léon Bourgeois, one that was premised on compulsory insurance.

A specialist of contemporary Germany, Fuster served as secretary at the 1902 Dusseldorf International Congress on Social Insurance and brought with him a French delegation including four members of the Musée's board of directors: Gigot, Siegfried, Cheysson, and Gruner.[81] In the context of European policy formation, social insurance congresses had grown to become major political events, and the French contingent—which included a cross section of elites—was escorted around to inspect the functioning of the German social insurance system. Upon their return, Fuster submitted a report that constitutes an example of the pragmatic approach taken by Musée social investigators. Rather than discounting the German model a priori because of prejudices against "state socialism," Fuster explained that the first-hand observations of the French delegation had shed new light on the German social insurance system: "The French, be they civil servants, industrialists, doctors, or sociologists, looked around in earnest and without prejudice, but perhaps with a shred of hidden regret when confronted with the strength and optimism of the Germans."[82] After attending the congress and conducting his own investigation, Fuster began to look favorably on the German system.[83] Later, at a public lecture at the Musée social in 1905, he demonstrated the efficiency of the compulsory law and its beneficial effect on national life, noting particularly that the Germans had accumulated sufficient funds to improve worker housing and public health services.[84] He insisted, moreover, that state socialism was an ideological notion that prevented those who had not actually visited Germany from seeing how decentralized the system actually was. Fuster urged French policy makers and reformers to go and observe the German system themselves.

Maurice Bellom, an editorialist for the *Journal des économistes* and *L'Économiste français* who was initially in agreement with Cheysson's strictly liberal ideas, also reversed his position after engaging in careful investigations of his own.[85] In a paper presented to the Société statistique de Paris in 1901, he compared the various forms of social insurance functioning in Europe and attempted to evaluate their influence on the population at large. The global results, he concluded, were not brilliant. In the area of health insurance, in France and England, where legislation was not compulsory, Bellom found that although improvements had been made, they were negligible and only skilled workers benefited from the voluntary insurance schemes. "Despite the extent to which forms of assistance to the sick were developed under the voluntary liberal system," he concluded, "one cannot deny that the intervention of lawmakers, as they imposed mandatory participation, was the only means of extending benefits to all workers." Bellom also contended that the current level of pension funds functioning in France was far below that which had been anticipated.[86] Upon further examination, employer-sponsored pension plans did not fare much better. Already in 1896, in a study requested by CAPS under the presidency of Jules Siegfried, the Office du travail had found that of 296,797 industrial firms surveyed, only 229 had employer-sponsored pension plans for workers. Moreover, among the largest of these firms, those employing more than five hundred workers, only 13.9 percent had established pension funds. Overall, an alarming 0.08 percent of the industrial firms included in the study, or a mere 4.35 percent of the total work force, benefited from employer-sponsored pension funds. Studies such as these offered mounting evidence that the solution to the problem of social welfare could not be found by relying solely on voluntary or employer-sponsored programs.

Finally, in 1906, Musée social president Jules Siegfried rallied to the principle of compulsory insurance after examining the results of the German and Belgian laws. In Germany, 13.5 million out of 14.5 million workers (93.1 percent) were covered by the 1889 law; whereas in Belgium, the results were simply not as successful: 700,000 out of 1,600,000 workers (43.8 percent) were covered. After two visits to Germany, one to the 1902 Dusseldorf congress, and a subsequent one to Berlin, Siegfried decided to change his opinion and vote for compulsory insurance:

> In my opinion, the success of the German law on the one hand and the relative failure of the Belgian law on the other, demonstrate beyond reasonable doubt that the easy solution [a nonmandatory solution] . . . is not enough. We must therefore turn to a mandatory system; this appears all the more necessary as it is the only means of ensuring cooperation from employers, without whom a pension law cannot produce serious results. For all of these reasons, I have been won over by the doctrine of *obligation*, along with the majority of the members of the Chamber.[87]

Like Bellom, Siegfried had concluded that industrial employers could not be depended upon to participate voluntarily in sufficient numbers to ensure workers' pensions. His decision represented a departure from the faith he had inherited from his Alsatian ancestors: that industrialists would voluntarily assume their social responsibility in the new industrial order. Siegfried therefore resorted to the law as the guarantor of social justice and invoked solidarism as the underlying justification for social legislation in a liberal democracy.

The Mutualist Response: "La Liberté dans l'obligation"

From 1902 until 1904, Léopold Mabilleau had led the FNMF in the belief that voluntary insurance provided by mutual aid societies could provide French workers and their families with the social protection they needed. By 1904, however, given the increasing momentum gained by proponents of compulsory insurance, and in light of CAPS's decision that same year to introduce a compulsory pension bill in Parliament, the mutualists were forced to reexamine their position. Mabilleau was the first to draw the hard conclusions. Despite all efforts, it was becoming increasingly clear that mutualism alone would not form a sufficient basis for social policy in the area of retirement pensions. Moreover, Mabilleau's chief ally in Parliament, Jules Siegfried, had decided to vote for compulsory insurance. Despite his reluctance, Mabilleau was forced to adopt a political compromise for the mutualist movement or run the risk of being left on the sidelines with no role whatsoever to play in the future pension law.[88]

At the 1904 Mutualist Congress held in Nantes, Mabilleau summoned his rhetorical skills and undertook the difficult task of convincing the French mutualists to accept the compulsory pension bill.[89] Mutualists, he argued, should support the premise of a compulsory law in exchange for being guaranteed a central role in the administration of the program. Despite his own misgivings, he succeeded in convincing the mutualist assembly and sent the following message to Parliament: "Find a way of reconciling the obligation to have insurance with the practice of freely choosing the means of obtaining that insurance, and we will be at your side to bring this social ideal into being."[90]

The consensus engineered by Mabilleau within the FNMF was a fragile one, however, and representatives of the Ligue nationale de la prévoyance et de la mutualité dissented openly. At the 1907 national congress in Nice, mutualists still believed that they could become the only authorized agents to administer the pensions. Jean Jaurès had warned them against such pretentions, predicting that it would lead only to paralysis and the bureaucratization of mutualism itself.[91] By 1909 they finally accepted that mutual aid societies would be designated as only one of several different possible agents of social insurance to be taken into consideration by the law.[92]

In his final analysis, Mabilleau conceded that mutual aid societies in France were stagnating; the movement had reached a saturation point, he suggested, with nearly five million mutualist members. At a public lecture at the Musée social in 1908, he admitted that although mutualism was still attracting new members, it was doing so at a much slower rate and had made almost no progress among industrial workers or the peasantry. In the end, he too invoked the principle of social solidarity to justify the compulsory nature of the law.[93] In defense of this new role for the state, he adopted the old republican analogy of the 1882 Ferry law on primary school education: "Fathers are under legal obligation to send their children to school: is that a form of constraint upon liberty? By having to learn how to read, the mind is liberated and freed! I cannot believe that it is any different in the area of *prévoyance*." Men should remain the "artisans of their own destiny"; and for that reason, he insisted that a choice be made available to citizens, even in the realm of social policy.

When all had been said and done, and despite the efforts of liberals who had struggled initially to keep the government from having a direct role in social policy, the compulsory legislation package on national pensions carried on the day on April 5, 1910. Before the vote, Léopold Mabilleau gave a public lecture at the Musée social in the presence of many members of Parliament. As long as there would be the freedom to choose between a private insurance agent, a mutual society, or a direct deposit fund to administer the pension, Mabilleau promised the cooperation of mutualists with the law, although he still reaffirmed his belief in the superiority of the system of voluntary insurance because of its educational and social value.

Alexandre Ribot, who presided over Mabilleau's lecture, explained how he too, after believing wholeheartedly in the educative value of individual initiative, had rallied to the principle of compulsory insurance: "We have to accept the assistance of mutual aid societies as works of good fortune; we must make room for them, not just a little room, but ample room for them to increase the extent of their investments, not under the guarantee, but under the supervision of the state." Ribot further described how, while participating in the Senate discussions, he came to the Musée social for advice. He learned that the results of the Belgian law were not what its promulgators had expected and that even Luigi Luzzatti had reached similar conclusions concerning Italy. This Italian statesman, who had long promoted liberal ideals, finally decided that obligation was necessary; and, Ribot added, he too had "allowed himself to be convinced." The Musée social's lecture series and discussion format had succeeded in disseminating information and having an impact on the opinions of legislators concerning pension policy.[94]

Despite the mutualists' acceptance of obligation, the final government bill did not grant any specific role to mutualism. Moreover, shortly after its final adoption, a series of administrative court decisions essentially blocked the implementation of the compulsory dimension of the law. The results of the long, intense debates, begun in the 1880s and temporarily subsiding only in the disappointing aftermath of the 1910 national pension law, had been fascinating but arduous. A compromise had eventually been reached between the voluntarist forces and the interventionists, who believed that only a compulsory, government-administered program could attain comprehensive national goals. Although this compromise ultimately failed in the case of the 1910 pension law, nothing was lost to posterity. These crucial decades of debate succeeded in paving the way for a specifically French model for administering social welfare that eventually formed the basis for the 1928 and 1930 Social Insurance laws and the 1945 Social Security Act. By 1910, although the political and institutional compromises had not yet been worked out, a consensus in favor of a hybrid system of social protection that was both compulsory and contributory had been reached in France.[95]

Although the Musée social reformers had maneuvered to place mutualism in the most favorable political light during the debates, their commitment to voluntary insurance had been put to a test. In the case of national pension policy, the mutualist movement proved to be more steadfastly liberal than were many of the social liberals at the Musée social. In the short run, social liberals seemed to have failed in their search for a nongovernmental solution to the formation of a national social policy. They were unable to argue convincingly what could have been a strong case, namely that mutualism provided a preexistent, decentralized structure that could be transformed into an agent of social welfare.[96] One of the strongest, yet curiously underdeveloped, arguments made in favor of mutualism was that its expansion would have eventually decreased the public assistance budget of local governments.[97] Their wavering, however, on the issue of government intervention and compulsory insurance clearly weakened the impact of social liberals as a group within the political arena.

Due to its multiple contacts in mutualist, business, and government circles, the Musée social provided an active forum for discussion and strategy throughout the parliamentary debates on pension policy. Its members defended the mutualist position on retirement pensions at a time when mutualism might have been easily dismissed from the debate because of political pressures within Parliament. Its public lectures and section meetings regularly attracted important politicians and high-level civil servants who sought the advice and expertise of Musée collaborators on the pending pension bills. The politicians who frequented the Musée social were "friends of mutualism" who sought a conciliatory attitude with the movement, once it became clear that the political choice for pension policy would be compulsory legislation. Mutualists themselves continued to consult the Musée on technical matters such as which statistical tables to use when setting up mutualist pension funds. Throughout this entire period, Musée social board members and administrators occupied key political positions both in the mutualist world and in government. In this example of social policy formation, the Musée social clearly combined its functions as a research center, a pressure group, and a forum for public debate.

6. The Modernity of Hygiene: Interventions in the City

❧

Once everyone owns property, the social question will be resolved. . . .
And architects will rub their hands together in satisfaction, like theater
box office cashiers the day of a sellout crowd. —M. PETRU, *L'Architecture
du Sud-Ouest*, 1894

Originating in a matrix of medicine, public administration, sociology,
and law, public hygiene deeply transformed how social reform was conceived and practiced at the Musée social and in French reform circles
generally throughout the nineteenth century and beyond. Leaving behind
eighteenth-century characterizations of hygiene as an individual moral
attribute, modern definitions evolved rapidly to include a social and public dimension. At first, as a matter of public sanitation, hygiene fell under
the purview of municipal engineers, the police, and public administrators, who attempted to reduce foul odors and to counteract the effects of
deadly vaporous miasmas in the air, water, and waste of crowded urban
centers. Later, biological science, particularly following the discoveries of
Pasteur, redirected the attention of hygienists to the disinfection of factories, sweatshops, schools, tenements, and other buildings where contagious microbes were thought to be lurking. By the end of the century,
the term *social hygiene* reflected a new focus, not on the physical environment, but rather on people as agents of infection and on prevention as a
necessary means of protection against illness.[1] These changing notions
of hygiene traced the new contours of an expanded and diversified public sphere in nineteenth- and early-twentieth-century France. Armed with
their theories of contagion and prevention, hygienists began to have a de-

termining impact on the formation of public policy and eventually the law in the areas of health, housing, and urban reform.

Largely as the consequence of Pasteur's model of contagion, matters of public health concerned every man, woman and child, regardless of their political beliefs or socioeconomic status. Transposed onto the social body, germ theory implied that individuals were not isolated monads, but were linked instead by the invisible and potentially threatening bond of infectious disease. This involuntary bond reduced every member of society to a common biological denominator and became a powerful tool for expressing how interrelated all segments of urban and industrial society truly were. After all, the material privileges and carefully erected boundaries of social class did not constitute an impermeable barrier against contagion. Rumors of "dresses that kill" circulated as bourgeois ladies voiced their fear of tuberculosis and ensuing alarm over the health conditions of the sweatshops that produced their finery.[2] Nor, by extension, could class privileges secure their bearers from the effects of social unrest, which had repercussions on every aspect of the economy and society. Whether the illness was physical or social, Émile Cheysson argued, all members of society were united "by a form of de facto solidarity, which allowed no one to feign disinterest for his own well-being." "Epidemics of social hatred are bred within the depths of sweatshops," he added. "They are no less contagious than tuberculosis or typhoid fever." Indeed, prominent reformers such as Léon Bourgeois and Georges Risler knew this to be true, since they had personally experienced the death of beloved family members due to contagious disease.[3]

As medical discoveries refined the fundamentals of hygiene, so too did reformers adopt new approaches and techniques to improve the standards of public health. New government agencies devoted to hygiene began the long march toward establishing a more coherent and effective public health policy in France. Hygiene evolved into a commanding social metaphor that fostered new representations of urban life, industrial society, and even democracy itself.[4] It served as a lever for transforming the traditionally defined relationship between the public and private spheres of liberal bourgeois society. During the period under consideration, questions of public hygiene challenged and ultimately altered the relationship between the individual and government by slowly discrediting the liberal notion of "the night-watchman state." According to this minimalist view of government, the state should merely be charged with surveillance, like a night watchman, to prevent unwarranted incursions into the private realm of property rights. Only gradually would the French state be entrusted with preserving the public interest. This chapter examines this complex process of change from the perspective of Musée social reformers who were engaged in housing reform, pragmatic politics, and the campaign to reform the nation's cities.

Hygiene as a Lever of Modernity

Although the social question was a consequence of industrialization, it had never been perceived by reformers solely as an industrial problem. Its effects on the laboring population had long been evident not only in the large textile and metallurgical factories but also in the densely populated neighborhoods of the nation's cities. As contemporary observers struggled to define the social question, their mission to improve the lot of workers and their families quickly grew to encompass the material surroundings in which they lived.

The question of worker housing rose to the top of the nation's reform agenda as a consequence of the surge in migration to the cities during the final third of the century. Between 1876 and 1881, it was estimated, 55,000 to 60,000 new inhabitants per year either migrated to, or were born in, the capital. By 1886, merely 25 percent of all heads of household had been born in Paris or the department of the Seine; whereas 70 percent came from the provinces, and 5 percent were foreign-born. Parisian workers were often migrants from the provinces, living in chambres garnies, furnished rooms often found in the cramped garrets of Haussmann-era buildings that were overcrowded, poorly ventilated, and overpriced. The director of municipal statistics in Paris, Dr. Jacques Bertillon, determined that by the year 1891, 14 percent of the city's population lived in conditions of "excessive overcrowding."[5]

As a consequence of this influx, the central districts of Paris were caught in an infernal cycle of congestion and competition for housing that caused rents to soar. Consequently, the caricature of the despised landlord-vulture known as "Monsieur Vautour" became a mainstay figure

...rie du Parti Socialiste (S. F. I. O.)

19.

Monsieur Vautour

ET

LA RÉDUCTION

DES

Loyers

Par PAUL LAFARGUE

Prix: 10 centimes

Au Siège du Conseil National, 16, rue de la Corderie

PARIS (IIIᵉ Arrondissement)

Figure 11. Paul Lafargue, *Monsieur Vautour et la réduction des loyers.*
Paris: Librairie du Parti Socialiste-SFIO, n.d., 1908 or 1909.
CEDIAS-Musée social, Paris.

of popular urban lore. Forced to relocate to the urban periphery, many workers found mediocre housing at lower prices, or sometimes built themselves make-shift dwellings that quickly deteriorated into slums. Bertillon's study also revealed that overcrowding in Paris coincided with the map of working-class neighborhoods, particularly the nineteenth and twentieth arrondissements. These phenomena only accentuated the pattern of social segregation that began with the urban renovation and elimination of traditional working class neighborhoods such as the Butte des Moulins during the Second Empire under the direction of Baron Georges Haussmann, a prefect of the Seine department. Paris was increasingly characterized by a concentration of commerce and manufacturing in the center city, and an unstable or elastic labor force amassed on its periphery. The infrastructure of the city was clearly insufficient to meet the housing needs of this new population of wage earners.[6]

Concern with the material conditions of workers' daily lives predated this late-nineteenth-century urban influx. Dr. Louis Villermé and Adolphe Blanqui's investigations of the 1830s and 40s had disclosed the human misery hidden behind the facades of old buildings where workers often lived in unlit, damp cellars with no source of heat. But their investigations were impressionistic and their language highly moralistic. Only later in the century did the more empirical techniques of hygienists—including doctors, public administrators, statisticians, and eventually architects and civil engineers—lead to more convincing studies, all of which were backed by an authoritative discourse of scientific inquiry and expertise. Hygienists' claims were further legitimized by more reliable statistics made available through the Paris Municipal Bureau of Statistics (1865) and by professional associations that helped clarify the goals and techniques of public hygiene, such as the Société de médecine publique et d'hygiène professionnelle (1877) and its official publication the Revue d'hygiène (1879). Beginning in 1876 in Brussels, international congresses on public hygiene convened reformers, professionals, and experts from around the world who were grappling with similar issues within their specific national contexts.[7]

The social investigations of hygienists suggested, moreover, a direct correlation between high mortality rates, illness, and social class. Bertillon juxtaposed maps used to determine overcrowding with those measuring mortality rates in each neighborhood. The results were striking. Overcrowding and high mortality rates were indeed interrelated, and both, he determined, were caused by poverty. Paul Juillerat, the head of the *casier sanitaire*, an innovative sanitary census bureau for the city of Paris, compiled copious statistical files on mortality rates and tuberculosis in the city. He opened a file on each insalubrious dwelling in which a death had occurred due to infectious disease. Subsequently, regular note was made of improvements and evolving sanitation conditions within the building, thus establishing for each dwelling "its own daily sanitary journal." Unlike their predecessors, who were concerned to reveal—often only to condemn—the private lives and morality of workers, investigators of the "postbacteriological period" such as Bertillon, Juillerat, and du Mesnil were interested in understanding the relationship between workers' living conditions and the etiology of diseases.[8]

Medical research, too, began to demonstrate a correlation between the spread of tuberculosis and the dampness, inadequate ventilation, and absence of light so frequently found in neighborhoods of the working poor. As a result, a new urban pathology ensued: the buildings in congested city neighborhoods were themselves considered to be disease-ridden. Already, after the cholera epidemics of 1832 and 1849, Paris had been commonly referred to as *une ville malade*, a sick city, where the problems of stench, refuse, and water contamination only added to the new plights of urban life. For this reason, public works projects soon incorporated sanitary improvements as well. Officials reasoned that perhaps the spread of disease could be controlled by installing a better sewer system and providing a more purified water supply.

Another result of this hygienic thinking was the 1850 vote of the Melun housing law. Each commune could henceforth establish a commission authorized to investigate complaints of unhealthy housing conditions. Although the law permitted inspections under these conditions and stated that landlords had a responsibility to maintain healthful dwellings, it was rife with loopholes and did not grant to the state or the municipality the right of eminent domain necessary for slum clearance. As a result, the law was ineffective. Moreover, the notables who had accepted positions on the departmental hygiene councils, created in 1848, had often proven to be apathetic, negligent, or guilty of merely seeking political favor from the prefect. Doctors often refrained from reporting infectious disease for fear that if they did so—thus breaking a publicly perceived code of confidentiality—they might ruin their private practices.[9] Was intervention in personal property and medical records warranted at all, and, if so, in what proportions and in what forms? In each instance, the shifting divide between public and private interests was a potentially volatile one.

The interrelated problems of insalubrious housing and social class became increasingly pressing once France was confronted with epidemic outbreaks of tuberculosis, an even more socially determined plight than cholera had been. The tenacity of tuberculosis in the nation's capital was described by Dr. du Mesnil as "the reprisal of misery against the egoism and indifference of the rich." Only "heroism," he added, could prevent those forced to live in such conditions from "contracting a hatred of society." [10] As a result of these intertwined developments, reformers who sought to resolve the social question eventually turned to the city itself as the primary target of their interventions.

It was initially the problem of worker housing, however, that most poignantly captured the complex set of issues raised by hygienists. Housing touched on issues of grave importance to republicans: public health, class relations, the economy, a gendered order in which women were relegated to a domestic role, and the establishment of a stable political regime. These concerns became particularly acute in the aftermath of the Commune, during which the working-class neighborhoods of northern Paris had proven to be hotbeds of resistance and revolutionary fervor. The problem of worker housing, therefore, provided the original matrix for republican social reform efforts. Jules Siegfried called it "the first of all social questions," without a resolution of which all other attempts to improve workers' lives would be futile.[11]

The physical structure of a house or an apartment building was perceived by reformers as a pivotal social site linking individuals to the world around them. As a commodity, housing occupies a crossroads of public and private interests and "has never ceased," as Roger-Henri Guerrand remarked, "to reflect personal and social values that are inextricably linked." [12] Social reformers wrestled with these very issues. Moreover, they set their goals higher than those that merely sought to make discernible improvements in the physical structure of buildings. Through housing reform, they also hoped to transform social relations within the Republic. Because worker housing posed a complex series of questions involving property rights, class identities, notions of public and private space, gender relations, the family, and the state, it constituted a prism through which the full spectrum of reform issues was refracted.

Republican Housing Reform

By the century's end, reformers had established an international network for discussing worker housing, a problem that had arisen simultaneously in every industrializing nation. During the 1889 Universal Exhibition, Jules Siegfried took the initiative of organizing the first International Congress on Low-Cost Housing (Congrès international des habitations à bon marché), where reformers from around the world could meet to discuss the interrelated concerns of public hygiene, comparative housing legislation, the achievements of industrial housing schemes, and private building societies. Carroll Wright, the first director of the U.S. Department of Labor, presided as the congress's honorary vice president. This housing congress involved many of the same men who organized the Congress on Industrial Accidents, also convened for the first time in 1889, and who set up the social economy exhibit showcasing paternalist worker housing projects such as those created by Mulhouse industrialists André Koechlin and Jean Dollfus. Their *cité-ouvrière* system of single-family dwellings made available for purchase by workers through annuity payments became legendary in reform circles. These *cités-ouvrières* were not built directly by industrial firms, but instead they were financed by private building societies, themselves capitalized by local industrialists. The worker housing of Mulhouse was presented by French reformers as a model of social entrepreneurship. In this spirit, Édouard Aynard had created the Société des logements économiques de Lyon, founded in 1886, which was partially financed by the municipality. That same year, M. Picard created the Société des petits logements in Rouen, and Eugène Rostand formed the Société des habitations salubres à bon marché de Marseille. Émile Cheysson and Émile Cacheux's Société des habitations ouvrières de Passy-Auteuil, created in 1882, had built sixty single-family homes with the most advanced hygienic features, including a central sewage connection.

Although the single-family model was generally considered to be impracticable in Paris, reformers retained two of its main features in their subsequent proposals: the need to surround dwellings wherever possible with gardens and courtyards; and the desirability of creating independent building societies to finance housing construction. Reformers surmised that, based on what industrialists had accomplished in cities such as Mulhouse, Lyon, and Rouen, capitalists could achieve similar results by creating limited stock building companies that offered investors a 4 percent yearly interest rate. Such schemes were intended as social philanthropy with a business edge. The creation of these building societies testifies to the prevalent belief among this first generation of liberal republican reformers that the Third Republic's social mission could yet be accomplished by relying on the wellspring of private initiative. This conviction led reformers like Jules Siegfried to turn initially to the nation's economic elites in the belief that they would indeed fulfill their social duty. If more capitalists had not previously expressed an interest in housing construction, Siegfried surmised, it was simply because they had not yet realized how profitable it could be.[13]

When confronted with the realities of reform, however, these same men quickly diversified their strategies. In the aftermath of the 1889 International Congress on Low-Cost Housing, the Société française des habitations à bon marché (hereafter SFHBM) was created in Paris, under the presidency of Jules Siegfried, to pursue even more ambitious efforts. As the future Musée social president Georges Risler later recalled when referring to Siegfried, Cheysson, Picot, Rostand, and Robert: "These great benefactors visited thousands of dwellings and, profoundly disturbed by what they saw, came to the conclusion that in the face of so terrible and so deep-seated an evil, private initiative alone was powerless."[14] The SFHBM therefore decided to seek legislative reform. It wanted the state to release governmental funds—such as those available through savings and deposit banks, worker pensions, or credit institutions—as seed capital for investment in private construction companies designed to build worker housing. Such an investment would constitute a new form of social philanthropy, one in which the government, in cooperation with the private sector, would produce a work of social betterment. This type of collaboration between the private and the public sectors was precisely the type of social welfare policy sought by social liberals.

The SFHBM formed another primary constituent network that led to the creation of the Musée social. Here we encounter yet again the familiar configuration of networking for reform in the parapolitical sphere.

The first meeting of the SFHBM was held in the Siegfried family home on March 1, 1890. All political and religious discussion was forbidden by its by-laws, and the government had granted it the status of a public service association. Forty-three members were present, including a stock cast of characters: the society's two vice presidents, Émile Cheysson and Georges Picot; its treasurer, Charles Robert; its general secretary, Anthony Roulliet; and members Émile Cacheux, Albert Gigot, Dr. Octave du Mesnil, Henry Fleury-Ravarin, Jacques Siegfried (Jules's brother) and Albert Trombert. As Jules Siegfried put it, since they "didn't want to appear to have any commercial interest in housing," members did not contribute substantial amounts to the newly formed society. Instead, they accepted 11 donations of 1,000 francs each; 22 "charter memberships" set at 300 francs each, entitling their donors to lifetime membership in the society; and 184 subscription memberships at 20 francs per year. These men, many of whom had met previously in Le Playist circles, continued to collaborate, "pursing the same goal by taking parallel paths." By 1893 the SFHBM had 386 members and was described in its bulletin as "a phalanx of collaborators and friends." [15]

Although the members of this network projected the image of a very informal group, they in fact had inroads into powerful circles that linked industry, parliament, philanthropy, medicine, and public administration. The SFHBM worked in concert with government agencies, such as the Office du travail, and advisory councils, such as the parliamentary Commission d'assurance et de prévoyance sociales and the Conseil supérieur du travail, both of which examined, modified, and ultimately supported a housing bill introduced before the Chamber of Deputies in 1892 by the newly appointed minister of commerce, Jules Siegfried. This bill ultimately gave rise to the passage of the 1894 law on *habitations à bon marché* (HBM), commonly referred to as the Siegfried housing law, which is the predecessor of the current legislation on French public housing, the *habitations à loyers modérés* (HLM).[16] The SFHBM also received a yearly subsidy from the Ministry of Education, and the count de Chambrun gave the group a 50,000 franc endowment, in recognition for which, he was named an honorary president. The society continued to meet at the Siegfried family home to discuss possible legislative strategies to improve worker housing. As Jules Siegfried wrote to his son in November 1891, "Yesterday we had a very interesting meeting at our home with Picot, Robert, Ravarin, etc.—together we outlined a legislative bill on worker housing that I might introduce in the Chamber. The purpose of the bill would be to facilitate the construction of worker housing by granting fiscal advantages from the state."[17]

Not only did the SFHBM members actively work toward the establishment of the Musée social—heralded by the SFHBM's bulletin as "an open temple to the cult of social science"—but the operating methods and goals of each group were similar: to act as a study bureau and research center as well as a "forum for action and propaganda." To this end, the SFHBM sponsored its own investigations of housing conditions in Paris. Rather than immediately turning to governmental agencies such as the Office du travail, the SFHBM considered itself to be in the vanguard of social research and preferred to rely on its own private network of expertise to perfect a "detailed monographic method" that it could recommend for future governmental studies.[18]

Like the Musée social, the SFHBM intended to act within the public sphere by inspiring a movement of opinion favorable to its goals. Social surveys, in this view, would "shake the public from its state of torpor" and provoke a collective "examination of conscience." Before seeking legislative action, the question of worker housing was widely discussed and publicized in congresses, meetings of *sociétés savantes*, public meetings, and the press. Jules Siegfried frequently lectured on the topic. Appearing at two republican organizations—the Association nationale républicaine and the Société des conférences populaires—he encouraged others to proselytize in a similar vein. He reproduced the text of his speech in pamphlet form and distributed it to the members of both groups. "The goal," Siegfried wrote to his son, "is to spread these lectures throughout the entire French nation, so that they can be read in the smallest villages."[19] In an effort to further popularize housing reform, the SFHBM sponsored design competitions to raise interest among architects in the construction of low-cost housing.

Finally, like the Musée social, the SFHBM intended to have an impact on legislation. Its membership worked for two years to draft the text of the legislative bill that gave rise to the Siegfried housing law of 1894. This legislative success marked a turning point for liberal reformers and altered the way they approached all other social problems. As indicated in the preamble to the bill: "The moment . . . seemed propitious in our country for undertaking the study of practical reforms to be obtained by virtue of the law." Although the bill was framed to stimulate private enterprise in the construction of low-cost housing through tax abatements and other fiscal incentives, it represented a departure from past reform practices because it invoked the principle of public subsidies to finance what was essentially a measure of social welfare.[20] Siegfried's bill further called for the establishment of a Conseil supérieur des habitations à bon marché and departmental committees—local SFHBMs—to promote the construction of worker housing. In order to be successful, the bill counted on the support of elites with a social conscience.

The process by which the Siegfried housing bill became law illustrates the powerful parapolitical configuration of reform activities in fin de siècle France. So successful was their strategy, or so it seemed at the time, that many SFHBM members enthusiastically joined the Musée social in an attempt to apply their skills to the full range of France's social problems. Before turning to the Musée social's work in this area, however, let us briefly examine the language of social reform used to argue in favor of the Siegfried housing law, since it exemplifies the tenor of public argument in late-nineteenth-century reform circles.

Worker Housing: Republican Rhetorics of Reform

Republican discourse on worker housing at the turn of the century was a blend of old and new rhetorics of reform. As Jules Simon proclaimed at a meeting of the SFHBM in 1890: "Whether one's perspective is that of social solidarity or the principles of Christian fraternity, whether one considers the anguishing question of depopulation, or whether one deems it to be in the general interest to improve social conditions as a way of avoiding class struggle and revolution, or even that it is the sentiment of duty that pushes us to work for others, one thing is certain: the question of housing is one of the most crucial ones that our civilization has to resolve."[21] Indeed, a complex discursive weave of old and new referents, combining moralistic overtures with scientific rationales, was used by republican reformers to justify their new directions in social policy.

Although many of the basic tools of social inquiry, such as the firsthand investigations of doctors and social philanthropists, were inherited from earlier in the nineteenth century, the context of housing reform had been transformed not only by economic and demographic changes but also by the advent of the Third Republic and the values the regime stood for. The preamble to the Siegfried housing bill reflected this hybrid rhetoric. An explicit form of public argument, the preamble was crafted by reformers in the SFHBM to justify the Republic's intervention in this area of social welfare. Even a cursory reading of this preamble reveals how the multiple layers of nineteenth-century reform discourse filter through in filigree, from Le Playist social thought to more explicitly republican notions of solidarity. It divulges the diversity of cultural discourses that were brought to bear on republican justifications for social welfare reform in fin de siècle France.

Le Playist overtones resound in the text. The home, for instance, is portrayed as a worthy object of reform since, much more than offering a mere physical structure for comfort and protection from the elements, it also provided an essential component of social cohesion. "A kind of center where traditions are preserved as in a trust, where its members can meet on a daily basis," a home was the place "where permanent bonds between the generations are formed." From a moral perspective, the text warned that insalubrious housing threatened to be "the solvent of family life." [22]

Housing reform would also purportedly help to remedy the old problem of *déracinement*. Home ownership had long been promoted by reformers as an antidote to the uprootedness of industrial workers. Traditionally, in ancien régime society or even throughout most of the nineteenth century, landed property had conferred certain rights on its owners. But to republican reformers such as Siegfried, the ideal of the citizen-landowner also implied moral notions of responsibility, personal investment, and autonomy that were central to the model of civic republicanism they were striving to promote.[23] Despite this long-standing rhetoric, Siegfried still found cause to worry that granting to workers mortgages that were payable by annuity—a practice commonplace in England, where workers were "accustomed to self-help and managing their own affairs"—might in France prove dangerous, given "our yet incomplete apprenticeship of the mores of freedom." He was finally convinced, however, that if a worker could be shown "even the distant possibility" of owning a home, he could be made into a citizen, "useful to himself, to his family, to his country." [24]

Siegfried and his associates at the SFHBM fully expected their legislative bill to beget new home ownership schemes, thereby reinforcing paternal authority within the family. Owning a home, Siegfried argued, turned a worker into "a head of household worthy of the name, that is to say moral and *prévoyant*, [a man who] sinks his roots into the earth and exerts authority over the members of his family." If home ownership were not possible, however, then a garden plot was the next best form of attachment to the land. Gardening his own plot, Siegfried explained, provided a man with "a healthy and fortifying activity"; he "soon forgets the way to the *cabaret*," enjoys his family and his dwelling, "becomes aware of his duties and . . . reconciles himself with society." Owning a garden also conferred well-being and morality on the family. It helped "home industry thrive" by "keeping women at home and bringing a supplemental wage to the family budget." For each of these reasons, Siegfried argued, Parliament should recognize the eminently social value of the proposed housing law.[25]

Social liberals' indecision about the role of the state in social policy was sometimes expressed in terms of gender anxiety. The state was thus portrayed as being in competition with the father, thereby potentially undermining his rightful role. Many reformers argued that the state should refrain from building worker housing or providing guarantees for social protection that would diminish the traditional paternal function. According to Georges Picot, "When the state fulfills a private service by entering into the intimate realm of family life, it absorbs the personality, subjects it, and finally domesticates it. This transformation would usurp the father's role," it would dissolve and break apart the moral force of the family.[26]

Issues of social class were also at the forefront of reformers' concerns. When the Conseil supérieur du travail examined the bill, some of its members, such as Auguste Keufer, protested that *cités-ouvrières* attempted to segregate workers and argued that it was inimical to social solidarity across class lines. The destruction of working-class neighborhoods in Paris, he complained, had been a disaster. Keufer invoked a romanticized vision of a bygone era when members of different social classes intermingled and when "wealthy families lived with workers, next door, or in the same house." Neighborhood residents knew each other's daily lives, he claimed, and wealthy families "realized that workers were honorable people." "There was," he concluded, a greater sense of "social solidarity between these two classes." [27] Jules Simon concurred, adding that neighborhoods, like classrooms, should be mixed: "I am an old school teacher," he explained. "I know that when you do not mix students, you only breed intolerance." Yet other members of the Conseil supérieur du travail were more concerned about civil rights. They opposed any housing scheme in which employers also acted as landlords. This, they warned, was bad for democratic life. Some employer-landlords had already abused their powers by preventing the distribution of specific newspapers within their buildings; the next thing they might do would be to obstruct citizens from exercising their civil right to vote. In this light, housing reform was once again presented as much more than a philanthropic concern for providing basic shelter. It was framed as an inherent social challenge, and its various ramifications for society and the polity were carefully spelled out and weighed by liberal republican reformers.

In his 1885 book Un devoir social et les logements ouvriers, which had a major impact on philanthropic circles, Georges Picot portrayed low-cost housing reform as part of a growing antisocialist arsenal. Of course, not all reformers shared his perspective. As with other reform issues, they generally agreed on the final goal, if not always on the strategies for achieving change. Dr. du Mesnil, for instance, feared that Siegfried's bill would not pass the Senate, where some provisions might be interpreted as an attack on private property and as an inroad for state socialism. When speaking to an audience of socialist workers, du Mesnil asked rhetorically, "Why should Parliament accept to exempt workers from taxes?" "Why use the Caisse des dépôts, the Caisse nationale de retraite, the Caisse d'épargne, the Caisse d'assurance en cas de décès et d'accidents . . . to build worker housing?" [28] Reformers had anticipated each of these questions. By lobbying for the use of public monies as a form of investment in workers' housing, their bill was calling for a substantial shift in state policy. The Senate stalled on the bill, sending it back to committee on June 19, 1894, with instructions to substantially revise the first seven articles. Predictably, senators wanted to know why it was even necessary to adopt a law on such things: Why should the national government get involved? Couldn't special independent committees content themselves with taking up the cause of low-cost housing?

In an article published in the Journal des débats after the Senate's decision to return the bill to committee, Georges Picot vented his outrage at what he labeled a "disdainful rejection" of those who wanted to improve workers' lives and to fight "against the socialist utopias that threaten us." Such frustration is what eventually led Picot to help found the Musée social as an independent agency that would attempt to influence the parliamentary process from the outside. The problems of overcrowding, alcoholism, and tuberculosis, Picot lamented, had not even been acknowledged in the Senate debate. The "humanitarian intent" of the bill had been mentioned by legislators merely to attack it. Picot argued that instead of blindly defending property, capital, employers, and the labor contract, the Senate should help stimulate private initiative and "develop the spirit of association" without which "a democracy remains a spectator to the struggle between the isolated individual and the all-powerful state and is continually tossed between anarchy and despotism." He concluded by echoing the sentiment of many republican reformers in France: "What we lack are public mores: let us educate the citizen" by associating him with plans for his own betterment, "by showing him the way to achieve the progress he desires." [29]

Jules Siegfried, on the other hand, was much less concerned about waging a war against socialist utopias. In fact, at the first public meeting of the SFHBM, held at the Hôtel Continental in Paris, Siegfried had described his intentions, not as charity but, as he put it, as "enlightened philanthropy, or ... *practical socialism*." More than a merely rhetorical statement, Siegfried's reference to "practical socialism" reveals the overarching pragmatism of his approach to social reform. Within both the Musée social and the SFBHM, Siegfried's staunchly pragmatic perspective on the politics of reform defies simple categorization. An adamant free-trader who opposed the Méline tariff, he nevertheless supported an activist role, particularly for local government. His belief in the preeminence of public well-being over the private rights of landlords (as in the case of eminent domain legislation) effectively undergirded all theorizing and organizing of the fledgling *État-providence*, though Siegfried himself remained uncomfortable with the state as the primary motor of change. A moderate republican who rejected Clemenceau's brand of Radicalism, Siegfried nonetheless enthusiastically supported Léon Bourgeois' 1895 cabinet and embraced the concept of republican solidarism. According to Siegfried, Bourgeois professed an open-minded Radicalism; they thus became allies in reform and personal friends. Bourgeois frequented the Siegfried family home for what André Siegfried referred to as his parents' republican *salon* and their "parliamentary dinners." Jules Siegfried was not averse to collaborating with socialists either; nothing in his political principles dictated more than a form of staunch, unfailing support for a democratic and secular republic. He appreciated Bourgeois' intention to create "a democratic progressive party" and to fight "the fear of socialism" by expressing "confidence in the spirit of democracy." His son André recounts that his father would have been perfectly at home in the English Liberal party, but he added, "Whether in his heart he was a conservative or a man 'of the Left,' I would be hard put to say." [30]

Because of his preoccupation with social reform, Siegfried was always closer to the progressive wing of the republican movement, although his positions in favor of free trade and business interests were appreciated by conservatives as well. An early supporter of Dreyfus, Siegfried was reclassified as a "leftist," a label that, according to his son, cost him his seat in the Senate in 1900.[31] A founding member of the Alliance démocratique républicaine, created in May 1901 in response to the constitution of the Radical party, Siegfried's politics gradually shifted again toward the right of the political spectrum to culminate in his 1919 election to Parliament as a member of the *bloc national*'s electoral list. Throughout, he remained a pragmatist. In the words of Nicholas Bullock and James Read, Siegfried's "policy of 'practical socialism' in reform politics may have lacked the rigor of liberal economics or socialist collectivism. But it had a logic which confirmed that social reform was more than simply a rearguard action in the face of the threat from the Left." [32]

Jules Siegfried therefore offers a profile of the changing nature of liberalism in France at the turn of the century. Moreover, he constitutes a key transitional figure in the history of republican social reform, since he bridged two generations of reformers, linking late-nineteenth-century social philanthropists to twentieth-century reform practitioners who were more concerned with efficiency and rational planning than they were with moral reform. Siegfried stands as an example of a public figure who felt strongly that in order to improve the well-being of an urban population, reformers needed to follow a dual approach, combining both hygienic living conditions and systematic urban planning. His personal experiences, moreover, taught him how to pragmatically implement his social vision.

Siegfried's Pragmatism

Born in 1837, Jules Siegfried was raised within the Alsatian industrial community of Mulhouse and inherited many of its values and social traditions. The son of a former cloth tradesman who had married into the Mulhousian industrial aristocracy, Siegfried earned a quick fortune in the cotton textile trade during the early 1860s, following a trip to the United States where he met with Abraham Lincoln and realized that the Civil War had created new opportunities for foreign cotton.[33] Having relocated to the port city of Le Havre for his business interests, Siegfried made that city his political base. Deciding to abandon business for public life, he served first as an assistant to the mayor and then as the mayor of Le Havre from 1878 to 1886. There he earned a national reputation for his innovative municipal policies. From Le Havre, Siegfried went on to enjoy a thirty-six year career in national politics as a deputy, a senator, and, briefly, as the minister of commerce. Lacking the vestments of higher education proved to be both an advantage and a disadvantage for Siegfried in political life.[34] A man of action who did not shy away from promoting controversial social proposals on the floor of the Parliament, he experienced some difficulty articulating his reform vision in national political circles. Much like his public-spirited Alsatian ancestors, he was most at ease within the arena of municipal affairs. From his first steps in public life, Siegfried was a creative outsider whose success in politics was ironically linked to the fact that he was not a prominent figure of any readily identifiable party other than that of "the Republic." [35]

His marriage in 1869 to Julie Puaux reinforced Siegfried's religious sentiment and influenced his decision to devote himself to public life and works of social betterment. The Siegfried family home, first in Le Havre and later in Paris, remained a center for their networking activities until World War I. The Protestant community was frequently invited, including Henri Monod, the director of public assistance, and Sarah Monod, the feminist leader who became the first president of the Conseil national des femmes françaises when it was founded in 1901. Their son André reminds us that their social circles revolved around religion and reform; the literary and artistic world, for instance, "didn't exist for them." Beyond the impact she had on her husband's devotion to the public interest, Julie Siegfried emerged as a significant figure of French bourgeois feminism during the early twentieth century.[36]

Convinced that the strength of cities was necessary to sustain national prosperity, Jules Siegfried, while mayor of Le Havre, directed the municipality to adopt an increasingly activist role and to create educational, public hygiene, and urban development projects. President of the Ligue de l'enseignement's chapter in Le Havre, Siegfried urged the group—contrary to the wishes of national founder Jean Macé, who did not want the league to become political—to draw up a petition in favor of free and compulsory primary schooling. He built a secular primary school in Le Havre as early as 1870, organized adult evening classes, and introduced vocational training schools for boys and girls. Moreover, he founded the first public high school for girls in France (1885).[37]

For Siegfried, education, public health, and housing reform were inextricably linked. His conviction, moreover, was rooted in a personal experience: after a nearly fatal bout with typhoid fever contracted in 1879 through contaminated water and faulty pipes in a recently constructed building, Siegfried's life was saved by one of the earliest successful blood transfusions performed in France. The health of the nation, Siegfried quickly came to believe, was not simply a private affair; it was an eminently public one, often connected to hygienic living conditions. Siegfried was convinced that if an entire block of houses was condemned for being insalubrious, then the municipal administration should be empowered to demolish them and thereby supersede the private interests of property owners. This view was consistent with his overarching philosophy—rooted both in his Alsatian industrial experience and in his social Protestantism—that the general well-being of the community was an essential factor in achieving both material progress and spiritual salvation. Therefore, he insisted that the municipal government's legitimate role included working toward the prevention of contagious illnesses such as typhoid fever. A self-taught hygienist, Siegfried later became a stalwart supporter in Parliament of measures promoting public health.

As mayor of Le Havre, Siegfried demonstrated his early concern with public hygiene. With the assistance of Dr. Gibert—his friend and the physician who had performed his blood transfusion—Siegfried opened Le Havre's Pasteur Hospital (1882) as well as France's first municipal bureau of public hygiene (1878).[38] This bureau became an administrative model in the annals of French public health because it centralized all public health decisions into a single office. However, it remained in operation for only four years. Entrusted with inspecting the sanitation conditions of private dwellings, the bureau was quickly dismantled as soon as Siegfried left municipal office because of pressure from local landlords.

Siegfried also brought in specialists to direct major road work and to plan new streets and urban expansion projects, including a design for the suburbs. In 1885 he hired the renowned sanitary engineer Alfred Durand-Claye to design a new sewage system for Le Havre. Siegfried's idea to introduce a system of city planning was not appreciated in all circles, however, since it seemed to question yet again the sacrosanct principle of private property. On a more idiosyncratic note, Siegfried's interest in public hygiene even extended to the area of diet and nutrition. Although his concern was rather obsessive and, in his son's words, recalled "the minutia of a Bouvard or a Pécuchet," Siegfried collected a vast amount of documentation on the subject of nutrition and hoped to have the city undertake surveys to develop rational menu plans for workers.[39]

Siegfried's accomplishments in the area of public hygiene were quickly noticed on a national level. Upon arriving in Paris in 1887, one of his first acts as a parliamentary deputy was to introduce a bill calling for the reorganization of hygienic services and the creation of a ministry of public health. This bill—which, after many false starts and permutations, ultimately gave rise to France's first public health law in 1902—would have required towns to routinely enforce basic health regulations and mandate municipal inspectors to enter all privately owned buildings to verify sanitation standards. The municipality would also have been granted increased powers not only to inspect but also to exercise eminent domain to repossess unsanitary housing and demolish slums. However, no immediate action was taken on his bill—a fact that is hardly surprising since the Parliament was still unprepared to accept such sweeping measures. The concept of a ministry authorized to intervene in health issues, which were still widely considered to be an exclusively private matter, appeared ridiculous and misplaced to many of his contemporaries.[40] Some even attributed Siegfried's unorthodox devotion to the public interest to the fact that he was merely a provincial deputy who had not yet adopted the more astute mores of the capital's political class. Such judgments, however, did not prevent Siegfried from resubmitting his bill in 1890. In the end, these early frustrations contributed to Siegfried's decision to pursue social reform through the parapolitical sphere, relying primarily not on Parliament but on voluntary associations such as the SFHBM and the Musée social. Siegfried continued along his unwavering path, pursuing housing and public health reforms by backing the 1906 and the 1908 housing laws, both of which assigned a greater role to municipal government in assisting private enterprise to construct low-cost housing.

Finally, however, Siegfried's pragmatism enabled him to gradually come to terms with some of the contradictions or failures of his initial approaches to reform. For one thing, he and his colleagues had to face the hard facts that their reliance on private initiative was simply an insufficient lever with which to accomplish their reform agenda. By the early years of the twentieth century, it had become obvious that the 1894 Siegfried law on low-income housing was not producing the desired results. The bill's promoters had been mistaken to count primarily on private initiative or the burgeoning social consciousness of the bourgeoisie to produce change. On paper, investment in worker housing, although perhaps not extremely lucrative, made good business sense. But the upper classes targeted by the law were simply not interested, since they could get a better return on their investments elsewhere. Industrialists had produced greater results in their paternalist company towns than had the reform-minded bourgeoisie with its paltry accomplishments in urban low-cost housing. Nevertheless, Siegfried and his colleagues in housing reform continued to push for legislation on the right to enforce eminent domain to ease slum clearance.

Although housing—that vital milieu of the family—had been the first target of their hygienic mission to prevent disease and moral destitution, reformers soon transposed the ideal of enforcing sanitary standards from the individual dwelling to the city itself. A catalyst of this movement, the Musée social rallied its networks, personnel, and years of experience for what ultimately proved to be its most ambitious and successful campaign.

A New Campaign for Public Hygiene

Social reformers affiliated with the Musée social were instrumental in launching a new campaign to popularize the goals of hygiene and to bring these concerns to the public eye. In February 1902, when a new comprehensive public health law was passed by the French Parliament, reformers and hygienists throughout the country took heart at this signal that public health had finally become a national priority. Like the 1894 public housing law, the new public health code of 1902 was also known as the Siegfried law in recognition of his sponsorship of the original 1887 bill on which the 1902 legislation was based. This 1902 public health law set uniform hygiene standards for the entire country and, for the first time, authorized public officials to inspect private dwellings for their salubrity. Opponents of the law cried foul, claiming that representatives of Paris would be able to enter their homes at will and open their "most secret drawers" under the pretext of searching for microbes. Others criticized the law for being a legislative trompe l'oeil, since it merely offered the *illusion* of radically improving national health standards. In reality, critics claimed, enforcement of the law had been entrusted to mayors, local health officials, and doctors, a situation that would only perpetuate the political snarls and stasis of the past. Nevertheless, the 1902 law did establish important new hygienic codes and procedures for modern France. It required smallpox vaccinations; the reporting of transmissible disease by doctors, midwives, and health officials; the disinfection of unsanitary buildings and apartments; and the establishment of a public health bureau, under the authority of the mayor, in every commune of more than 2,000 inhabitants. By extending the jurisdiction of public authorities in this way, the 1902 law promised to alter the relationship between personal privacy rights, property, and the state.[41]

Unsatisfied with certain provisions in the 1902 law (such as the lack of an eminent domain clause) and convinced that legislative action alone was insufficient for the successful implementation of any law, reformers at the Musée social once again turned to proselytizing civil society. A series of strategically related initiatives soon followed. In November 1902, the hygienist and engineer Édouard Fuster addressed an audience at the Musée social, summarizing the lessons he had learned from his many trips abroad to study social insurance. Instead of dispersing energy in so many single-issue groups, Fuster urged French public health associations to consolidate their forces into a single, powerful federation "to combat tuberculosis, alcoholism, [and] the insalubrity of dwellings." One large, integrated public health federation, he believed, would incarnate the hygienist conviction that all social problems, as well as their solutions, were interconnected.[42]

The timing of Fuster's announcement was critical. Speaking just two days before the official founding of the Fédération nationale de la mutualité française at the Musée social, Fuster intimated that the goal of improved public health would be more attainable if backed by the forces of French mutualism. A national federation of public health associations would provide the leadership, while the three million mutualists of France would supply the foot soldiers to spread the word and educate its members about the dangers of alcoholism, tuberculosis, and unhealthful housing, particularly as they affected the working-class family. If mutualists and hygienists joined forces, they could perhaps spark a grassroots movement to combat these scourges and improve the conditions of public health in France.[43]

Fuster's call to action was seconded by another innovator in the area of public hygiene: Georges Benoît-Lévy, who, in 1903, created the Association française des cités-jardins to promote new ideas in urban reform and town planning. The Musée social subsidized two study missions for Benoît-Lévy to go to England and the United States to report on the garden-city movements in those countries. Self-sufficient communities designed for single-family dwellings, garden cities offered a new approach to the containment of urban growth and were popularized in England, France, and the United States by the writings of Sir Ebenezer Howard. Influenced by utopian socialist thinkers such as André Godin, Howard's urban ideal was a small town, "surrounded by immense fields and forests belonging to the community where no construction would ever be permitted." Garden cities were conceived of as countercities; in response to chaotic urban development, they would be situated in pleasurable environments, enveloped by nature. A similar conception of cities surrounded by a "hygienic strip" of greenery inspired Musée social member Dr. Albert Calmette to propose, in 1903, that all French cities currently surrounded by military fortification walls dismantle them and reserve the space for parks, public health facilities, workers' gardens, and the general enjoyment of impoverished families.[44]

From social hygiene to garden cities, the emphasis of social reform had shifted: banished from the workplace, reformers had first turned to housing, then to the prevention of contagious illness, and finally to the city itself as a primary site of reform activities. Thereafter, they concentrated on the larger issues of public health, parks, town planning, zoning, the role of municipalities, and public architecture. They would eventually attempt to reform the structures of government itself. These new approaches to social and urban reform set the tone for the Musée's agenda in public hygiene until at least 1919, when the first French law on urban planning—the Cornudet law, the text of which had been drafted mainly within the sections of the Musée social—was approved by the Chamber of Deputies.

The Alliance d'hygiène sociale

Several important players at the Musée social heeded Édouard Fuster's summons and, in June 1904, helped found the Alliance d'hygiène sociale, a coalition of French public health groups intended to mobilize "all the branches, federations, [and] forces of social hygiene."[45] The Alliance d'hygiène borrowed the tentacular network model of voluntary associations linked together in local and regional federations. Like the Musée social, it was "a laboratory of ideas, a forum for propaganda, an instrument of organization." The familiar array of groups and men were there, including Mabilleau's Fédération nationale de la mutualité française (FNMF); Siegfried's Société française des habitations à bon marché; Gide's Association des cités-jardins, and Bourgeois's Association centrale française contre la tuberculose and his Association française pour la lutte contre le chomage. These voluntary associations coordinated their activities through educational channels, mutual aid societies, and the promotion of legislation on public health and housing. According to Siegfried, the Alliance d'hygiène provoked public awareness "of the great problems of existence in modern society, which are ever more dense, more complex and more alienated from nature."[46]

Following in the footsteps of the group's first president, Jean Casimir-

Périer, Léon Bourgeois headed the Alliance d'hygiène in 1907 and remained there until 1925 when he was replaced by Musée social president Georges Risler. Édouard Fuster and Eugène Montet were two of the alliance's first secretaries-general, and its vice presidents were Jules Siegfried and Léopold Mabilleau. Due both to shared personnel and interests, the Alliance d'hygiène—once referred to as "the strong arm of the Musée social"—and the Musée remained closely aligned throughout their existence. Both groups targeted issues of public health, urban life, the environment, and sanitary and affordable housing.[47]

But the Alliance d'hygiène had a particularly difficult task. The wide reach of its membership meant that the group navigated the choppy waters that separated charities—often Catholic associations under siege by the anticlerical republic—from staunchly secular groups such as the Ligue de l'enseignement. As Lion Murard and Patrick Zylberman have described it, the Alliance d'hygiène sought to win over the Catholic ladies who knitted and drank tea during their "Wednesdays of the Poor" without alienating the secular philanthropists, mutualists, doctors, and Radical freemasons who were also devoted to the cause of social hygiene. The Alliance d'hygiène, like the Musée social before it, cut across traditional political divisions—a particularly delicate feat in the wake of the Dreyfus Affair—to proclaim its cause of improving social hygiene as being above politics and in the public interest. With its message of prevention, the Alliance d'hygiène hoped to mobilize civil society but also to incite the government to adopt measures that would prevent the spread of illness rather than simply providing assistance once the harm had already been done.[48]

Instead of relying on public assistance, which was the dominant tendency in legislative circles, the Alliance d'hygiène promoted private initiative, voluntary insurance, and a decentralized structure for providing public health services. On these points, they were in line with the FNMF and the Musée social. Such an approach enabled the Alliance d'hygiène to attract both Catholic philanthropists who "were used to swimming against the tide" of the Radical republic, and middle-class mutualists and doctors who hoped for a liberal solution to the social question. The Musée social continued to support the Alliance d'hygiène sociale and, as had been the case of the FNMF, even invited the group to move its headquarters to its building at number five rue Las Cases in 1909 once its funding sources began to falter.[49]

Figure 12. Congress of Social Hygiene under the
presidency of Léon Bourgeois. Meeting Room, Musée social,
n.d. RV 923.041. Collection Roger-Viollet, Paris.

Léon Bourgeois and Jules Siegfried regularly joined forces within the
Alliance d'hygiène's annual congresses to publicly argue the solidarist
position as a justification for social legislation. Although one was a Radical and the other a moderate republican, their ideas of social policy were
nearly identical. Earlier, in his philosophical and social treatise *Solidarité*,
first published in serial form in 1895, Bourgeois proposed solidarism as
a rationale for social legislation: "Men live in society," he claimed. "Isolated man does not exist." As a consequence of this state of affairs, "an exchange of services is necessarily established between each man and every
other member of society." It is this exchange of services, he continued,
that constitutes "the quasi-contract of association linking all men" and
that is "the legitimate objective of social law."[50]

When Bourgeois had the opportunity to speak in public, promoting the
causes of public hygiene—whether concerning the prevention of tuberculosis, alcoholism, infant mortality, or the improvement of housing, diet,
or nutrition—he consistently linked the ideals of solidarity and social duty
to the state's obligation to engage in *prévoyance*. The state, he argued, must
"fight and prevent those ills for which the individual is not responsible,"
those ills that precede him and surround him. "Prevention, not public as-

The Modernity of Hygiene ~ 249

sistance," Bourgeois claimed, was the "directing principle of social hygiene." Siegfried echoed this approach, affirming that public assistance was the solution of the past, while prevention was "that of the future." When they campaigned for social legislation, both Bourgeois and Siegfried concurred that laws were simply not enough: "Individual initiative remained the true motor of all progress, the most reliable manifestation of what can be called 'the social instinct.' "[51]

The Musée social's Section on Urban and Rural Hygiene

With the Alliance d'hygiène sociale and the FNMF poised to organize campaigns in favor of public health and social insurance, the Musée social turned its attention to issues of urban development. On January 5, 1907, Jules Siegfried announced to the board of directors that, "in light of its interests," he considered "the Musée social qualified to initiate—along with the Alliance d'hygiène sociale, the Société française des habitations à bon marché, and the Société d'art populaire—a movement of public opinion" to promote the cause of *espaces libres* or *espaces verts*, those green, open-air spaces that provide cities with increased air and light in conformity with the standards of public health. Other Musée members quickly rallied to Siegfried's side. Georges Benoît-Lévy's interest in the garden-city movement made him a natural ally. Siegfried further hoped that such a movement of public opinion to protect park space would lead to widespread support for mandatory expansion plans for all French cities. Urban planning, he argued, would help avoid the public health problems that inevitably resulted when urban areas expanded in chaotic, haphazard fashion. It is within this context of a new urban thinking—that of joining public health concerns with a conservationist impulse to protect green spaces and promote urban planning—that the Musée social created its new urban and rural hygiene section (hereafter, hygiene section) with Siegfried as its president and Benoît-Lévy as its secretary.[52]

Since the beginning of the century, the interests and objectives of the Musée social had clearly evolved. The institution was much less a quiet think tank relegated to the margins of public life and devoted primarily to the study of social problems; it had become much more action oriented, developing its role as an agitator of public opinion. The new hygiene section met for the first time in January 1908 "with an eye to public action

Figure 13. Soccer being played along the Paris fortification walls
around 1900. RV 618.840. Collection Roger-Viollet, Paris.

and propaganda."[53] From the outset, the group discussed strategies for
the implementation of its two main goals: that French cities adopt rational methods of urban planning, and that public hygiene be a main feature
of any proposal for the redevelopment of the military fortification zone
surrounding Paris.

These military fortifications — or *les fortifs*, as they were referred to in
popular culture — essentially comprised a wall of masonry defenses and
bastions that surrounded the city (see figure 14). Forming a 35-kilometer
ring around Paris of 130 to 135 meters in width, the fortifications also included a military firing zone at least twice that wide, where, at least theoretically, all construction was prohibited. In reality, *la zone*, as this area was
also called, was a wasteland notorious for its ramshackle shanty towns inhabited by poor workers. Make-shift manufacturing shops were also set
up in or along its periphery. By 1926 the population of *la zone* was estimated
at 42,000 persons. This undeveloped area was sometimes depicted in quite
a different light by the more picturesque portrayals of popular song or
film, as a remnant of the countryside within the city. As one bourgeois
contemporary remarked, *les fortifs* were "the countryside of the misfortunate," and "the vacation spot of the poor," since they created the illusion
of being far from Paris.[54]

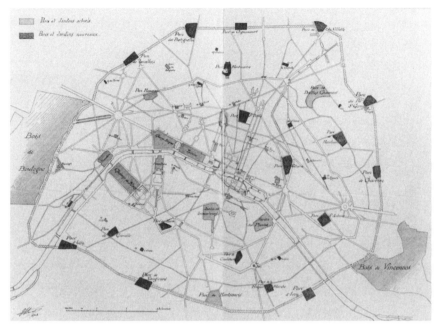

Figure 14. Eugène Hénard's plan for the creation of
parks and gardens in Paris. From his *Études sur la transformation
de Paris*, 1903. CEDIAS-Musée social, Paris.

Also referred to as the "Thiers fortifications," since they had been built
by Adolphe Thiers in the 1840s, this line of military defense walls served
to delineate the new post-Haussmannian boundaries of the city. Since
the nature of warfare had changed, however, the walls were no longer
needed as a defensive barrier, and discussions concerning their removal
were increasingly the focus of Paris municipal council meetings. These
discussions were highly charged since the eventual declassification of this
stretch of land from military to civilian use, and its transferal or sale from
the state to the city represented an opportunity for municipal real estate
development unlike any that was likely to occur again in the twentieth
century.

Defense of the Bois de Boulogne

Already in 1900, when plans to parcel off a portion of the military fortification zone along the periphery of the Bois de Boulogne were first made pub-

lic, adamant cries of protest were heard from sports enthusiasts, urban beautification advocates, historical preservationists, and hygienists interested in protecting open spaces in the capital. The Parisian press, notably the *Figaro*, denounced "the amputation of the Bois de Boulogne," and a defense committee was formed at the suggestion of Pierre de Coubertin. As Marie Charvet has argued, rather than focusing on questions of hygiene, however, these protest articles highlighted elitist concerns such as the need to defend a standard of living among the academicians, doctors, and writers of the posh sixteenth arrondissement that bordered directly on the Bois de Boulogne. The articles also revealed an elite anxiety concerning "the consequences of progress," suggesting that urban growth was perhaps "not synonymous with the advancement of civilization." [55]

The efforts of the committee to defend the Bois de Boulogne were seconded by other recently formed groups such as the Société pour la protection des paysages de France (founded in 1901 by Radical deputy, regionalist, and preservationist Charles Beauquier) and the Société pour le nouveau Paris (founded by modernist architect Franz Jourdain). Together they mounted campaign after campaign protesting what they deemed to be the Paris municipal council's incompetence in managing public spaces. Public health groups such as La Fédération des ligues contre la tuberculose and La ligue anti-alcoolique, and publications such as *La Presse medicale* and *Le Journal de auto* also joined this effort.[56] The campaign to defend the Bois de Boulogne animated a first wave of public opinion in support of preserving open spaces and paved the way for the intervention of reformers at the Musée social into the debate on the redevelopment of the fortification zone.

Redeveloping the Fortification Zone

Given this general context, it soon became obvious that not only did the Musée social's hygiene section have a plan for the redevelopment of the fortification zone, but its creation had been timed to coincide precisely with the 1908 Paris municipal elections. Among the new members of the hygiene section was the architect Eugène Hénard, an employee of the Paris municipal bureau of public works, who furnished the Musée social with its plan of action. Although relatively unknown at the time, Hénard quickly earned international stature as an urbanist for his "metropolitan visions," a series of studies, published between 1903 and 1908, for the extension of the city of Paris. One of these studies concerned the fortified zone and formed the basis of the hygiene section's subsequent proposals. Hénard's plan for the future of Paris featured the creation of nine large public parks and thirteen playing fields along the urban periphery as well as a boulevard—la grande Ceinture—which would encircle the city (see figure 14). Between Haussmann and Le Corbusier, only Eugène Hénard presented such a variety of proposals for the modernization of the capital, a combination of social objectives and urbanistic thought that inaugurated what has become known as "the French school of urbanism." [57]

Membership in the Hygiene Section

The composition of the hygiene section—which by 1911 included ninety-eight members, or nearly a third of the total membership of the Musée social—represented a departure from standard reformist practice at the Musée. Even a cursory glance at the list of members reveals that this was a strategically formed group. In addition to Hénard, the Musée's hygiene section participants combined professional expertise with a commitment to public service as members of national or local health advisory committees, municipal politicians, or members of the city administration.[58] Their networks also linked public health professionals and architects who had an interest in civic architecture and public hygiene with elected officials in local and national government and members of the public administration. Paris municipal councilors Fortuné d'Andigné, Paul Escudier, and Ambroise Rendu were key figures who ensured that the Musée social's proposals had spokesmen directly within the city council. Over the years, the Musée social had also benefited from the participation of Henri Hébrard de Villeneuve, a member of the Conseil d'État, who, in this case, argued for the interests of public hygiene before this conservative judicial body. Such varied and wide-reaching networks enabled the Musée's hygiene section to quickly acquire national visibility and promote concepts of city planning that eventually had an impact upon legislation. Never before in France had such a mixed group of experts combined efforts to promote public hygiene, urban development, and beautification projects. They employed a discourse of expertise in city planning that served to legitimize their intervention in municipal and national politics.

The form taken by the Musée's action in urban hygiene was largely a function of the composition of its membership. The section's six physician members included Louis Cruveilhier of the Pasteur Institute; Émile Roux, the dean of the Faculty of Medicine; and Maurice Letulle, who was also a member of the Public Hygiene Council for the Department of the Seine. The engineer, Georges Bechmann, was the honorary president of the water sanitation services of the city of Paris. Paul Juillerat, as a city official responsible for tracking the spread of tuberculosis, had fought for years to enforce the right of eminent domain over insalubrious housing and to develop a new building code that would rigorously enforce public health standards.

Among the architects in the section, Alfred Agache, Henri Prost, Robert de Souza, and Léon Jaussely all developed national and international reputations for their work in urban design. Louis Bonnier, a specialist in civic architecture, was also the director of architectural services and public works for the city of Paris. Because of his position within the city administration, Bonnier had direct ties to the prefect of Paris and served as a conduit for the flow of ideas developed within the hygiene section into Parisian governmental planning circles. Urban and rural preservationists also participated in the section: Fernand Cros-Mayrevieille and Charles Beauquier of the Société pour la protection des paysages de France combined their interests in environmental conservation with the promotion of national heritage (patrimoine). The 1906 Beauquier law created departmental committees to designate and preserve national landmarks and, in the words of the bill's sponsor, "consecrated the right of eminent domain for reasons of public beauty." The concerns of preservationists such as Beauquier for regional culture, rural conservation, and urban development amounted to a form of "national hygiene," a curious blend of historical and modern concerns with distinctly nationalist overtones.[59]

Hygienic Strategies

Since the general concept of urban planning was still embryonic in France when the Musée social's hygiene section adopted Eugène Hénard as its principal urban visionary, its members rallied around only one specific part of his overall plan: the preservation of public park space along the Paris periphery.[60] The creation of public parks, playing fields, and espaces *verts* became the hygiene section's battle cry during the municipal elections of 1908 as it attempted to influence candidates and stir up a movement of public opinion in its favor. Hénard's plan, reformers argued, represented the public good since it promoted the "superior interests of public hygiene." Any proposal that would turn over the fortified zone to private real estate speculators, they claimed, should be rejected. Siegfried and Rendu even called on the state to directly concede the land to the city, sacrificing any profit it might make since, as they argued, "it is in the national interest to make Paris the most beautiful city in the world." This element of the proposal was ultimately eliminated, however, since members of the hygiene section realized it would never pass in Parliament, where a majority of deputies and senators, who were from rural areas and provincial cities, were not well disposed toward granting fiscal advantages to the capital. Adopting a more moderate position, Juillerat and Rendu called for subjecting portions of the declassified military zone to a public use clause, thereby guaranteeing that those portions be reserved for hygienic purposes by institutions operating in the public interest such as hospitals, cemeteries, and parks.[61]

On April 2, 1908, the Musée social's hygiene section formally adopted as its own Hénard's plan for the redevelopment of the fortification zone. Submitted immediately by Rendu to the Paris municipal council, this proposal stated that it was in "the interest of public health" and "the imperious duty [of the state] not to sacrifice the health and prosperity of the capital to ephemeral financial needs." Portions of the proposal, including drawings of the proposed parks, were incorporated into a series of twelve thousand electoral posters that were put up in the Paris Métro and throughout the city in anticipation of the 1908 elections (see figure 15). Sponsored by the Musée social, the Alliance d'hygiène sociale, the Association des cités-jardins, and the Touring-Club de France, these posters were designed to place the Musée's proposal into public view and directly into the hands of all candidates, regardless of their political affiliation. To spread the good word, the Musée enlisted volunteers to attend public election meetings and "plead the cause of *espaces libres*." The Musée even sponsored an impromptu training session during which Hénard himself coached young conservationists on how to intervene in these meetings and what to say. The hygiene section did not seek to advance its plan

Figure 15. Poster designed by the Musée social's
urban and rural hygiene section for the Paris municipal
elections of 1908. CEDIAS-Musée social, Paris.

through endorsements by particular candidates, but instead attempted to bring its ideas directly to the people. Jules Siegfried later indicated that "the masses who avidly read the proposals adopted them as their own." [62]

In an electoral year when the left was still a dominant presence in municipal politics, Siegfried claimed proudly that the socialist candidates stamped the Musée social's posters with their own slogans in order to garner support in working-class neighborhoods.[63] Indeed, the Socialist Party's Fédération de la Seine had come out in support of preserving green spaces within the capital. Albert Thomas expressed the socialist position in a series of articles on the subject published in L'Humanité: "A revolutionary proletariat," he claimed, "will not be formed within infected dwellings and cities lacking air." "The artisans of the first Revolution descended from the faubourgs, where one could breathe." "We want the country to become a little more city-like and the city a little more country-like." [64]

The Musée heightened its propaganda efforts by organizing a public meeting at the Sorbonne in June 1908 devoted to "Les Espaces libres à Paris." Before an audience of nearly 1,500 people, the keynote speaker, liberal deputy and former minister Alexandre Ribot, explained that France had not done enough to promote public hygiene. It was true, he claimed, that thanks to the new housing laws of 1906 and 1908 the state was beginning "to understand its social duty in a new way." But there was much yet to accomplish. Citing the problem of establishing the right of eminent domain for reasons of public health and the lobby of propertied interests that continued to block its application, Ribot described the current situation as contrary to the general interest of preserving public health. A report by Dr. Landouzy listed 5,200 tuberculosis-infected dwellings in Paris for the year 1907, only fourteen of which had been demolished for public health reasons. It was time, Ribot resolved, to resurrect Jules Siegfried's old parliamentary bill on the right of eminent domain that would allow the state to repossess dangerous and unhealthy housing. "I might be accused of socialism," he conceded, "but what we are doing here is good socialism." "Instead of pushing towards class division and civil warfare," we are simply trying to rally "good French men who understand their social roles." With regard to the fortifications, he proclaimed that the state should not act as a real estate speculator. It was "in the national interest," he argued, for the state to turn over the land to the city at a reasonable cost. If France were to maintain "its force and its virility," then all

Frenchmen, regardless of politics, should join forces and fight the enemies of "hatred, alcohol, and tuberculosis." "We should all unite in this task," Ribot concluded, "leaving aside our passions, our hatred, our bitterness . . . to accomplish what is above all a patriotic and national task." The two salient characteristics of this speech—the appeal to national sentiment and the pretense of rising above politics—were recurrent themes of hygienist discourse before World War I.[65]

The next speaker, the lawyer Henri Robert, returned to ecologist and preservationist concerns. In agreement with the Société des amis des arbres, he declared that trees also needed protection from abuse. Robert lamented that during the 1900 Universal Exposition, the main public attraction at the colonial exhibit had been to watch elephants uproot trees with their trunks in the Bois de Boulogne. Public parks and gardens, he maintained, were to be respected. The fortification zone should be developed, but public park space must also be preserved; if not for ourselves, he said to his largely bourgeois audience, then for the "courageous working people," for whom the creation of these parks would constitute "a social service" and a means of "fighting alcoholism." The creation of public parks, he argued, constituted "true socialism," since everyone in a park is equally free to engage in leisure activities and relaxation. Public parks embodied an active, practical form of socialism "that helps, consoles and sustains"; they did not promote that deleterious kind of socialism that merely "cradles the people with its never-ending lullaby of human misery."[66]

The hygienists at the Musée social did not limit their arguments to this type of direct appeal to the public. In 1909 Jules Siegfried introduced the Musée's text as a bill to the Chamber of Deputies, presented in the name of "the population of Paris." Drafted within the Musée's hygiene section, the bill's preamble claimed that public opinion was against the idea of dividing up the fortified zone and selling it off in lots to real estate speculators. It further suggested that if the supporters of the bill had taken their proposals to the streets earlier, the Paris municipal council would never have been able to relinquish half of the Champs de Mars and the Temple marketplace to private developers without provoking a general uproar. In the intervening months, and thanks in large part, the text suggests, to the Musée social's efforts during the 1908 electoral campaign, "public spirit" with regard to this issue in the Paris region had been transformed. Now everyone understood that the fortified zone constituted "our last reserve of clean air" and that no one, at any price, should "allow that land to be occupied by seven-story buildings that resemble barracks." [67]

But as Marie Charvet has pointed out, the Paris municipal councilors were eager to wrest these urban reform issues away from the self-proclaimed experts at the Musée social and reclaim them as their own. They did not show up for the public meeting at the Sorbonne, and from that point on, they built a successful momentum to regain control of plans to develop the fortified zone. That being said, the meeting at the Sorbonne certainly revived debate within the council on the future of the fortifications. In December 1908, nationalist councilor Louis Dausset presented his own development proposal, which eventually carried the day. Dausset's project stipulated that the city purchase the fortified zone, which would be sold off in parcels and developed; that two circular boulevards be built; and that the remaining surface of the military zone be divided into a series of parks. An agreement to this effect was signed between the city and the state in 1912. Parliamentary ratification was granted only in 1919, at which time the demolition of the fortified walls began. In the end, the Paris municipal council reasserted its dominion over issues of urban space and carefully rejected the efforts of reformers who claimed competence in this domain. If the passage of Dausset's plan represented a failure for the Musée social, it was only a partial failure, however. First, the preservation of park space was incorporated into the Dausset plan, which, after several raucous meetings, finally received the Musée social's endorsement. Second, redevelopment of the fortified zone had constituted only one part of the Musée reformers' overarching goal, which was to achieve rationally planned urban development in the major cities of France.[68]

Public Parks and a Reinvigorated Nation

It is important to point out that despite the intense political haggling over the redevelopment of the fortification zone, a pervasive nationalist discourse—expressed in terms of "national hygiene"—ran as a common thread through all prewar discussion on public parks, playing fields, and physical exercise. The Musée social's first proposal, sent to the Paris municipal council in 1908, argued, for instance, that although the population of Paris had tripled since 1855, the French government had done very little to proportionately expand the capital's green spaces. Statistics could prove French "inferiority" in this realm, particularly in comparison to London and Berlin. How could the falling birthrate ever be reversed if hygienic living conditions did not exist in the country's premier city? An appeal to republican pride further reinforced this nationalistic argument: the monarchies of the past had done far more, the text proclaimed, than had the Republic to preserve the natural environment—which was, after all, a form of national heritage.

The Musée social had collected information on the preservation of *espaces verts* from its foreign correspondents such as William Willoughby, who sent a long report on the American national parks, urban beautification, and local playground associations. Musée hygienists were in awe of the combination of national interest and civic pride represented by American and British efforts to create national and local public parks and playgrounds. Nor is it surprising that so many of them admired Theodore Roosevelt for promoting the image of sportsman *qua* national patriot. In 1910, Musée social member Paul de Rousiers even prefaced the translation of Roosevelt's *American Ideals* into French. References to another of Roosevelt's essays, *The Strenuous Life*—referred to as "*la vie intense*"—were recurrent in the discourse of French cultural nationalism before World War I.[69] In a similar vein, Siegfried's legislative bill petitioned French deputies to promote outdoor activities and physical exercise. They could accomplish their goal, he claimed, by supporting efforts to preserve green spaces and to create public playgrounds and parks along the periphery of the nation's capital. Siegfried's bill announced, moreover, that the national value of physical exercise had been first recognized officially by the Third Republic when, in 1877, Jules Ferry and Paul Bert introduced the need for outdoor recreation and sport—based on the English model—in their reform proposals for French primary schools.

The discursive strategies of those who promoted the preservation of green spaces further revealed an anxiety concerning France's status as an imperial power. In 1910 another former Alsatian businessman and industrialist, Siegfried's successor to the presidency of the hygiene section, Georges Risler, extolled the benefits of physical exercise for young men by quoting former British prime minister Benjamin Disraeli: "A people that does not play will always be defeated by a people that plays." In addition to the obvious reference to physical exercise, the type of play in question here may also be understood as the race for imperial domination over England. Underlying this national and imperial construction of play—and by extension of playgrounds as training fields—was Risler's gendered proposition that France needed to champion a new, more vigorous type of manhood in order to produce a strong nation. If so many French men reached adulthood without having learned to enjoy sports and physical exercise, Risler surmised, this was the fault of the country's educational system, which encouraged young male students of bourgeois origin to use their recreational time to discuss "the most serious subjects of philosophy or politics" but reprimanded them for playing games of leap-frog or sliding on the ice, activities that were considered dangerous and "particularly ill-suited for intellectuals" and young men of their social condition. The French educational style revered "sonorous words" and rhetoric and all but ignored physical exercise. Such an educational system may have produced "the great number of our admirable orators of whom our nation is so proud," but it also caused in France "a dearth of practical-minded men," and it spawned entire generations that were incapable of turning "a rousing speech into a practical result." "It is not with the ephemeral values espoused by classical French education," Risler intoned, "that we create explorers and colonizers!" [70]

Others couched their support for green spaces, sports, and playgrounds in nationalistic terms that stressed eugenics, the preservation of the French "race," and the reversal of the falling birthrate, which was often attributed to physical degeneration.[71] In each instance, public hygiene and the concept of national interest were conflated into a pseudobiological discourse of physical revival that could barely disguise other prevalent anxieties in prewar France concerning gender identities and the uncertain reaches of imperial rule.

These multiple layers of discourse permeated the hygienist impetus for reform in prewar France. Hygienists had first called for the demolition of insalubrious housing, then for urban reform based on the principles of public health, such as revising the building code to create wider streets and to protect space between buildings for adequate sunlight, air, and ventilation. Their campaign to preserve green spaces, or the "lungs of Paris," as they were sometimes called, next led them to a broader conception of reform, one that championed the rational city, developed according to a master plan for urban development.[72]

Already in his 1909 bill submitted to Parliament, Jules Siegfried had called for the establishment of a planning commission for the Paris metropolitan region that would be entrusted with overseeing the comprehensive urban development of the Paris region. It would not be a political body, but one comprised of "members who offered very special guarantees of competence and experience," professional experts and technicians in urban development who had demonstrated their concern, not for the narrow concerns of partisan politics, but for the higher public interest. Only such experts would purportedly know "how to ascertain the common interests of Paris and its suburbs; to organize and beautify both areas; to improve roadways leading to and from the city . . . reducing the distances between city and suburb." [73]

Georges Risler continued to push for the establishment of a central urban planning commission for Paris, particularly since France appeared to be in danger of falling behind England, which had already adopted a town planning act in 1910. He agreed with Siegfried that such a planning commission should be composed of experts. But Risler argued the point to new heights. Rather than relying on "elected bodies," a planning commission, he felt, should exist almost entirely outside of government and should be composed of men who were "particularly competent in these matters." Neither the public administration nor elected political officials had been able to establish "a comprehensive plan conceived only in the general interest," since the first was subjected to heavy bureaucratic regulations and the latter was constrained by the politics of electoral districting and the electoral mandate itself. These institutions of government, Risler claimed, constituted "the major obstacle to the adoption of an overall vision . . . conceived in the general interest." [74] Inverting the republican assumptions that had given scope and authority to earlier reform impulses, Risler suggested that the mechanisms of parliamentary democracy were themselves blocking reform. Since they had proved to be inefficient, he implied, they should simply be bypassed. In the area of urban reform, this meant that the quickest way to achieve success was to work through channels leading directly to the Conseil d'État, which determined the building code, and the prefect of police, who oversaw public works. Little by little, as the sociologist Christian Topalov has argued, social problems "were depoliticized and sheltered from the artificial and dangerous controversies of the democratic process." It is also, in large part, for this reason that the architect Henri Prost—on the recommendation of Risler and other members of the Musée's hygiene section—enthusiastically went to work for the Maréchal Lyautey in Morocco, where the road leading to comprehensive town planning and urban development was cleared by imperial decree. When the hexagone proved to be too constraining, the colonial laboratory allowed for ample experimentation by combining what Gwendolyn Wright has termed "the dominant authority of colonialism and . . . the more subtle control of professional expertise."[75]

In 1911 the city of Paris did create a Commission d'extension de Paris, composed of municipal councilors, urbanists, and members of the city administration. Its report, published in 1913, was authored by Marcel Poëte; and although it contained many of the provisions that had been discussed over the course of five years at the Musée social, progress on its recommendations remained stalemated. It was not until the outbreak of World War I that some headway was made in urban planning at a time when, given the exigencies of wartime, the French state greatly expanded its role in the economy and in the realm of public welfare. Soon after the early and extensive German bombing campaigns that left the cities of Lille, Arras, and Reims in ruins, the Musée social's hygiene section presented a new proposal directly to the premier requiring "extension plans for the development of those cities destroyed by the enemy." "This painful situation of devastation," Risler later recalled, provided "an opportunity to bring victory to the ideas that had germinated in the hygiene section and had been the basis of a renaissance of urbanism." The Musée's proposal called for setting up commissions appointed by the police prefect that included technical experts or "men having proven their attachment to the city by their specialized studies." No city, their plan stipulated, should receive funds allocated for national disasters, or solidarity funds for reconstruction, until it presented a "rational and serious extension plan." The hygiene section even proposed sending its own members to the devastated cities to draw up an initial series of recommendations for reconstruction. As deputy Paul Doumer remarked, "It is a new country that needs to be rebuilt."[76]

In 1915 the deputy Cornudet introduced yet another bill requiring comprehensive urban plans for every city of more than 10,000 inhabitants. This time the bill passed the scrutiny of Parliament, though not until after the war had ended, in March 1919. The war reconstruction effort finally gave the proposal the necessary political impetus for passage. Cornudet later acknowledged that his bill had been largely drafted within the hygiene section of the Musée social. He explained, moreover, that he had been "a student of the Musée social" ever since his interest in urban reform was piqued while seated in the audience of the Musée's 1908 public meeting at the Sorbonne in defense of green spaces and the redevelopment of the fortified zone.[77] Although the city's legal acquisition of the fortifications in 1919 coincided with the Chamber's vote on France's first national city planning law, even this did not ensure that the proposals would be enacted.

The demolition of the fortifications, begun in 1919, was completed only in 1932; and no comprehensive plan was developed for this area. Instead, it was sold off in parcels, largely turned over to private developers, and served as the site for today's peripheral highway encircling the city. As Norma Evenson has argued, "What many had anticipated as a well-planned residential district, embodying abundant greenery and reflecting enlightened design concepts, had evolved into a dense wall of mediocrity encircling the city."[78] Instead of a "radiant city," Le Corbusier deplored how real estate speculation had nearly destroyed the aesthetic environment of Paris. "Profit prevailed," he lamented. "Nothing, absolutely nothing was done in the public interest. . . . This was a wasted adventure." Le Corbusier's pronouncements, made in 1935, were overly harsh, however, and did not take into account the development of stadiums, playing fields, or the more ambitious undertakings for the expansion of the suburban region such as Henri Sellier's innovative vision for the garden city of Suresnes. In fact, this period marks a crucial turning point in the history of urban thought in France by having introduced into law the concept of urban planning as well as that of concerted regional planning, sixteen years later, with the decree-laws of July 1935. This momentum, which germinated within the hygiene section of the Musée social, was built on a dynamic concern for hygiene, urbanism, planning, and the public interest. During the immediate postwar period, therefore, the collaborative efforts of reformers, urbanists, and public officials produced the new territorial and political entity of the greater Paris region.[79]

Important changes did occur within the urban laboratory of the Musée social and its affiliated organizations. In order to perceive these changes, however, it is necessary to place them within the broader context of reformist strategies since the advent of the Third Republic. Instead of focusing on one specific legislative battle or another, it is helpful to stand back and peer down the longer road that had been followed since the late 1880s. Although some have argued that France exhibited "sheer intransigence to change" with regard to municipal reform and civic improvement, the fact remains that this extraordinary gathering of minds and talents at the Musée social's hygiene section proved to be at least a theoretical testing ground for many of the modern conceptions of urban design and development that would mark the twentieth century.[80] These developments were also a tribute to the preceding years of experience in parapolitical reform groups. The extraparliamentary setting of the Musée's hygiene section allowed it to remain open to the cross-fertilization of ideas from an array of disciplines. Without necessarily having prepared the way—as had been suggested by Georges Risler—for a dismissal of parliamentary processes, the Musée's reformers generally did find fault with an overcentralized state that did not afford sufficient opportunity for input from the individuals comprising civil society. An underlying critique of the centralized French state is apparent in nearly every reform proposal that emanated from the Musée social. Even within the proposal for a commission of urban planning, provisions were made for the participation of private citizens. Once again, a hybrid concept of social reform predominated. These reformers went a long way, moreover, toward justifying an expanded definition of the public interest. Although they did not achieve immediate and satisfying legislative results, they did help change attitudes and even had an impact on legal thinking that advanced the subsequent elaboration of modern French social and urban policies.

Since the days when Jules Siegfried proclaimed worker housing to be the first of all social questions, both the terms of discussion and the actors in the unfolding drama of social policy debate in France had changed radically. The social question too had changed—or at least had been redefined. Since the 1880s, French reformers had gradually stopped seeing the social question as an amalgam, or a condition attributed to industrial society. They broke it down instead into discrete, interrelated social issues, treatable as symptoms of a larger, specifically modern plight.

As Christian Topalov has argued, these issues—alcoholism, tuberculosis, school attendance, apprenticeship, housing, town planning, and unemployment—were themselves defined by historical processes.[81] This new perception of the social question corresponded to equally new practices of intervention and to a change of reformist personnel as well. Instead of the moralistic language of the first generation of liberal republican reformers, which targeted the personal habits and behavior of workers in order to bring about change, the new, more specialized experts of the twentieth century directed their efforts toward the transformation of the physical urban environment. Their efforts, moreover, were no longer aimed primarily at the working class, but were designed instead to improve the lot of every member of society. At least that is how they presented their reforms to the public: in the name of the common good.

By defending the higher interests of society, reformers made a claim for objectivity, saying that they did not represent partisan political groups or social classes; they were experts and purported to be as objective as the science they served.[82] They would soon cultivate the notion and discourse of public service and social work. By speaking in terms of the public interest, moreover, they contributed actively to renegotiating the boundaries between the public and private spheres in modern France. On the other hand, the vigor with which reformers began to defend the public cause can be interpreted as the reverse image of their bourgeois preoccupation with the rituals and boundaries of private life. Seen from this perspective, their insistence on urban planning reflected an attempt to exert control over the slippery frontiers, not only of neighborhoods and cities, but also of social class. In this sense, reform efforts and discourse continued to be intimately linked to the intertwined construction of national, bourgeois, and middle-class identity. The bourgeoisie's gradual appropriation of urban space can be traced from the nineteenth-century preoccupation with building sewage systems and controlling the stench of refuse and human excrement to the twentieth-century utopia of the planned city and suburbs.[83] This was all part of the ongoing renegotiation of public and private space in twentieth-century France that served as a crucial backdrop to the rise of modern social policy.

Of course, the moralistic dimension of reform discourse did not disappear. But the reformers of the early twentieth century were less prone to attribute the causes of destitution, degeneracy, and disease to individual morality or behavior. In a sense, individuals were held to be less directly responsible than ever before for their distress. An individual forced to live in the squalor and unhealthy conditions of urban tenements and slums could do very little to turn a difficult situation around. The empirical studies of the past had revealed the concrete scope of the problem of poverty. By the early twentieth century, new techniques of social inquiry were being developed by urban professionals and used as prognostic devices to justify interventions into the city. Reformers were no longer social philanthropists speaking in defense of the Republic or of the industrial elite's social mission. Now they were doctors, engineers, architects, and civil servants acting as professionals, or at least attempting to establish their identities as such. While pursuing reformist goals, they mounted their own platform of professional interests — although often unarticulated to the public — on the foundations of early city planning. They promoted a language of expertise — reinforced by advances in medicine, statistics, and social science — designed to make themselves indispensable to social progress.[84]

The very notion of progress, moreover, was increasingly defined in technical and material terms. Rarely invoked as an abstract conceptual category to be filled with enlightened notions of reason and republican rights, progress was increasingly measured purely through its physical manifestations — bridges, roads, housing, parks, and the applications of medical science to public hygiene. This emphasis on material and scientific progress was particularly evident in the colonies, where reform experts at the Musée social increasingly turned their attention, as if extending the walls of their social laboratory to include the empire.[85] The multilayered reform discourse of these new professionals — at once moral, empirical, public-spirited, and nationalistic — mirrors the various dimensions of social policy debate in France on the eve of the First World War.

Conclusion

~

France, as it is sometimes suggested, is a country perpetually caught between "l'amour des grandes idées et la réalité des petits arrangements."[1] Such is one way of characterizing the French Republic's search for a renewed social contract during the late nineteenth and early twentieth centuries. Indeed, before World War I, the great republican ideals of social solidarity, the rights of citizenship, and equal treatment before the law, although widely heralded by reformers, did not always provide a sufficient basis for attaining their legislative goals. The reality of *petits arrangements,* as in the case of the greatly compromised 1910 pension law, proved disappointing to nearly everyone involved, from legislators to beneficiaries. In housing, and urban and public health reform, the legislative process had proven to be equally long, drawn-out, and frustrating.

Yet, the prewar debate on social reform in France was also infused with a far-reaching public debate on *les grandes idées.* Weighty philosophical questions concerning the social responsibility of the republican state and the rightful expectations of citizens to receive some form of social protection were discussed at great length, both inside and outside of Parliament, by workers and elites alike. The results of this public debate, although not readily visible in the legislative record, were in fact long-lasting. Here, we have come full circle, to reexamination of the received historiographical wisdom that has typically portrayed the prewar Republic's record in social reform as being "backward."[2] On closer analysis, the achievements of these prewar years appear much more significant than they might from the legislative record alone. Once again we are reminded that the lens through which one looks is also an instrument of measure. By shifting the focus of this study from the Parliament to the parapolitical sphere embodied by the Musée social, the outline of another configuration of the

French welfare state—one characterized not by "backwardness," but by progressivism—becomes readily apparent.

The rise of the French welfare state is undeniably a chronicle of ideals and compromises, both of which warrant our attention. The broad philosophical debate concerning the relationship of the individual to the state and the responsibility of government in the formulation of social policy took on new meaning within the context of the Third Republic. Consequently, the liberal reformers at the Musée social identified their quest for social reform with a certain ideal of the Republic. Although this ideal may have meant different things to different people, the pursuit of social reform in prewar France and the ensuing reformulation of the bond between individuals and the state were consistently framed within the context of republican citizenship. This social mission, moreover, was held to be the Republic's rightful inheritance from the French Revolution.

What did it mean to be a citizen of the Third Republic? Léon Bourgeois proposed the concept of solidarism as the philosophical embodiment of the new relationship of the individual to the state in republican France. Thereafter, the right to receive social protection in the form of pension subsidies, accident insurance, or free medical attention for the indigent was seen as a function of the new set of social responsibilities attributed to the republican state. The identification of social rights and benefits with the ideal of republican citizenship has had lasting effects until the present day.

By the same token, the reality of legislative compromise need not be interpreted as a failure of republican ideals, but rather as the reflection of an ongoing process of negotiation between the state and representatives of civil society. Unlike the pioneering status of Bismarckian Germany's social welfare laws, French social legislation was not initially decreed from on high. As such, France's protracted legislative battles reflect historic tensions between the impulses of a centralized state, an entrenched liberal order, and the demands of a variegated civil society that both resisted and claimed protection from the state. Thus, even the 1910 pension law can be viewed as having established the foundations for a social welfare compromise that would be successfully realized only during the interwar period and beyond. The 1910 law reflected "the social state" of France, in which groups such as the mutualists claimed their legitimate stake in the compromise. In this light, the rise of the French welfare state can be viewed as a process of negotiation whereby high-flown ideals were transformed into concrete realities. Although this process may have initially proved disappointing, it launched a thorough and lasting public debate, and crafted a complex welfare system that was the reflection of the divergent demands of French society.

A language of consensus on the goals of social welfare reform in France was therefore first established along the lines of a republican national identity. At the Musée social, reformers from diverse backgrounds who had pursued the goals of social reform for decades, some of them since the Universal Exhibition of 1889, embodied this search for a renewed republican social contract. In this light, the foundation of the Musée social—during the final years of the nineteenth century and under the semiofficial auspices of the republican government—responded to a social need to maintain national cohesion in a period of rapid social change spurred by an expanding market economy. In the eyes of the first generation of Musée reformers, typified by Jules Siegfried, the defense of the Republic constituted the *clef de voûte* (keystone) that not only held a political system of alliances in place but also served as an idiom, or initial language of exchange, in which to examine and perhaps resolve the social question. This republican idiom made sense to a broad spectrum of individuals from different social classes and walks of life who were thus able to collaborate in a common quest for social reform.

Another source of consensus on social welfare, evident in the history of the Musée social, is the profound questioning of the liberal credo that had long enjoyed official hegemony in France. Transformations in liberal thought occurred particularly during the final decades of the nineteenth century and had considerable impact on the areas of social welfare, public health, and the law. These changes testify, moreover, to the emergence of a new attitude among an important segment of French elites with regard to the state's role in society. The French state adopted a progressively more interventionist role and was accepted as a regulator of social relations. After *Rerum novarum* in 1891, social Catholics gave their assent to the Republic's more active role in social policy and added to the debate their deeply rooted cultural justifications for a protectionist state. Even those Musée members who were closest to the positions of laissez-faire liberalism recognized that it was not realistic to reject the state's newly conceived role of social responsibility. But by the same token, the partisans of this new social liberalism actively sought to maintain and protect the sphere of private initiative, which remained for them the wellspring of a vital society and economy. In the end, the reformers at the Musée social wanted a hybrid state, one that integrated the public and the private sectors, and that associated the freedom of enterprise with the protection of republican rights. The concept of "social law" gradually replaced the nineteenth-century notion of "social duty" in the vocabulary of Musée social reformers.

Musée social members also demonstrated ideological open-mindedness and a willingness to approach social problems from a multidisciplinary perspective. In the Musée's research sections, members committed themselves to work with those who sometimes professed divergent political views; yet together they upheld the general principles of social science, or, in the vocabulary of the day, the study of social facts, the method of direct observation, and the compilation of social statistics. Musée reformers sought to establish more scientific or empirical foundations—not credos, dogmas, or ideologies—on which they could base a new kind of social policy for modern France. They were aware, moreover, of the lack of cognitive tools available to them for understanding contemporary society. Consequently, they were open to all schools of thought and all forms of social experimentation. The heritage of Le Playist social science, for instance, greatly contributed to an increased understanding of industrial society and its problems at the turn of the century. More than the fear of social unrest or socialism, it is this advance in knowledge about social problems that best explains the work of the Musée social.

Throughout the period under examination, both old and new idioms of reform were evoked by Musée social reformers to justify the need to redefine the relationship of the individual to the state. The conviction, for instance, that societies could be consciously molded by the empirical interventions of social scientists, lawmakers, and other experts was premised on a rational, scientific worldview rooted in the Enlightenment. Pioneers of public health led this search for empirical standards. Consequently, this approach to reform resulted in the development of a language of expertise that was inimical to partisan politics, one that sought to rise above ideologies and to realize the objectivity of a science. In turn, the language of scientific hygiene was used to provoke a rethinking of the accepted cultural and political boundaries separating the private and the public spheres. The sanitary ideal that had been developed and pursued since the early nineteenth century launched a chain reaction of events that elevated certain matters of common concern—such as public health, sewer and drain installation, and the preservation of park space—to the level of "public interest," while the divisive and "particularistic" concerns of political ideology were supposedly of little concern to reformers.

Moreover, a new convergence of bourgeois reformers and middle-class professionals supported the push first to establish and then to broaden the legal definition of public interest. This concept, which had direct implications for debates on housing inspection, urban reform, and planning, also led to the prominence of a new generation of reformers. These social "experts"—including architects, doctors, engineers, urban planners, and municipal officials—laid the foundations in France for a language of efficiency and rational planning that would take on expanded dimensions during the interwar period, particularly during the postwar reconstruction. But the increasing professionalization of reform had injected yet another layer of complexity into the social welfare compromise. Influenced by the rise of the professional middle classes, new technical conceptions of welfare also became subject to the hidden agendas and pressures of those who sought to achieve more clearly defined social and professional identities. Thus, the Musée social's hygiene section, for instance, became as much of a professional springboard as it was a laboratory of ideas for urban reform. The increasing professionalization of reform also announced the advent of social work in France.[3]

The efficiency and rational planning movements, however, had edged away from one of the fundamental premises of social welfare reform in France since the late nineteenth century: the republican ideal. As soon as the notion of what constituted the public sphere was dissociated from republican values and notions of building a liberal democracy, reform threatened to become the preserve of experts whose vision was curiously divorced from a larger project for society. Instead, their utopia was a proto-technocratic one in which individuals, their lives, histories, and complexities were viewed as subordinate to an overarching standard. The ensuing conflict of interests between experts and participatory democracy is a familiar one, reminiscent of the American debate on these themes between Walter Lippmann and John Dewey. In France, the efficiency and rational planning movement, unlike what had preceded it, was not based on the democratic demands of civil society. Its proponents, moreover, often concluded that the parliamentary process was the summit of inefficiency and was therefore to be avoided. Voluntarily shielded from the sometimes chaotic forces of democracy, some Musée reformers preferred to work in the colonies, where they had greater latitude in decision making, fewer bureaucratic entanglements, and less conflict over negotiating the boundaries between the private and the public spheres.[4] Even public hygienists, during the interwar period, demonstrated a pronounced preference for an administrative and "statist" approach to reform, designed to circumvent the tangle of civil society. This approach, moreover, has been analyzed as a reaction on the part of officials against the doctrine of solidarism and its inherent inefficiency as a basis for establishing public health measures.[5]

But, finally, it was the Great War that radically redefined the context of reform. If prewar legislation seemed to suffer the lack of a clear political will to initiate change, the circumstances of postwar reconstruction ushered in a set of concerns that forged the basis for a new national consensus. The circumstances of total war, which directly involved both the civilian population and the military, provided a crucial momentum for the extension of welfare proposals to an ever-broader segment of the French population. Military pensions traditionally reserved for soldiers and the wounded were extended massively to benefit widows and orphans in the civilian population. These measures, which were justified before Parliament by arguments stressing nationalism, social solidarity, and maternalist and child welfare concerns, set the stage for the introduction of comprehensive welfare reform in France.

Pro-natalist arguments also played an increasingly important role in forging consensus on social welfare policy during the interwar years.[6] Based on a redefinition of national unity and solidarity that crossed class, gender, and political lines, such measures were not only framed as practical (the nation's survival would depend on increased birth and infant survival rates), but were popular as well. World War I ushered in a new set of social, economic, and human circumstances—particularly acute in face of the enormous casualties suffered by the French and the subsequent effects on demographic patterns—that broke through the wall of prewar reticence concerning universal benefits. As a result of this sharpened sense of the need to provide security, the French turned increasingly to the state to provide social services.

Within this new context, the social meaning of the Musée social changed yet again. Financially hurt by postwar economic strife, the Musée could no longer afford to finance its generous program of social research initiatives. After Jules Siegfried's death in 1922, the institution was led by George Risler, who turned his attention to pro-natalist concerns and to urban planning and reconstruction efforts. But the Musée social no longer served as a republican think tank during the postwar period. The momentum of reform had shifted; France entered a new, more state-driven phase of both social and economic development.[7]

Yet even during the interwar years, the manner in which social services were extended bore the mark of prewar systems of social insurance. Welfare legislation thus relied on a remarkable variety of instruments: private initiative, state subsidies, social insurance, collaboration with local municipal officials, and partnership with private institutions and agencies. This diversity of cultural traditions, procedures, and institutions became the hallmark of the "hybrid" welfare state in France.

Reformers at the Musée social who acted in the parapolitical sphere in fact laid the foundations for a universal system of welfare protection, but one that preserved a decidedly liberal flavor. Forged initially within the context of the early Third Republic, social insurance in France remained linked, moreover, to the concept of citizenship. Social insurance became a concrete demonstration of the abstract bonds of solidarity linking individuals to the Republic. As a result, republican citizenship and social insurance became closely intertwined. The Republic would be expected, eventually, to both ensure and insure the social protection of its citizens.

Therefore, rather than approaching the rise of the French welfare state as the linear and exponential growth of a bureaucratic structure, the history of the Musée social suggested that the boundaries of what constituted government were indeed fluctuating and permeable. We have been able to acknowledge, moreover, that the sources of welfare reform were multiple; they simultaneously were embedded within the past and projected a vision of the future. The origins of the French welfare state are complex indeed, stretching back to medieval attitudes toward charity and welfare, to social

Catholic pronouncements for a more just social order, and to the social Protestant conviction that salvation would be attained only by devotion to the collective welfare of the community. Every social welfare measure can be shown to embody a concept of the society it seeks to regulate.

As the structures of contemporary welfare states are strained—or in some cases, being dismantled—the complexities of policy making and consensus building are also unraveling, revealing their inner weave and thereby compelling us to understand them better. This process stands as a signal that fundamental change is occurring in the way we conceive of the collectivity, of society, and of relationships between individuals. As we reexamine the foundations of welfare, we are left to question the bonds of community and of national identity that persist. We are left to reexamine the "social mechanisms" of our own democracies and the substance of what constitutes our "fabric of citizenship." [8] These questions arise naturally from this study of the Musée social, which is rooted in the complex web of the informal and formal networks of civil society that ultimately gave rise to the French welfare state.

Although not a comparative project, this book has been written by an American observer of France. A cross-cultural perspective has therefore informed much of the research in this study. Even a historical investigation such as this one reverberates with meaning for a comparative understanding of contemporary French and American cultures. Thus, as I end this study, I find myself returning to current debates on social welfare policy, national identity, and culture invoked in the introduction to this book. Despite their similarities as two of the world's wealthiest and most industrialized nations that share fundamental political premises, France and the United States could hardly be more different with regard to the history of social welfare. Their divergent historical experiences partially explain, moreover, some of today's prevalent cultural misunderstandings.

For the French, "welfare," or the *État-providence*, has come to symbolize, in a nonabstract way, the bonds of citizenship that link individuals to the collectivity. These bonds are very concrete and are demonstrated by actual services that touch the daily lives of nearly every French citizen, regardless of social rank or income level. The *État-providence* is still commonly viewed as an extension of the fundamental rights of republican citizenship; it is the modern-day version of the French Republic's social contract. Merely by virtue of citizenship, one belongs to a larger societal entity; the social-welfare provisions are constant reminders of the ties that bind individuals to the society at large. This is something most French citizens take for granted. More importantly, the *État-providence* plays a fundamental role in social cohesion and is approached by lawmakers as a means of ensuring the "insertion" of individuals into society. Thus, for instance, the minimum subsistence wage for the indigent in France is labeled the *revenu minimum d'insertion*.[9]

In the American case, by contrast, we continue to tackle the problem of poverty as an issue separate from the question of our collective social identity. As a nation we have not formed the habit of thinking of ourselves as a single entity defined by collective social rights. Nor have we adopted, moreover, the forms of universal social insurance so prevalent in Europe today. Our identities as American citizens have never been tied to the concept of social services. Nor, consequently, have we turned to social welfare provisions to help us attain social cohesion. Therein lies a fundamental difference between the attitudes, expectations, and welfare practices of our two nations. The history of the Musée social helps to explain how this difference came about. It demonstrates how French reformers, a century ago, initiated a process that assigned to the welfare state the role of achieving social cohesion within an industrializing republic.

Notes

~

Introduction

1 Jeffrey Rosen, "Is Nothing Secular?" *New York Times Magazine*, 30 January 2000, 42.

2 For the American case, see Skocpol, *Social Policy in the United States* and *Protecting Soldiers and Mothers*; and Gordon, *Women, the State, and Welfare*. For the French and British cases, see Pedersen, *Family, Dependence, and the Origins of the Welfare State*.

3 Through strikes that shut down transportation systems throughout the country for weeks, the public rejected government plans to cut state-guaranteed benefits such as retirement pensions for public-sector employees, particularly in the railroad. See Touraine et al., *Le grand refus*. For an analysis announcing the advent of a thorough philosophical reconsideration of the welfare state in France (provoked by the possible need to refinance the system through personal tax levies), see Rosanvallon, *Nouvelle question sociale*, 9.

4 Lacey and Furner, "Social Investigation, Social Knowledge, and the State: An Introduction," in Lacey and Furner, eds., *State and Social Investigation*, 55; Clark, *Prophets and Patrons*. Today, the CEDIAS–Musée social functions as a not-for-profit association that, in addition to its research library, dispenses information on auxiliary social services such as drug rehabilitation programs, nursing homes, and geriatric programs, and offers continuing education courses to social workers.

5 The French Social Security *ordonnance* of October 4, 1945, unified the Social Insurance Funds, which had been made mandatory by the laws of 1928 and 1930. This unification, however, was not complete. Separate funds continued to exist, for instance, in the mines; and Family Allocation Funds maintained their independence. Funds were managed by committees composed of both representatives of the public administration and representatives of beneficiaries, who, beginning in 1946, were elected by wage-earners.

6 Ashford, *Emergence of the Welfare States*, 182–83.

7 Topalov, "From the 'Social Question' to 'Urban Problems,'" 327; and Horne, "Antichambre de la Chambre"; both in Topalov, ed., *Laboratoires du nouveau siècle*.

8 Elwitt, *Third Republic Defended*, 290.

9 Sewell's pioneering book, *Work and Revolution in France*, set an example of scholarship that incorporated the fundamental significance of language and symbolic meaning into the processes of historical change and the social adaptation of artisans. Also see

Sewell, "Toward a Post-materialist Rhetoric for Labor History"; and Reid, "Reflections on Labor History and Language"; both in Berlanstein, ed., *Rethinking Labor History*, 5–38 and 39–54; Berlanstein, "Working with Language," 426–40; and Ford, *Creating the Nation*.

10　For more on this subject and on the creation of a women's section at the Musée social, see Blum and Horne, "Féminisme et Musée social."

11　For an excellent review article on this subject, see Nord, "Welfare State in France," 821–38.

12　Ibid., 837.

13　Enacted by imperial decree, Bismarck's record included sickness insurance (1883); accident insurance (1884); and insurance for the elderly and the infirm (1889).

14　Mitchell, *Divided Path*.

15　Elwitt, *Third Republic Defended*; Elwitt, "Social Reform and Social Order."

16　Wright, *France in Modern Times*, 439.

17　See Berlanstein, *Big Business*; Reid, *Miners of Decazeville*; Devillers and Huet, *Creusot*; Noiriel, *Longwy*.

18　See Nye, *Crime, Madness, and Politics*; Ellis, *Physician-legislators*; Weissbach, *Child Labor Reform*; Fuchs, *Poor and Pregnant in Paris*; Stewart, *Women, Work, and the French State*.

19　Kuisel, *Capitalism and the State*, 1–30.

20　Logue, "Sociologie et politique"; Freeden, *New Liberalism*.

21　Sewell, *Work and Revolution*.

22　Nelson, Megill, and McCloskey, eds., *Rhetoric of the Human Sciences*, 4.

1. The Modern Sphinx

1　See my "Musée social à l'origine," 47–69; Elwitt, "Social Reform and Social Order," 431–51.

2　Throughout this book the term *social reformer* is used in its most general sense to refer to those men and women who devoted a significant portion of their public lives to reform efforts. My broad usage of this term is intended to highlight the fact that networks of social reform, although crucial to the early history of social welfare in France, defied neat political categorization and proved resistant to labeling, even by contemporaries. Men predominate in this study since women were barred from Musée social membership and, more generally, in the case of nineteenth- and early-twentieth-century France, from participation in influential reform circles. See Horne, "Libéralisme à l'épreuve de l'industrialisation," in Chambelland, ed., *Musée social en son temps*; D. Rodgers, *Atlantic Crossings*, 52. For a discussion of the reform efforts of women who were excluded from this all-male institution until 1916, see Blum and Horne, "Féminisme et Musée social."

3　See D. Rodgers, *Atlantic Crossings*, 16, 30–75.

4　For an important sociopolitical analysis of the social question in turn-of-the-century France, see: Stone, *Search for Social Peace*, 1–23.

5　Kalaora and Savoye, *Inventeurs oubliés*.

6 Gambetta, Speech of 18 April 1872, in *Discours et plaidoyers politiques*, 2:263 (underlined in the original); Topalov, "From the 'Social Question,' " 326.

7 E. Laurent, *Paupérisme*, cited by Hatzfeld, *Du Paupérisme*, 9; L. Chevalier, *Classes dangereuses*; J. Martin, *Fin des mauvais pauvres*; Dewerpe, *Monde du travail en France*, 53; Rabinbach, *Human Motor*.

8 Bezucha, *Lyon Uprising of 1834*; Sheridan, "Household and Craft in an Industrializing Economy," 107–28.

9 Procacci, *Gouverner la misère*, 13.

10 See Dewerpe, *Monde du travail*, for an overview. See also Woronoff, *Industrie sidérurgique en France*; Bouvier, "Panoramas du premier siècle"; Fridenson and Straus, eds., *Capitalisme français, xixe-xxe siècles*; Bergeron and Bourdelais, eds., *La France n'est-elle pas douée pour l'industrie?*

11 Coffin, *Politics of Women's Work*; Dewerpe, *Monde du travail*, 28; Reid, *Miners of Decazeville*; Trempé, *Mineurs de Carmaux*; Reddy, *Rise of Market Culture*; Fohlen, *Industrie textile*.

12 Noiriel, *Ouvriers dans la société française*; Moss, *Origins of the French Labor Movement*; Sewell, *Work and Revolution in France*; Kaplan and Koepp, eds., *Work in France*. For a slightly different interpretation, see Freedeman, *Triumph of Corporate Capitalism in France*. Also see Cottereau, "Distinctiveness of Working-Class Cultures," 111–54; Berlanstein, "Distinctiveness of the Nineteenth-Century French Labor Movement," 660–85.

13 Perhaps the classic formulation of this idea is to be found in Jules Meline's *Le retour à la terre et la surpopulation industrielle* (1905).

14 Peer, *Peasants, Provincials, and Folklore*, 3, 10–14, 170–73; S. Rodgers, "Farming Visions," 50–70.

15 For an insightful historical analysis of *"puissance paternelle,"* see Schafer, *Children in Moral Danger*, and, on Le Play and paternal authority specifically, 37–38.

16 Michelet, *Peuple*, 91, 98–99, 152; Rancière, *Nuit des prolétaires*; Audiganne, *Populations ouvrières*.

17 Simon, *Ouvrière*, 182; Scott, "L'ouvrière! Mot impie," 139–63.

18 Conceived in order to influence others and have an impact on public discourse, these texts contain, and were shaped by, a "social logic." See Spiegel, "History, Historicism, and the Social Logic of the Text," 68; Sewell, *Rhetoric of Bourgeois Revolution*, 36–37.

19 Procacci, *Gouverner la misère*, 13.

20 Desan, "Reconstituting the Social," 92.

21 Rosanvallon, *État en France*, 163, 95.

22 Sewell, *Work and Revolution*, 16–40; 162–93.

23 Rosanvallon, *État en France*, 98; Michelle Perrot, "Introduction," in Procacci, *Gouverner la misère*, 8.

24 In 1902 Albert de Mun contended, for instance, that state socialism was "the natural, inevitable product of individualism, that is to say, of a regime in which the rupture of social bonds brought with it the destruction of groups formed by local proximity or common interest." Cited in *Action populaire* (1902): 34. The *romans champêtres* of George Sand, such as *La mare au diable* (1889), exemplify this idealization of the countryside as

the site of social stability and happiness. On Michelet, see Gossman, *Between History and Literature*, 152–224.

25 Leroy, *Histoire des idées sociales en France*, 3:94, 101. See Pickering, *Auguste Comte*.

26 Le Play, *Réforme sociale*, 19–21, 29; Schafer, *Children in Moral Danger*, 40.

27 E. Chevalier, *Quelques mots sur la question sociale*, 3.

28 Sismondi, *Nouveaux principes de l'économie politique* (1819), cited by Procacci, *Gouverner la misère*, 136–39.

29 Saint-Simon, *Oeuvres complètes*; Ansart, *Sociologie de Saint-Simon*, 20; Jonas, *Mulhouse industriel*, 20.

30 William Sewell has suggested that the best translation of the term *industriel* at the time would be "producers" and has identified this oppositional coupling of "producers" and "idlers" as being rooted in the rhetoric of the French Revolution. Sewell, *Rhetoric of Bourgeois Revolution*, 200–202; quotes from Saint-Simon, *Social Organization*, 72–73.

31 See Walch, *Michel Chevalier*; Passy, *Leçons d'économie politique*, 209; Roncayolo, "Le temps des essais," 511–60; Jonas, *Mulhouse industriel*, 1:122–24.

32 The term *social economy* appeared in Jean-Baptiste Say's *Cours d'économie politique pratique* (1829). Other titles published at this same time included Charles Dunoyer's *Traité d'économie sociale* (1830), Pecqueur's *L'économie sociale* (1839), and Marbeau's *L'économie sociale* (1844). See Procacci, *Gouverner la misère*, 124–70; Rebérioux, "Naissance de l'économie sociale"; Gueslin, *Invention de l'économie sociale*.

33 Sismondi, *New Principles*, xxiii, xxvii–xxviii, 21–22; Sismondi, "Du sort des ouvriers dans les manufactures," 1.

34 See Procacci, *Gouverner la misère*, 52–53.

35 Villeneuve-Bargemont, *Économie politique chrétienne*; Blanqui, *Histoire de l'économie politique en Europe*, 337; Blanqui, "Tableau des populations rurales de la France," 1–15; Gérando, *De la bienfaisance publique*, 2:531; Gérando, *Visiteur du pauvre*, 9; Chambelland, "Aux origines de l'enquête sociale," 327–29. For an important analysis of these themes, see Lynch, *Family, Class, and Ideology*, 3–4, 9–10, 33–39.

36 Stone, *Search for Social Peace*, 5.

37 Pecqueur, *Théorie nouvelle d'économie sociale*, i–ii, 193, 195.

38 Kaplow, *Names of Kings*; Hufton, *Poor of Eighteenth-Century France*; Weissbach, "Oeuvre Industrielle, Oeuvre Morale," 99–120; Weiss, "Origins of the French Welfare System," 47–78; Duprat, "Pour l'amour de l'humanité."

39 See Duroselle, *Débuts du catholicisme social en France*.

40 On the Société de la morale chrétienne, see Duprat, *Usages et pratiques*, 1:485–571; on Jewish charities, see Dab, "Philanthropie laïque."

41 "Public assistance is a sacred debt. Society owes a form of subsistence to its misfortunate members, either by procuring them work, or by ensuring a means of existence to those who cannot work" (Article 21, "Declaration of the Rights of Man and of the Citizen," Preamble to the Constitutional Act of June 24, 1793).

42 Forest, *French Revolution and the Poor*.

43 Duprat, "Pour l'amour de l'humanité," 1:359. Duprat, *Usages et pratiques*, 1:3–10, 39–135.

44 Rosanvallon, *État en France*, 151.

45 The Caisse des dépôts et consignations was created in 1816; the Caisse d'épargne de Paris, in 1818; the Phénix fire insurance company, in 1819; the Compagnie royale d'assurance, in 1820; the Caisse générale des pensions et retraites, in 1825; the insurance company L'Union, in 1828. The law of June 5, 1835, authorized municipal governments to create and manage their own savings funds.

46 Thiers, *Rapport général*, 26 January 1850, and *Discours parlementaires*, 24 May 1850, 9:40. For other liberal views on the social question, see M. Chevallier, *Questions politiques et sociales*; Leroy-Beaulieu, *L'état moral et intellectuel*.

47 For a penetrating analysis of liberal attitudes toward the state, see Hazareesingh, *From Subject to Citizen*, particularly 162–232.

48 Although in its generic form, the term *philanthropy* can refer globally to all charitable and humanitarian organizations, it is used here in a more specific sense—hence the term *secular philanthropy*—to distinguish it from religious charity. See Bec et al., eds. *Philanthropies*, v–vi.

49 Duprat, *Amour de l'humanité*, 1:xx–xxxiv.

50 In addition, Duprat cites the Association de bienfaisance judiciaire, the Société de la charité maternelle, and the Amis des noirs as examples of secular philanthropy. Duprat, "Des lumières au premier XIXe siècle," 8. On the Société philanthropique de Paris, see Duprat, *Usages et pratiques*, 327–404.

51 Duprat, *Amour de l'humanité*, 1:xxxi–xxxiv.

52 Jonas, *Mulhouse industriel*, 1:117–46. For a history of this group based on original archives, see Ott, *Société Industrielle de Mulhouse*.

53 The petition followed a plea by a manufacturer from Guebwiller, J. J. Bourcart, who had spent a year in England and observed the movement in favor of a law limiting the workday and the age of children working in the textile mills. Mataja, "Origines de la protection ouvrière en France," 536.

54 Kott, "Enjeux et significations," 640–59.

55 Jonas, *Mulhouse industriel*, 1:145; Neufville, *Mouvement social protestant*, 27, 196; Simon, *Ouvrière*, 381; Weill, *Histoire du mouvement social*, 5.

56 Léon Harmel, *Manuel de la corporation chrétienne*, quoted in Haussonville, *Études sociales*, 345; Rabinow, *French Modern*, 170–71; Dumons and Pollet, *L'État et les retraites*, 287. On Le Play and social Catholic influences on turn-of-the-century natalism debates, see Pederson, *Family, Dependence, and the Origin of the Welfare State*, 60–65.

57 In 1827, for instance, a Dr. Gerspach defended a doctoral thesis at the Paris Faculty of Medicine entitled "Considerations on the Influence of Cotton Spinning and Weaving upon the Health of Workers." Although published in 1840, Dr. Louis-René Villermé's *Tableau de l'état physique et moral des ouvriers* was first commissioned by the Academy of Moral and Political Sciences in 1834. Rigaudias-Weiss, *Enquêtes ouvrières en France*; Reddy, *Rise of Market Culture*, 169–80; Sewell, *Work and Revolution in France*, 223–32.

58 Festy, *Mouvement ouvrier*; Faure, "Mouvements populaires"; Vigarello, *Propre et le sale*; La Berge, *Mission and Method*; Murard and Zylberman, *Hygiène*, 66–67; Aisenberg, *Contagion*, 32.

59 Rosanvallon, *État en France*, 129. See also Aisenberg, *Contagion*, 17–20; Mataja, "Origines de la protection ouvrière en France," 531; Lecuyer, "Maladies professionelles."

60 Bourdelais and Raulot, *Une peur bleue*; Kudlick, *Cholera in Post-Revolutionary France* and "Giving Is Deceiving," 457–81.

61 Abrams, *Social Surveys and Social Action*, quoted in Bulmer, Bales, and Sklar, eds., *Social Survey in Historical Perspective*, 3.

62 Rosanvallon, *Moment Guizot*, 232; Barksdale, "Liberal Politics and Nascent Social Science in France."

63 Lynch, *Family, Class, and Ideology*, 11; Leclerc, *Observation de l'homme*, 85.

64 Coleman, *Death Is a Social Disease*.

65 Villermé, *Tableau de l'état physique*, 30.

66 Guépin and Bonamy, *Nantes au XIXe siècle*, 292–96.

67 Lynch, *Family, Class, and Ideology*, 13, 58; Michelet, *Le Peuple*, 131–47.

68 Kang, "Lieu de savoir social."

69 Le Play, *Ouvriers européens*, 1:vii–viii; Brooke, *Le Play*.

70 Carroll Wright visited Le Play in Paris and acknowledged the "new inspiration" he received from him concerning "the true, fundamental principles of industrial and social development," one that would completely change his way of thinking. Le Play's influence is evident in Wright's work as a social statistician and in the monographic studies produced during the early years of the U.S. Labor Department (Wright to Edmond Delaire, in "Centenaire de Fréderic Le Play"). On Wright, see Leiby, *Carroll D. Wright and the Origin of Labor Statistics*. For an indication of Le Play's international impact, see *Centenaire de la Socété d'économie et des sciences sociales*; Zimmerman and Frampton, *Family and Society*; Trépanier, "Société canadienne d'économie sociale"; Savard, "Du Lac Saint-Jean au Texas"; Savoye, "École de Le Play et l'intelligentsia italienne"; Protasi, "Applicazioni pratiche della metodologia di ricerca sociale" and "Tra scienza e riforma sociale"; *Etudes Sociales*, special issue "Influence de Le Play en Espagne."

71 See Savoye, "Le Play et la méthode sociale;" Kalaora and Savoye, *Inventeurs oubliés*; Savoye, "Genèse de la sociologie d'intervention."

72 Cited by Gide, "Expositions d'économie sociale," 349.

73 Savoye, "Le Play et la méthode sociale," 17; Savoye, "Une réponse originale," 487.

74 Le Play, *Réforme sociale en France*, 1:30–31; See Silver, introduction to *Frédéric Le Play: On Family, Work, and Social Change*, 16.

75 Le Play, *Réforme sociale en France*, 1:32.

76 In the stem family, or *famille-souche*, property descended to a married son who remained within the ancestral household, whereas other (preferably married) sons achieved independence upon receipt of an inheritance and left the paternal home—even if to emigrate—to set up their own branch of the family. The stem family was, according to Le Play, the familial model best suited to urbanizing societies since, unlike the traditional partrarchal family, it allowed for a balance between association and individual freedom. Le Play coined the term *stem family*—a concept that would become central to his social theories—while studying the Mélouga, a peasant family of the Pyrénées in 1856. Le Play, *Réforme sociale en France*, 1:168; Le Play et al., *Les Mélouga*.

77 At the time, Le Play was not alone in his attempts to adjoin social investigations to his official and technical missions: Tocqueville's mission to study prison systems in the United States (1831–32) allowed him to gather material for his *Démocratie en Amérique;* and Michel Chevalier, although sent on an official mission to study the American railroads (1834–35), published his *Lettres sur l'Amérique du Nord* (1836) in addition to his commissioned technical report.

78 Savoye, "Le Play et la méthode sociale," 22–24.

79 Ibid., 32.

80 Ibid., 118.

81 Kalaora and Savoye, *Inventeurs oubliés,* 110, 113; "kernel of a new aristocracy," Le comte de Butenval, cited by Kalaora and Savoye, *Inventeurs oubliés,* 111. Even Louis Pasteur, who in March 1871 published "Pourquoi la France n'a pas trouvé d'hommes supérieurs au moment du péril," joined the chorus of critics who found reason to implicate French leadership, or lack thereof—in this case the public health authorities—in the disaster at Sedan. Cited by Murard and Zylberman, *Hygiène,* 41.

82 Rousier, *Élite de la société moderne;* Reid, "Industrial Paternalism," 579–607; Charle, *Histoire sociale de la France,* 306–7; Magraw, *Workers and the Bourgeois Republic,* 2:37.

83 Favre, *Naissance de la science politique,* 25, 29; Le Play, *Paix sociale après le désastre,* cited in Ribbe, *Le Play, d'après sa correspondance,* 225–26.

84 Leroy-Beaulieu, "Aspirations des ouvriers."

85 Nye, *Masculinity and Male Codes of Honor.*

86 Simon, *Ouvrière,* 124, 170.

87 See Noiriel, "Du patronage au paternalisme," 26; Noiriel, *Ouvriers,* 114; Reid, "Industrial Paternalism," 579–607; Parize, "Paternalisme et son influence politique"; Dumay, *Mémoires d'un militant;* Montgomery, *Workers' Control in America."*

88 Cited by Noiriel, *Ouvriers,* 114. On this point, also see Noiriel, "Patronage," 27.

89 In 1891, 80 French companies practiced profit sharing; by 1901, 120 did. Charle, *Histoire sociale de la France,* 309.

90 Conklin, *Mission to Civilize.*

91 Compayré. *Éléments d'éducation civique;* Stock-Morton, *Moral Education.*

92 Bert, *Instruction civique à l'école,* 2.

93 Thomas and Guérin, *Cours d'instruction civique,* 181. Pittman, *Léon Bourgeois,* 38–52. Also see Mabilleau, *Cours d'instruction civique* (1883), and *Cours de morale* (1883).

94 Simon, "Mon petit journal."

95 Gide was referring to the Institut de France, the Société d'économie politique (1842), the *Journal des économistes* (1841) and the Librairie Guillaumin. See Gide, "Economic Schools," 614, 629.

96 Gide, *Quatre écoles d'économie sociale,* 109, 133, 135.

97 Murard and Zylberman, *Hygiène,* 36.

98 Bourgeois, *Politique de prévoyance sociale,* 1:57; Gide, *Quatre écoles,* 112; Varlez, "Crise économique," 12–13.

99 E. Chevalier, *Quelques mots sur la question sociale,* 3; Levasseur, *Questions ouvrières,* 372; Gide, "Economic Schools," 625; Haussonville, *Études sociales,* 369.

100 Simiand, "Enquête trop oubliée"; Tilly, *Contentious French*, 360.

101 Barberet, *Travail en France*; Berlanstein, *Big Business*, 63; Reid, "Third Republic as Manager," 183–202; Reid, "Putting Social Reform into Practice," 67–87; Viet, *Voltigeurs de la République*.

102 This was particularly true of the Senate. Among the 36,000 communes of France, 27,000 had populations under 1,000; and among those, 16,000 had populations of under 500. Murard and Zylberman, *Hygiène*, 28.

2. Inventing a Social Museum

1 See my article, "Musée social à l'origine."

2 Donzelot, *Invention du social*; Rebérioux, "Élites intellectuelles," 29; Elwitt, *Third Republic Defended*, 155–69.

3 On the rhetoric of republican reform, see my article, portions of which are included in this chapter, "Presenting Modern France."

4 Hobsbawm, *Age of Capital*, 32–33; Greenhalgh, *Ephemeral Vistas*; Hamon, *Expositions*.

5 "Machine Palace" is a translation of the commonly used French term *Palais des machines*. The official designation of this building, however, was *Galerie des machines*, and I will refer to it as such throughout the chapter.

6 Spiegel, "History, Historicism," 68.

7 Barthes, "Eiffel Tower," 3–17; Ory, *Une nation pour mémoire*, 107. Familial imagery, such as the "republican family" or the "industrial family," was a recurrent feature of reform discourse.

8 Trachtenberg, *Incorporation of America*, 231.

9 Benedict, "Anthropology of World's Fairs," 129.

10 Benjamin, *Écrits français*, 295–96.

11 As early as 1885, Paul Cambon, a member of the republican establishment, lent credence to those very fears when he wrote to his friend Jules Ferry: "The general impression is that the Republic is at the end of its course. Next year we will have revolutionary excesses, then a violent reaction. What will come of it? A dictatorship of one sort or another." Paul Cambon, *Correspondence*, 1940, 261, cited by Mayeur, *Débuts de la Troisième République*, 166.

12 "To be honest, however, if General Boulanger governs France next year, I will have no longer any scruple or hesitation to follow you anywhere we will be able to flee." Georges Picot to Jules Simon, 25 September 1888, Archives nationales (AN) 87 Archives privées (AP) 6.

13 Berger to Simon, 25 April 1888, AN 87 AP 1.

14 Silverman, "1889 Exhibition."

15 Ory, *Une nation*, 148–49; Nelms, *Third Republic*, 47, 50–51, nn. 90–91. In the end, despite the official refusal of most monarchies to participate, almost every nation—with the exception of Germany and Montenegro—was represented by at least a commissioner or an official committee. Private exhibitors, on the other hand, represented every country, including Germany. Unsigned editorial, *Événement*, 17 June 1887; Garcia, "État républicain face au centenaire," 154.

16 Untitled editorial, *Événement*, 17 June 1887.

17 Nelms, *Third Republic*, 57; Ory, *Une nation*, 109.

18 "How not to celebrate the freeing of workers by the French Revolution? How not to rejoice at the emancipation of commerce and industry?" Picard, *Rapport général*, 9:8.

19 Ibid., 9:355–56.

20 Cheysson, "Économie sociale à l'Exposition," 1–2.

21 In 1884 a proposal to designate a Palace of Labor was quickly abandoned. Nelms, *Third Republic*, 21.

22 The social economy section was created by ministerial decree on June 9, 1887, and subsequently confirmed by decree on August 10, 1888. Picard, *Rapport général*, 1:324; Trombert, *Charles Robert*; A. Siegfried, *Mes Souvenirs de la IIIe République*.

23 Weiss, "Origins of the French Welfare System," 47–78.

24 Cheysson, "Institutions patronales," in Picard *Rapport du jury international*, 1:452.

25 Cheysson, "Musée social," 10.

26 Lockroy had asked the socialists Benoît Malon, Edouard Vaillant, and Jean-Baptiste Dumay to participate in the new section. Godineau, "Économie sociale" (1988) 70, 100–101.

27 Vogüé, *Remarques sur l'Exposition*, 203.

28 Cheysson, "Économie sociale à l'Exposition," 3; Bennett, "Exhibitionary Complex," 148; see also Bennett, *Birth of the Museum*.

29 Çelik, *Displaying the Orient*.

30 Cheysson, "Économie sociale à l'Exposition," 4; Picard, "Rapport général," 4:56.

31 AN F^{12} 3767, Procès verbaux, Commission d'organisation, 14 May 1888.

32 Simon, "Mon petit journal," and *Ouvrière*, 313; Reid, "Industrial Paternalism," 579; Bullock and Read, *Movement for Housing Reform*, 425–31.

33 For a discussion of the gendered notions of social reform and leisure time for workers, see my article, "In Pursuit of Greater France."

34 Lami, "Cercles d'ouvriers," 1:233.

35 Siegfried, "Cercles d'ouvriers," 12–13; Lami, "Cercles d'ouvriers," 2:238–39.

36 Say, "Economie sociale," vi.

37 Cheysson, "Économie sociale à l'Exposition," 4, 8, 11–13; Say, "Économie sociale," in Picard, ed., *Rapport général*, vi; Cheysson, *Musée social*, 11.

38 Vogüé, *Remarques*, 216–17.

39 Cheysson, "Économie sociale à l'Exposition," 17; Godineau, "Économie sociale" (1989), 85; Rebérioux, "Expositions universelles," 12.

40 Huxley, "Administrative Nihilism," 525–43; Freeden, *New Liberalism*, 33.

41 Picard, *Rapport général*, 9:108–9, cited by Ryckelynck, "Économie sociale," 104–5. See also Dogliani, "Laboratoire de socialisme municipal."

42 Cheysson, "Musée social," 1.

43 Musée social, *Inauguration*, 11. Rasmussen, "Congrès internationaux."

44 Procès-verbaux de la Commission d'organisation de l'Exposition d'économie sociale, 5 December 1888, AN F^{12} 3767; Godineau, "Économie sociale," 73.

45 Greenhalgh, "Education, Entertainment and Politics," 89; Le Play, "Exhibitions go

by," cited by Picard, *Rapport général*, 1:176. Proudhon had been inspired in the aftermath of the 1855 Exhibition to imagine his *Projet d'une exposition perpétuelle* that would function as a permanent encyclopedic display of human production.

46 There is now a rich body of research on the various forms and meanings of the museum as a cultural form. See, for instance, Dagognet, *Musée sans fin*; Sherman, *Worthy Monuments*; Karp and Lavine, *Exhibiting Cultures*; Lumley, *Museum Time-Machine*; Vergo, *New Museology*; Sherman, ed., *Museum Culture*; Bennett, *Birth of the Museum*.

47 Sherman, *Worthy Monuments*; Hudson, *Social History of Museums*, 46; Impay and Mac-Gregor, *Origin of Museums*.

48 Vachon, *Rapport sur les musées*; *Musée pédagogique*; Beurier, *Musée pédagogique*; Serrurier, *Les musées scolaires*; Demarty, *Formation et organisation*; Hudson, *Social History*, 24. Pelloutier also used the expression "musée social" in his *Histoire des bourses du travail*, cited by Julliard, *Fernand Pelloutier*, and Crubellier, *Histoire culturelle*, 313.

49 Cheysson, "Musée social," 3–5; Cheysson, "Exposition d'économie sociale," 62.

50 Cheysson, "Musée social," 11.

51 Bennett, "Exhibitionary Complex," 126, 135. Bennett's theories enable us to nuance earlier notions, influenced by Foucault, of the nineteenth century as an age of industrial discipline. See Perrot, "Three Ages of Industrial Discipline."

52 Cheysson, "Économie sociale à l'Exposition," 9.

53 Cheysson, "Institutions patronales," 351–52.

54 The association was formed on February 17, 1890. Its vice presidents were Jules Siegfried and Émile Cheysson; its secretary, Léon Caubert; and its treasurer, Charles Robert. See *Association du Musée d'économie sociale: Statuts*, 1–11; Cheysson, *Musée social*, 14; Ministère du commerce, Conseil supérieur du travail (hereafter CST), *Rapport relatif au Musée d'économie sociale*, 1–2; "Musée d'économie sociale," *Le Petit Havre*, 10 January 1893.

55 For a time, the association hoped to install the museum in the new wing of the Museum of Decorative Arts to be erected on the site of the old Cour des comptes. Cheysson, "Musée social," 7; Ministère du commerce, CST, *Rapport relatif au Musée*, 2–3; Lucas, "Apprentissage," 331; Cheysson, *Musée social*, 14; Cheysson, "Institutions patronales," 452.

56 Oscar Linder to Jules Simon, 6 September 1889, 8 April 1890, and 28 December 1892, AN 87 AP 5; Jules Siegfried to Jules Simon, 18 June 1891, AN 87 AP 18; CST; Savoye, "Continuateurs de Le Play," 315; Savoye, "Genèse de la sociologie d'intervention," 194, 254; Luciani and Salais, "Matériaux pour la naissance d'une institution."

57 Ministère du commerce et de l'industrie, CST, *Rapport relatif au Musée*, 4; Cheysson, "Musée social," 1–6. The first such establishment was the Musée des appareils destinés à prévenir les accidents du travail opened in Winterthur, Switzerland. In 1890 Dr. Migerka, a labor inspector and Austrian delegate to the Berlin Labor Conference, adopted this model and founded a museum in Vienna entirely devoted to the prevention of industrial accidents. Similar museums were also created in Amsterdam (1893), in Berlin (1903), and eventually in Paris (1905) at the CNAM. See Tolman, *Oeuvre de l'ingénieur social*, vi; Rivière, "Exposition d'appareils de protection," 446; "Musée

d'économie sociale," *Petit Havre*, 10 January 1893; Gruner, "Association . . . du Musée viennois."

58 Ministère du commerce et de l'industrie, CST, *Deuxième session; L'Éclair*, "Économie sociale"; May, "Enseignement social à Paris," 10–12.

59 "Musée d'économie sociale," *Petit Havre*, 10 January 1893.

60 Cheysson, *Musée social*, 15; *L'Éclair*, "Économie sociale"; Levasseur, *Resumé historique*, 7; Ministère du Commerce et de l'Industrie, CST, *Rapport relative au Musée*, 5; Cheysson, "Institutions patronales," 452; *Jules Siegfried: Sa vie et son oeuvre*, 42. The reference to a "musée d'enseignement" is in "Musée d'économie sociale," *Petit Havre*, 10 January 1893; Simon referred to the CNAM as the "Sorbonne de ouvrier" in *Ouvrière*, 419.

61 Siegfried, "Projet de loi ayant pour but la création d'un Musée d'economie sociale." Siegfried served as minister of commerce from December 6, 1892, until January 10, 1893, and again from January 11, 1893, until April 3, 1893. Yvert, ed., *Dictionnaire des ministres*, 614. Cheysson, *Musée social*, 14; Cheysson, "Musée social," 7. This legislative initiative was originally due to Jules Simon, who proposed in 1891 that Siegfried sign an amendment with him to that effect. Jules Siegfried to Jules Simon, 18 June 1891, AN 87 AP 18. Cheysson, *Oeuvres choisies*, 1:53.

62 Cheysson, *Musée social*, 13; Stone, *Search for Social Peace*, 104. Obligatory accident insurance had first been proposed by Félix Faure in 1888. Since 1853, retirement benefits had been granted to French civil servants who were *titulaires* (those who had obtained entitlement, or tenure, in their positions, approximately 350,000 at this time). The 1894 law is significant, therefore, because for the first time, private sector workers were guaranteed retirement benefits. Although private companies, the railroads and mines were closely tied to the state since they had to obtain a license, a *concession légale*, authorizing them to operate on French soil. Employers in these sectors also wanted to stabilize their largely rural workforce and therefore did not fight the legislation. Prost, "Providence sociale," 162.

63 Cheysson, *Musée social*, 15; André Siegfried, "La fondation du Musée social," lecture notes, Archives André Siegfried, Foundation nationale des sciences politiques, n.d.

64 BN, Nouvelles acquisitions françaises (NAF) 14114, ff. 303.

65 The Chambrun family dominated the political life of Lozère in almost dynastic fashion. See Pourcher, *Maîtres de granit*; Musée social, *Obsèques du Comte*, 4.

66 Chambrun, *Comte de Chambrun*, 34; Bader, *Comte de Chambrun*. Chambrun authored several works on the arts and music: *Le philosophe et la muse. Dialogues sur la musique* (1884); and, with Stanislas Legis, *Wagner*, 2 vols. (1895). See Blum, "Le comte de Chambrun, catholique."

67 Founded in 1764 by Monseigneur de Montmorency-Laval, the Cristalleries de Baccarat became a major company after 1822 when it was first purchased by the Parisian shareholder Pierre-Antoine Godard-Desmarest and later inherited by his son, Émile. See Birck, "Entre le patronage," 30; *Histoire de Baccarat*; BN, NAF 14114, ff. 313.

68 Comte de Chambrun to Kozakiewicz and Leroux, his personal secretaries, 6 April 1891. Archives du Musée social.

69 Trombert, *Charles Robert*, 2:203–4; Chambrun, *Aux montagnes d'Auvergne: Mes conclusions* (hereafter, *Conclusions*), 57; BN, NAF 25169, ff. 360–61; Count de Chambrun to Ernest Lavisse, 23 November 1893 and 16 May 1894, BN, NAF 25169, ff. 331–32 and 341–42; Bader, *Comte de Chambrun*, 90; Lichtenberger, "Musée social: Son but," 336–37; Blum, "Comte de Chambrun, catholique," 28.

70 Chambrun, *Conclusions* and *Aux montagnes d'Auvergne: Mes nouvelles conclusions* (hereafter, *Nouvelles conclusions*).

71 Chambrun, *Conclusions*, 98, and *Nouvelles conclusions*, 113.

72 Chambrun to Léopold Mabilleau, 2 March 1898, Archives du Musée social, cited in Blum, "Comte de Chambrun, catholique," 32.

73 Chambrun, *Conclusions*, 71, 81–85, 106; Birck, "Entre le patronage."

74 The comte de Chambrun had no descendants. Interview with Réné de Chambrun, 1985; Comte de Chambrun, "Testament," Article 1, 19 October 1897, Archives du Musée social.

75 Weisz, "Idéologie républicaine," 83–112; Prochasson, "Dick May et le social," 43–58.

76 Musée social, *Société du Musée social; Journal officiel de la République française*, 26, no. 239, Tuesday, 4 September 1894; note dictated by the comte de Chambrun to his secretary, 30 June 1894, Archives du Musée social.

77 Comte de Chambrun to Dick May, 11 June 1894, BN, NAF 26169, f. 345. Chambrun insisted that the term *musée* was intended to attract "la foule" (Chambrun, *Aux montagnes d'Auvergne*, 50).

78 Jules Siegfried to Jules Simon, 23 March 1895, AN 87 AP 7; Musée social, Procès-verbaux du Comité de direction, 28 December 1894.

79 "Discours de M. Jules Simon," in Musée social, *Inauguration*, 2.

80 Elwitt, *Third Republic Defended*, 155–69.

81 "Discours de Léon Bourgeois," in Musée social, *Inauguration*, xi; Hayward, "Solidarity," and "Official Social Philosophy."

82 Musée social, *Inauguration*, 30.

83 Perrot, *Ouvriers en grève*, 1:195.

84 "Discours de M. André Lebon," in Musée social, *Inauguration*, 26.

85 "Discours de M. Ribot," in Musée social, *Inauguration*, 11, 13–17.

86 Dupuy, "Discours," in Musée social, *Obsèques*, 10.

3. A Genealogy of Republican Reform

1 Cheysson, "Accidents du travail," 324.

2 Rodgers, *Atlantic Crossings*; Rasmussen, "Congrès internationaux."

3 Wuthnow, *Communities of Discourse*, 1–22; Kloppenberg, *Uncertain Victory*; Rodgers, "In Search of Progressivism," 113–32; Dawley, *Struggles for Justice*, 11.

4 Freeden, *New Liberalism*, 13; Kloppenberg, *Uncertain Victory*, 7; Collini, *Liberalism and Sociology*. Alfred Fouillée, in his book *La propriété sociale et la démocratie*, criticized the concept of private property. For a presentation that stresses the diverse currents of political economy and liberal thought in France, see Breton, ed., *Économie politique en France*.

5 Kloppenberg, *Uncertain Victory*; Logue, "Sociologie et politique," 141–62, and *From Philosophy to Sociology*; Bellamy, *Liberalism and Modern Society*; Elwitt, *Third Republic Defended*; Warchaw, *Paul Leroy-Beaulieu*; Horne, "Économie sociale et la naissance," and "Libéralisme à l'épreuve de l'industrialisation."

6 Parts of this chapter appear in my article, "Antichambre de la Chambre."

7 Topalov, "Champ réformateur," in Topalov, ed., *Laboratoires du nouveau siècle*, 366, 465–68.

8 Agulhon, *Cercle dans la France bourgeoise*; quote from Eley, "Nations, Publics, and Political Cultures," 304.

9 For similar studies of the American and German bourgeoisie, see Doyle, "Social Functions," 333–55; "associational trajectories" from Eley, "Nations, Publics, and Political Cultures," 313. Most prevalent Protestant and Jewish charities at the time—such as the Oeuvres de la Chaussée du Maine (1871), the Société des Visiteurs pour le relèvement des familles malheureuses (1896), and the Société philanthropique de l'Asile isréalite de Paris (1900)—proclaimed their autonomy from politics and religion and as such should more properly be considered examples of secular philanthropy (see Dab, "Philanthropie laïque").

10 Barksdale, "Liberal Politics and Nascent Social Science," 23; Duprat, *Pour l'amour de l'humanité.*

11 As Habermas has defined it, the public sphere is that "realm of our social life in which something approaching public opinion can be formed," where citizens can meet and confer "as a public body," with guaranteed freedoms of assembly, "about matters of general interest" ("Public Sphere," 49). Eley comments that "the public sphere makes more sense as the structured setting where cultural and ideological contest or negotiation among a variety of publics take place, rather than as the spontaneous and class-specific achievement of the bourgeoisie" ("Nations, Publics, and Political Cultures," 310). Tocqueville, *Democracy in America*, 2:513–17; "as bridges . . ." from Doyle, "Social Functions," 341.

12 This relationship worked both ways, since the involvement of civil servants within reform groups also afforded them a measure of autonomy from state service. Topalov, "Patronages," in Topalov, ed., *Laboratoires*, 390.

13 *La Réforme sociale* became the official publication of the Société d'économie sociale and the Unions de la paix sociale. Kalaora and Savoye, *Inventeurs oubliés*, 174. For more details on this split, see Savoye, "Continuateurs de Le Play."

14 For a detailed analysis of the Le Playist school and its various branches, see Kalaora and Savoye, *Inventeurs oubliés*.

15 May, "Enseignement social," 3.

16 Savoye, "Une réponse originale," 487.

17 Savoye, "Paroles et les actes," 63.

18 Duroselle, *Débuts du catholicisme social.*

19 Weill, *Histoire du catholicisme libéral*, 221, 226; Levillain, *Albert de Mun*; Mayeur, *Un prêtre démocrate.*

20 Silverman, *Origins of French Art Nouveau*, 47; McManners, *Church and State in France*, 81–93.

21 Pope Leo XIII's initiatives represented merely a brief hiatus in official Catholic policy. His successor Pope Pious X (1903) rejected modernist strands of Catholic thought, condemned the separation of church and state (1905), refused to allow French Catholics to form cultural associations under the 1901 law, and pursued a hard-line policy that further isolated French Catholics from public life. Mayeur, *Vie politique*, 146–53; Barthélemy-Madaule, *Marc Sangnier*; "Rerum novarum," in Carlen, *Papal Encyclicals*, 241–61.

22 A case in point is Paul Desjardin's Union pour l'action morale (1892), a group of republican intellectuals with liberal Catholic origins whose membership was expanded and radicalized by the Dreyfus Affair, leading to a split between those Catholic members who left the group to found Action Française and those who remained with the group's pro-Dreyfus majority. See Dab, "Bienfaisance et socialisme," in Topalov, ed., *Laboratoires*, 223. Droulers, *Politique sociale et christianisme*, 1:14; Weill, *Histoire du mouvement social*, 416.

23 *Action populaire*, 6; Droulers, *Politique sociale et christianisme*, 85, 107; Stone, *Search for Social Peace*, 202, n.70. With 250,000 members and 2,000 local committees, Action libérale populaire (which originated as the parliamentary group, Action Libérale, in 1901) attracted liberals, as well as clergymen and social Catholic members of Albert de Mun's Association catholique de la jeunesse française (1884), a group that had evolved to accept the Republic and embrace social reformism. Action libérale also gave financial support to Catholic congregations under siege by the Radical republic. Certain members of the Musée social's board of directors purportedly contributed to the speakers' fund of this group. Combeau, *Paris et les élections municipales*, 256–57, 258, n.68; Mayeur, *Vie politique*, 193–95. Also see Martin, "Creation of the Action libérale populaire."

24 Moon, *Labor Problem*, 341.

25 *Le Mouvement social*, January 1909, 2.

26 Lemire quoted in Mayeur, *Un prêtre démocrate*, 369. Raoul Jay was secretary general of the ANPPLT. Jay, *Protection légale*; Mayeur, *Un prêtre démocrate*, 329; Droulers, *Politique sociale et christianisme*, 85, 107; Stone, *Search for Social Peace*, 202. Quote from Jay, "Assurance ouvrière et les caisses nationales," 84.

27 Blondel, "Question sociale," in Blondel et al., eds. *Idées sociales et faits sociaux*, 33–37.

28 See Victorine B . . . , *Souvenirs d'une morte vivante*, 21.

29 Nicolet, *Idée républicaine en France*, 105–6.

30 For an account of how religion both modified and served as a conduit for republican ideas and national identity in Brittany, see Ford, *Creating the Nation*.

31 Hause, "Protestant Republicanism."

32 According to his son André's account, Jules Siegfried became more religious and made more public references to his faith after his marriage to Julie Puaux, the daughter of the Protestant minister François Puaux, who authored a seven-volume work on the history of French Protestantism, and the sister of Frank Puaux, director of *Revue chrétienne*. See A. Siegfried, *Jules Siegfried*; Ardaillou, "Foi Protestante."

33 The Siegfried family graciously invited me into their home to consult Jules Siegfried's personal diary, kept irregularly from the mid-1860s until 1893, and a series of family letters that chronicle personal life and several trips he made to the United States. J. Siegfried, *Misère*.

34 Neufville, *Mouvement social protestant*, 118; Hayward, "Solidarity," 261–84.

35 Gide, "Rôle pratique du pasteur," 25.

36 André Encrevé, for instance, has noted that during the founding period of the regime, Protestant peasants accepted the Republic earlier did than other peasant groups ("Protestants et la République"). See also Baubérot, *Retour des Huguenots*; Garrisson, *Homme protestant*.

37 Encrevé, "Protestants et la République," 41; Auspitz, *Radical Bourgeoisie*; Hayward, "Educational Pressure Groups."

38 Henri Monod and his family were frequently the target of Charles Maurras's polemics in the early years of Action Française. Paul Guieysse was regularly attacked by the *Libre Parole* as a "Dreyfusard" and a Protestant ("Paul Guieysse," APP BA 886). See Édouard Drumont, *La France juive* (1886); George Thiébaud, *Le parti protestant* (1896); Ernest Renauld, *Le péril protestant* (1898) and *La conquête protestante* (1900). Encrevé, *Protestants en France*, 202–16; Tannenbaum, *Action Française*.

39 In 1897 Guieysse was a member of the Central Committee of the Ligue des droits de l'homme. Also a member of the "Nature et Philanthropie" lodge, Guieysse reported that a majority of the Ribot cabinet (1889) belonged to the freemasonry and that he himself had never been such an active freemason before becoming minister of colonies in 1889. *Le Gaulois*, 20 April 1896; "Guieysse," APP BA 886; Hayward, "Educational Pressure Groups," 1–5.

40 *Association protestante*, 6–7. On Tommy Fallot and social Christian discourse, see Baubérot, *Retour des Huguenots*, 116–34; Neufville, *Mouvement social protestant*, 119–20; Joly, *Socialisme chrétien*.

41 *Association protestante*, 13.

42 The jury included Fallot, Gide, Lichtenberger, and Pressensé. *Association protestante*, 18.

43 Cited by Neufville, *Mouvement social protestant*, 121.

44 For more details on Julie Siegfried's social feminism, see Blum and Horne, "Féminisme et Musée social"; Klejman and Rochefort, *Égalité en marche*. On "integral feminism," see Offen, "Depopulation, Nationalism." On social maternalism and the rise of an *état maternel*, see Koven and Michel, "Womanly Duties."

45 *Association protestante*, 8.

46 Neufville, *Mouvement social protestant*, 121.

47 Gide, "Rôle pratique du pasteur"; *Association protestante*, 18–28.

48 Arboux, *Histoire de seize ans*, 177; J. Siegfried, "Rapport fait au nom de la Commission supérieure chargée d'examiner la proposition de loi," *Bulletin SFHBM* (1892): 501.

49 Neufville, *Mouvement social protestant*, 59–72, 81, 190; Gaumont, *Histoire générale*, 2:85–86; Stora-Lamarre, *Enfer de la IIIe République*.

50 Quotes from Silverman, *Art nouveau*, 49. Levasseur, *Questions ouvrières*, 372; Hayward,

"Solidarity" and "Official Social Philosophy"; Stone, *Search for Social Peace*, 36; Bourgeois, *Politique de la prévoyance sociale*, 1:57. Reformist socialists such as Georges Renard were won over to solidarism, although socialists and solidarists differed over their conception of property. See Dubois, "Solidarisme," 73–74.

51 Cantecor, *Morale théorique*, 319–27; Lemoine, *Livret d'enseignement moral*, 43–36; Michel, *Idée de l'État*, 586–87; "Un discours de Léon Bourgeois," *Le Temps*, 4 August 1894.

52 Solidarism's rich intellectual history, until recently neglected, is explored fully in Kristin A. Sheradin's Ph.D. dissertation, "Reforming the Republic: Solidarism and the Making of the French Welfare State." The legal notion of solidarity was introduced into the dictionary of the French Academy in 1798. Eichtal, *Solidarité sociale*, 3.

53 Hayward, "Solidarity," 262–63.

54 Institut de France, *Académie des sciences morales et politiques*, 376–412; Gide, *Histoire des doctrines économiques*, 633–37.

55 Levasseur, *Questions ouvrières*, 373.

56 Furlough, "Politics of Consumption," 93.

57 Elwitt, *Third Republic Defended* and "Social Reform and Social Order"; Stone, *Search for Social Peace*; Reid, *Miners of Decazeville*.

58 For the purposes of this analysis, the term *member* will refer to any individual whose name appeared on the following official membership lists: *Musée social: Statuts, organisation, services*, 5–12; "Personnel" in *Musée social* (1906), 1–18; "Personnel," *Musée social* (1911), 17–59. According to these lists, there were 96 members of the Musée social in 1896; 199 in 1906; and 340 in 1911.

59 Topalov, "Patronages," in Topalov, ed., *Laboratoires*, 358.

60 Haussonville, *Études sociales* and *Salaires et misères*; Levillain, *Albert de Mun*.

61 "Comité de défense." For a fuller discussion of this point, see chapter 5.

62 See Bourdeau, "Socialisme municipal."

63 Jolly, ed., *Dictionnaire*, 4:1548–50; Maitron, ed., *Dictionnaire*, 12:102–3; Ponsot, "Un militant socialiste."

64 Secretary of the Syndicat des journalistes socialistes, Daudé-Bancel signed the 1912 pact that put an end to the conflict that had split socialist and bourgeois cooperatives (Coston, *Dictionnaire de la politique française*, 2:161).

65 Prochasson, *Intellectuels, le socialisme*, 123.

66 Lichtenberger, "Congrès international pour la protection," 265; Stone, *Search for Social Peace*, 51.

67 For a contrary view, see Elwitt, "Social Reform and Social Order," 431–51; Elwitt, *Third Republic Defended*.

68 The Musée's section on rural and urban hygiene is examined in greater detail in chapter 6.

69 Robert and Cougny, eds., *Dictionnaire des parlementaires*, 1:948; 3:1332; Prévost et al., *Dictionnaire*, 12:1163; "Funérailles de M. Ernest Glasson," *Institut de France, Académie des sciences morales et politiques* (1907): 1.

70 Weill, *Historie du mouvement social*, 251.

71 Levasseur, *Questions ouvrières*, 770, 749–50; Maitron, *Dictionnaire biographique*, 11:57;

Gueslin, *Invention*, 235; Gaumont, *Histoire générale*, 213–14; Musée social, *Inauguration*, 36–38.

72   Musée social, *Obsèques*, 21.

73   Levasseur, *Questions ouvrières*, 751; Martin Saint-Léon, *Petit commerce français*, 73; Nord, *Paris Shopkeepers*.

74   See Watkins, *International Cooperative*; Seilhac, "Mouvement syndial en France," 325.

75   Birck, "Entre le patronage"; Chambrun, *Nouvelles conclusions*, 71; Berlanstein, *Big Business*; Viet, *Voltigeurs de la République*; Reid, "Putting Social Reform into Practice."

76   Stone, *Search for Social Peace*, 194.

77   Lévy-Leboyer, ed., *Patronat de la second industrialisation*; Thépot, ed., *Ingénieurs dans la société française*; Charle, *Histoire sociale*, 252.

78   Prévost et al., *Dictionnaire*, 16:1384; Gruner, "Association pour l'entretien du Musée viennois," 3–7. For more details on the Comité permanent and the debates leading to the 1898 accident compensation law, see chapter 6.

79   Charle, *Histoire sociale*, 254.

80   Gruner, "Responsabilité des accidents," 13, 18.

81   Charle, *Élites de la République*.

82   Nord, "Social Defense and Conservative Regeneration," 210–28. For more on these men, see chapter 5.

83   F. Charpin, "Albert Gigot," *La Réforme sociale* 1 (1913): 1.

84   AN C5544, Chambre des deputés, Commission d'assurance et de prévoyance sociales, *Procès-verbaux*, "Sociétés de secours mutuels," vol. 1, 5 April 1895. For a more complete discussion on the functioning of these networks with regard to mutualism, social insurance, and retirement pensions, see chapter 6.

85   Stone, *Search for Social Peace*, 50, 75.

86   Ellis, *Physician-legislators*, 100, 152; Nord, "Social Defense," 215–21.

87   Barnes, *Making of a Social Disease*.

88   Rabinow, *French Modern*; Gwendolyn Wright, *Politics of Design*; Cottereau, "Débuts de la planification."

89   For a sociological analysis of cultural elites during this period, see Charle, *Naissance des "intellectuels."* On the French university system and its *corps d'enseignants*, see Karady, "Professeurs de la République," 90–112; Weisz, *Emergence of Modern Universities*. Several prominent professors, particularly from the republican bastion of the École normale supérieure—such as Charles Péguy and Lucien Herr—were involved in socialist attempts to defend the interests of workers and define social justice. Herr became a member of the Parti ouvrier socialiste as early as 1890. See Goldberg, *Life of Jean Jaures*, 62. On the intellectual milieu of the École normale supérieure, see Prochasson, *Intellectuels, le socialisme*; Karady, "Normaliens et autres enseignants," 35–58; Charle, "Pour une histoire sociale."

90   Luchaire, "Funérailles de M. Ernest Glasson."

91   Favre, *Naissances de la science politique*; Osborne, *Grande école for the grands corps*.

92   Cottereau, "Distinctiveness of Working-Class Cultures," 152.

93   Weisz, "Idéologie républicaine," 95.

94 Bertholet, *Durkheim.*

95 Latour, *Pasteurization of France;* Charle, *Histoire sociale,* 220; Ellis, *Physician-Legislators,* 207–37; Nye, *Crime, Madness, and Politics;* Schneider, *Quality and Quantity,* 11–54.

96 Charle, *Histoire sociale,* 220; Ellis, *Physician-Legislators,* 111–44; Thoinet, *Bulletin de l'Académie nationale de médecine* [hereafter *Bulletin de l'ANM*], 31 July 1906; *Bulletin de l'ANM,* 13 December 1910.

97 Ellis, *Physician-Legislators,* 182–91.

98 "Éloge," *Bulletin de l'ANM,* 15 May 1917, 601–4; Lépine, "Louis Landouzy"; "Éloge," *Bulletin de l'ANM,* 15 January 1929, 56–62; Bianchon, *Grands médecins.*

99 Topalov, "Nouvelles spécialités," in Topalov, ed., *Laboratoires,* 432. I am indebted to Deborah Hurtt for illuminating discussions of French architecture and architects during this period.

100 Sutcliffe, *Autumn of Central Paris* and *Towards the Planned City;* Rabinow, *French Modern;* Gwendolyn Wright, *Politics of Design;* Gaudin, *Avenir en plan* and (ed.) *Premiers urbanistes.*

4. A Laboratory of Social Reform

1   The first meeting of the board, however, was held on June 25, 1894, at the Paris home of the comte de Chambrun, 12 rue Monsieur. *Musée social, procès-verbaux du Comité de direction* (hereafter PVCD), 25 June 1894.

2   Rust, "Business and Politics in the Third Republic."

3   Rosanvallon, *État en France,* 116–17.

4   Cheysson, *Oeuvres choisies,* 1:vii.

5   Board members in 1914 also included Henri Hébrard de Villeneuve, a member of the Conseil d'État and the Comité consultatif des chemins de fer; Georges Risler, the president of the Crédit immobilier de France and of the Conseil supérieur des habitations à bon marché; and René Stourm, a member of the Institut and the Société d'économie sociale, and Georges Picot's successor as the perpetual secretary of the Académie des sciences morales et politiques.

6   The other members of the Musée social's first administrative staff included a former secretary at the prefecture of police, M. Villin, who was hired as the Musée's first librarian, and Eugène Montet and Roger Merlin who oversaw the archives.

7   PVCD, 8 and 16 November 1894; François-Poncet, *Vie et l'oeuvre,* 13; Rebérioux, "Les 'élites intellectuelles,' " 23.

8   Salomon became Tolstoy's French translator. Tolstoy particularly appreciated the work of Paul de Rousiers and Léon de Seilhac. Leon Tolstoy to Charles Salomon, 19 October 1896, as cited in *Revue d'études slaves* 10 (1930): 205–12. The author thanks Mr. Pierre Mazon for this and other references to Charles Salomon. Salomon left the Musée in 1896 to become the administrator-delegate of the mines of Krivoj Rog in Russia and was replaced by François de Carbonnel, a law student and a graduate of the École libre des sciences politiques.

9   PVCD, 22 December 1900.

10 PVCD, 7 and 16 July 1897; Robert Pinot to Jules Siegfried, 10 July 1897, Archives Paul de Rousiers, Château de Rhus. The author thanks Antoine Savoye for this source. Pinot's

friend Charles Salomon later indicated, however, that Pinot had in fact been fired. "Une Education," *Le Temps*, 13 August 1927; Charles Salomon, "Correspondence," *Le Temps*, 8 October 1927, Musée social Archives.

11 Prévost et al., eds, *Dictionnaire de biographie*, 5:1367.

12 Between 1893 and 1896, Mabilleau had been a *chargé de mission* at the Ministry of Public Instruction. He had also been a *maître de conférence* at the Musée pédagogique. APP, BA 1165. He earned a yearly salary of 8,000 francs. PVCD, 25 September 1897. On Mabilleau's role in the mutualist world, see chapter 6.

13 PVCD, 25 September 1897, 12 March and 26 November 1898, 30 March 1901. A moderate republican political group, the Grand cercle républicain was created by Marcel Fournier, director of the *Revue politique et parlementaire*, with the active support of Jules Siegfried and René Waldeck-Rousseau. Mayeur, *Vie politique*, 170–71.

14 These fourteen seats went to the perpetual secretary of the Académie des sciences morales et politiques; the holders of the chair of social economy at the Faculté des lettres, the CNAM, and the École libre des sciences politiques; the director of the Office du travail and delegates from the Société d'économie sociale; the Société pour l'étude pratique de la participation aux bénéfices; the Société française des habitations à bon marché; the Centre fédératif du crédit populaire de France; the Comité central de l'Union coopérative des sociétés françaises de consommation; the Chambre consultative des associations ouvrières de production; the Ligue nationale de la prévoyance et de la mutualité; the Institut des actuaires; and the Office central des institutions charitables. PVCD, 25 June 1894.

15 André Siegfried, "Composition du Grand Conseil à sa fondation (1900)," Archives André Siegfried, FNSP, 4; Stone, *Search for Social Peace*, 50.

16 See Blum and Horne, "Féminisme et Musée social," 313–99.

17 *Musée social, Annales*, "Travaux des sections: Rôle des sections et caractère des procès-verbaux de leurs séances" (1902): 27.

18 Rivière, "Émile Cheysson," 229. In 1901 the board of directors discussed Audiffred's bill on voluntary social insurance. PVCD, 2 March 1901. For more information on Audiffred's and Siegfried's role in this debate, see chapter 6.

19 PVCD, 27 November 1896.

20 Blondel, *Études sur les populations*; Lachèvre, "La crise agraire."

21 See Dogliani, "Naissance d'un Musée social en Italie"; and Novick, "Le Musée social et l'urbanisme en Argentine, and *Influence de Le Play en Espagne*. Other institutions modeled on the Musée social were also created in London, Stockholm, and Budapest, as well as in Spain. Critchlow, *Brookings Institution*, 34. On Willoughby, see PVCD, 29 November 1895, 27 March 1896, 5 March 1898; *National Cyclopaedia*, 212–13. On Tolman, see Tolman and Hemstreet, *Better New York*, 158, 162; Tolman, *Municipal Reform Movements*. On Willink, see PVCD, 15 January and 12 February 1898; Willink, "Ingénieur social." On Varlez, see PVCD, 15 January 1898; Bureau international du travail, *Informations sociales* (the author thanks Sandra Dab for this source). On Stanley, who received a yearly fee of 2,000 francs, see PVCD, 10 December 1895, 29 October 1897. Musée social Archives, Box "Correspondents."

22 Muller to Salomon, 13 September 1897. Musée social Archives.

23 Salomon even encouraged Stanley to use the first person pronoun in his report, which, as Salomon wrote, "is not as hateful as French authors sometimes pretend it is." Salomon to Albert, 6 April 1897 and May 1897. Musée social Archives.

24 Muller to Chambrun, 18 January 1898. Musée social Archives, Box "Correspondents."

25 Willoughby, "Musée social in Paris."

26 Grave considered his work as a publisher to be the continuation of a form of anarchist "*propagande de tous les jours.*" The geographer Elisée Reclus paid Grave to go to Geneva (1883) to take over the administration of *Révolté*, which he brought back to Paris in 1883. Kropotkine remained his friend for many years. Maitron, *Dictionnaire biographique*, vol. 12, part 3 (1871–1914): 325–26.

27 Fonds de la Bibliothèque Martinet, purchased 29 March 1897. Musée social Archives; "Martinet." A member of the Comité central républicain during the Commune, Martelet signed the *affiche rouge* (red poster) of 6 January 1871 denouncing the government of the newly formed Third Republic for crimes of treason committed against the people of Paris. *Dictionnaire bibliographique*, vol. 7, part 2 (1864–71): 270–71.

28 As a bookseller, Delesalle thought of his work as a "continuation of propaganda and diffusion for syndicalist and revolutionary ideas." Located at # 16 rue Monsieur Le Prince beginning in 1908, his shop became a gathering place for intellectuals, militants, journalists, and writers of the Latin Quarter. See Maitron, *Dictionnaire biographique*, vol. 11, part 3 (1871–1914): 347–49.

29 Nettlau, *Michael Bakounine: Eine Biographie.* This colossal three-volume work served as the basis for Arthur Lehning's definitive biography of Bakounine. See Lehning, *Bakounine et les historiens.* The Austrian-born Nettlau, trained in philology, became a "historian-participant" of anarchist and socialist movements of nineteenth-century Europe. I thank Anthony Lorry for sharing with me his knowledge of Nettlau and anarchism during this period.

30 Julliard, *Fernand Pelloutier*, 173.

31 Métin, "Musée social," 564. The author thanks Venita Datta for this reference.

32 PVCD, 17 December 1898.

33 PVCD, 14 December 1894, 3 May and 28 June 1895; Willoughly, "Musée social," 62.

34 Lichtenberger, "Musée social: l'organisation et les services," 113–14. PVCD, 8 December 1894, 19 February 1897. See Martin Saint-Léon, *Rapport sur le projet de révision.*

35 Willoughby, "Musée social," 60.

36 Lichtenberger, "Musée social," 335.

37 Cheysson, *Musée social*, 22.

38 PVCD, 4 December 1896.

39 Other contributors to Desbuquois's almanac included Émile Cheysson, Maurice Dufourmantelle, Georges Picot, Hyacinthe Gailhad-Bancel, and the comte de Rocquigny. Droulers, *Politique sociale*, 80, 84–85 and n.112

40 May, "L'enseignement social," 16.

41 PVCD, 29 January 1897; Métin, "Musée social," 564.

42 PVCD, 23 November 1900. For more information on the Mutualism Service, see chapter 6.

43 Cheysson, "Musée social," 10–11.

44 PVCD, 2 November 1894. Unfortunately, only a few traces of these written consultations remain in the archives of the Musée social.

45 Lichtenberger, "Musée social: L'organisation et les services," 111.

46 Cited in ibid., 117.

47 Ibid., 122.

48 PVCD, 4 December 1896.

49 PVCD, 22 July 1895. It was considered rude to smoke cigars in the presence of ladies. Agulhon, *Cercle dans la France bourgeoise*, 52.

50 PVCD, 10 and 12 December 1895, 17 and 24 January and 7 November 1896; Lichtenberger, "Musée social: l'organisation et services," 121.

51 PVCD, 4 April 1900.

52 Cheysson, "Musée social," 11.

53 Chambrun to Léopold Mabilleau, 24 October 1898. Cited in Blum, "Comte de Chambrun, catholique," 31. Despite his protests, Chambrun did not prevent Fleury from participating in the Musée's study mission to England. See his report on the Algamated Engineers Union in Rousiers et al., *Trade-unionisme en Angleterre*, 255–92.

54 In 1897 Guieysse was a member of the Central Committee of the Ligue des droits de l'homme. "Guieysse," APP Ba 886 reports dated 24 February and 24 April 1901 and 21 October 1902. André Siegfried, *Mes souvenirs de la IIIe Republique*, 127–28. Jules Siegfried demonstrated his pro-Dreyfus sentiment when he invited the socialist Francis de Pressensé, president of the Ligue des droits de l'homme, to his home in Le Havre following a lecture at the Cercle Franklin. Murard and Zylberman, *Hygiène*, 193; Weill, *Histoire du catholicisme libéral*, 221, 226.

55 Eley, "Nations, Publics, and Political Cultures," 323.

56 "J'arrive de Besançon, où j'ai été faire une conférence pour ouvrir la série des conférences anti-socialistes que nous essayons d'organiser dans les diverses villes" (Georges Picot to Jules Simon, 14 February 1895, AN 87 AP 6).

57 Dubreuilh, "A la conquête des jeunes."

58 May, "Enseignement social à Paris," 16; Hauser, *Enseignement des sciences sociales*, 217. The municipal elections of May 1892, for instance, tallied 160,000 socialist votes and the election of 36 municipal councilors. The results of the legislative elections the following year confirmed this pattern, with 700,000 socialist votes and the election of 45 deputies representing all socialist factions. Bourdeau, "Mouvement syndical en France," 313. Georges Picot to Jules Simon, 30 July 1895, AN 87 AP 6; Picot, *Lutte contre le socialisme*.

59 Picot, *Socialisme, radicalisme et anarchie*, 25.

60 Georges Picot had unsuccessfully been a candidate on a moderate republican list for the Paris municipal elections of 1884 (quartier Chaussée d'Antin) and in the 1885 legislative elections in the department of Seine-et-Oise.

61 Picot, *La République—ses véritables adversair* [sic], 18.

62 Albert-Petit, "Georges Picot"; Coston, *Dictionnaire des dynasties bourgeoises*, 256–61.

63 May, "Enseignement social," 19.

64 Renard, "Musée social," 440–42.

65 Ibid., 441.

66 Picot, *Socialisme*, 26–27.

67 Guyot as quoted in Seilhac, *Congrès de legislation du travail*, 28; Cheysson, "Rapports des lois d'assurances ouvrières," 9.

68 Cited in an anonymous book review of Paul Deschanel's *Quatre ans de présidence: Annales*, ELSP, 1903, 542.

69 Chambrun, *Aux montagnes d'Auvergne: Mes conclusions*, 36, 44, 68–69, 71, 104–5.

70 Cheysson, "Rôle de l'État dans la question des habitations ouvrières," 24.

71 *Bulletin de la* SFHBM, Assemblée général du 12 mars 1893, 25.

72 Cheysson, "Économie sociale à l'Exposition," 19.

73 *Bulletin de la* SFHBM, 1893, 25.

74 Cited in an anonymous book review of Paul Deschanel's *Quatre ans de présidence*. *Annales*, ELSP, 1903, 542.

75 Picot, cited in Cheysson, "Georges Picot," 293; Picot, *Usage de la liberté*. Bismarck enacted, by imperial decree, sickness insurance (1883); accident insurance (1884); and insurance for the elderly and the infirm (1889).

76 Picot, "Usage de la liberté," 12, 28.

77 Ibid., 38–39.

78 Cheysson, *Homme social et la colonisation*, 14.

79 Cheysson, "Musée social," 1.

80 Fleury quote, as reported by Charles Gide, cited in C. Robert, "Économistes et coopérateurs"; Guyot quote cited in *Le Siècle*, 24 August 1900. Guyot also protested vehemently when the Musée social lent its meeting hall for the assembly of the Congrès international pour la protection légale des travailleurs; see Lichtenberger, "Congrès international," 264, n. 1; C. Robert, "Économistes et coopérateurs," 35.

81 See Sorel, *Réflexions sur la violence.*

82 Abbé Henri de Seilhac, interview with the author, Paris, 8 March 1988. I thank Abbot de Seilhac of Saint Thomas Aquinas Parish in Paris for his attempts to find documentation on his great uncle. Léon de Seilhac's name is missing, for instance, from the family genealogy furnished by the Departmental Archives of Corrèze.

83 Musée social, PVCD, 6 March 1896; Martin Saint-Léon, "Léon de Seilhac"; Julliard, *Fernand Pelloutier*, 129; Howorth, *Édouard Vaillant*, 151–52; Seilhac, *Monde socialiste: groupes et programmes*; Seilhac, *Le monde socialiste: Les partis socialistes politiques*; Seilhac, *Congrès ouvriers en France de 1876 a 1897*; Seilhac, *Congrès ouvriers en France; Deuxieme série*; Seilhac, *Syndicats ouvriers.*

84 Dubreuilh, "Congrès ouvriers."

85 Martin Saint-Léon, "Léon de Seilhac."

86 Lichtenberger, "Musée social: L'organisation et les services," 115–6.

87 Seilhac, *Enquête sociale*, 44, 159. Also see Scott, *Glassworkers of Carmaux.*

88   Seilhac, *Syndicats ouvriers, féderations;* Lichtenberger, "Musée social: L'organisation et les services," 116.

89   Rousiers mentions his conversation with Webb, who was also a historian of trade-unionism, in Rousiers, "Trade-unionisme anglais," 18; also see Rousiers, "Syndicats du bâtiment en Angleterre."

90   Rousiers, "Trade-unionisme anglais," 22.

91   Festy, "Ouvriers des docks," 166.

92   "C'est le corps de métiers le plus atteint par le machinisme qui fournit encore les hommes les plus intelligents et les plus capables" (Rousiers, "Syndicats du bâtiment," 68).

93   Magraw, *History of the French Working Class,* 22.

94   Rousiers, "Trade-unionisme anglais," 28.

95   Action populaire, *Guide social,* 1907, 320–22; Seilhac, *Grèves,* 250; Fontaine, *Grèves et la conciliation,* 27.

96   "L'élargissement de la loi de 1884: Capacité civile du syndicat," *Guide social* (1911), 153.

97   Seilhac, *Grèves,* 250.

98   Jay, *Forme nouvelle,* 1, 15.

99   "Acculturation," from Cottereau, "Distinctiveness of Working-Class Cultures," 112. Accordingly, Musée reformers rejected the claims of socialist cooperatives such as the Bourse des coopératives socialistes (1900), previously known as the Bourse des sociétés coopératives ouvrières de consommation (1895). See Furlough, *Consumer Co-operation,* 119–22.

100 The International Cooperative Alliance (ICA) was founded by British Christian Socialist Vansittart-Neale in 1892. Although its first official congress was held in London in August 1895, the organization was solidly implanted only with its second international congress, held in Paris in October 1896 at the Musée social. See "Alliance coopérative internationale," 8–9; Gaumont, *Histoire générale,* 2:205.

101 The ICA president was Charles Robert; the vice presidents were Henry Buisson, Comte de Rocquigny, and Eugène Rostand; the treasurer was Fitsch; and the secretary, Albert Trombert. It is not surprising that the French members of the ICA were also extremely active in other sectors of the social reform movement such as low-income housing, people's banks, and mutual aid societies. Musée social, *Semaine coopérative;* "Générosité du comte" *Émancipation,* 15 August 1897, 126; "Alliance coopérative internationale," 8–9; Nord, *Paris Shopkeepers,* 352–61; also see Daugan, *Histoire et législation des patentes.*

102 Musée social, *Semaine coopérative,* 57, 81. Siegfried explained that once the advantages of cooperation were understood, "revolutionary and socialist theories [would] lose their malevolent action." Clavel's speech in Musée social, *Semaine coopérative,* 10; "Discours de clôture de M. Jules Siegfried," 97.

103 *Cooperative News,* 14 November 1896; Musée social, *Semaine coopérative,* 30.

104 Renard, "Musée social," 442.

105 "First step," from Lagarde, "Revue des revues," 484; Pelloutier, "Mes conclusions sociologiques par le comte de Chambrun," and "La semaine politique et sociale."

106 Dubreuilh, "Le comte de Chambrun."

5. Voluntary Associations and the Republican Ideal

1 As will be further developed, the term *social insurance* refers to the various means of acquiring insurance or protection against such risks as illness, old age, and unemployment. See Stone, *Search for Social Peace*, 99–122.

2 Dreyfus, "Léopold Mabilleau et le mouvement mutualiste," 107–8; Dreyfus, *Histoire de la C.G.T.*

3 Dreyfus, "Opération patrimoine," Zeldin, *France*, 1:661–62; Dreyfus, *Mutualité: Une histoire*; Gibaud, *Mutualité à la Sécurité sociale*; Bennet, *Biographies de personnalités mutualistes*; Hatzfeld, *Paupérisme à la Sécurité, sociale*; T. Laurent, *Mutualité française*; Mitchell, *Divided Path*, 228–96; Gueslin, *Invention de l'économie sociale*, 167–212; Sewell, *Work and Revolution*; Hunt and Sheriden, "Corporatism, Association"; Wolloch, *New Regime*, 289–93; Weintrob, "From Fraternity to Solidarity."

4 Georges Picot to Jules Simon, AN 87, AP 6, 4 July 1895; Mabilleau, "Mutualité," 27; Tocqueville, *Democracy in America* (1945), 2:114–18. English friendly societies or American provident societies and contingency funds are sometimes compared to French mutual aid societies, although they were more firmly implanted in England and were primarily designed as financial institutions in the United States.

5 Laveille, *Histoire de la mutualité*, 61; Arboux, *Histoire de seize ans*, 131. See comments by Charles Dupuy in "L'avenir de la mutualité," *Musée social*, Series A, 24 (1898): 382; Société des industriels, "Retraites ouvrières, 91; Weill, *Histoire du mouvement social*, 450.

6 *Banquet offert à Léopold Mabilleau*, 39.

7 Martin Saint-Léon, "Compagnonnage, ses coutumes," 171; Mabilleau, *Mutualité française*, 10–11; Martin Saint-Léon, *Histoire des corporations*; Bennet, *Mutualité des origines*.

8 Wolloch, *New Regime*, 290; Amizade, *Class, Politics*, 71–72; Judt, *Marxism and the Left*, 63–65.

9 Dreyfus, "Léopold Mabilleau," 106. During this period, nearly ten percent of all mutualists were honorary members. Dreyfus, "Mutualité," 42; *Caisse des dépôts*, 76; Delorme and André, *État et l'économie*; Smiles quoted in Briggs, *Collected Essays*, 2:185.

10 AN, Chamber of Deputies, Comité d'assurance et de prévoyance sociales (CAPS), Series C, 5544, 1 January 1894; Gibaud, "Mutualité sous la Troisième République," 17–19; Dreyfus, "Mutualité," 31; *Banquet offert à Léopold Mabilleau*, 28, 30; Based on figures given by Léopold Mabilleau in 1898, Michel Dreyfus revised the number of industrial workers in mutual aid societies upward to 600,000–700,000 (out of 3,300,000 workers accounted for in the census), see "Avenir de la mutualité," *Musée social*, Série A, Circulaire 24, 22 December 1898, 573–96; Dreyfus, "Léopold Mabilleau," 107.

11 The 1898 law maintained the distinction between the three sorts of mutual aid societies: "free societies," "approved societies," and societies with public utility status, each of which were submitted to certain restrictions. Dreyfus, "Mutualité de Léopold Mabilleau"; Gibaud, "Mutualité sous la Troisième République."

12 Louis Varlez reported on Belgian mutual aid societies, "Service des correspondants," *Musée social* (1900): 36; 149–51; Fuster, "Résultats de la mutualité maladie"; Paul Langer (on the attitude of trade unions toward the Friendly Society Act of 1896), *Musée social*, Annales (1906): 370.

13 Blum, "Comte de Chambrun, catholique," 40. "L'Aiguille," a mutual society for the Paris sewing trades, see "L'industrie de la couture et de la confection à Paris," in *Musée social*, Series A, 14 (1897), 279; on "L'Avenir", a mutual society for saleswomen, see ibid., 281. On "La Mutualité maternelle," see ibid., 282; on a maternal mutual aid society established by the Chambre syndicale de la confection et de la couture, see *Musée social, Annales* (1903): 35; Stewart, *Women, Work, and the French State*.

14 Cheysson, "Mutualité familiale," 621–43; Cheysson, "Conference," in *Musée social*, 82; Cheysson, "Famille, l'association et l'État," in *Oeuvres choisies*, 2:145; AN, Series C, 5544, CAPS, *procès-verbaux*, 1 January 1894.

15 Cheysson, "Rôle de la femme dans la mutualité"; Cheysson, "Action sociale de la femme," 601. For comprehensive mutualist membership figures, see Table 2.

16 Guérin, "Settlement anglais," 357.

17 "Enquête sur les législations relatives au droit d'association," *Musée social*, Series A, 22 (1897): 499; "Discussions de la loi sur les sociétés de secours mutuels," *Musée social*, Series B, 20 (1898): 605–98. The 1884 law enabled unions to form their own mutual aid societies, but by 1903 only 8 percent declared to have done so. Gibaud, "Mutualité," 18.

18 Rivière, "Émile Cheysson," 229.

19 AN C 5544, CAPS, *procès-verbaux*, 5 April 1895; Mitchell, *Divided Path*, 231–45.

20 Jolly, *Dictionnaire des parlementaires* 1:410–11; Robert and Cougny, *Dictionnaire des parlementaires* 1:111–12; Labarre de Raillicourt, *Nouveau dictionnaire des biographies françaises*, 1:948, 3:1332; Musée social Archives, PVDC, 22 October 1897; Hamon, *Histoire générale de l'assurance*, 111. Ten of the original thirty-three CAPS members became Musée social reformers: Maruéjouls, Guieysse, Bourgeois, Audiffred, Léon Say, Louis Ricard, Poincaré, Raiberti, Siegfried, Émile Chevallier. AN C 5544, CAPS, *procès-verbaux*, 18 January 1894.

21 Société des industriels, *Retraites ouvrières et la mutualité*, 91.

22 Gibaud, "Mutualité," 18; Dreyfus, "Mutualité," 33–34; Dreyfus, *Mutualité*, 30–31; Cheysson and Dergas quoted in *Banquet offert à Léopold Mabilleau*, 19–20.

23 *Banquet offert à Léopold Mabilleau*, 29–30; Cheysson, *Assurances ouvrières*, 20. No French mutual aid society even approximated the wealth of the Boston Provident Institution for Savings, one of Massachusetts's main financial institutions. Story, *Harvard and the Boston Upper Class*, 11.

24 Fuster, "Évolution de l'assurance ouvrière," 388.

25 Cheysson, *Assurances ouvrières*, 54.

26 Varlez, "Assurance intégrale," 16; Bureau international du travail, *Informations sociales*, 160–61; Cheysson, *Assurances ouvrières*, 7; Levasseur, *Résumé historique*, 31–32.

27 Bellom, *Résultats de l'assurance ouvrière*; Gibon, *Retraites organisées*.

28 In 1908, the term "industrial accidents" was dropped altogether from the official title of the congress in favor of the "International Congress on Social Insurance," with its corresponding publication, the *Bulletin des assurances sociales*. Varlez, "Assurance intégrale," 16.

29 Cheysson, "Rapports des lois d'assurances," 8.

30 Cheysson, "Accidents du travail et la pension," 324.

31 Cheysson quoted in Ewald, *État providence*, 283; also see 284–85.

32 Jay, *Assurance ouvrière obligatoire*, 11.

33 Ewald, *État providence*, 317, 373.

34 Fuster, "Évolution de l'assurance ouvrière," 388.

35 Cited by Jay, *Assurance ouvrière obligatoire*, 11.

36 Varlez, "Assurance intégrale," 1894; Fuster, "Évolution de l'assurance ouvrière," 388.

37 AN C 5544, 5 February 1896.

38 Cited by Derosières, "Ingénieur d'État," 70.

39 Cited by Lavielle, *Histoire de la mutualité*, 16.

40 Cheysson, *Assurances ouvrières*, 9.

41 Martin Saint-Léon, "Retraites ouvrières doivent-elles être obligatoires?" 419.

42 Paoli, "Questions économiques et sociales," 141. For a thorough history of retirement pension debates in the early twentieth century, see Dumons and Pollet, *État et les retraites*.

43 "Texte de loi sur les sociétés de secours mutuels, délibérée et adoptée par le Sénat et par la Chambre des députés, promulguée le 1er Avril 1898," *Musée social*, Series A, 24 (1898): 586–96; "Discussions de la loi sur les sociétés de secours mutuels," *Musée social*, Series B, 20 (1898): 605–98.

44 "Législation et jurisprudence sociales en France," *Musée social*, Series A, 23 (1898): 513–67; "Section des assurances sociales," *Musée social*, Annales (1902): 212.

45 "Service de la mutualité," *Musée social*, Annales (1902): 250.

46 Musée social Archives, PVCD, 17 April 1896, 24 July 1896, and 21 May 1897.

47 *Banquet offert à Léopold Mabilleau*, 27.

48 Section des assurances sociales, *Musée social*, Annales (1902): 216–17.

49 Dreyfus, "Léopold Mabilleau et le mouvement mutualiste."

50 Gaumont, *Histoire générale de la coopération*, vol. 2; Maitron, *Dictionnaire biographique*, 13:3; APP, BA1165.

51 Cheysson, *Banquet offert à Léopold Mabilleau*, 19; "Léopold Mabilleau," *Avenir républicain*, 19 March 1911.

52 Lecture, 22 November 1898, *Musée social*, Series A (1898), 575–85; Arboux, *Histoire de seize ans*, 126.

53 Bourgeois's speech, *Banquet offert à Léopold Mabilleau*, 26. Musée social Archives, Mabilleau, "Les progrès récents de la prévoyance sociale," public lecture at the Musée social, 21 January 1898; Mabilleau, Rayneri, and de Rocquigny, *Prévoyance en Italie*.

54 "Service de la mutualité," *Musée social*, Annales (1902): 250–57; 381–86.

55 The Chamber of Deputies began discussing the first series of bills in June 1901. After sixteen sessions, they postponed further debate until a survey of all interested parties could be undertaken.

56 "Service de la mutualité," *Musée social*, Annales (1905): 413; Stone, *Search for Social Peace*, 112.

57 *Banquet offert à Léopold Mabilleau*, 14; "Service de la mutualité," *Musée social*, Annales (1902): 78–85.

58 *Banquet offert à Léopold Mabilleau*, 38.

59 Fuster, "Évolution de l'assurance ouvrière," 407.

60 *Banquet offert à Léopold Mabilleau*, 35; Cheysson's speech at the banquet following the creation of the FNMF, "Service de la mutualité," *Musée social, Annales* (1902): 436. Foundation and its statutes: "Service de la mutualité," *Musée social, Annales* (1902): 381–86. Also, see: Lavielle, *Histoire de la mutualité*; Mabilleau et al., *Prévoyance sociale en Italie*, xviii; Dreyfus, *Mutualité*, 36; Gibaud, "Musée social et mutualité."

61 Félix Raison, "Service de la mutualité," *Musée social, Annales* (1920): 250.

62 "Mutualists must federate and combine their forces" (cited in Dreyfus, *La mutualité: Une histoire*, 39; Gibaud, "Musée social et mutualité," 317).

63 Mabilleau was forced to resign as president of the FNMF in 1921 following a dubious business transaction of pillows and blankets intended as wartime charitable goods. "Les marchés de M. Mabilleau," *Matin*, 3 June 1921; "M. Mabilleau est inculpé," *Matin*, 18 June 1921.

64 President Loubet became an official member of the Musée social in 1906.

65 "Service de la mutualité," *Musée social, Annales* (1902): 83–84.

66 Société des industriels, *Retraites ouvrières*, 86.

67 Comité central républicain, *Revue comique normande*, 19 April 1902, 2.

68 *Musée social, Annales* (1902): 50.

69 Société des industriels, *Retraites ouvrières*, 72; Mitchell, *Divided Path*, 44–67.

70 Salaun, "Retraites ouvrières en Belgique," 169–99; Salaun, "Résultats de la loi belge," 405–23.

71 "La mutualité et l'assurance ouvrière," *Musée social, Annales* (1902): 421.

72 Cheysson, "Rapports des lois d'assurances," 8.

73 Paoli, "Questions économiques et sociales,"141.

74 "On enlève au travailleur son levier d'ascension sociale; on le rive au salariat, on l'enferme dans sa classe, puisqu'on lui retire les moyens d'en sortir" (Cheysson, "Rapport sur le projet de loi relatif au retraites ouvrières"); Cheysson, *Retraites ouvrières*.

75 Paoli, "Questions économiques," 141.

76 Martin Saint-Léon, "Retraites ouvrières," 427.

77 Dusart, "Obligation dans les retraites ouvrières," 336–50.

78 *Journal officiel: Débats Parlementaires: Chambre des députés*, 2nd session, 25 June 1901; Dumons and Pollet, *État et les retraites*.

79 Varlez, "Assurance intégrale," 5.

80 Musée social, *Contribution à la bibliographie des assurances sociales*. Other publications that attempted to establish a similar collection of references to foreign legislation include: *Bulletin de la Société de législation comparée*, 1891–92, 81; the publications of the International Congresses on Work Related Accidents; Bellom, *Lois d'assurance ouvrière à l'étranger*; Lavollée, *Classes ouvrières en Europe*.

81 PVCD, 28 June 1902.

82 Fuster, "Évolution de l'assurance," 404.

83 Fuster, "Vie ouvrière,"1.

84 "Service de la mutualité," *Musée social, Annales*, 1905, 434.

85 In 1897 the Société de législation comparée had discussed Bellom's theories on re-

tirement pensions for industrial workers. At that time, he espoused measures that were "anti-statist" and condemned the German model as a threat of state-socialism in France. Paoli, "Questions économiques et sociales," 41; *Musée social*, Series B (1897): 357.

86 Bellom, "Résultats de l'assurance ouvrière," 8, 24.

87 J. Siegfried, "Retraites ouvrières devant le Parlement," 133–34, 143.

88 Mabilleau, "Rapport présenté au 9e Congrès national," 120.

89 Gibaud, "La mutualité et les retraites ourvières," 74.

90 Lecture by Léopold Mabilleau, untitled, Musée social Archives, Box: "Grandes Conférences," 13 December 1909; Cheysson, *Retraites ouvrières*, 92.

91 Gibaud, "Mutualité et les retraites ouvrières."

92 Mabilleau, untitled lecture, 13 December 1909, Musée social Archives.

93 Mabilleau, "Comment réconcilier deux termes: La liberté individuelle et la solidarité sociale?" Musée social Archives, Box: "Grandes Conférences," 11 November 1908, 8, 12.

94 Mabilleau, "Mutualité et les retraites ouvrières," 51–52.

95 Ashford, *Emergence of the Welfare States*; Stone, *Search for Social Peace*, 122.

96 For more development of this theme, see Rabinow, *French Modern*, 197–210.

97 J. C. Cavé used this argument when he appeared before CAPS in 1894. AN C 5544, 2 February 1894.

6. The Modernity of Hygiene

1 Murard and Zylberman, *Hygiène*, 66–67, 71, 75; Schneider, *Quality and Quantity*, 117.

2 At the 1901 Tuberculosis Congress held in New York, Mr. Costello reported that 70 percent of the clothing exported from that city was infected with the tubercular bacillus. The daughter of English statesman Sir Robert Peel reportedly succumbed to tuberculosis contracted through "*un habit d'Amazone.*" Cheysson, "Travail des femmes," 384–85.

3 Léon Bourgeois's wife and daughter died of consumption (phthisis). Georges Risler lost a daughter (1899) and then a son (1902) to tuberculosis, prompting him to abandon his industrial firm and devote himself to social reform efforts. Musée social, *M. Georges Risler (1853–1941)*, 14; Murard and Zylberman, *Hygiène*, 457; Latour, *Pasteurization of France*; Rosanvallon, *État en France*, 130; Aisenberg, *Contagion*.

4 Leon Bourgeois expounded on these ideas in his compilation of essays and speeches entitled *La Politique de prévoyance sociale*.

5 The figures cited include seasonal migration. *Annuaire statistique de la ville de Paris et du département de la Seine* (1886), cited by Shapiro, *Housing of the Poor*, 55; Bertillon, *Essai de statistique comparée*, 6–7. For a summary of the considerable body of literature on migration, see Jackson and Moch, "Migration and the Social History of Modern Europe."

6 J. Siegfried, "Proposition de loi relative aux habitations ouvrières," 52; Mesnil, "L'Hygiène des habitations ouvrières," 304; Jacquemet, *Belleville au XIXe siècle*, 211.

7 On these early social investigators, see Perrot, *Enquêtes sur la condition ouvrière*; Rigaudias-Weiss, *Enquêtes ouvrières en France*; Blanqui, *Des classes ouvrières en France*; Vil-

lermé *Tableau de l'état physique*. A subsidiary function of the universal exhibitions was that such intellectual and political congresses served to publicly legitimate the concerns of their organizers and participants. See Rasmussen, "Congrès internationaux"; Bullock and Read, *Movement for Housing Reform*, 347; Murard and Zylberman, *Hygiène*, 41–65. In 1889, the Société de médecine publique created standing committees, including one on urban and rural hygiene and another, headed by Émile Cheysson, on demographics and statistics. Five years later the Musée social adopted this same institutional structure as its own.

8   "Postbacteriological period," Shapiro, *Housing of the Poor*, 78–83; Coleman, *Death Is a Social Disease*; Bertillon, *De la fréquence des principales causes de décès* and "Des logements surpeuplés à Paris," 111–126; "Sanitary journal," Bullock and Read, *Movement for Housing Reform*, 353; Barnes, *Making of a Social Disease*; Mesnil, *Hygiène à Paris*. Also see Juillerat, *L'hygiène du logement*; "Le logement et la santé"; "Sur le casier sanitaire."

9   Corbin, *Miasme et la jonquille*; Pinkney, *Napoleon III*, 23; Shapiro, *Housing the Poor*, 17, 21, 29; Murard and Zylberman, *Hygiène*, 24–26.

10   Du Mesnil as cited by Shapiro, *Housing the Poor*, 144; Bulletin SFHBM (1890): 19.

11   La Berge, *Mission and Method*; J. Siegfried, "Proposition de loi relative aux habitations ouvrières," 49.

12   Guerrand, *Origines du logement social*, 328.

13   Bulletin SFHBM (1890): 24, 37; Siegfried, "Proposition de loi relative aux habitations ouvrières," 84.

14   Risler, *Better Housing for Workers*, 4–5.

15   Bulletin SFHBM (1890): 1; (1893): 27.

16   Designed essentially for working-class families, *habitations à bon marché* can be translated as "low-cost housing"; whereas the newer designation, *habitation à loyers modérés*, can be translated as "low-rent housing."

17   Jules Siegfried was appointed as the minster of commerce in 1892 by Alexandre Ribot. For the committee's evaluation of the Siegfried bill, see Bulletin SFHBM (1894): 372–80; Jules Siegfried to Jules Siegfried, fils., 6 November 1891. Siegfried Family Archives (AP).

18   This study, undertaken by Drs. du Mesnil and Mangenot focused on the 13th arrondissement of Paris and was later published as part of a larger work entitled *Étude d'hygiène et d'économie sociale*.

19   Jules Siegfried to Jules Siegfried, fils, 11 December 1891, AP.

20   Jules Siegfried, "Proposition de loi," Bulletin SFHBM (1892): 51. Essentially, reformers wanted the state to grant fiscal advantages to the private constructors of low-cost housing and to authorize Caisse des dépôts, the central deposit bank, to lend money to constructors at preferential rates.

21   Bulletin SFHBM (1890): 470.

22   Siegfried, "Proposition de loi relative aux habitations ouvrières," 49, 53.

23   For a discussion of the evolution of the rhetorics of ownership and property, see Carol M. Rose, *Property and Persuasion*, 58–62.

24   Siegfried, "Proposition de loi relative aux habitations ouvrières," 58.

25   Roulliet, "Loi sur les habitations ouvrières," 244; Siegfried, "Proposition de loi relative aux habitations ouvrières," 63.

26   Cited by Guerrand, *Origines*, 299.

27   Conseil supérieur du travail, 29 June 1892, *Bulletin* SFHBM (1892): 475.

28   Mesnil, "Hygiène des habitations ouvrières," 304.

29   *Bulletin* SFHBM (1894): 227.

30   "Practical socialism," Siegfried, "Discours de M. Jules Siegfried," *Bulletin* SFHBM (1890): 16; Bullock and Read, *Movement for Housing Reform*, 340; "Le Banquet de Melun," *La Petite République* [s.d.], Dossier Léon Bourgeois, Fonds "Actualité," Archives of the Bibliothèque de la Ville de Paris; A. Siegfried, *Mes souvenirs de la IIIe République*, 106, 119, 124.

31   André Siegfried, *Mes souvenirs de la IIIe République*, 127–28.

32   Bullock and Read, *Movement for Housing Reform*, 341.

33   On the trip (which cost him his entire savings of 10,000FF) Siegfried took a copy of Gerando's *Bienfaisance publique* to read on the boat. "Hommage à la mémoire de Jules Siegfried," *Alsace française*, 10 February 1937, 34; A. Siegfried, *Mes souvenirs de la IIIe République*, 13–14.

34   According to his son André, although Jules Siegfried "never had any intellectual culture and never worried about acquiring any," he was "remarkably well-informed . . . but the disinterested life of the mind was foreign to him" (*Mes souvenirs de la IIIe République*, 10.)

35   A. Siegfried, *Jules Siegfried*, 8; Archives André Siegfried, "L'homme d'affaires," (notes for a speech about Jules Siegfried), Fondation nationale des sciences politiques.

36   Hause and Kenny, *Women's Suffrage and Social Politics*; Blum and Horne, "Féminisme et Musée social," 315–402.

37   "Obsèques de M. Jules Siegfried," *Le Petit Havre*, 30 September 1922; "Le fondateur du premier bureau d'hygiène en France," *Alsace française*, 10 February 1937, 34; Bullock and Read, *Movement for Housing Reform*, 340; Auspitz, *Radical Bourgeoisie*, 86, 160.

38   "Le fondateur du premier bureau d'hygiène en France," *Alsace française*, 10 February 1937, 36.

39   A. Siegfried, *Jules Siegfried*, 46–47; Bullock and Read, *Movement for Housing Reform*, 340.

40   A. Siegfried, *Jules Siegfried*, 45.

41   "Secret drawers," cited by Shapiro, *Housing the Poor*, 149; and Murard and Zylberman, *Hygiène*, 209. "Trompe l'oeil" in Murard and Zylberman, *Hygiène*, 237. On the history of 1902 Siegfried law, see ibid., 209–41. For a thorough discussion of the provisions of this law, see Shapiro, *Housing the Poor*, 147–58, and 200, n. 47 for a clear legislative chronology.

42   Fuster quote, Musée social, Comité de direction, procès-verbaux, 8 November 1902.

43   Murard and Zylberman, *Hygiène*, 444–45.

44   Benoît-Lévy, *La cité-jardin*; *Cités-jardins d'Amérique*; "Les cités-jardins aux États-Unis"; and "Les garden cities: Port Sunlight"; Howard, *Garden Cities of Tomorrow*; Howard cited by Benoît-Lévy, "Les garden cities: Port Sunlight," 12.

45   V. Dubron in the opening speech at the Second Congress of the Alliance in 1905. Cited

by Hayward, "Official Social Philosophy of the French Third Republic," 40. Musée social members Émile Cheysson, Jules Siegfried, Léopold Mabilleau, Georges Risler, Leon Bourgeois, Georges Picot, and Albert Gigot were all involved with the founding of the Alliance d'hygiène sociale.

46 Other groups in the Alliance d'hygiène included the Association des industriels de France contre les accidents de travail; the Ligue contre la mortalité infantile; the Ligue nationale contre l'alcoolisme; the Ligue française d'hygiène scolaire; and l'Association polytechnique. Hayward, "Léon Bourgeois and Solidarism," 40–41; also see Murard and Zylberman, Hygiène, 446. "A laboratory of ideas" and Siegfried quote, Alliance d'hygiène sociale, Congrès de Roubaix 13–14.

47 "Strong arm," Murard and Zylberman, Hygiène, 450.

48 "Wednesdays of the Poor," ibid.

49 "Swimming against the tide," ibid., 452. For the political interpretation of the Alliance d'hygiene sociale, ibid., 452; for funding, ibid., 469.

50 Bourgeois, Solidarité, 136–40.

51 Alliance d'hygiène sociale. Congrès de Roubaix, 16, 18; Siegfried, "Les retraites ouvrières devant le Parlement," 331.

52 Musée social, Comité de direction, procès-verbaux, 5 January 1907, 4 May 1907, 29 June 1907, 16 November 1907; 21 December 1907; 4 January 1908. Siegfried attributed these ideas on urban planning to the architect J. C. N. Forestier, see Le Musée social, Mémoires et documents (1907), 328. On this Section d'hygiène urbaine et rurale, see also Cormier, "Extension, limites, espaces libres"; Osti, "Musée social et l'urbanisme," 117–25; Magri, Les laboratoires de la réforme.

53 Section d'hygiène urbaine et rurale, Séance constitutive, 14 January 1908, Le Musée social, Annales (1908), 56.

54 O'Brien, "L'embastillement de Paris," 63–82; Evenson, Paris: A Century of Change, 206, 272; "vacation spot of the poor," Robert, "Discours à la Sorbonne," Grands conférences, Musée social Archives (1908), 5.

55 My information in this section on the Bois de Boulogne draws on Marie Charvet's work, particularly her "Question des fortifications de Paris," 23–44.

56 Ibid., 28.

57 Wolf, Eugène Hénard; Rabinow, French Modern, 254–57. For the "French school of urbanism," see Jean-Louis Cohen, "Les visions métropolitaines d'Eugène Hénard," preface to Hénard, Études sur les transformations de Paris, viii. See also Hénard, Études sur les transformations de Paris, 23–54; Poëte, Une vie de cité; Au jardin des Tuilleries; and Introduction à l'urbanisme. Marcel Poëte, the director of the Musée historique de la ville de Paris, who became the other dominant contemporary figure in French urbanism, was also a member of the Musée's hygiene section.

58 Cottereau, "Débuts de la planification urbaine," 362–92.

59 Wright, Politics of Design; "right of eminent domain," "Les espaces libres à Paris," Conference à la Sorbonne, 5 June 1908, typed report, Musée social Archives: Grands Conférences; "national hygiene," Nord, "Social defence and conservative regeneration," 217–18.

60 Foreign architects whose work in early urban planning influenced the hygiene section included Josef Stübben, Camillo Sitte, Edmund James, and Émile Vandervelde. Cormier, "Extension, limites," 19; Sutcliffe, *Autumn of Central Paris.*

61 "The most beautiful city in the world," SHUR, *Le Musée social, Annales,* 13 March 1909, 125; 12 April 1908, 127; 23 January 1908, 59–60.

62 "Ephemeral financial needs," SHUR, *Le Musée social, Annales,* 2 April 1908, 127–28. The associations who were asked to sign the poster also included the Société de médecine publique, the Ligue nationale contre l'alcoolisme, the Federation des sociétés anti-tuberculeuses, and the Société des paysages. Siegfried, "Proposition de loi concernant les fortifications," 73–77.

63 Combeau, *Paris et les élections municipales,* 261–67.

64 Thomas, "Espaces libres," 1; "Élections municipales," 3; "Manoeuvre à dénoncer," 1.

65 "Discours de M. Ribot," in "Espaces libres à Paris," 224–31.

66 "Conférence de Me. Henri Robert," in "Espaces libres à Paris," 221–22.

67 Siegfried, "Proposition de loi concernant les fortifications," 73–77.

68 Charvet, "Question des fortifications," 23–44. Eugène Hénard and the Society for Public Medicine refused to endorse Dausset's project. A former schoolteacher and one of the founding members, during the Dreyfus Affair, of the Ligue de la patrie française, Dausset presented his candidacy several times as a Nationalist for the Chamber of Deputies. His entrance into the Paris municipal council in 1900, with the support of the Ligue de la patrie française marked a new power dynamic within the council since the nationalist coalition, for the first time, occupied more seats than the left. The left regained its predominance from 1904 to 1908. But after having long been dominated by the left, the Paris municipal council moved definitively to the right with the 1909 elections. See Combeau, *Paris et les élections municipales.*

69 SHUR, *Le Musée social, Annales,* 8 July 1908, 330; SHUR, *Le Musée social, Annales,* 10 November 1910, 406–7; Roosevelt, *Idéal américain;* Nord, "Social Defence," 218.

70 SHUR, *Le Musée social, Annales,* 24 November 1910, 411–12.

71 SHUR, *Le Musée social, Annales,* 1912, 87–88; André Lichtenberger, "La lutte pour la race, espaces libres et terrains de jeux," *L'Opinion,* 24 December 1910, 801–3; Lucien March, "Pour la race: Infertilité et puericulture," *Revue du mois,* 10 (1910): 551–82.

72 SHUR, *Le Musée social, Annales,* 20 January 1911, 67.

73 The Commission supérior d'amènagement de l'agglomération parisienne operated under the aegis of the Ministry of the Interior. Siegfried, "Proposition de loi concernant les fortifications," 75–76.

74 SHUR, *Le Musée social, Annales* (1909): 54–60.

75 Topalov, "From the 'Social Question,' " 328; Gwendolyn Wright, *Politics of Design,* 81–160; 84. For a highly suggestive analysis of the Musée social's ideas on planning and their influence on urban design in the colonies, see Vacher, *Projection coloniale et ville rationalisée.*

76 SHUR, *Musée social, Annales,* 2 May 1918, 260.

77 Although Cornudet's bill quickly passed the Chamber in 1915, the bill was not ac-

cepted by the Senate until 1919, and it was then amended in 1924. SHUR, *Musée social, Annales* (1915): 197.

78   Evenson, *Paris: A Century of Change*, 275

79   Le Corbusier quotes from *The Radiant City* in Evenson, *Paris: A Century of Change*, 275; Baudoui, "Aux origines du Comité supérieur d'amènagement," 215–16; Blum, "Musée social au carrefour?"; Charvet, "De l'hygiènisme àl'urbanisme." I thank Scott Haine for his thoughtful comments on these points.

80   "Sheer intransigence," Wright, *Politics of Design*, 00.

81   Topalov, "From the 'social question,'" 125; Topalov, *Naissance du chômeur*, 116–91.

82   Topalov, "From the 'social question,'" 327.

83   Corbin, *Miasme et la jonquille*; Reid, *Paris Sewers and Sewermen*; Guerrand, *Les Lieux*; Guerrand, *Murs citadines*.

84   Topalov, "From 'the social question,'" 327.

85   For a discussion of how some Musée social reformers extended their prescriptions for France to the colonial empire, see my article "In Pursuit of Greater France," 21–42.

Conclusion

1   "The love of grand ideals and the reality of petty settlements" (Rosanvallon, *Nouvelle question sociale*).

2   Philip Nord has called for a substantial revision, if not an outright disavowal of this standard view. See Nord, "Welfare State in France," 837.

3   Guerrand, *Brève histoire du service social*.

4   Phillips, "Neo-Corporatist Praxis in Paris," 405; Wright, *Politics of Design*.

5   Murard and Zylberman, "Raison de l'expert," 339.

6   Koven and Michel, eds., *Mothers of a New World*; Susan Pederson, *Family, Dependence, and the Origins of the Welfare State*.

7   Kuisel, *Ernest Mercier*; Maier, *Recasting Bourgeois Europe*.

8   Briggs, *Collected Essays*, 2:182.

9   Rosanvallon, *Nouvelle question sociale*, 68.

Bibliography

∼

MANUSCRIPT SOURCES

Archives nationales, Paris (AN)

Jules Simon, 87AP

Albert Sorel, ABxix 3085

Étienne Lamy, 333AP

F¹² 3767 Commerce et industrie

F¹² 3829 Commerce et industrie

C 5544 Procès-verbaux des assemblées nationales, Chamber of Deputies, Comité d'assurance et de prévoyance sociales, manuscript notebooks

Archives privées (AP)

Siegfried family. Personal diaries of Jules Siegfried (1861–93), some in manuscript form, others typed, newspaper clippings, photos, letters

Bibliothèque historique de la Ville de Paris

Fonds "Actualités"

Dossiers Jules Simon, Georges Picot, Léon Bourgeois

Dossier Musée social: Demande en reconnaissance d'utilité publique: exposé des motifs (25 Juin 1894), dépôt légal Seine, 3199

Bibliothèque nationale, Paris (BN)

Nouvelles acquisitions françaises (NAF) 25169.

Correspondance d'Ernest Lavisse

Bureau de l'enregistrement de la Ville de Paris, Actes notaires

Fondation nationale des sciences politiques (FNSP)

Archives d'André Siegfried (articles, handwritten and typed notes, speeches, newspaper clippings), 6SI6 dr4

Musée social Archives, Paris

Boxes: Alliance d'hygiène sociale; Comités d'expositions françaises d'économie sociale; Correspondants; Fondation du Musée social; Grandes Conférences; Mabilleau, Léopold; Risler, Georges; Section d'hygiène urbaine et rurale (see inventory by Anne Cormier); Siegfried, Jules

Diverse Correspondence: Chambrun, Comte Aldebert de; Mabilleau, Léopold; Salomon, Charles; Siegfried, Jules

Procès-verbaux du Comité de direction (PVCD), 1894–1914

Procès-verbaux du Grand Conseil, 1899–1914

Préfecture de Police Archives, Paris (APP)

Ba 1007

Ba 1165

SECONDARY SOURCES

Abrams, Mark. *Social Surveys and Social Action.* London: Heinemann, 1951.

Action populaire. *Guide social.* Lille, Paris, then Reims: [n.p.], 1904–13/14.

———. *Manuel social pratique.* Reims: Action populaire; Paris: Lecoffre, 1908.

———. *Action populaire: Propagande périodique* Lille: Imprimerie de l'Action populaire, 1902.

Agulhon, Maurice. *Le cercle dans la France bourgeoise.* Paris: Armand Colin, 1977.

Aisenberg, Andrew. *Contagion: Disease, Government, and the "Social Question" in Nineteenth-Century France.* Stanford: Stanford University Press, 1999.

Albert-Petit, A. "Georges Picot." *Débats,* August 18, 1909.

"Alliance coopérative internationale," *L'Émancipation. Journal d'économie politique et sociale, Organe des associations ouvrières et du Centre régional coopératif du Midi,* 15 January 1897, 8–9.

Alliance d'hygiène sociale. *Congrès de Roubaix, 19–22 octobre 1911: "De la ville-taudis à la cité-jardin."* Agen: Imprimerie moderne, 1911.

Amizade, Ronald. *Class, Politics, and Early Industrial Capitalism: A Study of Mid-nineteenth-century Toulouse, France.* Albany: SUNY, 1981.

Ansart, Pierre. *Sociologie de Saint-Simon.* Paris: Presses universitaires de France, 1970.

Arboux, Jules. *Histoire de seize ans.* Paris: Fischbacher, 1907.

Ardaillou, Pierre. "Foi protestante, Action sociale et convictions républicaines." In Colette Chambelland, ed. *Le Musée social en son temps,* 75–101. Paris: Presses de l'École normale supérieure, 1998.

Ashford, Douglas, *The Emergence of the Welfare States.* Oxford: Basil Blackwell, 1986.

Association du Musée d'économie sociale: Statuts. Paris: Imprimerie Chaix, 1890.

Association protestante pour l'étude pratique des questions sociales. Paris: Fischbacher, 1889.

Audiganne, Armand. *Les populations ouvrières et les industries de la France.* 2 vols. Paris: Capelle, 1860.

Auspitz, Katherine. *The Radical Bourgeoisie, the Ligue de l'Enseignement, and the Origins of the Third Republic, 1866–1885.* Cambridge: Cambridge University Press, 1982.

B..., Victorine. *Souvenirs d'une morte vivante.* Paris: François Maspero, 1977.

Bader, Clarisse. *Le comte de Chambrun.* Paris: Calmann-Lévy, 1889.

Banquet offert à Léopold Mabilleau. Paris: Imprimerie Émile Kapp, 1902.

Barberet, Joseph. *Le travail en France: Monographies professionnelles.* 7 vols. Paris: Berger-Levrault, 1886–90.

Barksdale, Dudley Channing. "Liberal Politics and Nascent Social Science in France: The Academy of Moral and Political Sciences, 1803–1852." Ph.D. diss., University of North Carolina, 1986.

Barnes, David. *The Making of a Social Disease: Tuberculosis in 19th-century France.* Berkeley: University of California Press, 1995.

Barthélemy-Madaule, M. *Marc Sangnier: 1873–1950*. Paris: Éditions du Seuil, 1973.

Barthes, Roland. "The Eiffel Tower." In *The Eiffel Tower and Other Mythologies*, 3–17. New York: Hill and Wang, 1979.

Baubérot, Jean. *Le retour des Huguenots*. Paris: Éditions du Cerf, 1985.

Baudoui, Rémi. "Aux origines du Comité supérieur d'aménagment et d'organisation générale de la région parisienne: Débats et réflexions." *Vie sociale* 3–4 (1999): 315–27.

Bec, Colette, Catherine Duprat, Jean-Noel Luc, and Jean-Guy Petit, eds. *Philanthropies et politiques sociales en Europe (XVIe-XXe siècles)*. Paris: Anthropos, 1994.

Bellamy, Richard. *Liberalism and Modern Society: A Historical Argument*. University Park: Pennsylvania State University Press, 1992.

Bellom, Maurice. *Les lois d'assurance ouvrière à l'étranger*. 2 vols. Paris: A. Rousseau, 1892–1908.

———. *Les résultats de l'assurance ouvrière à la fin du XIXe siècle. Communication faite à la Société de statistique de Paris, 20 mars 1901*. Nancy: Imprimerie Berger-Levrault, 1901.

Benedict, Burton. "The Anthropology of World's Fairs." In Burton Benedict ed., *The Anthropology of World's Fairs*. Berkeley: Scholars Press, 1983.

Benjamin, Walter. *Écrits français*. Paris: Gallimard, 1991.

Bennet, Jean. *Biographies de personnalités mutualistes (XIXe-XXe siècles)*. Paris: Mutualité française, 1987.

———. *La mutualité des origines à 1789*. Paris: C.I.E.M., 1982.

Bennett, Tony. *The Birth of the Museum: History, Theory, Politics*. London: Routledge, 1995.

———. "The Exhibitionary Complex." In Nicholas B. Dirks, Geoff Eley, and Sherry B. Ortner, eds. *Culture/Power/History: A Reader in Contemporary Social Theory*. Princeton: Princeton University Press, 1994.

Benoît-Lévy, Georges. *La cité-jardin*. Paris: H. Jouve, 1904.

———. *Cités-jardins d'Amérique*. Paris: H. Jouve, 1905.

———. "Les cités-jardins aux États-Unis." *Le Musée social: Annales* (1905): 64–75.

———. "Les garden cities: Port Sunlight." *Le Musée social: Mémoires et documents*, 1 (1904): 1–40.

Bergeron, Louis, and Patrice Bourdelais, eds., *La France n'est-elle pas douée pour l'industrie?* Paris: Belin, 1998.

Berlanstein, Lenard R. *Big Business and Industrial Conflict in Nineteenth-Century France: A Social History of the Parisian Gas Company*. Berkeley and Los Angeles: University of California Press, 1991.

———. "The Distinctiveness of the Nineteenth-Century French Labor Movement." *Journal of Modern History* 64 (1992): 660–85.

———. ed. *Rethinking Labor History*. Urbana: University of Illinois Press, 1993.

———. "Working with Language: The Linguistic Turn in French Labor History: A Review Article," *Comparative Studies in Society and History* 33, no. 2 (1991): 426–40.

Bert, Paul. *L'instruction civique à l'école*. Paris: Picard-Bernheim et Cie., 1882.

Bertholet, Jean-Michel. *Durkheim: L'avènement de la sociologie scientifique*. Toulouse: Presses universitaires du Mirail, 1995.

Bertillon, Dr. Jacques. *Essai de statistique comparée du surpeuplement des habitations à Paris et dans les grandes capitales européénes*. Paris: Imprimerie Chaix, 1894.

———. *De la fréquence des principales causes de décès à Paris pendant la seconde moitié du XIXe siècle et notamment pendant la période 1886–1905*. Paris: Imprimerie municipale, 1906.

———. "Des logements surpeuplés à Paris en 1896." *Bulletin de la Société de médecine publique et d'hygiène professionelle* (1899): 111–26.

Beurier, A. *Le Musée pédagogique et la Bibliothèque centrale de l'enseignement primaire*. Paris: Imprimerie nationale, 1889.

Bezucha, Robert J. *The Lyon Uprising of 1834: Social and Political Conflict in the Early July Monarchy*. Cambridge: Harvard University Press, 1974.

Bianchon, Horace (pseud. of Dr. Maurice de Fleury). *Nos grands médecins d'aujourd'hui*. Paris: Société d'éditions scientifiques, 1891.

Birck, Françoise. "Entre le patronage et l'organisation industrielle: Les cristalleries de Baccarat dans le dernier quart du XIXe siècle." *Genèses: Sciences sociales et histoire* 2 (1990): 29–55.

Blanqui, Adolphe-Jérôme. *Des classes ouvrières en France pendant l'année 1848*. 2 vols. Paris: Pagnerre, 1849.

———. *Histoire de l'économie politique en Europe depuis les anciens jusqu'à nos jours*. Paris: Guillaumin, 1837.

———. "Tableau des populations rurales de la France en 1850." *Journal des économistes*, 28 (1851): 1–15.

Blondel, Georges. *Études sur les populations rurales de l'Allemagne et la crise agraire*. Paris: Larose, 1897.

———. "La question sociale et le devoir social." In Georges Blondel, Auguste Souchon, Étienne Martin Saint-Léon, Charles Combes, Maurice Dufourmantelle, and Emmanuel Rivière. *Idées sociales et faits sociaux*, 19–48. Paris: A Fontemoing, 1903.

Blum, Françoise, and Janet Horne. "Féminisme et Musée social: (1916–1939)." *Vie sociale* 8–9 (1988): 313–99.

———. "Le comte de Chambrun, catholique, mécène des protestants?" In Colette Chambelland, ed. *Le Musée social en sons temps*, 27–41. Paris: Presses de l'École normale supérieure, 1998.

———. "Le Musée social au carrefour?" *Vie sociale* 3–4 (1999): 99–108.

Bourdeau, Jean. *L'Évolution du socialisme*. Paris: Alcan, 1901.

———. "Le mouvement syndical en France et le Congrès corporatif de Tours, du 14 au 19 septembre 1896." *Le Musée social*, ser. A, no. 15 (1897): 293–321.

———. "Le socialisme municipal." *Revue des deux mondes* 160 (1900): 180–210.

Bourdelais, Patrice, and Jean-Yves Raulot. *Une peur bleue: Histoire du choléra en France, 1832–1854*. Paris: Payot, 1987.

Bourgeois, Léon, ed. *Essai d'une philosophie de la solidarité*. Paris: Félix Alcan, 1902.

———. *La politique de la prévoyance sociale*. 2 vols. Paris: Charpentier, 1914–1918.

———. *Solidarité*. Paris: Armand Colin, 1896.

Bouvier, Jean. "Panorama du premier siècle de l'ère 'industrielle' en France." In Fernand Braudel and Ernest Labrousse, eds. *Histoire économique et sociale de la France*, 4:00 (1): 9–21. Paris: Presses universitaires de France, 1982.

Breton, Yves, ed. *L'économie politique en France au XIXe siècle*. Paris: Economica, 1991.

Briggs, Asa. *The Collected Essays of Asa Briggs*. 2 vols. Brighton, Sussex: Harvester Press, 1985.

Brooke, M. Z. *Le Play: Engineer and Social Scientist*. London: Longman, 1970.

Bulmer, Martin, Kevin Bales, and Kathryn Kish Sklar, eds. *The Social Survey in Historical Perspective, 1880–1940*. Cambridge: Cambridge University Press, 1991.

Bulletin de la Société française des habitations à bon marché. Paris: Imprimerie Chaix, 1890, 1891, 1892, 1893, 1899.

Bullock, Nicolas, and James Read. *The Movement for Housing Reform in Germany and France: 184—1914*. Cambridge: Cambridge University Press, 1985.

Bureau international du travail, *Informations sociales* 36, no. 4 (1909): 160–161.

Caisse des dépôts et consignations, 1816–1986. Paris: Caisse des dépôts et consignations, 1988.

Cantecor, Georges. *Morale théorique et notions historiques*. Paris: Librairie classique Paul Delaplane, 1900.

Carlen, Claudia, comp. *The Papal Encyclicals, 1878–1903*. Wilmington, N.C.: McGraw Publishing House, 1981.

Çelik, Zeynep. *Displaying the Orient: Architecture of Islam at Nineteenth-Century World Fairs*. Berkeley: California University Press, 1992.

"Centenaire de Frédéric Le Play." Letter from Carroll D. Wright to Edmond Delaire. *La Réforme sociale* 1 (1906): 594–95.

Centenaire de la Société d'économie et des sciences sociale: Recueil d'études sociales à la mémoire de Frédéric Le Play. Paris: Éditions A. et J. Picard et Cie., 1956.

Chambelland, Colette. "Aux origines de l'enquête sociale." *Vie sociale* 7 (1986): 327–29.

———, ed. *Le Musée social en son temps*. Paris: Presses de l'École normale supérieure, 1998.

Chambrun, Comte Joseph-Dominique-Aldebert de Pineton de. *Le comte de Chambrun: Ses études politiques et littéraires: Comptes rendus de la presse*. Paris: Calmann-Lévy, 1889.

———. *Aux montagnes d'Auvergne: Mes conclusions sociologiques*. Paris: Calmann-Lévy, 1893.

———. *Aux montagnes d'Auvergne: Mes nouvelles conclusions sociologiques*. Paris: Calmann-Lévy, 1893.

Charle, Christophe. *Les élites de la Rèpublique, 1880–1900*. Paris: Fayard, 1987.

———. *Histoire sociale de la France au XIXe siècle*. Paris: Éditions du Seuil, 1991.

———. *Naissance des "intellectuels" (1880–1900)*. Paris: Fayard, 1990.

———. "Pour une histoire sociale des professions juridiques: Note pour une recherche." *Actes de la recherche en sciences sociales* 76–77 (1989): 117–19.

Charpin, F. "Albert Gigot," *La Réforme sociale* 1 (1913): 286.

Charvet, Marie. "De l'hygiénisme à l'urbanisme: La question des fortifications de Paris de 1880 à 1910." Ph.D. diss. Paris: École des hautes études en sciences sociales, 1999.

———. "La question des fortifications de Paris dans les années 1900: Esthètes, sportifs, réformateurs sociaux, élus locaux." *Genèses* 16 (1994): 23–44.

Chénu, Alain, ed. Epilogue: "La famille-souche: Questions de méthode." In Frédéric Le Play, Émile Cheysson, Bayard, Fernand Butel, *Les Mélouga: Une famille pyrénéene au XIXe siècle*, 177–230. Paris: Nathan, 1994.

Chevalier, Louis. *Classes dangereuses, classes laborieuses à Paris pendant la première moitié du dix-neuvième siècle*. Paris: Plon, 1958.

Chevalier, Michel. *Les questions politiques et sociales*. Paris: Revue des deux mondes, 1850.

Chevallier, Eugène. *Quelques mots sur la question sociale: Conférence faite dans deux cercles républicains.* Châteauroux: Imprimerie Aupetit, 1882.

Cheysson, Émile. "Les accidents du travail et la pensions aux ayants droit des ouvriers tués." *La Réforme sociale* 2 (1898): 322–33.

———. "L'action sociale de la femme de la mutualité." *La Réforme sociale* 1 (1902): 584–607.

———. *Les assurances ouvrières: Leçon d'ouverture à l'École libre des sciences politiques, 15 novembre 1892.* Paris: Librairie Guillaumin et Cie., 1894.

———. "L'économie sociale à l'Exposition universelle de 1889." *La Réforme sociale* 2 (1889): 1–19.

———. "L'Exposition d'économie sociale en 1889: Programme-situation actuelle." *Revue des institutions de prévoyance* 3 (1889): 62–66.

———. "La famille, l'association, et l'État." In Cheysson, *Oeuvres choisies,* 2:147–61.

———. "Georges Picot: Nécrologie," *Le Musée social: Annales* (1909): 287–97.

———. *L'homme social et la colonisation, Conférence faite au Muséum d'histoire naturelle, 4 mai 1897.* Paris: Paul Ollendorff, 1897.

———. "Institutions patronales." In Picard, ed., *Ministère du commerce: Exposition universelle internationale de 1889. Rapports du jury international, Groupe de l'économie sociale* 2:351–516. Paris: Imprimerie nationale, 1892.

———. "Le Musée social." *Congrès international des accidents du travail à Milan,* 1–14. Milan: H. Reggiani, 1894.

———. *Le Musée social: Fondation de Chambrun.* Paris: Arthur Rousseau, 1914.

———. "La mutualité familiale." *La Réforme sociale* 2 (1901): 621–43.

———. *Oeuvres choisies.* 2 vols. Paris: Arthur Rousseau, 1911.

———. "Les rapports des lois d'assurances ouvrières et de la santé publique." Ministère du commerce et de l'industrie. Exposition universelle 1900. *Congrès international des accidents du travail et des assurances sociales, 5e session, tenue à Paris du 23 au 30 juin 1900,* 1:381–90. Paris: C. Béranger, 1901.

———. *Les retraites ouvrières.* Paris, Guillaumin, 1905.

———. "Le rôle de la femme dans la mutualité." *Le Musée social: Mémoires et documents* (1905): 313–42.

———. "Le rôle de l'État dans la question des habitations ouvrières," *Bulletin de la Société française des habitations à bon marché* 1 (1893): 23–39.

Clark, Terry Nichols. *Prophets and Patrons: The French University and the Emergence of the Social Sciences.* Cambridge: Harvard University Press, 1973.

Coffin, Judith G. *The Politics of Women's Work: The Paris Garment Trades, 1750–1915.* Princeton: Princeton University Press, 1996.

Coleman, William. *Death Is a Social Disease: Public Health and Political Economy in Early Industrial France.* Madison: University of Wisconsin Press, 1982.

Collini, Stefan. *Liberalism and Sociology: L. T. Hobhouse and Political Argument in England, 1880–1914.* Cambridge: Cambridge University Press, 1979.

"Comité de défense et de progrès social: Séance du 15 mars 1895." *La Réforme sociale* 1 (1895): 749–67.

Combeau, Yvan. *Paris et les élections municipales sous la Troisième République.* Paris: L'Harmattan, 1998.

Compayré, Gabriel. *Éléments d'éducation civique et morale.* Paris: P. Garcet, Nisius et Cie., Éditeurs, 1881.

Conklin, Alice. *A Mission to Civilize: The Republican Idea of Empire in France and West Africa, 1895–1930.* Stanford: Stanford University Press, 1997.

Corbin, Alain. *Le miasme et la jonquille: L'odorat et l'imaginaire social, XVIIIe-XIXe siècles.* Paris: Aubier Montagne, 1992.

Cormier, Anne. "Extension, limites, espaces libres: Les travaux de la Section d'hygiène urbaine et rurale du Musée social." Diplôme d'études approfondies, École d'architecture Paris-Villemin, 1987.

Coston, Henri. *Dictionnaire de la politique française.* 4 vols. Paris: Librairie française, 1970–82.

———, ed. *Dictionnaire des dynasties bourgeoises et du monde des affaires.* Paris: Éditions Alain Moreaud, 1975.

Cottereau, Alain. "Les débuts de la planification urbaine dans l'agglomeration parisienne." *Sociologie du travail* 4 (1970): 362–92.

———. "The Distinctiveness of Working-class Cultures in France, 1848–1900." In Ira Katznelson and Aristide Zolberg, eds. *Working-Class Formation: Nineteenth-Century Patterns in Western Europe and the United States,* 111–56. Princeton: Princeton University Press, 1986.

Critchlow, Donald T. *The Brookings Institution, 1916–1952.* DeKalb.: Northwestern Illinois University Press, 1985.

Crubellier, Maurice. *Histoire culturelle de la France, XIXe-XXe siècles.* Paris: Armand Colin, 1974.

Dab, Sandra. "Bienfaisance et socialisme." In Topalov, ed., *Laboratoires du nouveau siècle,* 219–35. Paris: Presses de l'École des hautes études en sciences sociales, 1999.

———. "La philanthropie laïque, facteur d'intégration des juifs sous la IIIe République." In Colette Bec et al., eds. *Philanthropies et politiques sociales en Europe (XVIIe-XXe siècles),* 105–12. Paris: Anthropos, 1994.

Dagognet, François. *Le musée sans fin.* Paris: Champ Vallon, 1984.

Daugan, J. *Histoire et législation des patentes des grands magasins.* Rennes: Imprimerie des arts et manufactures, 1902.

Dawley, Alan. *Struggles for Justice: Social Responsibility and the Liberal State.* Cambridge: Belknap/Harvard University Press, 1991.

Delorme, Robert, and Christine André. *L'État et l'économie: Un essai d'explication de l'évolution des dépenses publiques en France (1870–1980).* Paris: Éditions du Seuil, 1983.

Demarty, Joseph. *Formation et organisation des musées scolaires.* Clermont-Ferrand: [author] 1894.

Derosières, Alain. "L'ingénieur d'État et le père de famille: Émile Cheysson et la statistique." *Annales des mines* 2 (1986): 66–80.

Desan, Suzanne. "Reconstituting the Social After the Terror: Family, Property and the Law in Popular Politics." *Past and Present* 164 (1999): 81–121.

Devillers, Christian, and Bernard Huet. *Le Creusot: Naissance et développement d'une ville industrielle, 1782–1914.* Paris: Champs Vallon, 1981.

Dewerpe, Alain. *Le Monde du travail en France, 1800–1950*. Paris: Armand Colin, 1989.

Dogliani, Patrizia. "Un Laboratoire de socialisme municipal: France, 1880–1920." Ph.D. diss., Université de Paris VIII, 1991.

———. "La naissance d'un Musée social en Italie." In Colette Chambellard, ed., *Le Musée social en son temps*, 359–64.

Donzelot, Jacques. *L'invention du social: Le déclin des passions politiques*. Paris: Fayard, 1985.

Doyle, Donald H. "The Social Functions of Voluntary Associations in a Nineteenth-Century American Town." *Social Science History* 1, no. 3 (1977): 333–55.

Dreyfus, Michel. *Guide des centres de documentation en histoire ouvrière et sociale*. Paris: Les Éditions ouvrières, 1983.

———. *Histoire de la C.G.T.: Cent ans de syndicalisme en France, 1895–1995*. Brussels: Éditions Complexe, 1995.

———. "Léopold Mabilleau et le mouvement mutualiste français et international." In Colette Chambelland, ed. *Le Musée social en son temps*, 103–18. Paris: Presses de l'École normale supérieure, 1998.

———. "La Mutualité de Léopold Mabilleau: Fondateurs et militants du mouvement mutualiste sous la IIIe République." In *Mutualité et protection sociale: Colloque national d'Albi*, 29–44. Paris: Mutualité française, 1988.

———. *La mutualité: Une histoire maintenant accessible*. Paris: Mutualité française, 1988.

———. "Opération patrimoine de la Mutualité." *Revue des études coopératives mutualistes et associatives* 25 (1988): 37–44.

Droulers, Paul. *Politique sociale et christianisme: Le Père Desbuquois et l'Action populaire*. 2 vols. Paris: Les Éditions ouvrières, 1969.

Dubois, Pascal. "Le Solidarisme," Ph.D. diss., Université de Lille II, 1985.

Dubreuilh, Louis. "Le comte de Chambrun." *La Petite République socialiste*, 9 February 1899.

———. "Les Congrès ouvriers," *La Petite République socialiste*, 14 March 1899.

———. "À la conquête des jeunes," *La Petite République socialiste*, 10 January 1895.

Dumay, Jean-Baptiste. *Mémoires d'un militant du Creusot (1841–1905)*. Paris: François Maspero; Grenoble: Presses universitaires de Grenoble, 1976.

Dumons, Bruno, and Gilles Pollet, *L'État et les retraites*. Paris: Éditions Belin, 1994.

Duprat, Catherine. "Des Lumières au premier XIXe siècle: Voie française de la philanthropie." In Colette Bec, Catherine Duprat, Jean-Noel Luc, and Jacques-Guy Petit., eds., *Philanthropies et politiques sociales en Europe (XVIIe-XXe siècles)*, 3–16. Paris: Anthropos, 1994.

———. *"Pour l'amour de l'humanité": Le temps des Philanthropes: La philanthropie parisienne des Lumières à la monarchie de Juillet*. 2 vols. Paris: Éditions du C.T.H.S., 1993.

———. *Usage et pratiques de la philanthropie: Pauvreté, action sociale et lien social, à Paris, au cours du premier XIXe siècle*. 2 vols. Paris: Comité d'histoire de la Sécurité sociale, 1996–97.

Duroselle, Jean-Baptiste. *Les débuts du catholicisme social en France, 1822–1870*. Paris: Presses universitaires de France, 1951.

Dusart, J. "L'obligation dans les retraites ouvrières," *L'Association catholique* 1 (1906): 336–50.

Eichtal, Eugène d'. *La solidarité sociale: Ses nouvelles formules*. Paris: Alphonse Picard et Fils, 1903.

Eley, Geoff. "Nations, Publics, and Political Cultures: Placing Habermas in the Nineteenth

Century." In Nicholas B. Dirks, Geoff Eley, and Sherry B. Ortner, eds. *Culture/Power/History: A Reader in Contemporary Social Theory*, 297–35. Princeton: Princeton University Press, 1994.

Ellis, Jack D. *The Physician-Legislators of France: Medicine and Politics in the Early Third Republic, 1870–1914*. Cambridge, New York: Cambridge University Press, 1990.

Elwitt, Sanford. *The Making of the Third Republic: Class and Politics in France, 1868–84*. Baton Rouge: Louisiana State University Press, 1975.

———. "Social Reform and Social Order in Late 19th Century France: The Musée social and its Friends." *French Historical Studies* 11, no. 3 (1980): 431–51.

———. *The Third Republic Defended: Bourgeois Reform in France, 1880–1914*. Baton Rouge: Louisiana State University Press, 1986.

Elwitt, Sanford, and Lawrence Goldman. "Debate: Social Science, Social Reform and Sociology." *Past and Present* 121 (1988): 209–19.

Encrevé, André. "Les protestants et la République." *L'Histoire* 7 (1981): 21–46.

———. *Les protestants en France de 1800 à nos jours: Histoire d'une réintégration*. Paris: Stock, 1985.

Encrevé, André and Michel Richard, eds. *Les protestants dans les débuts de la Troisième République (1871–1885), Paris, 3–6 octobre 1978: Actes du colloque*. Paris: Société de l'histoire du protestantisme francais, 1979.

"Les espaces libres à Paris." *Le Musée social: Mémoires et documents* 7 (1908): 177–232.

Evenson, Norma. *Paris: A Century of Change, 1878–1978*. New Haven and London: Yale University Press, 1979.

Éwald, François. *L'État providence*. Paris: Bernard Grasset, 1986.

Fallot, Tommy. *Le Christianisme social: Études et fragments*. Paris: Fischbacher, 1911.

Faure, Alain. "Mouvements populaires et mouvement ouvrier à Paris, 1830–1834," *Le Mouvement social* 88 (1974): 51–92.

Favre, Pierre. *Naissances de la science politique en France (1870–1914)*. Paris: Fayard, 1989.

Festy, Octave. *Le mouvement ouvrier au début de la monarchie de Juillet*. Paris: Édouard Cornely, 1908.

Fohlen, Claude. *L'industrie textile au temps du Second Empire*. Paris: Plon, 1956.

Fontaine, Arthur. *Les grèves et la conciliation*. Paris: Librairie Armand Colin, 1897.

Ford, Caroline. *Creating the Nation in Provincial France: Religion and Political Identity in Brittany*. Princeton: Princeton University Press, 1993.

Forest, Alan. *The French Revolution and the Poor*. Oxford: B. Blackwell, 1981.

François-Poncet, André. *La vie et l'oeuvre de Robert Pinot*. Paris: Armand Colin, 1927.

Freeden, Michael. *The New Liberalism: An Ideology of Social Reform*. Oxford: Clarendon Press, 1978.

Freedeman, Charles E. *The Triumph of Corporate Capitalism in France, 1867–1914*. Rochester: University of Rochester Press, 1993.

Fridenson, Patrick, and André Straus, eds. *Le capitalisme français, XIXe-XXe siècle: Blocages et dynamismes d'une croissance*. Paris: Fayard, 1987.

Fuchs, Rachel. *Poor and Pregnant in Paris: Strategies for Survival in the Nineteenth Century*. New Brunswick: Rutgers University Press, 1992.

"Funérailles de M. Ernest Glasson." *Institut de France, Académie des sciences morales et politiques* (1907): 1.

Furlough, Ellen. *Consumer Cooperation in France: The Politics of Consumption, 1834–1930.* Ithaca and London: Cornell University Press, 1991.

———. "The Politics of Consumption: The Consumer Cooperative Movement in France, 1834–1930." Ph.D. diss., Brown University, 1987.

Fuster, Édouard. "L'évolution de l'assurance ouvrière en Europe et le Congrès de Dusseldorf," *Le Musée social: Annales* (1902): 387–409.

———. "Les résultats de la mutualité maladie en Allemagne." *Le Musée social: Annales* (1904): 183–88.

———. "Vie ouvrière et les assurances sociales en Allemagne." *Le Musée social: Annales* 1902): 1–2.

Gambetta, Léon. *Discours et plaidoyers politiques de M. Gambetta.* 11 vols. Paris: G. Carpentier, 1881–88.

Garcia, Patrick. "L'État républicain face au centenaire: Raisons d'État et universalisme dans la commémoration de la Révolution française." In Jacques Bariety, ed. *1889: Centenaire de la Révolution française: Réactions et représentations politiques en Europe.* Berne: Lang, 1992.

Garrisson, Janine. *L'homme protestant.* Paris: Éditions Complexe, 1986.

Gaudin, Jean-Pierre. *L'avenir en plan: Technique et politique dans la prévision urbaine, 1900–1930.* Seyssel: Champs Vallon, 1985.

———, ed. *Les premiers urbanistes français et l'art urbain, 1900–1930.* Paris: École d'architecture Paris-Villemin, 1987.

Gaumont, Jean. *Histoire générale de la coopération en France.* 2 vols. Paris: Fédération nationale des coopératives de consommation, 1923.

Gérando, Baron Joseph Marie de. *De la bienfaisance publique.* 4 vols. Paris: J. Renouard and Cie., 1839.

———. *Le visiteur du pauvre.* Paris: Colas, 1820.

Gibaud, Bernard. "La mutualité et les retraites ouvrières: Trois articles de Mabilleau et Jaures." *La Révue de l'économie sociale* 4 (1985): 73–84.

———"Le Musée social et mutualité: L'ambivalence d'un parrainage." In Colette Chambelland, ed. *Le Musée social en son temps,* 317–30. Paris: Presses universitaries de l'École normale supérieure, 1998.

———. *De la Mutualité à la Sécurité sociale: Conflits et convergences.* Paris: Éditions ouvrières, 1986.

———. "La Mutualité sous la Troisième République." In *Mutualité et protection sociale: Colloque national d'Albi,* 15–27. Paris: Mutualité française, 1988.

Gibon, Alexandre. *Les Retraites organisées par les compagnies houillères au profit des ouvriers mineurs.* Paris: Guilaumin, 1895.

Gide, Charles. "The Economic Schools and the Teaching of Political Economy in France." Reprint from *Political Science Quarterly* 5, no. 4. New York: Ginn and Co., 1890.

———. "Les expositions d'économie sociale: Passé et avenir (1867–1909). *La Réforme sociale,* 2 (1906): 349–58.

————. *Histoire des doctrines économiques.* 7th ed. Paris: Sirey, 1947.

————. "Du rôle pratique du pasteur dans les questions sociales." Association protestante pour l'étude pratique des questions sociales. Paris: Fischbacher, 1889.

————. *Quatre écoles d'économie sociale.* Geneva: Stapelmohr, 1890.

Godineau, Laure. "L'économie sociale à l'Exposition de 1889." *Le mouvement social* 149 (1989): 71–88.

————. "L'économie sociale à l'exposition universelle de 1889." Master's thesis, Université de Paris-VIII, 1988.

Goldberg, Harvey. *The Life of Jean Jaurès.* Madison: University of Wisconsin Press, 1962.

Gordon, Linda. *Women, the State, and Welfare.* Madison: University of Wisconsin Press, 1990.

Gossman, Lionel. *Between History and Literature.* Cambridge: Harvard University Press, 1990.

Greenhalgh, Paul. "Education, Entertainment, and Politics: Lessons from the Great International Exhibitions." In Peter Vergo, ed., *The New Museology.* London: Reaktion Books, 1989.

————. *Ephemeral Vistas: The Expositions Universelles, Great Exhibitions, and World's Fairs, 1851–1939.* Manchester: Manchester University Press, 1988.

Gruner, Édouard. "L'Association pour l'entretien du Musée viennois d'hygiène industrielle." *Bulletin du Congrès des accidents du travail* 1, no. 6 (1890): 3–7.

————. *La responsabilité des accidents au point de vue chrétien: Lu à la séance du mercredi 16 juillet 1890 au Congrès de l'Association protestante pour l'étude pratique des questions sociales,* 1–19. Nîmes: Imprimerie de H. Michel et G. Gory, 1891.

Guépin, Ange, and E. Bonamy. *Nantes au XIXe siècle: Statistique topographique, industrielle et morale.* Nantes: P. Sebire, 1835; reprint Nantes: Presses de l'Université de Nantes, 1981.

Guérin, Joseph. "Un settlement anglais: Note sur Toynbee Hall." *Le Musée social,* Series B, Circulaire no. 12 (1897): 345–77.

Guerrand, Roger Henri. *Les lieux: Histoire des commodités.* Paris: Éditions de la Découverte, 1985.

————. *Murs citadines: Histoires de la culture urbaine, XIXe-XXe siècles.* Paris: Quai Voltaire, 1992.

————. *Les origines du logement social en France.* Paris: Éditions ouvrières, 1967.

————. *Propriétaires et locataires: Les origines du logement social en France (1850–1914)* Paris: Quintette, 1987.

Guerrand, Roger Henri and Marie-Antoinette Rupp. *Brève histoire du service social en France, 1896—1976.* Toulouse: Privat, 1978.

Gueslin, André. *L'invention de l'économie sociale: Le XIXᵉ siècle français.* Paris: Economica, 1987.

Habermas, Jürgen. "The Public Sphere." *New German Critique* 3 (1974): 49–55.

Hamon, Georges. *Histoire générale de l'assurance en France et à l'étranger.* Paris: Assurance moderne, 1895–96.

Hamon, Philippe. *Expositions: Littérature et architecture au XIXe siècle.* Paris: José Corti, 1989.

Hatzfeld, Henri. *Du Paupérisme à la Sécurité sociale: Essai sur les origines de la Sécurité sociale en France, 1850-1940.* Paris: Armand Colin, 1971.

Hause, Steven C. "Protestant Republicanism, Protestant Morality, and the Politics of Social Control in France, 1860-1910." Paper presented at the Society for French Historical Studies, Wilmington, Delaware, March 1994.

Hause, Steven C., with Anne R. Kenny. *Women's Suffrage and Social Politics in the French Third Republic*. Princeton: Princeton University Press, 1984.

Hauser, Henri. *L'enseignement des sciences sociales: État actuel de cet enseignement dans les divers pays du monde*. Paris: A. Chevalier-Maresq, 1903.

Haussonville, le comte de. *Études sociales: Misères et remèdes*. Paris: Calmann-Lévy, 1886.

———. *Salaires et misères des femmes*. Paris: Calmann-Lévy, 1900.

Hayward, J. E. S. "Educational Pressure Groups and the Indoctrination of the Radical Ideology of Solidarism, 1895–1914." *International Review of Social History* 8 (1963): 1–17.

———. "The Official Social Philosophy of the French Third Republic: Léon Bourgeois and Solidarism, 1895–1914." *International Review of Social History* 6 (1961): 19–48.

———. "Solidarity: The Social History of an Idea in Nineteenth-Century France." *International Review of Social History* 4 (1959): 261–84.

Hazareesingh, Sudhir. *From Subject to Citizen: The Second Empire and the Emergence of Modern French Democracy*. Princeton: Princeton University Press, 1998.

Hébrard de Villeneuve, Henri. "Les espaces libres et les terrains de jeux." In Alliance d'hygiène sociale, *Congrès de Roubaix, 19–22 octobre 1911: "De la Ville-taudis à la Cité-jardin,"* 116–29. Agen: Imprimerie moderne, 1911.

Hénard, Eugène. "Les espaces libres à Paris." *Le Musée social: Mémoires et documents* 7 (1908): 74–75.

———. *Études sur les transformations de Paris et autres écrits sur l'urbanisme*. Paris: Librairies-imprimeries réunies, 1903. Reprint, Paris: L'Équerre, 1982.

Hénard, Eugène, and Jules Siegfried. "Les espaces libres à Paris: Les fortifications remplacées par une ceinture de parcs." *Le Musée social: Mémoires et documents* 4 (1909): 73–92.

Histoire de Baccarat. 3 vols. Baccarat: Compagnie des Cristalleries de Baccarat, 1984.

Hobsbawm, Eric. *The Age of Capital, 1848–1875*. 2nd ed. New York: New American Library, 1979.

Horne, Janet. "L'antichambre de la Chambre: Le Musée social et ses réseaux réformateurs, 1894–1914." In Christian Topalov, ed., *Laboratoires du nouveau siècle: La "nébuleuse réformatrice" et ses réseaux en France, 1880–1914*, 121–40. Paris: Éditions de l'École des hautes études en sciences sociales, 1999.

———. "L'économie sociale et la naissance du Musée social." In André Gueslin and Pierre Guillaume, eds., *De la charité médiévale à la Sécurité sociale*, 107–16. Paris: Les Éditions ouvrières, 1992.

———. "In Pursuit of Greater France: Visions of Empire Among Musée Social Reformers, 1894–1931." In Julia Clancy-Smith and Frances Gouda, eds., *Domesticating the Empire: Race, Gender, and Family Live in French and Dutch Colonialism*, 21–42. Charlottesville: University Press of Virginia, 1998.

———. "Le Libéralisme à l'épreuve de l'industrialisation: La Réponse du Musée social." In Colette Chambelland, ed., *Le Musée social en son temps*, 13–26. Paris: Presses de l'École normale supérieure, 1998.

———. "Le Musée social à l'origine: Les Métamorphoses d'une idée," *Le Mouvement social* 171 (1995): 47–69.

————. "Presenting Modern France: The Rhetoric of Reform at the 1889 Universal Exhibition." In Robert T. Denommé and Roland H. Simon, eds., *Unfinished Revolutions: Legacies of Upheaval in Modern French Culture*, 139–162. University Park: Pennsylvania State University Press, 1998.

Horne, Janet, and Françoise Blum. "Féminisme et Musée social: 1916–1939. *Vie sociale* 8–9 (1988): 315–402.

Horne, Janet, and Antoine Savoye. "A la jonction du travail social et de la sociologie: Les 'social surveys' américains." *Vie sociale* 5–6 (1988): 213–36.

Howard, Sir Ebenezer. *Garden Cities of Tomorrow*. London: Faber and Faber, 1951.

Howorth, Jolyon. *Édouard Vaillanti: La création de l'unité socialiste en France: La politique de l'action totale*. Paris: EDI: Syros, 1982.

Hudson, Kenneth. *A Social History of Museums: What the Visitors Thought*. Atlantic Highlands, N.J.: Humanities Press, 1975.

Hufton, Olwen H. *The Poor of Eighteenth-Century France, 1750–1789*. Oxford: Clarendon Press, 1974.

Hunt, Lynn, and George Sheriden. "Corporatism, Association, and the Language of Labor in France, 1750–1850," *Journal of Modern History* 58 (1986): 815–21.

Huxley, T. H. "Administrative Nihilism." *Fortnightly Review* 10 (1871): 525–43.

Impay, Oliver, and Arthur MacGregor, eds. *The Origins of Museums: The Cabinet of Curiosities in Sixteenth and Seventeenth Century Europe*. Oxford: Clarendon Press, 1985.

L'influence de Le Play en Espagne. Special issue of *Les Études sociales*. 129 (1999): 5–40.

Institut de France. *Académie des sciences morales et politiques*. 2 (1903): 376–412.

Jackson, James H., Jr., and Leslie Page Moch. "Migration and the Social History of Modern Europe." *Historical Methods*, 22, no. 1 (1989): 27–36.

Jacquemet, Gérard. *Belleville au XIXe siècle: Du faubourg à la ville*. Paris: Éditions de l'École des hautes études en sciences sociales, 1984.

Jay, Raoul. *L'assurance ouvrière et les caisses nationales de retraites pour la vieillesse*. Paris: Revue parlementaire et politique, 1895.

————. *L'assurance ouvrière obligatoire*. Paris: Librairie de la Société du receuil général des lois et des arrêts, 1899.

————. "L'assurance ouvrière obligatoire." *Revue d'économie politique* 13, no. 1 (1899): 105–17.

————. *La protection légale des travailleurs*. Paris: Sirey, 1904.

————. *Une forme nouvelle d'organisation du travail par les groupements professionnels*. Paris: Librairie de la Société du recueil général des lois et des arrêts, 1901.

Jolly, Jean, ed. *Dictionnaire des parlementaires français: Notices biographiques sur les ministres, députés et sénateurs français de 1889 à 1940*. 8 vols. Paris: Presses universitaires de France, 1960–77.

Joly, Henri. *Le socialisme chrétien, les origines, la tradition, les hérésies, théologiens, prédicateurs, missionnaires, la crise de 1848, les dernières écoles*. Paris: Hachette, 1892.

Jonas, Stéphane. *Le Mulhouse industriel: Un siècle d'histoire urbaine, 1740–1848*. 2 vols. Paris: L' Harmattan, 1994.

Judt, Tony. *Marxism and the Left in France: Studies on Labour and Politics in France, 1830–1981.* Oxford: Clarendon Press, 1986.

Juillerat, Paul. *L'hygiène du logement.* Paris: C. Delagrave, 1909.

———. "Le logement et la santé." *Musée social: Annales* (1909): 114–18.

———. "Sur le casier sanitaire des maisons de Paris." In *Congrès international d'hygiène et de démographie 1900,* 360–65. Paris: Masson et Cie., n.d.

Jules Siegfried: Sa vie et son oeuvre social: Hommage rendu à l'occasion du 100e anniversaire de sa naissance (février 1837-février 1937). Paris: Musée social, 1937.

Julliard, Jacques. *Fernand Pelloutier et les origines du syndicalisme d'action directe.* Paris: Éditions du Seuil, 1971.

Kalaora, Bernard, and Antoine Savoye. "Frédéric Le Play, un sociologue engagé." Epilogue to Frédéric Le Play, ed. *Ouvriers des deux mondes: Études publiées par la Société d'économie sociale à partir de 1856,* 320–33. Thomery: À l'enseigne de l'arbre verdoyant, 1983.

———. *Les inventeurs oubliés: Le Play et ses continuateurs aux origines des sciences sociales.* Seyssel: Éditions Champ Vallon, 1989.

Kang, Zheng. "Lieu de savoir social: La Société de statistique de Paris au xixe siècle, 1860–1910." Ph.D. diss., École des hautes études en sciences sociales, 1989.

Kaplan, Steven Laurence, and Cynthia J. Koepp, eds. *Work in France: Representations, Meaning, Organization, and Practice.* Ithaca: Cornell University Press, 1986.

Kaplow, Jeffry. *The Names of Kings: The Parisian Laboring Poor in the Eighteenth Century.* New York: Basic Books, 1972.

Karady, Victor. "Normaliens et autres enseignants à la Belle Époque: Note sur l'origine sociale et la réussite dans une profession intellectuelle." *Revue française de sociologie* 13, no. 1 (1972): 35–58.

———. "Les professeurs de la République: Le marché scolaire, les réformes universitaires et les transformations de la fonction professorale à la fin du XIXe siècle." *Actes de la recherche en sciences sociales* 47–48 (1983): 90–112.

Karp, Ivan, and Steven D. Lavine, eds. *Exhibiting Cultures: The Poetics and Politics of Museum Display.* Washington: Smithsonian Institution Press, 1991.

Klejman, Laurence, and Florence Rochefort. *L'égalité en marche: Le féminisme sous la Troisième République.* Paris: Presses de la Fondation nationale des sciences politiques, Édition des femmes, 1989.

Kloppenberg, James T. *Uncertain Victory: Social Democracy and Progressivism in European and American Thought, 1870–1920.* New York and Oxford: Oxford University Press, 1986.

Kott, Sandrine. "Enjeux et significations d'une politique sociale: La société industrielle de Mulhouse, 1827–1870." *Revue d'histoire moderne et contemporaine* 34 (1987): 640–59.

Koven, Seth, and Sonya Michel. *Mothers of a New World: Maternalist Politics and the Origins of Welfare States.* New York: Routledge, 1993.

———. "Womanly Duties, Maternalist Politics, and the Origins of the Welfare States in France, Germany, Great-Britain, and the United States." *American Historical Review* 95 (1990): 1076–108.

Kudlick, Catherine Jean. *Cholera in Post-Revolutionary Paris: A Cultural History.* Berkeley: University of California Press, 1996.

———. "Giving Is Deceiving: Cholera, Charity, and the Quest for Authority in 1832." *French Historical Studies* 18, no. 2 (1993): 457–81.

Kuisel, Richard F. *Capitalism and the State in Modern France: Renovation and Economic Management in the Twentieth Century.* Cambridge: Cambridge University Press, 1981.

———. *Ernest Mercier: French Technocrat.* Berkeley: University of California Press, 1967.

Labarre de Raillicourt, Dominique, ed. *Nouveau dictionnaire des biographies françaises et étrangères.* 2 vols. Paris: D. Labarre de Raillicourt, 1974.

La Berge, Ann Elizabeth. *Mission and Method: The Early Nineteenth-Century French Public Health Movement.* Cambridge and New York: Cambridge University Press, 1992.

Lacey, Michael J., and Mary O. Furner, eds. *The State and Social Investigation in Britain and the United States.* Cambridge: Woodrow Wilson Center Press and Cambridge University Press, 1993.

Lachèvre, Léon. "La crise agraire: Une mission française en Allemagne." *L'Abeille cauchoise,* 30 October 1897.

Lagarde, Paul. "Revue des revues." *La Revue socialiste* 1 (1894): 481–85.

Lami, Étienne O. "Cercles d'ouvriers, récréations et jeux." In Picard, ed., *Ministère du commerce, de l'industrie et des colonies: Exposition universelle internationale de 1889 à Paris. Rapports du jury international: Groupe de l'économie sociale,* 2:231–81. Paris: Imprimerie nationale, 1891.

Latour, Bruno. *The Pasteurization of France.* Cambridge: Harvard University Press, 1988.

Laurent, Émile. *Le paupérisme et les associations de prévoyance.* 2 vols. Paris: Guillaumin, 1865.

Laurent, T. *La mutualité française et le monde du travail.* Paris: C.I.E.M., 1973.

Lavielle, Romain. *Histoire de la mutualité: Sa place dans le régime français de la Sécurité sociale.* Paris: Librairie Hachette, 1964.

Lavollée, René. *Les classes ouvrières en Europe: Études sur leur situation matérielle et morale.* 3 vols. Paris: Guillaumin, 1884–97.

Leclerc, Gérard. *L'observation de l'homme: Une histoire des enquêtes sociales.* Paris: Éditions du Seuil, 1979.

Lecuyer, Bernard. "Les maladies professionelles dans les Annales d'hygiène publique et de médecine légale, ou une première approche de l'usure au travail," *Le Mouvement social* 124 (1983): 45–70.

Lehning, Arthur. *Bekounine et les historiens.* Geneva: CIRA Éditions Noir, 1979.

Leiby, James. *Carroll D. Wright and the Origins of Labor Statistics.* Cambridge, Mass.: Harvard University Press, 1960.

Lemoine, Georges. *Livret d'enseignement moral: Esprit laïque, exposé méthodique.* Paris: C. Delagrave, 1901.

Lépine, J. "Louis Landouzy." *Revue de médecine* 35, no. 5–6 (1916): 279–84.

Le Play, Frédéric. *La constitution essentielle de l'humanité.* Tours: Mame, 1881.

———, ed. *Ouvriers des deux mondes: Études publiées par la Société d'économie sociale à partir de 1856.* Introduction and epilogue by Bernard Kalaora and Antoine Savoye. Paris: À l'enseigne de l'arbre verdoyant, 1983.

———. *Frédéric Le Play on Family, Work and Social Change.* Edited, translated, and with an introduction by Catherine Bodard Silver. Chicago: University of Chicago Press, 1982.

———. *La méthode sociale: Abrégé des "Ouvriers européens."* Tours: Mame, 1879. Reprint with an introduction by Antoine Savoye. Paris: Méridiens-Klincksieck, 1989.

———. *Les ouvriers européens.* 9 vols. Tours: Mame, 1877–79.

———. *L'organisation du travail, selon la coûtume des ateliers et la loi du Décalogue.* Tours: Mame, 1870.

———. *La paix sociale après le désastre.* Tours: Mame, 1871.

———. *La réforme sociale en France déduite de l'observation comparée des peuples européens.* 2 vols. Paris: Plon, 1864; New York: Arno Press, 1975.

Le Play, Frédéric, Émile Cheysson, Bayard, and Fernand Butel. *Les Mélouga: Une famille pyrénéene au XIXe siècle.* Textes réunis par Alain Chénu. Paris: Nathan, 1994.

Leprun, Sylviane. "Paysages de la France extérieure: La mise en scène des colonies à l'Exposition du Centenaire." *Le Movement social* 149 (1989): 99–128.

Leroy, Maxime. *Histoire des idées sociales en France.* 3 vols. Paris: Gallimard, 1954.

Leroy-Beaulieu, Paul. "Les aspirations des ouvriers et leurs projets de réforme sociale." Rapport de la délégation française à l'Exposition de Vienne. *Revue des deux mondes* (1875): 133–68.

———. *De l'état moral et intellectuel des populations ouvrières.* Paris: Guillaumin, 1868.

Levasseur, Émile. *Questions ouvrières et industrielles en France sous la Troisième République.* Paris: Arthur Rousseau, 1907.

———. *Résumé historique de l'enseignement de l'économie politique et de la statistique en France de 1882 à 1892.* Paris: Librairie Guillaumin, 1893.

Levillain, Philippe. *Albert de Mun, catholicisme français et catholicisme romain du Syllabus au Ralliement.* Rome: École française de Rome, 1983.

Lévy-Leboyer, Maurice, ed. *Le patronat de la seconde industrialisation.* Paris: Éditions ouvrières, 1979.

Lichtenberger, André. "Congrès international pour la protection légale des travailleurs." *Musée social: Revue mensuelle* 3, no. 8 (1900), 261–96.

———. "Le Musé social: L'organisation et les services." *Le Musée social* 4 (1900): 109–26.

———. "Le Musée social: Son but, son organisation, son oeuvre." *Le Musée social: Revue mensuelle* 40, no. 10 (1933): 333–49.

Logue, William. *From Philosophy to Sociology: The Evolution of French Liberalism, 1870–1914.* Dekalb: Northern Illinois Press, 1983.

———. "Sociologie et politique: Le libéralisme de Célestin Bouglé." *Revue française de sociologie* 20, no. 1 (1979): 141–62.

Lucas, Charles. "L'apprentissage." In Alfred Picard, ed. Ministère du Commerce. *Exposition universelle de 1889. Rapports du jury international. Groupe de l'économie sociale,* 1:277–331.

Luchaire, M. "Funérailles de M. Ernest Glasson." *Institut de France, Académie des sciences morales et politiques* (1907): 1.

Luciani, Jean, and Robert Salais. "Matériaux pour la naissance d'une institution: l'Office du travail (1890–1900)." *Genèses: Sciences sociales et histoire* 2 (1990): 83–108.

Lumley, Robert, ed. *The Museum Time-Machine: Putting Cultures on Display.* London: Routledge, 1988.

Lynch, Katherine Ann. *Family, Class, and Ideology in Early Industrial France: Social Policy and the Working-Class Family, 1825–1848.* Madison: University of Wisconsin Press, 1988.

Mabilleau, Léopold. *Cours d'instruction civique.* Paris: Hachette, 1883.

———. *Cours de morale.* Paris: Hachette, 1883.

———. *Dixième Congrès national de la mutualité française: Les retraites et la mutualité.* Nancy: Imprimerie nancéienne, 1909.

———. *La mutualité française: doctrines et applications.* Bordeaux: Imprimerie de G. Delmas, 1904.

———. "Rapport présenté au 9e Congrès national de la mutualité," "Service de la mutualité." *Le Musée social: Annales* (1907): 119–31.

———. "La mutualité et les retraites ouvrières." *Le Musée social: Annales* (1910): 51–52.

Mabilleau, Léopold, Charles Rayneri, and Comte de Rocquigny. *La prévoyance en Italie.* Paris: Armand Colin, 1898.

Magraw, Roger. *A History of the French Working Class.* 2 vols. Oxford: Blackwell, 1992.

Magri, Susanna. *Les laboratoires de la réforme de l'habitation populaire en France: De la Société française des habitations à bon marché, à la section d'hygiène urbaine et rurale du Musée social, 1889–1909.* Paris-La Défense: Ministère de l'équipement, du logement, des transports et du tourisme, 1996.

Maier, Charles S. *Recasting Bourgeois Europe: Stabilization in France, Germany, and Italy in the Decade After World War I.* Princeton: Princeton University Press, 1975.

Maitron, Jean, ed. *Dictionnaire biographique du mouvement ouvrier français.* 20 vols. Paris: Les Éditions ouvrières, 1964–83.

March, Lucien. "Pour la race: Infertilité et puericulture." *Revue du mois* 10 (1910): 551–82.

Martin, B. F. "The Creation of the Action Libérale Populaire: An Example of Party Formation in Third Republic's France." *French Historical Studies* 9, no. 4 (1976): 660–89.

Martin Saint-Léon, Étienne. *Cartels et trusts.* Paris: Lecoffre, 1903.

———. "Le compagnonnage, ses coutumes, son rôle social." *Le Musée social: Annales* (1902): 171–72.

———. *Histoire des corporations de métiers.* Paris: Librairie Félix Alcan, 1922.

———. "Léon de Seilhac." *Le Musée social: Mémoires et documents (supplement)* 3 (1 April 1920): 1–7.

———. *Le petit commerce français, sa lutte pour la vie.* Paris: J. Gabalda, 1911.

———. *Rapport sur le projet de révision du catalogue alphabétique et d'achèvement du catalogue méthodique de la Bibliothèque du Musée social.* Paris: Imprimerie Farant, 1897.

———. "Les retraites ouvrières doivent-elle être obligatoires? À propos d'un livre récent." *L'Association catholique* 2 (1906): 413–27.

Martin, Jean-Baptiste. *La fin des mauvais pauvres: De l'assistance à l'assurance.* Seyssel: Champ Vallon, 1983.

Mataja, Victor. "Les origines de la protection ouvrière en France." *Revue d'économie politique* 9 (1895): 529–34.

May, Dick. "L'enseignement social à Paris." *Revue internationale de l'enseignement* 26 (1896): 1–45.

Mayeur, Jean-Marie. *Les débuts de la Troisième République, 1871–1898*. Paris: Éditions du Seuil, 1973.

———. *Un prêtre démocrate, l'abbé Lemire, 1863–1928*. Tournai: Castermann, 1968.

———. *La vie politique sous la Troisième République*. Paris: Éditions du Seuil, 1984.

McManners, John. *Church and State in France, 1870–1914*. London: S.P.C.K. for the Church Historical Society, 1972.

Meline, Jules. *Le retour à la terre et la surpopulation industrielle*. Paris: Hachette, 1905.

Mesnil, Dr. Octave du. *L'hygiène à Paris: L'habitation du pauvre*. Paris: J. B. Baillière et fils, 1890.

———. "L'hygiène des habitations ouvrières." Conférence faite le 30 avril 1892 au Congrès de la Fédération des ouvriers socialistes de France. *Bulletin de la Société française des habitations à bon marché* (1892): 304–26.

———. "L'habitation du pauvre à Paris," *Revue d'hygiène* 4 (1882): 956–64.

Mesnil, Dr. Octave du, and Dr. Mangenot. *Étude d'hygiène et d'économie sociale: Enquête sur les logements, professions, salaires et budgets*. Paris: Imprimerie Chaix, 1899.

Métin, Albert. "Le Musée social." *La Revue blanche* 2 (1896): 564–65.

Michel, Henry. *L'idée de l'État*. Paris: Hachette, 1896.

Michelet, Jules. *Le Peuple*. Paris: Comptoir des Imprimeurs Unis, 1846; reprint, Paris: Flammarion, 1974.

Ministère du commerce et de l'industrie. Conseil supérieur du travail. *Deuxième session, 1892 (juin-juillet)*. Paris: Imprimerie nationale, 1892.

———. Conseil supérieur du travail. *Première session (février 1891). Compte-rendu des séances, rapports des commissions et résolutions votées*. Paris: Imprimerie nationale, 1891.

———*Rapport relatif au Musée d'économie sociale présenté au nom de la deuxième commission par M. Linder*. Paris: Imprimerie nationale, 1892.

Mitchell, Allan. *The Divided Path: The German Influence on Social Reform in France After 1870*. Chapel Hill: University of North Carolina Press, 1991.

Montgomery, David. *Workers' Control in America: Studies in the History of Work, Technology, and Labor Struggles*. Cambridge: Cambridge University Press, 1979.

Moon, Parker Thomas. *The Labor Problem and the Social Catholic Movement in France: A Study in the History of Social Politics*. New York: MacMillan, 1921.

Moss, Bernard. *The Origins of the French Labor Movement, 1830–1914: The Socialism of Skilled Workers*. Berkeley: University of California Press, 1976.

Le Mouvement social. Revue catholique internationale. Paris: [n.p], 1909.

Murard, Léon, and Patrick Zylberman. *L'hygiène dans la République: La santé publique en France ou l'utopie contrariée, 1870–1918*. Paris: Fayard, 1996.

———. "La raison de l'expert ou l'hygiène comme science sociale appliquée." *Archives européenes de sociologie* 26 (1985): 58–89.

Le Musée pédagogique, son origine, son organisation, son objet, d'après les documents officiels. Paris: Imprimerie nationale, 1884.

Le Musée social. Paris: Arthur Rousseau, 1914.

Le Musée social, Paris: Musée social, 1906.

Le Musée social, Paris: Musée social, 1911.

Le Musée social: Annales. Paris: Musée social, 1902–14.

Musée social: Circulaire. Série A. Paris: Musée social, 1896–98 (Jan. 1896–Dec. 1898): nos. 1–24.

Musée social: Circulaire. Série B. Paris: Musée social, 1896–98 (June 1896–Oct. 1898): nos. 1–20.

Musée social: Fondation Chambrun. Paris: Arthur Rousseau, 1908.

Le Musée social: Mémoires et documents. Paris: Arthur Rousseau, 1902–21.

Le Musée social: Organisation et services. Paris: Arthur Rousseau, 1900.

Musée social. *Le concours de la participation aux bénéfices.* 30 May 1897. Paris: F. Didot, 1897.

———. *La fête du travail. Dimanche 3 mai 1896.* Paris: Calmann-Lévy, 1896.

———. *La fête pour le concours des associations ouvrières et patronales. 19 juin 1898.* Paris: Calmann-Lévy, 1898.

———. *Le concours entre les syndicats agricoles au Musée social. 31 October 1897.* Paris: Calmann-Lévy, 1897.

———. *La contribution à la bibliographie des assurances sociales.* Paris: Rousseau, 1898.

———. *M. Georges Risler (1853–1941).* Paris: Musée social, 1941.

———. *Inauguration. 25 mars 1895.* Paris: Calmann-Lévy, 1895.

——— *Les lauréats du travail agricole (20 octobre 1898).* Paris: Calmann-Lévy, 1898.

——— *Obsèques du comte de Chambrun: Fondateur du Musée social, 1821–1899.* Paris: Calmann-Lévy, 1899.

———. *Une semaine coopérative. 25 octobre-1er novembre 1896.* Paris: Calmann-Lévy, 1896.

———. *Société du Musée social, Décret du 31 août 1894, Statuts, demande en reconaissance d'utilité publique.* Paris: Imprimerie nouvelle, Association ouvrière, 1894.

———. *Statuts, organisation, services.* Paris: Firmin-Didot, 1896.

The National Cyclopaedia of American Biography. New York: James T. White and Co., 1892–1901.

Nelms, Brenda. *The Third Republic and the Centennial of 1789.* New York: Garland Publishing, 1987.

Nelson, John S., Allan Megill, and Donald N. McCloskey, eds. *The Rhetoric of the Human Sciences: Language and Argument in Scholarship and Public Affairs.* Madison: University of Wisconsin Press, 1987.

Nettlau, Max. *Michael Bakunin: Ein Biographie.* 3 vols. Copy # 36. London: Privated printed (reproduced by Autocopyist), 1899–1900.

Neufville, Agnès de. *Le mouvement social protestant en France depuis 1880.* Paris: Presses universitaires de France, 1928.

Nicolet, Claude. *L'idée républicaine en France: Essai d'histoire critique, 1789–1924.* Paris: Gallimard, 1982.

Noiriel, Gérard. *Longwy, immigrés et prolétaires: 1880–1980.* Paris: Presses universitaires de France, 1984.

———. *Les ouvriers dans la société française, XIXe-XXe siècles.* Paris: Éditions du Seuil, 1986.

———. "Du patronage au paternalisme: La restructuration des formes de domination de la main-d'oeuvre ouvrière dans l'industrie métallurgique française." *Le Mouvement social* 144 (1988): 17–36.

Nord, Philip. *Paris Shopkeepers and the Politics of Resentment.* Princeton: Princeton University Press, 1986.

———. "Social Defence and Conservative Regeneration: The National Revival, 1900–14." In Robert Tombs, ed., *Nationhood and Nationalism in France: From Boulangism to the Great War, 1889–1918*, 210–28. New York: HarperCollins Academic, 1991.

———. "Welfare State in France, 1870–1914." *French Historical Studies* 18, no. 3 (1994): 821–38.

Novick, Alicia. "Le Musée social et l'urbanisme en Argentine." In Colette Chambelland, ed., *Le Musée social en son temps*, 331–58.

Nye, Robert. *Crime, Madness, and Politics in Modern France: The Medical Concept of National Decline.* Princeton: Princeton University Press, 1984.

———. *Masculinity and Male Codes of Honor in Modern France.* New York: Oxford University Press, 1993.

O'Brien, Patricia. "L'embastillement de Paris": The Fortification of Paris During the July Monarchy." *French Historical Studies* 9, no. 1 (1975): 63–82.

Offen, Karen. "Depopulation, Nationalism and Feminism in Fin-de-Siècle France." *American Historical Review* 89 (1984): 648–76.

Ory, Pascal. *Une nation pour mémoire: 1889, 1939, 1989. Trois jubilés révolutionnaires.* Paris: Presses de la Fondation nationale des sciences politiques, 1992.

Osborne, Thomas. *A Grande école for the Grands corps: The Recruitment and Training of the French Administrative Elite in the Nineteenth Century.* Boulder, Colo., New York: Social Science Monographs, dist. by Columbia University Press, 1983.

Osti, Giovanna. "Le Musée social et l'urbanisme au début du siècle." *Vie sociale* 3 (1984): 117–25.

Ott, Florence. *La Société industrielle de Mulhouse, 1826–1876: Ses membres, son action, ses réseaux.* Strasbourg: Presses universitaires de Strasbourg, 1999.

Paoli, Louis. "Questions économiques et sociales." *L'Émancipation.* 15 September 1897.

Parize, René. "Le paternalisme et son influence politique au Creusot (1899–1939)." Ph.D. diss., Université de Toulouse II, 1981.

Passy, Frédéric. *Leçons d'économie politique faites à Montpellier par M. Frédéric Passy, recueillies par MM. Émile Bertin et Paul Glaize. 1860–1861.* Paris: Guillaumin, 1862.

Pecqueur, Constantin. *Théorie nouvelle d'économie sociale et politique.* 1842; reprint New York: B. Franklin, 1971.

Pederson, Susan. *Family, Dependence, and the Origins of the Welfare State, 1914–1945.* New York: Cambridge University Press, 1993.

Peer, Shanny. *Peasants, Provincials, and Folklore in the 1939 Universal Exposition.* Albany: SUNY Press, 1998.

Pelloutier, Fernand. "*Mes conclusions sociologiques* par le comte de Chambrun." *La Démocratie de l'Ouest*, 16 November 1893.

———. "La semaine politique et sociale: *Nouvelles conclusions sociologiques.*" *L'Avenir social*, 1893.

Perrot, Michelle. *Enquêtes sur la condition ouvrière en France au 19e siècle.* Paris: Microéditions Hachette, 1972.

———. *Les ouvriers en grève: France, 1871–1890.* 2 vols. Paris, La Haye: Mouton, 1974.

———. "The Three Ages of Industrial Discipline in Nineteenth Century France." In

John M. Merriman, ed., *Consciousness and Class Experience in Nineteenth Century Europe.* New York: Holmes and Meier, 1980.

Philipps, Peggy A. "Neo-corporatist Praxis in Paris." *Journal of Urban History* 4 (1978): 397–415.

Picard, Alfred, ed. Ministère du commerce, de l'industrie et des colonies. *Exposition universelle internationale de 1889 à Paris. Rapport du jury international. Groupe de l'économie sociale.* 3 vols. Paris: Imprimerie nationale, 1891–92.

————, ed. Ministère du commerce, de l'industrie et des colonies. *Exposition universelle internationale de 1889 à Paris. Rapport général.* 9 vols. Paris: Imprimerie nationale, 1891–92.

Pickering, Mary. *Auguste Comte: An Intellectual Biography.* New York: Cambridge University Press, 1993.

Picot, Georges. *La lutte contre le socialisme révolutionaire.* Paris: Armand Colin, 1896.

————. *La République - Ses véritables adversair* [sic]. *Discours prononcé à Gien, 11 décembre 1892.* Gien: Imprimerie Paul Pigelet, 1892.

————. *Socialisme, radicalisme et anarchie: Conference faite à Sancerre, 11 novembre 1894.* Sancerre: Typographie lithographie Michel Pigelet, 1895.

————. *L'usage de la liberté et de devoir social: Comité de défense et de progrès social, séance d'ouverture,* January 9, 1895. Excerpt from *La Réforme sociale.* Paris: Comité de défense et de progrès social, 1895.

Pinkney, David. *Napoleon III and the Rebuilding of Paris.* Princeton: University of Princeton Press, 1958.

Pittman III, Paul March. *Léon Bourgeois et les origines du solidarisme.* Mémoire de D.E.A. Paris: Institut d'études politiques, 1987.

Poëte, Marcel. *Au jardin des Tuilleries: L'art du jardin, la promenade publique.* Paris: Picard, 1924.

————. *Introduction à l'urbanisme, l'évolution des villes, la leçon de l'antiquité.* Paris: Boivin and Cie., 1929.

————. *Une vie de cité: Paris de sa naissance à nos jours.* 4 vol. Paris: Picard, 1924.

Ponsot, Pierre. "Un militant socialiste du XIXe siècle: Jean-Baptiste Dumay." *Revue socialiste* 188 (1965): 517–22.

Pourcher, Yves. *Les maîtres de granit: Les notables de Lozère du XVIIIe siècle à nos jours.* Paris: Olivier Orban, 1987.

Prévost, Michel, Jean-Charles Roman d'Amat, and Henri Tribout de Morembert, eds. *Dictionnaire de biographie française.* 19 vols. Paris: Letouzey et Ané, 1933–99.

Procacci, Giovanna. *Gouverner la misère: La question sociale en France, 1789–1848.* Paris: Éditions du Seuil, 1993.

Prochasson, Christophe. "Dick May et le social." In Colette Chambelland, ed. *Le Musée social en son temps,* 43–58. Paris: Presses de l'École normale supérieure, 1998.

————. *Les intellectuels, le socialisme et la guerre.* Paris: Éditions du Seuil, 1993.

Prost, Antoine. "La Providence sociale." In Jean-Pierre Rioux and Jean-François Sirinelli, eds., *La France d'un siècle à l'autre, 1914–2000: Dictionnaire critique,* 161–70. Paris: Hachette, 1999.

Protasi, Maria Rosa. "Le applicazioni pratiche della metodologia di ricerca sociale di F. Le

Play e della sua scuola in Italia dall'unità alla prima guerra mondiale." *Società e storia* 77 (1997): 581–617.

———. "Tra scienza e riforma sociale: Il pensiero e il metodo d'indagine sociale di F. Le Play et dei suoi continuatori in Italia (1857–1914)." *Studi Storici: Rivista trimestrale dell'istituto Gramsci* 37 (1996): 813–45.

Rabinbach, Anson. *The Human Motor: Energy, Fatigue, and the Origins of Modernity.* New York: Basic Books, 1990.

Rabinow, Paul. *French Modern: Norms and Forms of the Social Environment.* Cambridge: MIT Press, 1989.

Rancière, Jacques. *La nuit des prolétaires.* Paris: Fayard, 1981.

Rasmussen, Anne. "Les congrès internationaux liés aux expositions universelles de Paris (1867–1900)." 7 (1989): 23–44.

Rebérioux, Madeleine. "Les 'élites intellectuelles' et la question sociale." In Madeleine Rebérioux and Gilles Candar, eds. *Jaurès et les intellectuels,* 19–39. Paris: Éditions de l'Atelier, 1994.

———. "Les expositions universelles: Voir Paris ou mourir." *Revue de l'économie sociale* 19 (1990): 7–18.

———. "Naissance de l'économie sociale." *Revue de l'économie sociale* 1 (1984): 9–16.

Reddy, William M. *The Rise of Market Culture: The Textile Trade and French Society, 1750–1900.* Cambridge: Cambridge University Press, 1984.

Reid, Donald. "Industrial Paternalism: Discourse and Practice in 19th Century French Mining and Metallurgy." *Comparative Studies in Society and History* 27 (1985): 579–607.

———. *The Miners of Decazeville: A Geneology of Deindustrialisation.* Cambridge: Harvard University Press, 1985.

———. *Paris Sewers and Sewermen: Realities and Representations.* Cambridge: Harvard University Press, 1991.

———. "Putting Social Reform into Practice: Labor Inspectors in France, 1892–1914," *Journal of Social History* 20 (1986): 67–87.

——— "The Third Republic as Manager: Labor Policy in the Naval Shipyards." *International Review of Social History* 30 (1985): 183–202.

Renard, Georges. "Un musée social." *La Revue socialiste* (1894): 440–42.

Ribbe, Charles de. *Le Play d'après sa correspondance.* Paris: Firmin-Didot, 1884.

Rigaudias-Weiss, Hilde. *Les enquêtes ouvrières en France entre 1830 et 1848.* Paris: Félix Alcan, 1936.

Risler, Georges. *Better Housing for Workers in France.* Paris: Centre d'informations documentaires, 1937.

———. "Les espaces libres dans les grandes villes et les cités-jardins." *Le Musée social: Mémoires et documents* (1910): 349–404.

———."Les plans d'amenagement et d'extension des villes." *Le Musée social: Mémoires et documents.* (1912): 301–52.

Rivière, Louis. "Émile Cheysson." *La Réforme sociale* 1 (1910): 225–33.

———. "Une exposition d'appareils de protection pour les travailleurs de New York," *La Réforme sociale* 2 (1906): 446–47.

Robert, Adolphe, and Gaston Cougny, eds. *Dictionnaire des parlementaires français: Comprenant tous les membres des Assemblées françaises et tous les ministres français depuis le 1er mai 1789 jusqu'au 1er mai 1889.* 5 vols. Paris: Bourloton, 1889–91.

Robert, Charles. "Économistes et coopérateurs," *L'Émancipation* 13 (1899): 34.

Rodgers, Daniel T. *Atlantic Crossings: Social Politics in a Progressive Age.* Cambridge: Belknap Press of Harvard University Press, 1998.

———. "In Search of Progressivism." *Reviews in American History* 10, no. 4 (1982): 113–32.

Rodgers, Susan Carol. "Farming Visions: Agriculture in French Culture." *French Politics, Culture, and Society* 18, no. 1 (2000): 50–70.

Roncayolo, Marcel. "Le temps des essais: Techniques et représentations du territoire." In André Burguière and Jacques Revel, eds., *Histoire de la France: L'espace français,* 511–50. Paris: Éditions du Seuil, 1989.

Roosevelt, Theodore. *L'idéal américain.* Paris: Armand Colin, 1910.

Rosanvallon, Pierre. *La crise de l'État-providence.* Paris: Éditions du Seuil, 1981.

———. *L'État en France de 1789 à nos jours.* Paris: Éditions du Seuil, 1990.

———. *Le moment Guizot.* Paris: Gallimard, 1985.

———. *La nouvelle question sociale: Repenser l'État-providence.* Paris: Éditions du Seuil, 1995.

Rose, Carol M. *Property and Persuasion: Essays on the History, Theory, and Rhetoric of Ownership.* Boulder, Colo.: Westview Press, 1994.

Roulliet, Anthony. "Une loi sur les habitations ouvrières." *Le Bulletin de la Société française des habitations à bon marché* 3 (1890): 244–63.

Rousiers, Paul de. *L'élite de la société moderne.* Paris: Armand Colin, 1914.

———. "Les syndicats du bâtiment en Angleterre." *Le Musée social,* series A, 4 (1896): 57–71.

———. "Le Trade-unionisme anglais et les causes de son succès." *Le Musée social,* series A, 2 (1896): 18–38.

Rousiers, Paul de, with de Carbonnel, Festy, Fleury, and Wilhelm. *Le Trade-Unionisme en Angleterre.* Paris: Armand Colin, 1897.

Rust, Michael Jared. "Business and Politics in the Third Republic: The Comité des forges and the French Steel Industry." Ph.D. diss., Princeton University, 1973.

Ryckelynck, Xavier. "L'économie sociale dans le rapport d'Alfred Picard sur l'Exposition universelle de 1889." *Revue de l'économie sociale* 19 (1990): 97–107.

Saint-Simon, Henri de. *Catéchisme des industriels.* 2 vols. Paris: Imprimerie de Sétier, 1823–24.

———. *Oeuvres complètes.* 6 vols. Paris: Anthropos, 1955.

———. *Social Organization, the Science of the Man, and Other Writings.* Edited and translated by Felix Markham. New York: Harper and Row, 1964.

Salaun, Georges. "Les résulats de la loi belge sur les retraites ouvrières."*Le Musée social: Annales* (1902): 405–23.

———. "Les retraites ouvrières en Belgique." *Le Musée social: Mémoires et documents* (1901): 165–99.

Savard, Pierre. "Du Lac Saint-Jean au Texas: Claudio Jannet à la recherche de l'Amérique idéale." *Revue française d'histoire d'outre-mer* 77, no. 288 (1990): 3–19.

Savoye, Antoine, "Les continuateurs de Le Play au tournant du siècle." *Revue française de sociologie* 22, no. 3 (1981): 315–44.

———. "L'école de Le Play et l'intelligentsia italienne: Une relation de longue durée (1846–1914)." *Richerche di Storia Sociale e Religiosa* 29, no. 57 (2000): 87–115.

———. "Genèse de la sociologie d'intervention." Ph.D. diss., University of Paris x, 1979.

———. "Les paroles et les actes: Les dirigeants de la Société d'économie sociale, 1883–1914." In Topalov, ed. *Laboratoires du nouveau siècle: La nébuleuse réformatrice et ses réseaux en France, 1880–1914*, 61–94. Paris: Éditions de l'école des hautes études en sciences sociales, 1999.

———. "Le Play et la méthode sociale." Introduction to Frédéric Le Play, *La méthode sociale: Abrégé des "Ouvriers européens."* Tours: Mame, 1879; reprint Paris: Méridiens-Klincksieck, 1989.

———. "Une réponse originale aux problèmes sociaux: L'ingénierie sociale (1885–1914)." *Vie sociale* 8–9 (1987): 485–505.

Say, Léon. "Économie sociale: Rapport général." In Picard, ed., *Ministère du commerce: Exposition universelle internationale de 1889: Rapport général.* 1: v-cxlviii. Paris: Imprimerie nationale, 1891.

Schafer, Sylvia. *Children in Moral Danger and the Problem of Government in Third Republic France.* Princeton: Princeton University Press, 1997.

Schneider, William H. *Quality and Quantity: The Quest for Biological Regeneration in Twentieth-Century France.* Cambridge, New York: Cambridge University Press, 1990.

Scott, Joan Wallach. *The Glassworkers of Carmaux: French Craftsmen and Political Action in a Nineteenth-Century City.* Cambridge: Harvard University Press, 1974.

———. "'L'ouvrière! Mot impie, sordide . . .': Women Workers in the Discourse of French Political Economy, 1840–1860." In *Gender and the Politics of History*, 139–163. New York: Columbia University Press, 1985.

Seilhac, Léon de. *Congrès de legislation du travail, tenu à Bruxelles du 27 au 30 septembre 1897.* Paris: Firmin-Didot, 18978.

———. *Les congrès ouvriers en France de 1876 a 1897.* Paris: Librairie Armand Colin, 1899.

———. *Les congrès ouvriers en France; Deuxième série (1893–1906) Création de la Conféderation générale du travail.* Paris: V. Lecoffre, 1906.

———. *Les grèves* Paris: Librairie Victor Lecoffre, 1903.

——— ed. *Manuel pratique d'économie sociale.* Reims: Action populaire; Paris: Roustan, 1905.

———. "Le mouvement syndical en France et le Congrès de Tours." *Le Musée social*, Series A, circ. 15 (1897): 293–325.

———. *Une enquête sociale: La grève de Carmaux et la Verrerie d'Albi.* Paris: Perrin et Cie., 1897.

———. *Le monde socialiste: Groupes et programmes.* Paris: Armand Colin, 1896.

———. *Le monde socialiste: Les partis socialistes politiques; les congrès socialistes politiques; les diverses formules du collectivisme.* Paris: V. Lecoffre, 1904.

———. *Syndicats ouvriers, féderations, bourses du travail.* Paris: Armand Colin, 1902.

———. *Utopie socialiste.* Paris: Bloud, 1908.

Serrurier, J. *Les musées scolaires: Exposition universelle de 1889. Monographies pédagogiques.* Paris: Imprimerie nationale, 1889.

Sewell, William H., Jr. *A Rhetoric of Bourgeois Revolution: The Abbé Sièyes and "What Is the Third Estate?"* Durham: Duke University Press, 1994.

———. *Work and Revolution in France: The Language of Labor from the Old Regime to 1848.* Cambridge: Cambridge University Press, 1980.

Shapiro, Ann-Louise. *Housing of the Poor of Paris, 1850–1902.* Madison: University of Wisconsin Press, 1985.

Sheradin, Kristin A. "Reforming the Republic: Solidarism and the Making of the French Welfare State." Ph.D. diss., University of Rochester, 2000.

Sheridan, George, Jr., "Household and Craft in an Industrializing Economy: The Case of the Silk Weavers of Lyons." In John Merriman, ed., *Consciousness and Class Experience in Nineteenth-Century Europe,* 107–28. New York: Holmes and Meier, 1979.

Sherman, Daniel, ed. *Museum Culture: Histories, Discourses, Spectacles.* Minneapolis: University of Minnesota Press, 1994.

———. *Worthy Monuments: Art Museums and the Politics of Culture in Nineteenth Century France.* Cambridge: Harvard University Press, 1989.

Siegfried, André. *Jules Siegfried (1836–1922).* Le Havre: Société des bibliophiles havrais, 1942.

———. *Mes souvenirs de la IIIe République: Mon père et son temps, Jules Siegfried, 1836–1922.* Paris: Éditions du Grand Siècle, 1946.

Siegfried, Jules. *L'alcoolisme. Discours prononcé à la séance de la Ligue nationale contre l'alcoolisme, le 17 novembre 1895.* Paris: Imprimerie Noizette, 1895.

———. *Le Cercle Franklin du Havre.* Le Havre: Imprimerie T. Leclerc, 1877.

———. *Les cercles d'ouvriers: Conférence faite au Havre, 29 novembre 1874.* Le Havre: Imprimerie de F. Santallier, 1874.

———. "L'expropriation pour cause d'insalubrité publique." In Alliance d'hygiène sociale. *Congrès de Roubaix, 19–22 octobre 1911: "De la ville-taudis à la cité-jardin,"* pp. 197–217. Agen: Imprimerie moderne, 1911.

———. *Les habitations à bon marché.* Paris: Masson, 1897.

———. *Les habitations à bon marché.* Paris: Librairie Félix Alcan, 1914.

———. *Les habitations à bon marché, Conférence du 9 décembre 1891.* Paris: Dole, 1892.

———. *La misère: Son histoire, ses causes, ses remèdes.* Paris: Ballière, 1877.

———. "Projet de loi ayant pour but la création d'un Musée d'économie sociale au Conservatoire national des arts et métiers," no. 2641, Chambre des députés, 5s legislature, séance de 1893. Annexe au procès-verbal de la séance du 13 mars 1893. Paris: Matteroz, Imprimeur de la Chambre des députés, 1893.

———. "Proposition de loi concernant les fortifications de la ville de Paris," in "Les espaces libres à Paris: Les fortifications remplacées par une ceinture de parcs," *Musée social: Mémoires et documents* 4 (1909): 73–77.

———. "Proposition de loi relative aux habitations ouvrières," déposé le 5 mars 1892 sur le bureau de la Chambre des députés, *Bulletin de la Société française des habitations à bon marché,* 1892.

———. "Les retraites ouvrières devant le Parlement," *Le Musée social: Mémoires et documents* 3 (1906): 129–43.

Siegfried, Jules, and Eugène Hénard. "Les espaces libres à Paris. Les fortifications remplacées par une ceinture de parcs." *Le Musée social. Mémoires et documents* 4 (1909): 73–92.

Silver, Catherine Bodard, ed. *Frédéric Le Play on Family, Work and Social Change*. Chicago: University of Chicago Press, 1982.

Silverman, Debora. *The Origins of French Art Nouveau, 1889–1900: Nature, Neurology, and Nobility*. Berkeley and Los Angeles: University of California Press, 1989.

———. "The 1889 Exhibition: The Crisis of Bourgeois Individualism." *Oppositions: A Journal for Ideas and Criticism in Architecture* 8, no. 45 (1977): 71–91.

Simiand, François. "Une enquête trop oubliée sur une crise méconnue." In *Mélanges d'économie politique et sociale offerts à Edgard Milhaud*. Paris: Presses universitaires de France, 1934.

Simon, Jules. *L'Ouvrière*. Paris: L. Hachette and Cie, 1860; Reprint Brionne: Gérard Monfort, 1977.

———. "Mon petit journal," *Le Temps*, 9 March 1890.

Sismondi, Jean-Charles-Léonard Simonde de. *New Principles of Political Economy*. Translated and annotated by Richard Hyse, with a foreword by Robert Heilbroner. New Brunswick, N.J.: Transaction Publishers, 1991.

———. "Du sort des ouvriers dans les manufactures." *Revue mensuelle d'économie politique* 3 (1834): 1–3.

Skocpol, Theda. *Protecting Soldiers and Mothers: The Political Origins of Social Policy in the United States*. Cambridge: Belknap Press of Harvard University Press, 1992.

———. *Social Policy in the United States: Future Possibilities in Historical Perspective*. Princeton: Princeton University Press, 1995.

Société des Industriels et des Commerçants de France. *Les retraites ouvrières et la mutualité*. Excerpt from *Revue internationale du commerce, de l'industrie et de la banque*. Paris: Librairie Guillaumin, 1905.

Sorel, Georges. *Réflexions sur la violence*. Paris: Librairie de Pages libres, 1908.

Spiegel, Gabrielle M. "History, Historicism, and the Social Logic of the Text in the Middle Ages." *Speculum* 65 (1990): 59–86.

Stewart, Mary Lynn. *Women, Work, and the French State: Labour Protection and Social Patriarchy, 1879–1919*. Kingston, Ont.: McGill-Queen's University Press, 1989.

Stock-Morton, Phyllis. *Moral Education for a Secular Society: The Development of Morale Laique in 19th Century France*. Albany: State University of New York Press, 1988.

Stone, Judith. *The Search for Social Peace: Reform Legislation in France, 1890–1914*. Albany: State University of New York Press, 1985.

Stora-Lamarre, Annie. *L'Enfer de la IIIe République: Censeurs et pornographes (1881–1914)*. Paris: Imago, 1990.

Story, Ronald. *Harvard and the Boston Upper Class: The Forging of an Aristocracy, 1800–1870*. Middleton: Wesleyan University Press, 1980.

Sutcliffe, Anthony. *The Autumn of Central Paris: The Defeat of Town Planning, 1850–1970*. Montreal: McGill-Queen's University Press, 1971.

———. *Towards the Planned City: Germany, Britain, the United States and France, 1780–1914*. New York: St. Martin's Press, 1981.

Tannenbaum, Edward. *The Action Française*. New York: Wiley, 1962.

Thépot, André, ed. *L'ingénieur dans la société française*. Paris: Éditions ouvrières, 1985.

Trépanier, Pierre. "La Société canadienne d'économie sociale de Montréal, 1888–1911: Sa fondation, ses buts et ses activités." *Canadian Historical Review* 67, no. 3 (1986): 343–67.

Thiers, Adolphe. *Discours parlementaires de M. Thiers*. 16 vols. Paris: Calmann-Lévy, 1879–89.

———. *Rapport général, présenté au nom de la Comission de l'assistance et de la prévoyance publiques, Assemblée législative, 26 January 1850*. Paris: Paulin, Lheureux, 1850.

Thomas, Albert. "Les élections municipales." *L'Humanité*, 8 April 1908.

———. "Espaces libres." *L'Humanité*, 5 November 1907.

———. "Manoeuvre à dénoncer—Parisiens, prenez garde!" *L'Humanité*, 28 April 1908.

Thomas, Jean, and Aléxis Guérin. *Cours d'instruction civique et morale: Rédigé conformément au programme officiel du 22 janvier, 1881*. Paris: C. Delagrave, 1882.

Tilly, Charles. *The Contentious French*. Cambridge: Harvard University Press, 1986.

Tocqueville, Aléxis de. *Democracy in America*. 2 vols. J. P. Mayer, ed. Garden City, N.Y.: Anchor Books, 1969.

Tolman, William H. *Industrial Betterment*. New York: Social Service Press, 1900.

———. *Municipal Reform Movements in the United States*. New York: Fleming H. Revell, 1895.

———. *Social Engineering*. New York: McGraw, 1909.

———. *L'oeuvre de l'ingénieur social*. Paris: Vuiblet et Nony, 1910.

Tolman, William H., and Charles Hemstreet. *The Better New York*. New York: Baker and Taylor, 1904.

Topalov, Christian. "From the 'Social Question' to 'Urban Problems': Reformers and the Working Classes at the Turn of the Twentieth Century." *International Social Science Journal* 125 (1990): 319–36.

———, ed. *Laboratoires du nouveau siècle: La "nébuleuse réformatrice" et ses réseaux en France, 1880–1914*. Paris: Éditions de l'École des hautes études en sciences sociales, 1999.

———. *Naissance du chômeur, 1880–1910*. Paris: Albin Michel, 1994.

Touraine, Alain, et al. *Le grand refus: Réflexions sur la grève de décembre 1995*. Paris: Fayard, 1996.

Trachtenberg, Alan. *The Incorporation of America: Culture and Society in the Guilded Age*. New York: Hill and Wang, 1982.

Trempé, Rolande. *Les mineurs de Carmaux (1848–1914)*. 2 vols. Paris: Éditions ouvrières, 1971.

Société canadienne d'économie sociale de Montréal, 1888–1911: Sa fondation, ses buts et ses activités." *Canadian Historical Review* 67, no. 3 (1986): 343–67.

Trombert, Albert. *Charles Robert, sa vie, son oeuvre*. 2 vols. Paris: Librairie Chaix, 1927.

Vacher, Hélène. *Projection coloniale et ville rationalisée: Le rôle de l'espace colonial dans la constitution de l'urbanisme et France, 1900–1931*. Aalborg, Denmark: Aalborg University Press, 1977.

Vachon, Marius. *Rapport sur les musées et les écoles d'art industriel dans les différents pays d'Europe*. 4 vols. Paris: Imprimerie nationale, 1885–90.

Varlez, Louis. "L'assurance intégrale." In *Congrès international d'Anvers: Législation douanière et la règlementation du travail*, Section II, 6th Question: "La classe ouvrière a-t-elle intérêt à une règlementation officielle du travail?" 1–35. Gand: n.p., July 1894.

———. "La crise économique: L'école libérale et l'école réaliste." Reprint from *Revue universitaire*. Brussels: H. Lamertin, 1895.

Vergo, Peter, ed. *The New Museology*. London: Reaktion Books, 1989.

Viet, Vincent. *Les voltigeurs de la République: L'inspection du travail en France jusqu'en 1914*. Paris: CNRS, 1994.

Vigarello, Georges. *Le propre et le sale: L'hygiène du corps depuis le Moyen Age*. Paris: Éditions du Seuil, 1985.

Villeneuve-Bargemont, Alban de. *Économie politique chrétienne, ou recherches sur la nature et les causes du paupérisme en France et en Europe, et sur les moyens de le soulager et de le prévenir*. 3 vols. Paris: Paulin, 1834.

Villermé, Dr. Louis-René. *Tableau de l'état physique et moral des ouvriers employés dans les manufactures de coton, de laine et de soie*. J. Renouard, 1840; Paris: UGE, 1971.

Vogüé, Marquis Émile Melchior de. *Remarques sur l'Exposition du centenaire*. Paris: Plon, 1889.

Walch, Jean. *Michel Chevalier, économiste saint-simonien, 1806–1879*. Paris: Librairie philosophique J. Vrin, 1975.

Warchaw, Dan. *Paul Leroy-Beaulieu and Established Liberalism in France*. Dekalb: Northern Illinois University, 1991.

Watkins, W. P. *The International Cooperative Alliance, 1895–1970*. London: International Cooperative Alliance, 1970.

Weill, Georges. *Histoire du catholicisme libéral en France, 1828–1908*. Paris, Geneva: Ressources, 1979.

————. *Histoire du mouvement social en France, 1852–1924*. Paris: Librairie Félix Alcan, 1924.

Weintrob, Lori Robin. "From Fraternity to Solidarity: Mutual Aid, Popular Sociability, and Social Reform in France, 1880–1914." Ph.D. diss., University of California, 1995.

Weiss, John. "Origins of the French Welfare System: Poor Relief in the Third Republic, 1871–1914." *French Historical Studies* 13, no. 1 (1983): 47–78.

Weissbach, Lee Shai. *Child Labor Reform in Nineteenth-Century France: Assuring the Future Harvest*. Baton Rouge: Louisiana State University Press, 1989.

————. "*Oeuvre Industrielle, Oeuvre Morale*: The Sociétés de Patronage of Nineteenth-Century France." *French Historical Studies* 15, no. 1 (1987): 99–120.

Weisz, George. *The Emergence of Modern Universities in France, 1863–1914*. Princeton: Princeton Univerity Press, 1983.

————. "L'idéologie républicaine et les sciences sociales: Les durkheimiens et la chaire d'histoire d'économie sociale à la Sorbonne." *Revue française de sociologie* 20 (1979): 83–112.

Willink, Tjeenk. "L'ingénieur social aux établissements van Marken," *Le Musée social: Chronique du Musée social* 10 (1901): 337–49.

Willoughby, W. F. "Labor Legislation in France Under the Third Republic." *Quarterly Journal of Economics* 15 (1901): 390–415, 551–77.

————. "Le mouvement en faveur des espaces libres et l'esthétique urbaine aux États-Unis." *Le Musée social: Mémoires et documents* (1910): 296–314.

————. "The Musée social in Paris." *Annals of the American Academy of Political and Social Science* (1896): 58–63.

Wolf, Peter M. *Eugène Hénard and the Beginning of Urbanism in Paris, 1900–1914*. The Hague, Paris: Centre de recherche d'urbanisme, 1968.

Wolloch, Isser. *The New Regime: Transformations of the French Civic Order, 1789–1820s.* New York: W.W. Norton, 1994.

Woronoff, Denis. *L'industrie sidérurgique en France pendant la Révolution et l'Empire.* Paris: Éditions de l'École des hautes études en sciences sociales, 1984.

Wright, Gordon. *France in Modern Times.* 2nd ed. Chicago: Rand McNally, 1974.

Wright, Gwendolyn. *The Politics of Design in French Colonial Urbanism.* Chicago: University of Chicago Press, 1991.

Wuthnow, Robert. *Communities of Discourse: Ideologies and Social Structure in the Reformation, the Enlightenment, and European Socialism.* Cambridge: Harvard University Press, 1989.

Yvert, Benoît ed. *Dictionnaire des ministres de 1789 à 1989.* Paris: Perrin, 1990.

Zeldin, Theodore. *France, 1848–1945.* 2 vols. Oxford: Clarendon Press, 1973–77.

Zimmerman, Carle Clark, and Merle E. Frampton. *Family and Society: A Study of the Sociology of Reconstruction.* New York: D. Van Nostrand, 1935.

Index

Index ~ 345

Société française pour la protection des paysages de France, 132, 253, 255
Société nationale d'agriculture, 124, 145
Société philanthropique, La, 35, 71, 108, 121, 170
Société protestante de prévoyance et de secours mutuels, 117
Société statistique de Paris, 41, 218
Solidarism, 50, 93, 102, 107, 114–15, 118–20, 125, 138, 195, 219, 239, 249, 270, 274, 294 n.50
Sorel, Georges, 123, 178
Spencer, Herbert, 2, 77, 169, 176
Stanley, Albert, 153–54
State, 9, 29, 33, 60; attitudes of reformers toward, 104; interventionist conception of, 11, 32, 64, 77, 85–86, 90, 102, 109, 113, 120, 134, 139, 173, 203, 213–16, 219–21, 249; providential role of, 3, 32–33, 102, 111, 139, 174; relationship to society, 38, 55, 82, 95, 139, 172; sociological function of, 39
Strauss, Paul, 122, 132, 155
Strikes, 94, 155–56, 179–81, 183, 189
Syndicalism: revolutionary, 157, 195–96; *syndicalistes*, 124, 178

Thiers, Adolphe, 33, 169, 252
Thomas, Albert, 123, 258
Tolman, William Howe, 153
Topalov, Christian, 5, 121, 263, 267
Touring-Club de France, 256
Trade unions. *See* Labor associations
Tuberculosis, 135–36, 225, 229–30, 239, 246, 249, 255, 258–59, 267, 306 n.2 and n.3

Union d'études des catholiques sociaux, 112, 134
Union libérale républicaine, 169
United States, 2, 5, 9, 56, 99–101, 116, 152–54, 156–57, 241, 276; garden cities in, 246; voluntary associations in, 195

Universal Exhibition of 1889, 3, 10, 15, 43–44, 54–80, 122–23, 128, 204, 231, 271; in defense of industrial progress, 62; housing reform and, 231; museological function of, 79; women and, 198–99
Universal Exhibition of 1900, 123, 125, 145, 195, 259
Universal (male) suffrage, 41, 64, 73, 90, 105, 130, 150, 164
Urban planners, 136–37, 273. *See also* Architects
Urban planning, 11, 22, 124, 132, 137, 190, 240–43, 247, 250–51, 254–60, 263–67, 243; city growth and, 4, 19; Cornudet law of 1919 on, 204; French school of, 254; reconstruction and, 264–65, 273–75
U.S. Department of Labor, 41, 153–54, 231

Vaillant, Édouard, 123, 178
Varlez, Louis, 15, 153, 204–5, 207, 217
Vogüé, Count Louis de, 123
Vogüé, Marquis Eugène-Melchoir de, 124, 149
Voluntary associations, 11, 76, 104–6, 111, 120, 148, 161–65, 175, 194, 244, 247; as bridge between public and private sectors, 106; and the republican ideal, 193–95; in United States, 195. *See also* Mutualism

Waldeck-Rousseau, René, 52, 121
Webb, Beatrice, 156, 183
Webb, Sidney, 156, 180, 183
Weill, Jeanne (pseud. Dick May), 91, 171
Welfare: assistance, 29, 32–33; Catholic roots of, 32; reform, 1, 4–8, 103, 273–75; republican justification for, 236
Welfare state, 1–8, 270–77; foundations of modern French, 11, 58; hybrid nature of, 275; ultimate goals of, 2. *See also* État-providence
Willoughby, William, 153–54, 157–58, 261

Janet R. Horne is Associate Professor of French at the University of Virginia.

Material from the following previously published articles has been incorporated in this volume.

Chapter 2: "Le Musée social à l'origine: Les métamorphoses d'une idée, 1889–1900," Le Mouvement social 171 (August–September 1995): 49–72; and "Presenting Modern France: The Rhetoric of Reform at the 1889 Universal Exhibition," in Unfinished Revolutions: Legacies of Upheaval in Modern French Culture, ed. Robert Denommé and Roland Simon (College Park: Pennsylvania State University Press, 1998).

Chapters 2 and 4: "In Pursuit of Greater France: Visions of Empire among Musée Social Reformers," in Domesticating the Empire: Race, Gender, and Family Life in French and Dutch Colonialism, ed. Julia Clancy-Smith and Frances Gouda (Charlottesville: University Press of Virginia, 1998), 21–42.

Chapter 3: "L'Antichambre de la Chambre: Le Musée social et ses réseaux réformateurs, 1894–1914," in Laboratoires du nouveau siècle: La "nébuleuse réformatrice" et ses réseaux en France, 1880–1914, ed. Christian Topalov (Paris: Éditions de l'École des hautes études en sciences sociales, 1999), 121–40; and "Le libéralisme à l'épreuve de l'industrialisation: La réponse du Musée social, in Le Musée social en son temps (Paris: Presses de l'École normale supérieure, 1998).

Library of Congress Cataloging-in-Publication Data
Horne, Janet R. (Janet Regina)
A social laboratory for modern France : the Musée social
and the rise of the welfare state / Janet R. Horne.
p. cm.   Includes bibliographical references and index.
ISBN 0-8223-2782-1 (cloth : alk. paper)
ISBN 0-8223-2792-9 (paperback : alk. paper)
1. France — Social policy.   2. Musée social (Paris,
France) — History.   3. Welfare state — History.
4. Social problems — France — History.   I. Title.
HN425.5 .H67   2001   361.6'1'0944 — dc21   2001040642